Policy Studies Institute

CONSTITUTIONS IN DEMOCRATIC POLITICS

Policy Studies Institute

Constitutions in Democratic Politics

Edited by
Vernon Bogdanor
Fellow of Brasenose College, Oxford

Gower

Aldershot · Brookfield USA · Hong Kong · Singapore · Sydney

Published by
Gower Publishing Company Limited
Gower House
Croft Road
Aldershot
Hants GU11 3HR
England

Gower Publishing Company
Old Post Road
Brookfield
Vermont 05036
USA

British Library Cataloguing in Publication Data
Constitutions in democratic politics.
   1. Constitutional law   2. Democracy
   I. Bogdanor, Vernon
   342.2'2   JF51

ISBN 0 566 05575 9

Typeset by Guildford Graphics Limited, Petworth, West Sussex
Printed in Great Britain at the University Press, Cambridge

Contents

Contributors

Vernon Bogdanor is a Fellow of Brasenose College, Oxford and Senior Visiting Fellow of the European Centre for Political Studies.

S.E. Finer was formerly Gladstone Professor of Government and Public Administration at the University of Oxford.

Ghiţa Ionescu was formerly Professor of Government at the University of Manchester. He is President of the International Political Science Association's Research Committee on European Unification.

Richard Hodder-Williams is Reader in Politics at the University of Bristol, and was Visiting Professor of Political Science at the University of California, Berkeley, 1984–85.

Campbell Sharman is Senior Lecturer in the Department of Politics, University of Western Australia.

W.H. Morris-Jones was formerly Director of the Institute of Commonwealth Studies at the University of London. He served on the staff of the Viceroy of India as Constitutional Adviser in 1947.

Geoffrey Marshall is a Fellow of The Queen's College, Oxford.

Lawrence W. Beer is Fred Morgan Kirby Professor of Civil Rights at the Department of Government and Law, Lafayette College. He was Fulbright Visiting Professor, 1986–87, at the Faculty of Law, Hokkaido University, Japan.

David Hine is a Student (Fellow) of Christ Church, Oxford.

Kurt Sontheimer is Professor of Political Science at the Geschwister – Scholl – Institut of the University of Munich.

Guy Carcassonne is Professor of Public Law at the University of Rheims. Since 1986, he has been an adviser on constitutional questions to the socialist group in the National Assembly.

Guy Hermet is Research Director at the Fondation Nationale des Sciences Politiques in Paris, and Professor at the Institut d'Études Politiques in Paris.

Christopher Hughes was formerly Professor of Politics at the University of Leicester.

Emanuel Gutmann is Professor of Political Science at the Hebrew University of Jerusalem.

Olof Ruin is Lars Hierta Professor of Government and Head of the Political Science Department at the University of Stockholm.

Robert Senelle is Professor of Constitutional and Administrative Law at the University of Ghent.

Jan Vis is Professor of Constitutional Law at the University of Groningen, and a member (for D'66) of the First Chamber (Upper House) of the Dutch Parliament. He was a member of the Royal Commission 1982 on constitutional reform.

Roger Morgan was from 1978 to 1986 Head of the European Centre for Political Studies at the Policy Studies Institute. He is currently a Research Fellow of the Centre for International Studies at the London School of Economics.

Preface

This book is one of the last to be produced by the European Centre for Political Studies, which the European Cultural Foundation brought into existence in 1978, in collaboration with the Policy Studies Institute, and supported with generous financial assistance (including a special ad hoc grant for this project) until 1986. I am very glad that the subject of the Centre's final conference in November 1986, which was part of the process leading to this book, should have been the absolutely fundamental one of the relationship between democratic politics on the one hand and the constitutional 'rules of the game' on the other. In contrast to the traditional assumption in democracies, that 'the constitution' could be seen as a timeless and unchanging framework of rules, and in some way above the battles of day-to-day politics, events have forced us in recent years to see that constitutional problems are among the most acute ones faced by many democracies (including the United Kingdom for one), and that the relationship between 'constitutional' and 'political' matters is somewhat different from what we had supposed it to be.

The idea of a systematic comparative study of this phenomenon came from Vernon Bogdanor. I am very grateful to him for having, among his many other contributions as a Senior Visiting Fellow of the Centre, pursued this idea through the stages of planning and commissioning the various chapters, and supervised their discussion and revision to form the present book. The conference at PSI, where part of this discussion occurred, was brilliantly and constructively chaired by Sir Zelman Cowen and Dr David Butler; I am grateful to them and to all the other participants. Thanks are also due to Amanda Trafford for taking care of all the administrative arrangements, to Sally Walker, Nick Evans, and other members of the PSI staff, and to Margaret Cornell for another superb editorial operation.

Roger Morgan
October 1987

Foreword
Rt. Hon. Sir Zelman Cowen

This book makes its appearance at a time historically significant for students of constitutions: the bicentenary of the American Constitution. Between May and September 1787, the founding fathers fashioned the instrument which (with some important additions) became the Constitution of the United States. A century later, after further important amendments had been made, Mr Gladstone described that constitution as 'the most wonderful work ever struck off at a given time by the brain and purpose of man'. Whether or not that great claim would command universal acceptance, the United States Constitution surely occupies a very special place among constitutions.

This historic occasion might of itself justify a more general examination of modern constitutions and constitutional issues. There are also more immediate reasons. While, in some countries, in the post-war world, as Vernon Bogdanor writes, politics were widely thought to be dominated by socio-economic problems, with constitutional matters assuming a marginal importance, it is not so now. Issues of a constitutional character have re-emerged, and in various forms and contexts are seen to have a fresh significance.

I was pleased to act as Chairman for part of the conference at which the papers which form the chapters of this book were presented. They have been revised in the light of the excellent debates they generated, and now, with an introduction and conclusion, they provide a valuable body of information, analysis and viewpoint on public issues of contemporary interest and significance.

1 Introduction
Vernon Bogdanor

I

One of the more striking features in the recent experience of many democracies is the re-emergence of constitutional issues in states whose institutions were thought to be highly stable, as well as in less well-established democracies. In the post-war world politics was widely thought to be dominated by socio-economic problems, with constitutional matters being of marginal importance. Amongst political scientists too, there was a reaction against the study of constitutions which was held to be static, formal and legalistic, in favour of analysing the socio-economic realities which allegedly underpinned constitutional life. Constitutions, in short, were seen largely as epiphenomena, expressions of an underlying political culture, and it was this political culture which ought to be the prime object of analysis.[1]

Yet, in the 1970s and 1980s, politicians and political scientists in a number of countries have had to concern themselves with the problems of constitutional change. Of the countries discussed in this book, six – Belgium, Canada, the Netherlands, Portugal, Spain and Sweden – have adopted new constitutions – or what are in effect new constitutions – since 1970. In Belgium, as Robert Senelle shows, the adoption of the new constitution – the so-called State reform – is an on-going process which began in 1970 and is still not complete. In Portugal and Spain, of course, as well as in Greece, new constitutions have been adopted as a necessary stage in the transition from dictatorship to democracy.

Even where constitutional change has not gone so far as to lead to the adoption of a new constitution, the subject has nevertheless been a matter for intense debate in a number of democracies. In Britain and Israel, two of the three democracies, together with New Zealand, which lack written – or more accurately, codified – constitutions, there have been passionate and heated disputes on constitutional issues. In Britain, much of the agenda of politics in the 1970s was determined by the constitution as governments sought to grapple with the problems raised by Britain's entry into the European

Community, Northern Ireland and devolution and, more generally, by the weakening of party allegiances; and in both Britain and Israel, political movements have arisen which put at the forefront of their programme the demand for constitutional change – in Britain the Liberal/SDP Alliance, and in Israel the Democratic Movement for Change, which enjoyed a short-lived efflorescence in the general election of 1977.

In Australia and Italy (and in an earlier period in Japan), democracies with well-established constitutions, the issue of constitutional change was felt to be sufficiently important to warrant the setting up of non-partisan constitutional commissions to make recommendations and proposals for the future; and, although in none of these countries have major changes yet occurred, the possibility of change is by no means to be excluded. In Switzerland also, Total Revision of the constitution has been widely discussed.

Finally, the European Community, not a state but, in Roger Morgan's words, a 'would-be polity', an experiment in multi-national co-operation, has, in the Treaty of Rome, what amounts to a constitution – an organisation chart indicating the main institutions of the Community and how they are to interact with each other. In the Community also, much time and effort has been spent in recent years on constitutional matters, especially since direct elections to the European Parliament in 1979 have served to expose the considerable contrast between the new democratic legitimacy of the Parliament and its pitifully weak powers. And, although the hopes of the more radical reformers in the Community, symbolised by the 1984 Draft Treaty whose inspiration was the late Altiero Spinelli, have not been realised, nevertheless the 1986 Single European Act was, in effect, a major constitutional amendment to the Treaty of Rome, and one whose consequences could be very far-reaching.

In the four remaining countries considered in this book – France, India, Germany and the United States – pressure for constitutional change has not been a central issue in politics but is, nevertheless, a matter of concern to small if often significant minorities of opinion-formers. Such attempts at constitutional reform as have been made have been unsuccessful, and the United States, and perhaps also France, can be cited as examples of countries whose constitutions – the one the oldest still in existence, the other only thirty years old – have adapted reasonably well to the processes of social and economic change.

What is clear is that the functioning of democratic institutions has become intertwined with the working of constitutions to an extent which could hardly have been imagined twenty or thirty years ago. It has become increasingly the case, therefore, that an understanding of the role which the constitution plays in a country's politics is vital to an appreciation of the working of modern democratic government. The purpose of this book, therefore, is to seek an answer to the questions: Why and how have recent political conflicts come to take on a constitutional form? Why has there been a demand for constitutional change in hitherto stable democratic systems? And perhaps such an inquiry can cast light on a further and more difficult question: What role does the constitution play in a modern democratic state?

II

Constitutions are not, of course, confined to democratic states. Indeed, the vast majority of the 159 member states comprising the United Nations possess codified constitutions, although less than a third of these can fairly claim democratic credentials. The latter can, declares S.E. Finer with pardonable exaggeration, be counted on one's fingers and toes. Conversely, three countries which are indubitably democracies – Britain, Israel and New Zealand – lack, as we have seen, codified constitutions.

In the modern world, constitutions are almost ubiquitous and they are indeed part of the tribute which vice pays to virtue. For there *is* a conceptual connection, not so much between the constitution as a document and democracy, but between modern constitutionalism and the idea of a liberal democracy. Whether a country has a codified constitution is hardly something of great importance to the political scientist. Whether it achieves the aims which constitutions are intended to help achieve, is a matter of far greater moment. For codified constitutions are, after all, valued as a means to the end of limiting governmental power; and, in a democracy, limiting also the power of the people to whom government is responsible. The Founding Fathers in drawing up the American Constitution had, after all, two aims, not one. The first was to draw up a structure of government which could serve to protect the people from government, from the danger of a tyranny of the majority in the legislature; but the second aim was to protect the people from themselves.

Thus, the relationship between constitutionalism and liberalism, as Ghiţa Ionescu points out, is by no means a simple or straightforward one. To live under an effectively working constitution is not the same as living under a regime of moral *laissez-faire*. Constitutional government presupposes a certain set of virtues amongst the ruled; and these virtues must include self-restraint, a willingness not to push the pursuit of one's aims beyond a certain point. In the 1930s, Mr Justice Stone declared that the United States Supreme Court ought not to see itself as the sole guardian of the constitution. While the other branches of the Constitution were limited by institutional restraints, by checks and balances, the only restraint which limited the Court was its sense of self-restraint. By analogy, one might argue that in a democracy in which the people are, in effect, sovereign, the only effective restraint in the last resort is likely to be that of the people over themselves. Constitutions thus both liberate and bind; they provide for a framework of ordered freedom within a set of rules which prevents both majorities and their elected representatives from doing what they might otherwise wish to do.

The term 'constitution', as S.E. Finer shows, is to be understood in positivistic terms as a code of rules which aspire to regulate the allocation of functions, powers and duties among the various agencies and officers of government, and defines the relationships between these and the public. Yet, even defined in these terms, the existence of a constitution, in so far as it is observed, serves to limit power. For, to allocate functions, powers and duties is also, *ipso facto*, to limit power. There must be some gain to the citizen, however minimal, in living under a constitution which regularises the way in which power is exercised; even where government is authoritarian, it matters that it is not arbitrary.

Yet, a number of democratic constitutions today contain more than a mere organisation chart of functions and powers; they contain Bills of Rights, which may also include a charter of social and economic rights, something characteristic of constitutions of the twentieth century, although generally honoured more in the breach than in the observance.[2] Christopher Hughes goes so far as to refuse the title of 'constitution' to a document without 'a Catalogue of Rights and directive principles incorporated'; and, in the case of Britain and Israel, two countries without codified constitutions, such pressure as exists to adopt one is based less on the desire to possess a clear-cut organisational chart delimiting the institutions of government than on a feeling that rights would be better protected under a codified constitution than they are at present.

The concept of a constitution is closely bound up with the notion of the limitation of government by law, a source of authority higher than government and beyond its reach. An enacted constitution is a means – although, as the examples of Britain, Israel and New Zealand show, not an essential means – of securing this end. The law, it is suggested, is logically prior to government, and therefore constitutes a standard by which the actions of government are to be evaluated. It is, in Christopher Hughes's words, this 'appeal to a pre-existing law' which 'is the essence of constitutionalism'.

Yet analysis of constitutions cannot be restricted simply to the document called 'the Constitution', or to constitutional law. For a working constitution in a democracy implies reference to certain norms and standards which lie beyond and outside the document itself, and which cannot easily be inferred from it by someone who is not steeped in the history and culture of the country concerned. When conduct on the part of a government or some other public body is dubbed 'unconstitutional', what is often meant is not necessarily that the law has been broken, but rather that the action is out of keeping with the style or, more broadly, the 'way of life' of a country. Thus, when in 1975 in Australia, the Governor-General, Sir John Kerr, dismissed the Prime Minister, Gough Whitlam, he found himself the subject of criticism that he had acted unconstitutionally. What was implied by the criticism was not that he had acted against the law, but that he had acted contrary to the norms of Australian – or indeed – parliamentary government. There was no doubt that Sir John Kerr enjoyed the legal power to dismiss the Prime Minister; what was at issue was whether the exercise of the power was consistent with the ethos of parliamentary government as understood in Australia. The question is very far from being a simple one, however, for it relates, as Campbell Sharman shows, to the difficult issue of the extent to which the government of Australia should be seen as one in which only the lower house enjoys democratic legitimacy, as in Britain; or whether, by contrast, the federal element in the Constitution means that the upper house, enjoying democratic legitimacy on a different basis, is entitled to block supply. What difference does the federal element in the Australian Constitution make to the operation of the norms of parliamentary government? The appeal to convention cannot yield an unambiguous answer.

This kind of appeal – to constitutional conventions – can, of course, also be raised in countries without codified constitutions.[3] When, in Britain, it is suggested that the policies of the Conservative Government towards local authorities since 1979 raise constitutional questions, what is meant is not that these policies are in any sense illegal, but rather, as my own chapter in this book shows, that they breach hitherto accepted understandings, albeit tacit, as to how relationships between central government and local authorities should be ordered. These tacit understandings, which, in Sidney Low's graphic phrase, are so often misunderstood, may not be written down;[4] yet they exert a normative influence upon those concerned with central/local relations comparable to, and perhaps greater than, the influence exerted by a constitutional document. What makes Britain together with Israel and New Zealand, constitutional democracies, despite the absence of codified constitutions, is this very fact that their governments in general feel under pressure to conform to such norms; when accused of unconstitutional action their defence is not that the term 'unconstitutional' is without meaning, but that their actions can, despite appearances, be defended in constitutional terms.

In every working democratic system – whether it enjoys a codified constitution or not – conventions will have an important role to play. Indeed, there is no reason to believe that they will play a larger role in countries lacking codified constitutions than in countries which do have them. In the United States, for example, the electoral college, by convention, accepts the mandate which it is given by the voters in the presidential election. Were it to disregard its mandate, it would not be acting illegally – the Supreme Court would not declare its action void – but it would be acting unconstitutionally because it would be offending against norms which lie at the very basis of the American system of government. Similarly, in Switzerland, a central feature of government is the 'magic formula' by which the seats in the Federal Cabinet are divided on the basis 2:2:2:1, between the four main political parties. This formula is, arguably, at least as important as any provision in the Swiss constitution – it is, in Christopher Hughes's words, 'a constitution in itself' – but it is not part of the law, and so could be abandoned without risking any repercussions from the courts.

Constitutional conventions are the means through which constitutional law is brought into contact with political reality. For their meaning is dependent upon the configuration of power in a society and upon popular assumptions about how that power should be regulated. In pre-twentieth century constitutions, little or nothing is said about those basic constitutional rules which are constitutive of democratic practice – rules such as those providing for fair and free elections, free scope for the activities of political parties, pressure groups, the press, etc. Today, such matters may be regulated by law, but they may also depend upon convention. Until the Second World War, those constitutions drawn up in London for the dominions omitted to state the basic rules of cabinet responsibility, for these were treated as matters of convention. On the Continent also, nineteenth-century liberal constitutions tended to omit any firm statement of these rules. By contrast, the constitutions of the New Commonwealth countries drawn up after 1945 were replete with statements of what had previously been left to convention – often with unhappy results. For the interpretation of some of the fundamental rules of government will legitimately alter as assumptions about government change. Attitudes towards the House of Lords or towards the role of elected representatives or of political parties offer good examples illustrating the difficulty of putting any definitive statement of the basic rules of constitutional democracy in any single, time-bound document.

Thus, in addition to the basic meaning of 'constitution' – a document containing, at the very least, a code of rules setting out the allocation of functions, powers and duties among the various agencies and officers of government – there is a wider meaning of constitution, according to which every democratic state has a constitution. This wider meaning comprehends the normative attitudes held by the people towards government, their conception of how power ought to be regulated, of what it is proper to do and not to do. There are, as it were, pre-constitutional norms regulating government, and it is upon these that the health and viability of democratic systems will depend.

There is, however, an added complication. For the conventions may themselves be derived from pre-constitutional norms which have been written down – as, for example, with the American Declaration of Independence, the French Declaration of the Rights of Man and the Citizen, Britain's Magna Carta, Israel's Law of Return. Sometimes the precise details of these documents may be hardly known – there are probably few in Britain who could offer an accurate account of what Magna Carta actually contains – but this matters little since these half-remembered documents are important not in themselves but for the ideals which they are held to encapsulate and which come to be so widely diffused amongst the members of a society.

III

Lawyers and political scientists have classified constitutions in a large variety of different ways; but perhaps one of the most important questions that need to be asked about a constitution concerns the relationship which it has to a country's past. Are there in fact constitutional norms derived from the past, commanding widespread acceptance and capable of guiding a country's constitutional evolution? Or, by contrast, is the constitution of a country *reactive*, reacting against a past of dictatorship and terror, and attempting to establish anew the norms of constitutional government? Countries which seem to make a break with their past may, nevertheless, be examples of the first category. Both the United States and India saw their constitutions as marking a new beginning; yet the United States Constitution was deeply influenced by British constitutional ideas, while the Indian Constitution, as W.H. Morris-Jones shows, owes a good deal to the British Government's Government of India Act 1935, denounced by nationalists at the time as something totally inadequate to India's constitutional needs. Moreover, a country whose constitutional development has been anything but smooth may nevertheless possess norms which are serviceable because they command the consent, however generalised, of the vast majority of the citizens. The French Declaration of the Rights of Man is a clear example.

A problem only arises where the immediate past is seen in so negative a light that it is difficult to find appropriate norms from the past. Thus, the Constitution of the Fifth Republic in France, the Constitutions of Italy, the Federal Republic of Germany and Japan, as well as those of Portugal and Spain, can only be understood in terms of a rejection of the previous regime, and of the conditions which are held to have given rise to it. The Basic Law of the Federal Republic is a reaction, not only against the Nazi regime, but also against the Weimar Republic, whose weaknesses were, in the view of the Bonn Founding Fathers, responsible for the collapse of democracy in Germany. While in France, the Fifth Republic Constitution as Guy Carcassonne shows, represents a reaction, not only against the Fourth, but against a whole conception of republican government, highly influential since the Revolution. So it is that the central theme of the Federal German Constitution is the attempt to re-establish a *Rechtsstaat* after the experiences of the Nazi period, while the Fifth Republic Constitution is preoccupied almost exclusively with redefining the relationship between legislature and executive, a relationship which, in the view of its founders, had become seriously distorted under previous parliamentary regimes.

These constitutions are essentially negative constitutions, a product not of enthusiasm or ideology, but of disenchantment. Lacking a serviceable past, these modern founding fathers undertook their work imbued with a pessimistic view of the human condition, and (except in France and Portugal) with a marked distaste for anything redolent of populism or majoritarianism. There was, in the constitutions of the immediate post-war period – the Fourth Republic in France, the Italian and the German (as well as the Japanese) – an understandable revulsion against any philosophy which exalted the political abilities of the average citizen; there was 'one rather striking divergence from the American, if not from the British, climate of opinion. Nowhere on the Continent is there to be found any genuine "belief in the common man" as that belief is taken for granted in the United States.'[5] Perhaps it is for that very reason that the Italian, German and Japanese Constitutions have proved so much more durable than their predecessors in Central and Eastern

Europe between the wars, marked by a massive positive enthusiasm for national self-determination and for the fulfilment of social and economic rights. Optimism, no doubt, is rarely a good guide to constitution-making.

A further distinction needs to be made amongst this class of constitutions, between those, as in Italy, Germany, Japan and France, which mark a sharp *break* with the previous regime and those, as in Portugal and Spain, where there is a *transition* – which may be more or less smooth – between an authoritarian regime and a constitutional one. Guy Hermet's chapter illustrates how, in the case of the new Spanish Constitution, the transition had to be engineered from above, by those, such as Adolfo Suarez, who were, in a sense, compromised by their association with the previous, Franco, regime. Moreover, the constitution had to be drawn up by non-elected leaders, who could not be responsible to the Spanish people, and who, fearing – with some justification – the enemies of democracy more than its friends found themselves making concessions which the electorate would almost certainly have rejected if presented to them publicly. Spain illustrates a double paradox in many respects typical of constitution-making during the transition from one regime to another: the first is that the constitution was handed down from above by those who had prospered under a previous non-constitutional regime; the second is that to secure acceptance of the new democratic constitution, it had to be drawn up by methods which were far from democratic.

Nevertheless, if constitutional norms are derived from the past they also point towards the future. For the ideals embodied in the constitution provide an agenda of political change, change that is needed if the ideals are to be realised. A constitution does not allow a liberal democracy to rest content with its inheritance from the past, but serves as an indication of what remains still to be achieved. Thus, in the Federal Republic of Germany, as Kurt Sontheimer shows, the idea of the *Sozialstaat* in the Basic Law acts as a powerful stimulus to that conception of society favoured by the Social Democrats. In the European Community, above all, the idea of a 'union of peoples' has given a powerful dynamic to those reformers who seek to change the institutions of the Community so as to approximate more closely to this ideal – the ideal of European Union. It serves to legitimise new thinking about the structure of the Community, and graphically illustrates that the constitutionalist, far from being hide-bound by convention and precedent, may also have to become a reformer if the ideals contained in the constitution are to become a reality. It is, perhaps, this openness of constitutional life, an unwillingness to countenance a definitive conception of political reality – or of human nature – which is the defining characteristic of a truly liberal constitutionalism.

IV

It is clear, therefore, that constitutions cannot be understood without looking at what lies behind them – at the political processes which gave them birth, and at the historical experience which conditioned the thinking of their founders. The constitution itself will be an expression of these concerns rather than a generator of constitutional values. Its meaning and its prospects for stability will depend upon factors outside itself.

For a constitution, if it is to survive, must remain congruent with the broad way of life of a community, a way of life whose meaning, as we have seen, is to be found as much in pre-constitutional norms as in the document itself. A constitution is either a summation of the past, or a reaction against memories too painful to be endured. In either case, it is a repository of a society's hopes for its future. When those hopes are no longer seen as realistic or plausible, or when they seem to be incomplete, there will be pressure for constitutional change.

But constitutions can, no more than other expressions of political life, be divorced from considerations of political power. In origin, they are often, as so many of these essays show, the product not of a universal consensus which it would be impossible to reach, but of the victory of one side in a political battle, or of one interpretation of political reality following a deep-seated conflict of political forces. There may be, as was the case in, for example, the United States after 1787 and France after 1958, powerful forces which oppose the constitution, but, if the political environment is favourable enough, it will come to gain general acceptance and respect, partly no doubt as a result of the operation of the forces of inertia.

In general, the less specific the constitution, the more it will be able to accommodate social change and new alignments of political forces. The American Constitution is striking, indeed unique in this respect, in having been able, primarily through the agency of judicial interpretation, to convert what was a document intended to govern the activities of small communities of gentlemen farmers into one suitable for a continent and superpower of 230 million people. Such longevity is partly to be explained by the drafting of the constitution itself, a model for all constitution-makers. Indeed, the two fundamental principles of drafting set down by Edmund Randolph, and quoted by Richard Hodder-Williams (p. 77), still stand as the best advice ever given to those faced with the task of drawing up a constitution.

The longevity of the American Constitution is not only to be explained by its merits as a written document, however, but also by the role which it plays in American social and political life. For, as Hodder-Williams points out, it has played a vital part in forging the unity of the nation. Although the product of a homogeneous political culture, the Constitution has also been the instrument through which allegiance to a multi-cultural and multi-racial society, vastly different from that imagined by the Founding Fathers, has been maintained. In the United States, it is the Constitution itself which is the *pouvoir neutre* which Benjamin Constant believed should lie beyond the aspirations of particular social groups and political factions; and the very identity of Americans is bound up with respect for their Constitution, or perhaps rather with the ideals for which it is assumed to stand.

The American Constitution is assisted in performing this task by the loose and inchoate structure of American political parties. Because the American political process does not yield responsible party government in the British sense, leadership on major issues, and especially on race, has often been given by the Supreme Court. Indeed, in any list of the major milestones of American political development since the Second World War, two judicial decisions – *Brown v. Board of Education* (1954) and *Baker v. Carr* (1962) – would have to be given a prominent place. Where there has been a vacuum of political leadership, the court has, perforce, filled the vacuum. For this very reason, however, it is dangerous, as Geoffrey Marshall points out, to generalise from American experience. In almost every other democracy, the constitution, the Bill of Rights and the judiciary play a far smaller role than they do in the United States.

The power, which the American courts enjoy, of judicial review – a power which is nowhere mentioned in the Constitution, but which was taken by the Supreme Court in the case of *Marbury v. Madison* (1803) – could easily lead the unwary to believe that the American system of government was one of government by judiciary. Yet such an accusation would betray a misunderstanding of what courts can be expected to achieve. Because judges are appointed by presidents, they may well, in the long run reflect public perceptions of the proper scope of the law. It is not that judges will follow opinion in the crude sense of their judgments being affected by election returns, but the court will be affected by public opinion in a more long-term sense, since the electorate will, through the presidents which it chooses, deeply influence the composition of the court. While, therefore, the court may be expected to resist any temporary outbreak of hysteria or intolerance, it would be unwise to place very much faith in its ability to stand out against intolerance which is prolonged and intense. Courts are no more able than any other bodies in democratic societies to stand aloof from deep-seated popular currents of opinion.

This argument can be reinforced from a perusal of American constitutional history. It is noticeable that, whenever there have been major shifts of political power in the United States – and especially during the years immediately after the Civil War and during the New Deal – the court has accommodated itself to new power relationships. One could indeed write a commentary to the major Amendments to the Constitution, showing how each batch of amendments has involved the recognition of a new distribution of power in the country. For, if a constitution, in the broadest sense of the term, refers to the normative way of life of a community, then it is not to be expected that its interpretation will remain static when patterns of living change. The fundamental principles of a good constitution can be expected to hold good through time, but its interpretation will not.

A constitution, then, is not something that can be defended only, or even mainly, by the courts. Whether the restraints which a constitution imposes are effective or not will depend to a very limited degree upon the operation of courts and judicial machinery, but rather upon extra-legal factors, and primarily upon whether there are mechanisms of free and fair elections and the alternation – or at least the possibility of alternation – of parties in government. It is noteworthy that parties and elections are not mentioned in most of the constitutions considered in this volume – and in those newer constitutions such as the Federal German and the Fifth Republic Constitution which *do* mention parties, this mention is fleeting and more symbolic than substantive. For this reason, the analysis of constitutions cannot hope to get very far unless it looks at the political and social forces which lie behind the constitution, and at the way in which these forces have developed, and this is something which constitutional lawyers with their sometimes rigid classification of constitutions often fail to do. If the *raison d'être* of a constitution is the limitation of power, it is important to remember that the limitations imposed by a constitution cannot be enforced by the courts alone. As Montesquieu appreciated, it is only power which can check power.

The standpoint from which the present volume has been compiled, therefore, is that the study of constitutions cannot be divorced either from history or from politics, and that the reasons for constitutional

change must be sought in the perceptions of those whom a constitution is intended to regulate – the political leaders of a country
and the parties to which they belong. Yet, in democracies, political
parties reflect the views of those whose votes they seek, and so
in the perceptions of political parties can be seen a reflection of
the wishes of the voters themselves. Political parties can, as it were,
hold up a mirror to the preoccupations of the electorate in democratic
countries. So the analysis of constitutional change is the analysis
not only of political power relationships, but also of the changing
aspirations of those living in democratic communities as they seek
to realise the age-old ideals of constitutional government.

Notes and references

1. See, for example, Robert A. Dahl, *A Preface To Democratic Theory* (Chicago: University of Chicago Press, 1963).
2. In 1930, one constitutional analyst could write. 'Au xxᶜ siècle, le sens social, du droit, ce n'est plus une doctrine, ce n'est plus une école juridique, c'est la vie elle-même'. B. Mirkine-Guetzévitch, *Les Constitutions de L'Europe Nouvelle*, 2nd edn (Paris: Librairie Delagrave, 1930), p. 35.
3. See on this subject Geoffrey Marshall, *Constitutional Conventions* (Oxford University Press, 1984).
4. Sidney Low, *The Governance of England* (T. Fisher Unwin, 1904), p. 12.
5. Carl Friedrich, 'The Political Theory of the New Democratic Constitutions', in Arnold J. Zurcher (ed.), *Constitutions and Constitutional Trends Since World War II*, 2nd edn (New York: New York University Press, 1955), p. 33.

PART A
THE HISTORY AND THEORY OF CONSTITUTIONS

2 Notes towards a history of constitutions
S.E. Finer

I

The pre-history

Preambular

I define 'Constitutions' positivistically as 'Codes of rules which aspire to regulate the allocation of functions, powers and duties among the various agencies and offices of government, and define the relationships between these and the public'.[1] Many constitutions go further than that and include substantive rules of personal conduct to be followed by the citizens. These are in no way necessary to the fulfilment of a constitution's purpose. The simple proof of this is that the oldest of our written constitutions, the American, has managed to regulate the political life of the country for two centuries without benefit of such substantive rules of personal conduct; and the reverse, namely that a substantial body of nothing but such substantive rules, contained in the Pentateuch, was inadequate to regulate the political life of the Jews of biblical times, which they left in an uneasy limbo between monarchy and some forms of non-monarchy. What political rules the Jews adopted came from outside the Mosaic code.[2]

Trying to arrive at a meaning of 'constitution' by way of etymology is misleading. The word is a Roman Law term meaning special kinds of laws and ordinances made by the Roman Emperor, which entered the medieval European vocabulary via the Church, was so used in France and in England and elsewhere in the twelfth and thirteen centuries and – in brief – connoted precisely the opposite to what we intend by the word today.[3] If we have to ground our definition on etymology we should get much nearer the truth by looking at the history not of the Latin but of a German term, viz. *Grundgesetz*, i.e. the basic or fundamental law (as contrasted with the derivative laws made under it).

Certain commonplace distinctions are misleading. In particular:

(a) A rigid constitution is not necessarily a written one. The constitution of France under the ancien régime was completely rigid, but entirely customary. By the same token a written constitution is not necessarily rigid; all depends on the difficulty of the amending and/or interpretative process.

(b) (i) 'Limited', in the term 'limited government', may mean one or both of two distinct things. The first is a limitation on the way it arrives at and implements its decisions, and we may call this a procedural limitation. Or it may mean a limitation on the area within which it may make decisions. The Jewish monarchy was unquestionably limited as to the substance of what it might do, for it might not infringe the substantive content of the Mosaic code. But this code gave no guidance on foreign affairs, the army, taxation, police, and the organisation of the judiciary etc. etc., and within these areas it could and often did act in a thoroughly unbridled, and indeed tyrannical, fashion.[4] The same is true of the relationship between the Caliph-al-Islam and the Sharia code. Few rulers could have acted as despotically as Al-Mansur or Haroun ar-Raschid, but the sphere within which they could so act was limited. (ii) 'Limited government' does not necessarily require a comprehensive and/or written constitution. The Roman Republic's government was procedurally limited. The feudal monarchies were limited both procedurally and substantively but none of them had codified written constitutions.

Observations

(a) Do not let us be misled by the alleged existence among certain peoples of the notion that some higher moral power exists which transcends positive law. That notion is well attested and well-nigh universal. Thus, Indian kings and princes are said to have been subject to constraints of '*Dharma*' ('righteousness'), and the Egyptian Pharaohs subject to '*Ma'at*' or 'Justice', and Chinese Emperors to '*Ti'en*' or 'Heaven'. But as none of these terms were specific, they had no cash value.[5] (The Egyptians did not even have codes of law!)[6] A belief in the existence of a transcendent criterion like the above only acquires a cash value to the extent that it is expressed in detailed and specific terms. The Mosaic Law was quite specific, and to the extent that it was so, it limited the monarch. Similarly with the Islamic Sharia law. But both, as noted above, covered only a limited area of human activity.

Some care to think that such transcendent values or conceptions do indeed have a cash value in that they establish standards of justice or fair play in the ruler, his associates, possibly even in the community. This may readily be granted, but to make this equate

with or even approximate to a constitutional limitation is the reverse of the truth. For though the 'higher law' be unwavering, not so the rulers' responses. While one ruler feels morally obliged to follow the notion, his successor flouts it. (The Emperor Han Wen-ti conscientiously pursued Confucianist ideals, hence his name, 'civilisation'; but his ferocious successor, Han Wu-ti defied them, hence his name, meaning 'war'.) Alternatively, a ruler might follow the moral imperative simply for fear of alienating his associates and officials, or even his subjects. But while some have done this, others have done the reverse – with varying fortunes. In brief: the outcome of such vague transcendent ideals is not the consistency of rule which we associate with the supremacy of a constitution but just the reverse – a series of arbitrary decisions *via* a fluctuating succession of rulers.
(b) The distinction between fundamental political rules and rules made under or in accord with them is equally ancient and widespread. It is even found in Imperial China. There a distinction was drawn between *chih-tu*, which means something like an institution which is desirable and has an intrinsic value, and a *fa-shu*, which means a method, device (I think, literally, a 'law writing').[7] For Europe, McIlwain strains every resource to prove the existence of this distinction among the Ancient Greeks by a tortured explication of Plato's *Politicus*.[8] This was not at all necessary, for the distinction is clear in the practice of the Athenian Constitution where the *nomos*, or law, is held to be so fixed that it can be changed only by a special procedure, whereas the *psephismata*, or decrees, were simply the resolutions passed by the ordinary vote of the Assembly. The general belief was that a *nomos* was immutable: and individuals who proposed something that went contrary to it could be impeached for what the text translates as 'illegality'.[9]
(c) However, the cash-value of both (a) and (b) above depends on the two things I have already mentioned: first, specificity and second, enforceability. This itself breaks down into (i) an authoritative device for signalling that the fundamental law has been breached and (ii) sanctions which will punish such a breach.
About these requirements we may observe that one or other and frequently both were lacking in many and probably all customary constitutions.
(i) As to the absence of an authoritative signalling device, there was none when the Gracchi defied the Roman Senate, or when King John disagreed with his barons, or the Bourbons quarrelled with their Parlements or the Chinese Emperors contradicted the Confucian establishment. In none of these cases was there a neutral and authoritative arbiter who could signal an assault on the fundamental law, only two sides who blamed one another.

(ii) On some such occasions, one side succeeded in imposing its view on the other by means of some sanction or other – usually of a primitive kind. The Great Charter was enforced on John and Henry III by the establishment of committees of barons; the Bourbons were able to quell the Parlements by the *lit de justice* or the quaint device of 'exile'.[10] But the dispute between Chinese Emperors and mandarins ended up, in most cases, in violence,[11] and such was the outcome in England in the dispute between Charles I and the Parliament.

Written constitutions

When? Basically, constitutions come to be written down in two different sets of circumstances, the first when it seems necessary to replicate the old customary constitution and the second – the exact opposite – when it is deemed desirable to innovate and replace it.

(i) The main, if not the only examples of the first of these occasions are the planting of colonies. The constitutions of the Greek *poleis* in Asia Minor and Magna Graecia offer excellent examples. Since an assorted (and often ill-assorted) collection of individuals were being sent off to establish themselves in an alien environment, the mother-city had to give them a plan as to who was to do what, the entitlement to land, and so forth. Examples of these plans survive.[12] Of course, the constitution of the colony did not exactly replicate the original constitution, it had to be adapted to the local conditions. (Parenthetically, I think that this colonisation movement, and the consequent necessity for devising a constitution and writing it down, was the origin of Greek political science. It is no accident, in my opinion, that rational thought about government begins in Ionia: this was the first area of colonisation. When you translate accepted custom into writing, you have to think; and as you think you are changing the polity into an artefact. The Greeks were the first people ever to do this and Ionia was first among the Greek colonisation areas.) The planting of the English colonies in North America followed a similar course; their charters were based on the conventions of the home country.

(ii) But equally, a people may decide to write out its constitution as a deliberate revolutionary break with the old customary one, in order to reflect the new political or social situation and to create new ground rules. Such was the case with the individual thirteen North American colonies in 1776, and even more, the (by then) confederated states in 1787 when they decided on a new and federal union. Similarly with the French National Assembly of 1789, and for that matter, the Convention and the Directory after it. Similar again is the case of the Latin American colonies (excepting Brazil) when they revolted from the Spanish Empire between 1811 and 1822; and for that matter, the Spaniards themselves when they instituted their 1812 Constitution, which provided much of the inspiration for those Spanish-American constitutions.

I think I am prepared to generalise to the extent of saying:

(i) the first appearance of a written constitution in a country *always* reflects a break in institutional continuity, and

(ii) once the constitution is written it is *always* written thereafter; either there are amendments or new constitutions in their entirety, but never a return to the old unwritten constitution except in the rare event of such a revulsion against the new constitution that it is abrogated and the situation simply reverts to the status quo ante. This is what happened in England in 1660. Another example is Spain where the country reverted to its traditional constitution after Ferdinand VII abrogated the 1812 Constitution in 1820, and again, (after its temporary restitution) between 1823 and 1833.

Why? One reason why has already been provided: *ne obliviscéris* – lest you forget your old constitution or, alternatively, lest you forget the New Order. But this merges with a more pregnant and urgent mode of the imperative of *ne obliviscéris*: the written constitution is envisaged, not just as a general reminder, but as a simultaneous signalling device *and* self-acting sanction for its provisions. This aspiration – or perhaps intention is the better word? – comes out transparently in the following excerpt from the French Declaration of the Rights of Man and the Citizen of 1789. It says that the National Assembly has declared these Rights, so that *inter alia*:

> This declaration, perpetually present to all members of the body social, shall be a constant reminder to them of their rights and duties;
>
> So that, since it will be possible at any moment to compare the acts of the legislative authority and those of the executive authority with the final end of all political institutions, those acts shall thereby be the more respected.

Where? Constitutions in the sense I have defined them in my opening paragraph originated in Europe and nowhere else in the world. The reason is that no other region threw up and perpetuated and institutionalised the combination of two notions – the limitation of government by overriding law, and justice arrived at by a *lis inter partes*. The first of these notions is not European at all, but Jewish. The second is indeed European and derives principally from Rome rather than Greece, but was then re-invented by the Germanic tribes in the Middle Ages, and those two traditions were synthesised on the Continent (but not in England) by the 'Reception' of Roman Law that took place from the thirteenth century onwards.

The Jewish contribution   The Jewish monarchy is the first limited monarchy known to the world. The Jewish tribes were united, after Moses, by their common observance of the Mosaic code. The interpretation of this code was left, at first, to the *Shofetim*, translated in English as the 'Judges'. These were heroic-charismatic leaders. The last of them was the prophet Samuel. Defeat at the hands of the Philistines provoked the tribesmen to demand to 'be like other nations' i.e. to have a king. The Bible retains two opposite traditions respecting this. One represents Samuel as reprehending the people for, so to speak, deserting God, the other shows him deliberately calling on Saul and then on David at God's behest, and anointing them. The contest between the two traditions is carried on through the Old Testament and never so much as in the Prophets. But in the conflicts of the two traditions one thing is quite clear. At best, the king is a redundancy; he is there to protect his people from conquest (organising them accordingly) and to protect the cult. For the rest, behaviour is ordained from God through the Mosaic Laws. The monarch's infraction of or backsliding from these laws absolves the people from their obedience, as the Prophets never cease to preach and a number of revolutions demonstrate.[13] Monarchy therefore is limited, not in its means of execution, nor in a number of matters not covered in the Mosaic Laws, but in respect of all the matters that are covered by these.

The tradition that kings are limited by a divine law which is outside them and uncreated by them was appropriated by the Christian Church – but without the Mosaic Law (from which it dispensed its followers). It substituted a code of its own which, incidentally, was nowhere near as specific and detailed. But for all that, it did insist that monarchy was limited by the divine laws, of which it claimed to be the unique repository and interpreter.

The Roman and the feudal contributions   Throughout their history the Romans developed a peculiar and powerful appetite for – if I may use an expressive common phrase – 'doing things by the book'. I will not go into the reasons for this which are partly due to the very nature of citizenship (a notion, invented by the Greeks, whose essence is partnership in a co-operative enterprise) and partly due to the way subjects were incorporated into its rule under a charter of their province or *civitas*, as the case might be. At all events, citizen and subject alike were answerable only in respect of pre-existing laws. The notion, as everyone knows, was most highly developed in the sphere of private, or civil, law. Public law was relatively underdeveloped, in the sense that very wide discretion was given to magistrates in respect of public offences. Yet even in the case of subjects, the rule of law began to obtain when, in the later republic, it became possible for aggrieved subjects to come to Rome and have ex-governors tried for malpractice. Now the point here is that the subject's mode of complaint against the Governor was assimilated to the civil law's procedure of a *lis inter partes* i.e. the subject could take on the authorities, on equal terms.

We can see the process working even under the Principate, c. AD 100, in the letters of Pliny the Younger where he describes the cases in which he is engaged, prosecuting governors for malfeasance.[14] While Roman law survived and was codified in the Eastern Empire it died out in Western Europe (save in a barbarised form in certain southerly regions) during the Dark Ages. It was supplanted by German customary law, of a primitive, restricted and barbarous nature. But these barbarians had a respect, almost a mystical respect, for the sanctity of law, despite the poverty of its subject matter, procedures, and penalties. As the Dark Ages emerged into feudalism this generalised respect for law attached itself to the specific laws that arose out of the nascent feudal relationships. The essence of these relationships was that private rights and public duties were compounded together and political relationships were founded upon the basis of contract; so that in the event, rights and duties under public law were assimilated to the same processes etc. as those under private law, and both were treated as a *lis inter partes*. I repeat: a public relationship could be contested as a *lis inter partes* between subject and suzerain, for it had been assimilated under feudalism to the same sphere as a private action.[15]

In no other region in the entire world but Europe did this happen. On the Continent development was affected by the renascence of Roman Law (and to the disadvantage of the subject). There the inquisitorial procedure of Rome, fiscal absolutism, and the privileged status of the bureaucracy in the special administrative courts that arose in the Late Roman Empire were all eagerly resuscitated by the monarchs and territorial princes. In England, on the other hand, which rejected the reception of Roman Law, the adversary procedure, trial by jury, and the prerogative writs made it possible for the citizen to stand up to the Crown: as witness the famous cases under James I, Charles I, and finally James II, respecting the limitations on the royal prerogative.

Yet whether in England or in Europe, charges had to be laid under a law. In state trials that law was very widely drawn, admittedly; but for all that, the notion was that law and not the arbitrary personal whim of the executive had prevailed. Often the trial was rigged, as in the case of the Templars by Philip the Fair of France, but it was, ostensibly, a condemnation by law.[16]

Western Europe, in short, was the only region in the entire world that developed a respect for procedural guarantees in law and envisaged the possibility of the subject challenging the government as a litigant, by 'due process'. Without such a deep-rooted sentiment of the sanctity of law – not just of law in general but of laws in their specific substance – the notion of the constitution as a Basic Law, a *Grundgesetz*, could never have been anything more than the pious obeisances to *Ma'at*, or *Ti'en*, or *Dharma*, as the case might be; pious and well-meaning but without any cash value at all.

II

The history

The number of written constitutions of sovereign states today is nearly two hundred: if one were to add together their many former constitutions the total might be, perhaps, five times as great. It would take volumes to scrutinise these in any detail. All I can do here is to suggest the lines of such an inquiry. They are: (i) The modal constitutions, from 1776 to 1812. (ii) The great families deriving from these in the nineteenth century, in terms of the governmental structures, *modus operandi*, suffrage, and Declarations of Rights. (iii) The democratisation of those constitutions after 1918 and the emergence of a totally new pattern, the Soviet one. (iv) The post-1945 wholesaling of constitutions to the ex-colonial countries of Africa and Asia along the modal patterns, together with hybrid forms. It would be a formidable task for the historian: he would have to combine the chronological and developmental framework with the analytical and its discussion of origins, structures, the suffrage and the Declarations of Rights, as well as having to comment on the practical import of these constitutions, many of which are dishonoured and even more perverted, and where few even of the remainder operate exactly as the written texts lay down.

The modal constitutions 1776–1812

The first of all the modal constitutions is, of course, the traditional British constitutional monarchy. The second is the 1787 federal Constitution of the United States of America. This is particularly noteworthy for three innovations in the theory and practice of government: I mean the mutual independence of the Presidency and the legislature, a 'Bill of Rights', and the invention of federalism (since what had passed for this so far is what we today would call 'confederalism').[17] The third was the 1791 French unicameral Constitution, based on a restricted suffrage, with a weak executive power in the King. Though it was not operative for long, and in its short life broke down the original conception of a formal separation of powers between the executive and the legislature by making ministers responsible to the legislature and effectively denying the Crown its veto powers, this constitution was to influence the people of Spain in 1812, and, later, certain other European states.[18] The fourth constitution to act as a model was the now forgotten Spanish Constitution of 1812 which was itself partly derived from the French 1791 Constitution;[19] together with the United States model it was to act as a pattern for the new Spanish American Republics.

Till circa 1900

The spread of written constitutions As Napoleon's grip weakened, more and more countries adopted their own written constitutions. In Europe, it was the northern and western countries which led off, followed by the *sui generis* Switzerland in 1848 and Piedmont in the same year, and then spreading eastward to Germany in 1867–70, Austria-Hungary in 1867, and finally Russia (in a way) in 1905. Greece had had a written constitution since 1843. As the Balkans were liberated from the Ottoman Empire in the last third of the century, they too, of course, adopted written constitutions.

Meanwhile between 1811 and 1823, the Spanish colonies in Central and South America adopted written constitutions as and when they obtained independence, and this process continued through the century as the originally very large and conglomerate republics broke up into succession states.

In Canada, Australasia and South Africa, the British colonies, originally governed under statutes laid down by the mother country, obtained increasing autonomy and by the end of the century were on the brink of the formal independence that would be guaranteed in 1931 under the Statute of Westminster. All, then, had written constitutions excepting New Zealand which, by a freak, was governed under a number of organic laws dating from the colonial period, one of which, however, had the appropriate title of 'The Constitution Act 1852'.

Finally, the constitution mania spread to Asia. The Turks received a written constitution in 1876, but this lasted only a few months and they were without a constitution until the 1876 one was revived and modified by the Young Turks in 1908. Japan received a constitution in 1889, Persia in 1906, China in 1912.

The great 'families' of constitutions The first great 'family' was the British. Its 'Dominions' (as opposed to the Crown Colonies) were successively endowed with Westminster-type constitutions. But there was one highly significant modification to the type: federalism. The former colonies in Canada and Australia had originally been separate dependencies of the Crown. In 1867 the Canadian Confederation was accomplished, and the new federal state endowed with a federal government, but with a cabinet system. The same occurred in Australia in 1901. South Africa was perhaps an even better case for federation, since account had to be taken of the Boer states as well as the English ones and some solution had to be found for the situation consequent on the Boer War. In the event, in 1909, the Union was endowed with a largely unitary, and only quasi-federal, type of constitution.

The second great family was the American presidential-cum-federal type, which powerfully influenced the new Latin American Republics. But one must not overrate American influence. In fact – if one can generalise about twenty republics – these constitutions were also powerfully influenced by the Spanish 1812 Constitution. However, with their (often) federal form, their separately elected and extremely powerful presidency, their nominal adhesion to the principle of the separation of powers, these constitutions more clearly belong to the American rather than the European types of constitutions. (Brazil is quite exceptional. It was a monarchy and operated along the lines of the Portugese Constitution of 1822, except that it was federal. That Portugese Constitution was itself derived from the Spanish 1812 Constitution.)

Now come two different European families. The first, modelled partly on the French 1791 Constitution and partly on the British constitution (bicameral, unlike the French) was what we may style constitutional monarchy-cum-cabinet government. It was to be found, in its various avatars, in France, Belgium, the Netherlands, and Scandinavia. Italy, unified in stages, adopted the 1848 Statute of Piedmont, which itself followed this same common pattern. Swizerland's 1848 constitution was *sui generis*.

But in Germany and in Austria-Hungary a quite different pattern was created. Here the ministers were appointed, dismissed by and responsible to the Crown and not the legislature. The cabinet had to win the consent of the legislature, but it was not responsible to it. These two Central European monarchies struck a balance between the irremovable and free-standing hereditary head of state, on the one hand, and the elected legislature, on the other.

As constitution mania reached the Asian countries, they made selective choices. The Japanese Constitution of 1889 was modelled directly on the *Kaiserreich*. The Chinese Constitution of 1912, which never came into force, was modelled on the American pattern. The Young Turks of 1908 re-adopted the West European cabinet pattern.

Modus operandi of the constitutions The Latin American republican constitutions, save in Uruguay, Chile, and Colombia, never 'bit' and the subcontinent was delivered over to *caudillismo*. The Brazilian monarchy and (from 1889) Republic was, however, stable. So too were the ex-British colonies which were able to work their Westminster-type constitutions without difficulty, since they had been acclimatised to them for decades. The chief interest must centre on the way the Western European constitutional monarchies performed. It must be rememberd that, for most of the century, suffrage was highly restricted, and also that legislatures in these countries (Holland excepted) were innovations. Their tradition for at least two hundred years had been one of a royal bureaucracy. In short, new-fangled legislatures were grafted on to time-honoured and very powerful bureaucracies. This was clearly expressed in the texts of the German and Austro-Hungarian Constitutions, but it proved to be the working practice in most of the constitutional monarchies too: there, the Crown took a high degree of interest in politics so that the practical effect was one of a balance between the crown-cum-bureaucracy and the legislature, and not the omnipotence of the latter. Only in France was this pattern broken, under the Third Republic, and not even there until the MacMahon crisis of 1877.

Citizens' rights Citizens' rights were recognised on two planes – the extension of the suffrage, and the declarations of rights enshrined in the various constitutions. Universal suffrage and extensive Bills of Rights were a feature of the Latin American constitutions from the outset. They were quite worthless. As in today's spate of new Third World constitutions, they were the modish tribute that vice pays to martyred virtue. In ironical contrast, in the British Dominions where there were no bills of rights in the constitutions, the common law freedoms were upheld by the courts as faithfully as in Britain.

In Europe, from the very outset, notwithstanding Bentham's remark that natural and imprescriptible rights were 'nonsense on stilts', it became *de rigueur* to follow the example of the French 1789 Declaration of the Rights of Man and the Citizen and insert

State	Date of Bill of Rights	Date of universal male suffrage
Austria	1867	1907
Belgium	1831	1891–2
France	1789	1848/1870
Germany	1918	1867/1870
Italy	1848/1870	1912
Norway	1814	1905
Poland	1921	1921
Spain	1812 (highly temporary)	1812 (ditto)
USA	1801	c. 1850
USSR	1918	1918

something similar in their constitutions. These declarations therefore come much earlier than universal suffrage. (But the dates varied according to special historical circumstances; for example, the foundation of a new state, Germany, in 1867/70.) The table above shows the general drift. (It is illustrative, not exhaustive.)

The inter-war years
The interest here is entirely European. The story is a simple one: the rise and extension of the West European-type of parliamentary democratic constitution, and the emergence of two entirely new constitutional models which by 1939 threatened, between them, to expunge it for ever.

The year 1918 witnessed the fall of the two Central European monarchies and in their place, and that of their succession states, the adoption of republican constitutions, universal male, and in some places female, suffrage, the assertion of legislative sovereignty over the executive, the elaboration of Declarations of Rights, and the extension of such constitutions to revived states like the Baltic States, Czechoslovakia and Poland. Some of these constitutions, such as those of Weimar Germany and Poland, incorporated the most refined devices contrived by liberal-democratic theory. In general, Western parliamentary democracy had now reached its highest historical point.

From this period, however, a very striking change occurs in the character of the 'rights' embodied in many of these constitutions. Hitherto, with minor exceptions, they had comprised procedural guarantees and civil liberties. Now they began to include substantive and material rights. The development occurred almost simultaneously through the Mexican and Russian revolutions of 1917 and the German revolution of 1918. The Mexican Constitution of 1917 provided for free universal education and in article 123 – which was set apart so as to emphasise its importance – also guaranteed minimum wages and the right of workers to unionise and strike, and promised a comprehensive social security system including health and welfare programmes. The 1918 Constitution of the RSFSR (Part I) was much more modest; it did not go far beyond promising free universal education, and the USSR was to have to wait until the 1936 Stalin Constitution before it was promised substantive rights superior to those of Mexico. But neither of these sets of 'rights' could hold a candle to Part II of the Weimar Constitution which consisted of no less than 56 separate articles, which were grouped under the headings of 'the individual', 'social life', 'education', and 'economic life' (which included social security). One finds similar though less lengthy lists of such rights in others among the new constitutions of Europe; thus the 1921 Yugoslav Constitution (Part III), the 1921 Polish Constitution (Chapter V) and the 1922 Constitution of Romania (Part II).[20]

Even by 1933 many of these constitutions had given way to some kind of authoritarian or autocratic rule; Italy, the Baltic Republics, Finland, Austria, Hungary, Poland had all succumbed. Of all the new states only Czechoslovakia had a vigorous democracy. In South-eastern Europe the parliamentary system was increasingly debilitated, distorted and corrupted.

At the same time, two new constitutional models had emerged. One was the Soviet model, based on the 1918 Constitution of the Great Russian Soviet Socialist Republic. The other was the corporatist-autocratic model found in Italy and Portugal, and reaching its full potency in Nazi Germany in 1933. These two models, which were supposedly antithetical, shared certain major characteristics. Both were authoritarian. Both were totalitarian. And both incorporated into the constitution the supremacy of one single monopolistic official political party. The last is the great governmental invention of the twentieth century.

The Soviet model did not spread; it was not permitted to. The Nazi-Fascist model did. By 1939, either by conquest or contagion, it had established itself in some weak or strong form over the whole of Europe outside England, France, Belgium, the Netherlands, Norway, Sweden, Denmark and Switzerland.

The post-war era
For a historian of constitutions the central fact of this era must surely be the creation of about a hundred successor states to the

European empires, and the central question: Which of the models on offer would they follow?

The defeat of the Axis powers had eliminated the Nazi-Fascist model. But it had enabled the Soviet authorities to impose their own model on the whole of Eastern Europe and when China followed this path in 1949, it become one of the great 'export-models' of the world.

By now, the American model was no longer for emulation. It is significant that the Americans imposed a Western European cabinet-type system and not their own presidential type on conquered Japan; and they also allowed the Germans to opt for *Kanzler-demokratie*. So, in Europe, the western-type parliamentary model was revived: and unexpectedly, perhaps, it began to thrive as it had never done in the pre-war years.

The liquidation of the European empires occurred in and after 1960, by which time France had rejigged its parliamentary system into the semi-presidential system of the Fifth Republic. Thus the models which the colonial powers were likely to offer their succession states as they conceded them independence were, basically, the Westminster type and the French presidential type. This represents fairly faithfully the initial distribution of constitutional patterns in the Third World. But, once independent, the succession states took their own course and, sometimes by choice (Algeria, Guinea), the new states opted for something resembling the Soviet model.

Elsewhere, revolution and rebellion led by Marxist forces had the same result: as in the remnants of the Portuguese empire in Africa, or in South-East Asia. At the same time, many of the Westminster or French-presidential type regimes moved in an authoritarian direction, above all by incorporating into their constitutions the monopoly of a single official party. Finally, many of the original Western-type constitutions were overthrown by military *coups* or armed uprisings led by persons who openly espoused the Soviet model and adopted it for their own authoritarian purposes. Thus the contagion of the Soviet constitutions was leaked into these originally west European-type constitutions, revolutionising their nature.

Only two points need be added to this sketch of the Third World constitutions. The first is that all of them concede universal suffrage. The second is that all of them contain Declarations of Rights. Not only that; in many of them, these declarations run to several pages in length. The most striking example is the Indian Constitution of 1949. Articles 12–35 comprise a list of 'Fundamental Rights' and another list of 'Directive principles of state policy'. The latter are not enforceable in the courts but must be applied by legislators when they enact the laws. Together, these articles incorporate provisions relating to equality; freedom; defence against exploitation; freedom of religion; non-discrimination in culture and education; property rights; an adequate standard of living; equal pay for equal work as between men and women; the right to work and employment; and free and compulsory education. It is a formidable list, but it is only the most complete exemplar of what has become well-nigh universal, as indicated by the internationalisation of the matter. For in December 1948 the United Nations adopted and proclaimed the Universal Declaration of Human Rights, no less, in thirty clauses which posits the right of everybody, everywhere, to such things as work, just and favourable remuneration, an adequate standard of living including social security, health and welfare provision, and much else besides.[21] In view of the stark contrast between the rights here declared and the exact opposite that actually obtains in practically all the states on the globe, one does not know whether to howl with laughter or with anguish. The historian of constitutions would therefore be well advised to introduce into his analysis, beginning with the French Revolution Constitutions of 1791, a distinction which we have not so far made. It is the elementary one between working constitutions, façade constitutions and purely nominal constitutions.

This would take me far beyond the already over-ambitious scope of this chapter. All that needs to be said here is that the constitutions falling into the first of these categories can be counted, almost, on one's fingers and toes.

Notes and references

1. S.E. Finer, *Five Constitutions* (Penguin, 1979), p. 15.
2. See, for example, J. Bright, *A History of Israel*, 3rd edn (Philadelphia, 1981), pp. 183ff.; H. Jagersma, *A History of Israel from Alexander the Great to Bar Kochba* (SCM Press, 1985), pp. 79–135; H. Ben Sasson, *A History of the Jewish People* (Weidenfeld and Nicholson, 1976), Part II (H. Tadmor), pp. 91–124, Part III (M. Stern), pp. 217–38. And see note 4 below.
3. Extensively illustrated by C.H. McIlwain, *Constitutionalism, Ancient and Modern* (Cornell University Press, 1940).
4. Particularly the later Hasmoneans: see Josephus (tr. Whiston), *Antiquities of the Jews*, Book XII, Chapter XIff.
5. For *Dharma*, S.J. Tambieh, *World Conqueror and World Renouncer* (Cambridge University Press, 1976), pp. 32–72. For *Ma'at*, see B.G. Trigger *et al.*, *Ancient Egypt: a social history* (Cambridge University Press, 1983), pp. 74–76; H. Frankfort, *Kingship and the Gods* (University of Chicago Press, 1978), pp. 51–60. For *Ti'en*, see K–C Hsiao, *A history of Chinese political thought* (Princeton University Press, 1979); W–T Chan, *A source-book in Chinese philosophy* (Princeton University Press, 1963), pp. 22–23, 45, 78; and H.G. Creel, *The origins of statecraft in China*, Vol. I (University of Chicago Press, 1970), Chapter 5, 'The mandate of Heaven'.

6. J. A. Wilson, *The Culture of Ancient Egypt* (University of Chicago Press, 1956), pp. 172–73.
7. Ch'ien Mu, *Traditional Government in Imperial China* (Chinese University Press, Hong Kong, 1982)
8. McIlwain, *op. cit.*
9. Aristotle, *Politics*, 1292A:33; *The Constitution of Athens* (ed. P.J. Rhodes) (Penguin, 1984), 26.2; 41.2; and p. 89. 'Illegality' is the *'graphi paranomon'*, on which see V. Ehrenberg, *The Greek State* (Methuen, 1974), pp. 73–74. In the 4th century BC the sharp distinction between the *nomoi* and the *psēphismata* was effaced (*ibid.* pp. 56–7).
10. F.L. Ford, *Robe and Sword* (Harper Torchback, 1965), pp. 82–85.
11. So with the collapse of the Former Han, after 47 BC; of the Latter Han, after AD 159; of the T'ang, after 884; and of the Ming, 1620–44.
12. The prime example is the 'Stele of the Founders' of the colony of Cyrene, discovered some sixty years ago. For the text and a discussion, see J.V.A. Fine, *The Ancient Greeks* (Harvard University Press, 1983), p. 89.
13. The literature is vast of course, but the entire matter is summarised in the authoritative text, Fr Roland de Vaux, *Ancient Israel, its life and institutions.* (London, 1973), Part II, Chapter II, pp. 91–99, 'The Israelite concept of the state'. For the overthrow of rulers because they infringed the cult, see among many examples the destruction of Queen Jezebel at the hands of Jehu (2 Kgs 9:30ff.) and that of Queen Athaliah of Judah (2 Kgs 11).
14. *Letters of the Younger Pliny* (tr. Radice) (Penguin, 1969), especially the case of Marius Priscus, pp. 67–70.
15. You had to go to a higher court; so that subordinates to the Emperor or the King, should these be your immediate rulers, could be sued by proceedings in the Court of the Emperor or King, as the case might be. The problem was: what happened if you wanted to sue the agent of the Emperor or the King, for there were no courts higher than theirs! This was got around in various ways. Thus, in Imperial Rome though you certainly could not sue the Emperor you could sue the Emperor's fisc. For the various complicated modalities in medieval England, see Sir Paul Vinogradoff (ed.), *Oxford Studies in Social and Legal History*, Vol. VI, xii; L. Ehrlich, *Proceedings against the Crown (1216–1377)*. (Oxford, 1921).
16. M. Barber, *The Trial of the Templars* (Cambridge University Press, 1978).
17. Cf E.A. Freeman, *History of Federal Government*, Vol. I (Macmillan, 1863), who gets this right, and J.A.O. Larsen, *Greek Federal States* (Oxford University Press, 1968), who gets it quite wrong.
18. It can be conveniently found in L. Duguit and H. Monnier, *Les Constitutions de la France depuis 1789*, 5th edn (Paris, 1932).
19. For an analysis and commentary see, L.S. Agesta, *Historia del constitucionalismo espanol* (Madrid, 1955), pp. 41–114.
20. The texts can be found in B. Mirkine-Guetzévitch, *Les Constitutions de l'Europe nouvelle*, 2nd edn (Paris, 1930).
21. To be found in J. de Blank (ed.), *Human Rights* (Heinemann, 1967), pp. 17–23.

3 The theory of liberal constitutionalism
Ghiţa Ionescu

Où la morale ne gouverne pas, le bonheur se perd par la démence, l'adversité par l'avilissement. La volonté de tout un peuple ne peut rendre juste ce qui est injuste. (Benjamin Constant, *Principes de politique applicables à tous les gouvernements représentatifs*, Paris, 1815)

If in the history of political thought there is such a thing as a 'theory of liberal constitutionalism', one of the few theories which this elusive appellation could be made to fit is that of Benjamin Constant. Formal confirmation of this statement can be found only too obviously in the chronology of the history of political ideas, and in the concurrent history of political semantics. For it can be demonstrated that Constant's theory, especially when it is interpreted with some empathy, succeeds in reconciling these two terms, or still better in introducing a conceptual hyphen between them. In the formula 'liberal-constitutionalism', the dialectical hyphen saves the two terms from the two opposite dangers which their co-habitation threatens, that is, from either ingesting each other in a final pleonasm or, on the contrary, becoming increasingly antithetical.

Let us take first the danger of pleonasm. If 'constitutionalism' is the theory which posits first the reciprocal toleration by all citizens of the rights and freedoms of the other citizens, and secondly the limitation of government by means of checks and balances, these same conditions will be found to be inherent in the liberal state. Hence the tautology.

But if the citizens, egged on by belief in the continuous progress of the emancipation of the individual through permissive education and reform, which is basic to liberalism, abuse their individual and collective rights and freedoms, thus endangering those of others and the constitutional order itself, then obviously there will be a clash between the liberalism which undermines and the constitutionalism which defends the public order.

The relations between constitutionalism and liberalism, however, as well as the genuine meaning of each of these two concepts, receive their ultimate clarification only when they are projected on to the background of the history of ideas and of political terminology. It is bad enough that daily political language uses basic terms such as democracy, republic, or nationalisation in senses detached from, or indeed opposed to, their etymological legitimation. But nowadays political theory itself and a revived philosophy of history suffer from such an acute epidemic of anachronism that immunisation against it should be undertaken more vigilantly than ever before.

So, for the word *liberal* first. Its birth certificate dates from the appellation given to a group of deputies in the Spanish Cortes of Cádiz of 1812 (*los liberales*). The name spread like wildfire throughout Europe and from Europe, later, to end up in Britain, where it was applied to the first professional political party ever to exist, a professionalism which was the key to its success. Therefore to write, as, for example, Professor C.B. Macpherson and many other political philosophers – and especially the successors of Harold Laski, who relished the idea of accusing liberalism of guilt by association with capitalism – that 'the earliest liberals in the Anglo-American tradition were, in my view, the theorists and activists of the English Civil War and Commonwealth periods, ranging from the Levellers to Cromwell and Milton and other republicans'[1] is sheer historical nonsense.

As for the noun 'liberalism' as distinct from the adjective 'liberal', the definition of which is notoriously elusive,[2] the first precise use of the expression occurs in Madame de Staël's observation that the political thought of Benjamin Constant should be called 'le libéralisme'. Some fifty years later the expression also appeared in the English philosophical vocabulary to describe the uneasy trinity of Benthamite utilitarianism, old English radicalism, and Continental liberalism, under the equally uneasy authority of John Stuart Mill.

Sartori, although fully recognising in his by now classic *Democratic Theory* that the *word* had appeared only in the nineteenth century, proposes the ingenious theory:[3]

> this was unfortunate. Being born too late the term has not had time to take root... Too late, not only because the term liberalism was coined after liberalism, as yet unnamed, had already produced its results, if not the essential part of itself, but above all, because at that moment history had begun to move fast, so fast that the liberals did not succeed in making up for the great amount of time that had been lost between the clandestine party and the official baptism.

This is, as I said, an ingenious and generous interpretation. But obviously it is playing with words, or at least with one word.

Constitutions themselves – another word which acquires its real meaning only in the ninteenth century – are a consequence of the autonomy of politics: for as human beings are supposed to organise and conduct their lives on their own, it becomes imperative that they should put down in black and white how they intend to organise it (indeed *laissez-faire* itself is a conception of organisation). And in so far as the conduct of their affairs by all individuals living in a unit of man-made rule should not and cannot be monopolised by their representatives, elected to govern or even to 'administer' them, the role of the liberal constitution is to enumerate once again the 'rights' of the individual and the duties of the government towards the individual. But such was the vogue of constitutions in the nineteenth century, and even more in the twentieth, that there soon emerged the difference between states-with-a-constitution, and constitutional states, i.e. those in which the state and its agencies are kept under the control of the citizens by means of checks and balances.

The crisis of the Church in the sixteenth century and the subsequent emergence of the nation-state (in essence a fragmentation of the Christian fraternity into national jealousies) gave a new priority to public law and political organisation. But it was all based on 'virtue' – and the first revolutions in modern history were effected by the Puritans in God's name. The American Founding Fathers were happy to have left behind them 'the extream Corruption prevalent ... in this rotten old State' and contrasted it with the 'glorious publick Virtue so predominant in our rising Country'.[4] The Jacobins never ceased in their quest for 'vertu'. Moreover, the two eighteenth-century revolutions also promised happiness to their peoples.

The new concern of all individuals with the 'pursuit of happiness' was to extend the sphere of rights and freedoms as far as possible and to 'protect' them, indeed to 'guarantee' them as securely as possible against the interference of public law. To be sure, the experience of royal and imperial absolutism and the strife of religious intolerance fully justified the attempts of Locke and Montesquieu to estabish a new, constitutional, rule of law. The initial purpose of the American and French Revolutions was to ensure the people's freedom through a constitution – and already the dominant preoccupation was with rights, namely, how to 'protect' or 'guarantee' them by law. As the constitutional pattern gradually established itself, it became evident that the 'guarantee' of the sphere of autonomy of the citizen was its principal object; and that the means of fulfilling this essential condition consisted, on the one hand, of the structures and functions of political representation of individuals, and, on the other, of the separation of powers between the legislative, the executive and the judiciary.

As for *constitutionalism*, it naturally became the doctrine which, in the secular age of the autonomy of politics inherent in the principles of 'national sovereignty' and 'sovereignty of the people', demanded that this kind of state should have a written Law which would set out the rights and obligations of citizens and the institutions established to make them work, with all the checks and balances required to watch over the proper functioning of state and society on behalf of the people. Therefore, in many respects, *constitutionalism* and *liberalism* were historical and doctrinal twins, the one in charge of order, the other in charge of progress. Moreover, as it happened, Benjamin Constant soon came to be considered, in France at least, as a founding father of constitutionalism as well as of liberalism. We had better therefore now turn to him.

Cutting sovereignty down to size

Benjamin Constant (1767–1830) has, like Rousseau, his Swiss compatriot and Protestant co-religionist, a many-sided reputation. The reputation of both men has in any case been affected by the great contrast between the admiration felt for their work and their public stance, and the criticism of their private lives. Benjamin Constant was a gambler, a duellist (when afflicted in his old age by a bad leg he fought his duels sitting in a chair), and, above all, an incorrigible womaniser.

Although twice secretly married, he had seduced the most brilliant women of the particularly brilliant European intellectual society of his time (with the exception of Madame Récamier, whose rejection tortured his last years). Yet at the same time he had conducted a long-lasting love affair with Madame de Staël, whose loyal companion he had been in her struggle against the Jacobins and Napoleon, and during her long years of exile. Seldom has the symbiosis between two lovers been more complete. On the physical level, they had a daughter, Albertine, the future duchesse de Broglie; while on the intellectual level it still remains very difficult to disentangle their respective contributions to each other's works and ideas, so interwoven are they. But there is this difference, that most of Constant's political philosophy was published in the thirteen years after Madame de Staël's death.

These were also the years when Constant won recognition in France as one of the most famous parliamentarians in its history, as its constitution-maker (the constitution of 1815 was called 'la Benjamine'), and as its most dedicated and most disinterested liberal leader – he never wanted to be a minister. At his death, the national funeral brought all Paris out into the streets. Victor Hugo wrote, with due poetic licence, that 1830 was the year of the death of three popes: Pius XII, Goethe, the pope of literature, and Constant, the pope of liberty.

As a writer, Constant remains, through the novel *Adolphe*, and the *Journaux Intimes*, one of the sharpest analysts of the mysteries of the pursuit of love (Stendhal grew up in his shadow). As a political philosopher, he succeeded in giving unity not only to the particularly dialectical notion of Liberal, torn as it is between its dual aims of securing individual freedom and public order, but also to the questions he had posed to himself in his own work. In that sense his work contrasts with that of his predecessor Rousseau, forever bleeding from the wounds of the contradictions he himself inflicted on it. And it focused more precisely on the specific problems of liberalism than that of his successor, Tocqueville, who had already witnessed the submergence of liberalism in the deep waters of egalitarian democracy.

Constant published three major but slender works: *De l'esprit de conquête et de l'usurpation* (1814), which contains in embryo the subseqently published *De la liberté des anciens comparée à celles des modernes* (1819); *Principes de politique applicables à tous les gouvernements représentatifs* (1815) and *De la religion considérée dans sa source, ses formes et ses développements* (five volumes, 1824–31). This is slight, compared with the massive output of Rousseau, John Stuart Mill, or Tocqueville. Moreover, Constant's whole style and approach is somewhat more rhetorical than academic. Finally, the fact that he deliberately elevated the discussion to the most abstract sphere of political, moral, and religious concepts, and turned a strangely blind eye to the economic (industrialisation) and social (class conflicts) phenomena of contemporary French and British society could leave him open to the charge of utopianism.

On the other hand, it can be argued that only when measured on the scale of the ultimate problems of the human condition, and notably that of the quest for justice, can the economic, social and political problems be seen in their actual, and much reduced, size, and in their much more relative significance. In that case this possibly utopian exploration, shows its major continuity, as it passes like a red thread from the work of Constant to that of Tocqueville, Unamuno (who was actually a member of the Spanish Liberal Party), to T.H. Green, who was a liberal, and more recently to Isaiah Berlin, Giovanni Sartori and John Rawls.

There is, I believe, more logic in Constant's apparently haphazard and *ad hoc* works than meets the eye. The logic of the argument of his work is confirmed by that of its gestation. The one subject that Constant ruminated over throughout his life was religion. It was the first subject he ever wrote about while still an adolescent, and it was the subject of his last published work (the final volume came out posthumously). This was not unusual for an alert intellect of his period, since the separation from the old religion left every idealistic mind (as distinct from the materialistic Helvetius or his pupil, Bentham) tortured, after the first joys of liberation from the discipline of the Church, by what appeared terrifyingly as the final black hole of rationalism. Even Robespierre had had to create a Goddess to whom to devote his need for prayer.

Constant's essay on religion obviously leads on to an anti-clerical and pantheistic conclusion, but the main line of the argument is the affirmation of what he calls 'the religious sentiment', which he describes as the essence, the initial spark of 'those principles of justice and of pity which no human beings can cease to observe without degrading and denying their very nature'.[5] Once we discover this premiss of Constant's reasoning, and once we realise that for him the basic feeling of every individual human being is 'this mysterious sentiment', the religious sentiment, through which we find 'in the physical world all that belongs to nature, to the universe, to its immensity; and in the moral world all that arouses pity or enthusiasm; the spectacle of a virtuous action, of a generous sacrifice ... of the sorrows of others assisted or assuaged ... contempt for vice ... and resistance to tyranny ...', then it becomes easier to follow his liberal trend of thought. It is a trend which begins and ends with the individual and his conscience in the world – in the world, not only in society, it is the idealistic liberal trend of thought.

Once we are aware of the depth from which his theory of liberal constitutionalism sprang, we are no longer surprised to find Constant stating at the very beginning of his *Principes de politique* that:[6]

> since a constitution is the guarantee of the freedom of a people, everything that is related to that freedom is constitutional, but nothing which is not related to it is constitutional; that to extend the constitution over everything was to open up dangers for it everywhere, and to surround it with shoals; *that there are basic foundations which national authorities could not touch.*

The limitation of the constitution is then logically presented by Constant as the consequence of the prior limitation of the sovereignty of the people. Thus:[7]

> When one assumes that the sovereignty of the people is unlimited, one is setting up and throwing into human society in haphazard fashion a degree of power too great in itself, and which is an evil regardless of in whose hands it is lodged. It is the degree of power which is at fault, not those who wield it. One must act against the weapon, not against the arm which brandishes it. *Some bodies are too heavy for the hands of men to bear their weight* ... Of necessity there is some part of human existence which remains individual and independent, and which by right falls outside all social competences. Sovereignty exists only in a limited and relative manner.

Further, Constant extends this principle of limitation in an apparently more controversial way to human law itself:[8]

> No authority on earth is unlimited, neither that of the people, nor that of those who claim to represent it, nor that of kings, under whatever title they reign, not even that of the law, which being only the expression of the will of the people or of the kings, according to the kind of government, must be circumscribed within the same limitations as those of the authority which issues it ... No duty can bind us ... to those laws which not only restrict our legitimate liberties but order us to act in ways which run counter to those eternal principles of justice and pity which no man can cease to observe without degrading or denying his very nature ... The will of a whole people cannot make just what is unjust.

I suggested that this critique of the law itself might seem controversial, indeed bordering on anarchy. But it is clear that Constant is situating the laws made by human beings under those *principles of justice and of pity* which are sown in every human being by that mysterious 'sentiment of religion', the ultimate source of individual morality. In his recent study on Constant, P. Manent asked whether the limitations he placed on sovereignty were of a 'historical' or of a 'natural' order, that is to say, did they derive from the historical mutation perceived by Constant between the society of the *Anciens* and of the *Modernes*, or from the, by then, seemingly obsolete Law of Nature?[9] The answer, this time, is categorically in favour of the latter. The 'bodies which are too heavy for the hands of men to bear their weight', 'the basic foundations which national authorities cannot touch' and 'the principles of justice and pity which no man can cease to observe' emanate directly from the religious sentiment. Even if this sentiment is emancipated from the established church, it is still that 'certain inclination to know the truth about God and to live in society' described by St Thomas Aquinas, who also concludes in his *Summa Theologica* (1a, 2ae, 94, 2) that 'in this respect there come under the Natural Law all actions connected with such inclinations'.[10]

But another argument which Constant adduces for considering sovereignty, and the will of the people, as inherently relative, derives, as Manent shows, from historical considerations. This is the argument that in so far as the way of life of people and peoples changes with the expansion of knowledge, information and circulation, themselves fostered by human science and the technical means it offers for such an expansion, it is inconceivable that the way of life of human beings, and their understanding of it, should remain the same. One of the reasons why Rousseau's model of democracy is unachievable, and therefore misleading, is to be found, argues Constant, in the historical confusion he made between the life of the *Anciens* (the Greeks and the Romans) and the *Modernes* (the Europeans since at least the eighteenth century). This, combined with the geographical confusion he, and especially his interpreters, entertained, namely the belief that the kind of direct democracy perhaps appropriate for his federal, transnational, cantonal and diminutive fatherland, Switzerland, could be applicable to a vast, unitary country, with a homogeneous, indeed nationalistic, population like that of France, has had disastrous effects on modern politics ever since the French Revolution, when applied to the larger nation-states. According to Constant, civil liberty and political representation are what the Greeks and the Romans did not have either in their way of life or in their politics — and what modern societies must have. Representation works both ways in a modern society, in the interests both of the government and of the citizens. As regards the government, it is inconceivable that it could work in the modern world on the basis of the permanent deliberations and unanimous decisions taken in an *agora*, or even, more relatively, in a *forum*. Representation implies a selection, indeed later a professionalisation, of those who offer themselves to implement the policies approved by the majority of the population through accurate methods of popular consultation operated by the liberal method of government. This corresponds also to the existential requirements of those citizens 'who only wish to be left alone in the perfect independence of their occupations, of their projects, of their spheres of activity'.[11] The complex of individual activities is at the basis of modern society, the duty of government being only to see that they work freely.

Commerce (whose transnational effects of *communication* in all senses of the word Constant describes most perceptively as the motor of transnationalisation, which we know to have become inevitable in our days), and industry (which he mentions but whose supreme importance he fails to understand in spite of the work of his contemporary Saint-Simon) are the arteries of modern society. This is a particularly creative society – and individual creativity requires freedom and peace. The barrack-room mentality of despotism and militarism goes against the grain of such a society. 'The trading nations of modern Europe, industrious, civilised, situated in areas sufficiently large for their needs, and entertaining with other peoples relations which if interrupted would cause a disaster, have nothing to expect from military conquests,' he says. But, as though replying to the utilitarians, he adds: 'To defend the new system, it is not the identity of interests which should be demonstrated, but the universality of disinterestedness.'[12] And, as a general conclusion to his analysis of the difference between ancient and modern society,

Constant provides this cryptic sentence: 'The effect of all this is that individual existence is less involved in political existence.'[13] The full significance of this sentence will be easier to discuss in the general conclusions that I shall draw at the end of this chapter.

One more limitation which Constant considers necessary to prevent national sovereignty or the will of the people from becoming the tyranny which it is bound to become if left to itself, is at the top of the system – whereas free representation is at its base. Constant believes in the necessity of placing a *neutral* institution at the very top, that is *over* the political system, a kind of supreme, even if powerless, referee. The best example, in his view, is constitutional monarchy.[14]

> The royal power (by which I mean that of the head of the state, whatever title he bears) is a neutral power . . . . Constitutional monarchy creates this neutral power in the person of the head of the state. His ultimate interest is to see that no one power [legislative, executive and judiciary] should overthrow the other, but that all powers should support each other, be in agreement and act in concert.

The monarch:[15]

> stands high above human agitation, and it was the masterpiece of political organisation to have created in the very heart of those differences of opinion without which no liberties can flourish, an intangible sphere of security, of majesty, of impartiality, which allows these differences to manifest themselves without danger so long as they do not overstep certain boundaries, and which, as soon as danger arises, puts an end to it by legal and constitutional means, free of any taint of arbitrariness.

With all these limitations on the functioning of national sovereignty or the will of the people, Constant's theory of liberal constitutionalism transforms sovereignty into an open-ended and ever adjustable ceiling over the free functioning of a society itself under permanent rejuvenation. What holds the system together is not the outside power of institutions or their means of coercion, but the internal cohesion of the myriad individual consciences of free men who want their creative faculties to be unimpeded by anyone. Instead, they conduct their relations with others, and with society as a whole, on the plane of ethics, higher than that of politics, and which itself springs, in each of them, from the religious sentiment innate in any human being, which is what distinguishes the human species from all other animals.

As I said at the beginning, Constant's theory of floating constitutionalism, anchored only on the root of the religious origin of individual ethics, is the only *pure liberalism* – in other words liberalism without any of the qualifications which have since transformed it like that particularly controversial expression, liberal-democracy, two notions which are uneasy bedfellows. And only Constant's theory of liberal constitutionalism escapes the internal contradiction between the moral order required by constitutionalism, and the amoral progressive permissiveness which in our time goes under the name of liberalism and does so much to undermine it.

Why were Constant's ideas far less widely known than they obviously deserve? One reason was mentioned earlier: his writings do not really amount to an *oeuvre* of political philosophy. Another reason is the pronounced lack of sympathy of politically and ideologically triumphant utilitarian, materialistic liberalism for idealistic liberalism, indeed the clear incompatibility between the two theories. Constant's political writings are hardly known in Britain or the United States. In France too, although he is regarded with veneration and his roots are still alive in French individualism, Constant somehow fell between two stools. His theory of religious sentiment independent of the churches placed him between the two major, rival, schools of thought in his country: the rationalistic-atheistic, on the one hand, and the Catholic-clerical, on the other, whose deep-rooted dislike of his Protestantism, and especially of his kind of pantheism, has always been obvious.

Command and commandment in modern politics

Even those few who accept Constant's theory of the ultimate religious inspiration of ethical behaviour in the individual citizen might consider it to be somehow unoriginal. They might well ask what is the difference between his theory and Locke's much firmer article of faith in, for instance, the *Letter Concerning Toleration*, where, while seeking the institutional separation of the church from the state so as also to ensure true religious freedom, he continues to regard the individual's obligations towards the state and towards God as indivisible, *in foro interno*, and *in foro externo*; and where he goes so far as to refuse toleration to those who deny the existence of a divine power, because the 'promises, covenants and oaths which are the bonds of human society can have no hold upon an atheist. The taking away of God, though but even in thought, dissolves all.'

To my mind, the fundamental difference beteween the theory of Locke and that of Constant, apart from the fact that the latter's 'mysterious religious sentiment' is much more equivocal than Locke's firm faith in God, is that while Locke was writing *before* Voltaire, Rousseau and Helvetius and before the French Revolution, on which he was to have such a powerful even if indirect influence, Constant was writing *after* that 'break' in the history of politics.

In the history of political philosophy two consequences follow from the 'break' caused by the French Revolution: secularism, either as agnosticism or as straightforward atheism, has ever since replaced, first in France and then in Europe, the religious stance of the state. Hence liberalism, born after the revolution, should be historically predisposed to make agnosticism, if not atheism, preside over its political philosophy. Indeed, in the most current definition, liberalism is political agnosticism. The second consequence is that liberalism is born in direct opposition to its historical contemporary, the other philosophy descended from the French Revolution, namely Hegel's dialectical system, which finds its supreme synthesis in the state. In contrast, the supreme mission of liberalism is to limit and control the dangerous power of the state by means of constitutional arrangements; and liberalism proclaims the individual human being to be the centre of political power, whereas Hegel subjects him to the all-powerful state. The first permanent opposition opened up in European politics by the French Revolution was therefore that between the worshippers of the state and the worshippers of the individual human being.

It is, of course, logically gratifying that both liberalisms, the economic and the political – for we must not forget that there are two different kinds – take the individual as the free agent of the actions they want to interpret and orient. But underneath that apparent identity of views there runs the profound difference between the inherent materialism of economic liberalism, in which the motive of human activity is *interest*, with its corollary, the maximisation of profit, and the inherent idealism of political liberalism, in which the motive of human action is self-fulfilment, i.e. one's achievement in one's own conscience. In good logic, the difference between economic and political liberalism is bridged at the base because they have a common ethical motivation – at first more noticeable, as Benjamin Franklin and Max Weber have shown, in Protestantism (Catholics considered interest as sinful for a slightly longer time). And it is bridged at the top by the recognition ever since the time of Aristotle, that politics must provide the framework of human association within which commerce and industry can flourish.

But Bentham and his utilitarians gave to liberalism a decisively materialistic twist by granting to the economic concepts of interest and the maximisation of profit an absolute ethical character, and what was worse, but inevitable, a directly hedonistic orientation. 'The pursuit of pleasure and the avoidance of pain' not only runs counter to Aquinas's maxim of the law of nature: 'do good and avoid evil', but relativises all virtues[16] – and above all relativises *justice* (which Bentham characteristically defined as 'a portion of benevolence in disguise'). The relativisation of the concept of justice, which is nothing if not unique and universal, is the greatest crime committed by both triumphant nineteenth-century materialist ideologies: utilitarianism and historical materialism. For, since they were materialistic, they could not be other than atheistic, or at least crassly agnostic in the case of utilitarianism.

Justice originally sprang from the will of gods and of God, when Moses proclaimed the Ten Commandments. And Jesus subsumed them into two, which in their divine flexibility formed the ethical background of Western civilisation, the 'internalised norms' of people brought up in both religions. Nowhere is the continuity of the Old and the New Testaments more explicitly acknowledged than in the affirmation of moral commandment as 'the Law'. It is not surprising therefore that, as long as these commandments remained the norm for the execution of supreme justice, there was no need for constitutions. Carl J. Friedrich demonstrated this essential point in his insufficiently known book: *Transcendent Justice: the Religious Dimension of Constitutionalism*.[17]

There were therefore, to repeat, two liberalisms: one materialistic – that of Bentham, John Stuart Mill, Elie Halévy – and one idealistic – that of Constant, Tocqueville, T.H. Green. To the perennial clash of views between the two *Weltanschauungen*, which have detested each other since the days of Plato and Democritus, one must now add their fundamental modern divergence on the significance and validity of the idea of progress. Believing almost messianically in progress – that is, in the unstoppable advance of human reason, science and wealth – Bentham threw out all 'old' moral obligations in order to replace them with new and more 'rights'. Utilitarian liberalism became synonymous with progressive permissiveness, in all its hedonistic significance, and with self-interest in all its egoistic significance. The simple, and what is worse, inflammatory, slogans of materialistic liberalism, seemingly confirmed by the 'progress' of the scientific and industrial revolution, triumphed over idealistic liberalism, both in power and in popularity. The grey squirrels of materialistic liberalism extirpated the idealistic red squirrels all over Europe. The first Liberal Party, and the first Liberal government, were formed in Bentham's country. Materialistic parties followed everywhere in Europe and in the United States, where the principles of progressive permissiveness spread rapidly in education and civic culture. This advance was accompanied by that of constitutionalism, representation, the key to constitutionalism, being extended to most European countries, nearly always based on universal manhood suffrage.

Towards a constitutional society
The citizen, also by his behaviour helps to establish the content of
constitutional principle. (W.H. Morris-Jones, in *American Political
Science Review*, 1957)

Nevertheless, the triumph of English liberalism was short-lived,
almost ephemeral. To quote Dangerfield, it seemed to die a strange
death. Torn from without between socialism and conservatism, and
from within between the instinct for political order and the moral
disorder of the 'pursuit of pleasure and the avoidance of pain',
utilitarian liberalism lost its erstwhile commanding political position.

Now, we are told, liberalism, both economic and political, is
making a comeback in the wake of the crisis of socialism. But, oddly
enough, liberalism is coming back as the new politics of the Right,
as in Britain, the United States and the Federal Republic of
Germany. One may therefore ask whether it is only a coincidence
that the new economic liberalism (Hayek, Friedman) has been
adopted by the *traditionalist* parties, whose unmodernised creeds
have preserved, at least implicitly, the traditional moral principles
and respect for religious values? Is it a coincidence that the deliberately self-styled 'moral majority' or 'libertarians' are now situated
at the conservative end of the political spectrum, but on the liberal
side of economic doctrines and programmes? Or is it once again
the confirmation of the warnings issued in their time by Plato,
Aristotle, Aquinas, Machiavelli, Locke, Montesquieu and the idealistic liberals, that political organisations which reject their moral
commandments lose, as a result, their right to command?

After the First World War, the Western constitutional system
had, in a joint effort with the liberal political movement, triumphed
in the whole of Western Europe. But it soon became evident that
the liberal system was in difficulties. The collapse of the transatlantic
laisser-faire economy, and the even more dramatic collapse of the
liberal constitutional systems in Italy and Germany, which led to
the Second World War, and afterwards to the eventual transformation of the liberal state into the welfare state – all these developments were used by the adversaries of liberalism as so many proofs
of its death.

It soon became obvious that these calculations were, *pace* Mark
Twain, 'premature'. In states with an electoral system based on
just proportional representation, minuscule liberal parties were and
are the pivot on which governments turn; they occupy the 'centre'.
And, from another point of view, after a quarter of a century, the
tide of public opinion has turned again towards liberalism and against
state interventionism (although by now, as in a farce, the liberals

have moved towards some *dirigisme* and it is the conservatives who uphold *laisser-faire* principles).

Moreover, *economic* liberalism, although modernised internally by the new welfare society and externally by international trade and financial and monetary agreements, continues to uphold the 'market' as the *sine qua non* of the healthy and normal functioning of economic activities. The real distinction between the modern and the obsolete states of the world of today is that between market (and therefore constitutional pluralistic) and non-market (and therefore monolithic dictatorial) states.

If the liberal *political* system was in trouble in the constitutional states, it was for subtler and deeper reasons than those hurled at it by its adversaries. One was that, having sunk all its energies, indeed its very *raison d'être*, in establishing the constitutional system, once this had been achieved, liberalism could have faded away like the Cheshire Cat in the atmosphere it had itself created in the nineteenth century. This did happen in France, where to this day there is no party going by the name of 'liberal', and where liberal parties have called themselves, in an intelligently functional way, 'of the centre'.

But in so far as the world in the age of planetary communication became interdependent, and yet was still divided into market and non-market states, the first mission of liberalism was now to extend the economic system of market liberalism and the political system of constitutional pluralism as widely as possible, so as to enable the whole world to adapt itself freely to the new demands of world trade and interdependence. And the second task of liberalism in Europe, its birthplace, was to pave the way, in the new world formed by massive geo-political regional units, for the regional unit of the European union. From this point of view, the European liberal parties are fulfilling their duty impressively.

The third new task of the inherently pragmatic liberalism was to oppose the growth of the unnatural *ideologies*, which provide the alibi for the monolithic dictatorial states, and with which these latter have tried to undermine the foundations of the constitutional pluralistic states. But it is precisely here that liberalism developed its real troubles. For liberalism itself sought to become an ideology, and like all other ideologies, a materialistic one with demagogic slogans. 'Progressive permissiveness' became the ideological slogan of liberalism, with the accent laid on the negation of ethics, and its replacement by hedonistic-utilitarian catchwords, in rivalry with those of the post-1968 'Marxists'. But the repetition of inflammatory slogans in the changed circumstances of the mid-twentieth century proved to be disadvantageous to liberalism. For, from the philosophical, political, and last but not least, the moral point of view, those slogans and ideas were out of tune with the real developments of the modern world.

From a philosophical point of view, the very word 'progress', in which the nineteenth century had so fervently believed, was, after the new epistemological pessimism of science, after Stalinism, Fascism and Nazism, after the First and Second World Wars, after Vietnam and the development of nuclear weaponry, badly shaken. The credibility of 'progress' was less convincing.

Politically too, 'progressive permissiveness', with its overtones of egoism and hedonism, ran counter to the mentality of a citizenry prepared to make socio-economic sacrifices and to let the state curb some citizens' rights, provided it could redress some of the blatant injustices of the industrial society. The demand for further political permissiveness for the individual sounded paradoxical in the *dirigiste* conditions of the welfare state, even if of welfare-state liberalism. In addition, the new political psychology of the more sceptical citizenry in the constitutional states was inclined to *attach less importance to politics*, to believe less and less in its autonomy, and to demand that it should concentrate on fostering the activities of society rather than controlling them. Both the theory and the practice of the supra-political Communist states had demonstrated the dangers of the autonomy of politics only too clearly.

But it was on the moral plane that the modern liberal slogan of 'progressive permissiveness' encountered its gravest challenges. Here the heritage of hedonistic utilitarianism has had deleterious effects on the education, and subsequently on the behaviour, of people within the framework of liberal constitutionalism. The utilitarian slogan of the 'pursuit of pleasure and the avoidance of pain' was taken increasingly literally in a society which put more and more temptations in the way of a public moulded by a purely secular education. The phenomenon was general in the Western European constitutional states which tried to follow the glittering example of the United States. By 1968 the whole Western hemisphere had entered into a general moral crisis.

It was at this moment that the materialistic liberal ideology of progressive permissiveness came into conflict with its twin: constitutionalism. Indeed, it can even be said that the two former partners have now started actively to oppose each other: the constitutional system is asking citizens to observe the laws and abide by the civic and other virtues, while the ideologies of progressive permissiveness still continue to try to 'liberate' man from 'old prejudices' and/or 'class injustice'.

And yet the more one looks at the history of constitutionalism, the more one realises that true constitutionalism is bound to be liberal. Featherweight-light in structure, miraculously flexible in its adaptability to all economic and social requirements (as it had proved to be in welfare Sweden, Britain and the Federal Republic of Germany, in planning France and now in 'socialist' Spain, and as it may prove in the future unification of national sovereignties into one single European constitution), fitting human life itself, and not only civic and political life, the liberal constitutional state is perennial. Its dual link politically with the individual, economically with the market, renders it so *normal* that any attempt to replace it soon shows up its intrinsic abnormalities for human life. Even democracy, with its egalitarian overtones, its tyranny of the majority, and its collectivistic bent, must be tightly corseted in liberal constitutionalism if it is not to degenerate into the dictatorship of direct democracy.

Thus the general conclusion of these remarks can be summed up in the following syllogism. If, first premiss, the constitutional liberal state is guided by individuals, and if, second premiss, individuals are guided by their moral conscience, *ergo* the constitutional-liberal state is guided by the moral conscience of individuals; or conversely it can only thrive if the moral conscience of the individual citizens is in harmony with the moral principles which underlie it.

Notes and references

1. C.B. Macpherson, 'Liberalism as trade-offs' in *The Rise and Fall of Economic Justice* (Oxford University Press, 1987), p. 46.
2. Even nowadays the OED does no more than indicate that it derives from 'liberal', while in his *Dictionary of Modern Thought*, Lord Bullock gives this painstaking, but ultimately question-begging description: 'liberalism in its most characteristic contemporary expression emphasizes the importance of conscience and justice in politics, advocates the rights of racial and religious minorities and supports civil liberties and the right of the ordinary individual to be more effectively consulted in decisions which affect him'.
3. Giovanni Sartori, *Democratic Theory* (New York, 1965), p. 357.
4. Benjamin Franklin, writing in 1774, quoted in Henry Steele Commager, *The Empire of Reason* (Oxford University Press, 1977), p. 146.
5. All quotations in this paragraph are from Benjamin Constant, *De la religion*, in *Oeuvres* (Paris, Pleiade, 1957), pp. 1413–14 (my translation).
6. In *Oeuvres, op. cit.*, p. 1099, my italics.
7. *Ibid.* p. 1104, my italics.
8. *Ibid.* pp. 1109–1110.
9. P. Manent, *Les libéraux, textes choisis et présentés* (Paris, 1986), pp. 68–108. See also the recent article by María Luisa Sánchez Mejía, 'Actualidad de Benjamin Constant, un liberal olvidado', *Revista de Occidente*, No. 68, January 1987, pp. 100–12.
10. Quoted in A.P. d'Entrèves, *Natural Law* (London, 1970), p. 44.
11. *De l'esprit de conquête*, in *Oeuvres, op. cit.* p. 1045.
12. *Ibid.* p. 1060.

13. *Ibid.* p. 1088.
14. *Principes de politique,* in *Oeuvres, op. cit.* p. 1113.
15. *Ibid.* p. 1116.
16. Hence Alastair MacIntyre's beautiful title for the tragedy of the Enlightenment: *After Virtue.*
17. Duke University Press, 1969.

PART B
THE BRITISH, AMERICAN AND COMMONWEALTH CONSTITUTIONS

4 Britain: The political constitution
Vernon Bogdanor

I

En Angleterre, on reconnaît au parlement le droit de modifier la constitution. En Angleterre, la constitution peut donc changer sans cesse, ou plutôt elle n'existe point. Le parlement, en même temps qu'il est corps législatif, est corps constituant. (Tocqueville: *De la Démocratie en Amerique*, Pt I, Ch. 6)

If by 'constitution' we mean simply the rules, whether statutory or not, regulating the powers of government and the rights and duties of the citizen, then Britain, like other civilised states, has always possessed a constitution; but clearly this was not what Tocqueville had in mind when he made his famous declaration that Britain had no constitution. What, then, did he mean?

There are two senses in which it is correct to say that Britain has no constitution. First, Britain lacks a single specifically enacted document containing the main rules which regulate the powers of government and the rights and duties of the citizen. Second, since Parliament in Britain is sovereign, no distinction can be drawn between 'ordinary' laws and 'constitutional' laws, laws of fundamental importance which can be changed only through some special legislative procedure. Of these two senses of the term 'constitution', it is the second which is of greater significance. That Britain knows nothing of fundamental law is far more important than the fact that it has no enacted constitution. Nevertheless it is the absence of an enacted constitution that is the first feature to strike the student of British government.

Why is it that Britain lacks an enacted constitution? It is, with Israel and New Zealand, one of only three democracies without such a document. The reason is not difficult to find. Constitutions are generally drawn up to symbolise the birth of a nation, a new beginning in the aftermath of war or revolution. A constitution marks the start of a new political order, a new epoch in a nation's development. A document, so it is generally held, is an essential pre-requisite to the legitimation of a new regime, since it lays out the goals which the political community is expected to pursue and the means by which they may be attained. A constitution, therefore, marks a sharp discontinuity in the history of a state, a radical break with previous practice.

England, however, has been spared such discontinuities since the seventeenth century. Its progress has been evolutionary, unpunctuated by revolutionary upheaval or foreign occupation. The English people have hardly ever felt the need to ask themselves whether they ought to summarise their historical experience in a fundamental document. England's whole constitutional experience seems to show that there is neither any need for, nor any virtue in, an enacted constitution. England, so it might appear, has been constructed in a different way from most other democracies, and in a more durable way. English exceptionalism has been providential, a matter for congratulation and not for regret.

What was true of England was not, of course, necessarily true of Britain or 'the United Kingdom', to give the state its official title. For the United Kingdom came into existence as a result of specific and datable acts – the Articles of Union of 1706 abolishing the Scottish and English Parliaments, and establishing one Parliament of Great Britain; the Union with Ireland Act of 1800 abolishing the Irish Parliament but providing for Irish representation in the new Parliament of the United Kingdom; and the Anglo-Irish Treaty of 1922, removing the 26 counties of the Irish Free State from the jurisdiction of the Parliament of the United Kingdom. All these measures, it might be argued, were of the nature of constituent instruments creating the state as it has existed since 1922, the date when the present borders of the United Kingdom were delimited. Yet the courts, not only in England, but also in Scotland, have never accepted that the Acts of Union with Scotland or Ireland legally restrict Parliament's legislative powers. The courts have held that questions of obligation deriving from the Acts of Union are not legally justiciable. (*Ex p. Canon Selwyn* (1872) 36 J.P.54; *MacCormick v. Lord Advocate* (1953) S.C.396; *Gibson v. Lord Advocate* (1975) S.L.T. 134). If these Acts create obligations, then they are obligations which rest upon convention, rather than law; they are to be understood as obligations of honour, rather than legal limits upon the power of Parliament. For practical purposes, nevertheless, the legal effect of the Acts of Union has been assimilative. England as the largest of the units comprising the United Kingdom has been able to impose its own particular conception of constitutional development upon Scotland and Northern Ireland.

What is the significance of the fact that Britain lacks an enacted constitution? In his unpublished lectures on the Comparative Study of Constitutions, the constitutional lawyer A.V. Dicey distinguished between historic and non-historic constitutions. A historic constitution such as the English (as Dicey persisted in misnaming the British Constitution), was distinctive not only by its antiquity, but also through its originality and spontaneity. It was the product, not of deliberate design, but of historical development.

The characterisation of the British Constitution as a 'historic' constitution is, so it is suggested, more accurate than the common description of it as unwritten. The expression 'unwritten Constitution' was, in Dicey's view, nothing more than a lay and popular one. It is, of course, true that the articles of the British Constitution are not to be found, as are the articles of, for example, the American, French or Belgian Constitutions, in any definite documents or enactments; yet this, for Dicey, was 'a mere matter of form'.[1] For considerable parts of the British Constitution are in fact to be found in written documents or statutes. The Magna Carta, the Bill of Rights, the Act of Settlement and the Parliament Acts, all contain a good deal of the British Constitution, in the sense of providing norms for the regulation of government activity and the rights of citizens. There seems no *a priori* reason why the vast jumble of statutes, judicial decisions, precedents, usages and conventions, which comprise the British Constitution, should not be reduced to a single parliamentary enactment. The essential substance of the constitution need not be changed through its translation into written form.

One important provision of a written British constitution, however, would have to be that it could always be amended or repealed in exactly the same way as any other Act of Parliament. Such a provision would be needed to give effect to the principle of the sovereignty of Parliament which was, for Dicey, 'from a legal point of view the dominant characteristic of our political institutions'.[2] Indeed, there is a sense in which the British Constitution can be summed up in eight words: What the Queen in Parliament enacts is law. The essence of the British Constitution is thus better expressed in the statement that it is a historic constitution whose dominating characteristic is the sovereignty of Parliament, than in the statement that Britain has an unwritten constitution. But precisely because the sovereignty of Parliament is the central principle of the British Constitution, it has seemed pointless to rationalise it in an enacted constitution which could forbid nothing, nor could it provide a list of basic freedoms which governments would be unable to infringe.

That the British Constitution is not to be found in a single document is a fact of more interest to the constitutional lawyer than to the political scientist; that Parliament is sovereign is a fact of central importance to both. For it follows from the sovereignty of Parliament that Britain know no distinction between ordinary laws and constitutional laws, laws with a status higher than mere ordinary laws, the amendment of which requires some special legislative procedure. There is, in Britain, a single process for all legislation which requires but a simple majority in the House of Commons (the Lords can in theory delay a non-money bill, but this is a power which they have not used since the time of the 1949 Parliament Act). When Tocqueville stated that, Parliament having the right to change the Constitution, there was no Constitution, he meant that Britain knew nothing of fundamental law. Statutes concerning the organisation of government or the rights of the citizen can be passed or repealed by the same simple majority procedure as is required for all other legislation. Thus the term 'unconstitutional' cannot in Britain mean contrary to law; instead it means contrary to convention, contrary to some understanding of what it is appropriate to do. But, unfortunately, there is by no means universal agreement on what the standards of appropriateness are or ought to be. As Sidney Low put it in 1904, 'British government is based upon a system of tacit understandings. But the understandings are not always understood.'[3] It is perhaps easier to secure consensus and stability in such a system than in one based upon constitutional principles where interpretations of what the constitution requires will often vary with the political beliefs of the interpreter. But in Britain, doctrinal disagreement can be masked by attachment to a common stock of historical precedents; the standard of appropriateness is *internal* to the system, not external to it. For there is no objective reference point, no *pouvoir neutre* beyond Parliament which is able to erect a standard for what is constitutional.

Yet, although legally supreme, Parliament is in reality largely controlled by the government of the day. In the contemporary world of disciplined parties, the House of Commons is an electoral college rather than a genuine legislative body; and in practice, the supremacy of Parliament serves to legitimise the omnicompetence of government. Britain, *pace* Maitland, has substituted the authority of the Crown for a theory of the state.[4]

II

The ability of a government unilaterally to alter the rules of the political game could, in theory, allow for a very considerable abuse of power. Yet the abuse of power has been the exception and not the rule in British twentieth-century politics. The basic reason for this is that, for most of the twentieth century, the British Constitution has remained above politics. Whatever other differences there have been between the political parties, they did not seek to dispute the fundamental rules through which political activity was regulated. Even in the 1930s when political conflict was at its sharpest, there was surprisingly little questioning of Britain's constitutional arrangements. The only period in the twentieth century when the Constitution has genuinely been under strain were the years 1910–14 when the dispute over Irish Home Rule and the Ulster question threatened the very foundations of the political system and might easily have led to civil war. Indeed, some historians believe that the impasse over Ulster would have had this consequence, had it not been for the coming of the First World War in August 1914.

No other issue has so menaced the civic order of Britain this century. Nevertheless, there have been two other periods when constitutional quesitions formed a central part of the agenda of politics – the thirty years before the First World War, and the period since 1969. These were years of constitutional *ferment* in British politics, years in which the contours of the constitution were blurred and its future seemed uncertain.

Britain adopted universal male suffrage for men over 21, and universal female suffrage for women over 30, in 1918. (Women aged between 21 and 30 were enfranchised in 1928.) Yet, the real battle over the suffrage had been won much earlier – in 1884, 1867 or perhaps even in 1832; and from the 1880s, constitutional reformers began to turn to other issues, and in particular to a consideration of the relationship between the new democratic electorate and the institutions of government.

A.V. Dicey's classic *Introduction to the Study of the Law of the Constitution* was first published in 1885 at the beginning of this period of constitutional ferment. For the eighth edition published in 1915 – the last edition for which he was personally responsible – Dicey contributed a long introduction surveying the constitutional debates of the previous thirty years: women's suffrage, Home Rule, proportional representation and the referendum. These constitutional issues formed a central part of the political agenda in the three decades before the First World War. For there was a deepseated disagreement both within and between the parties on the future shape of British democracy. Until 1911, it was uncertain whether Britain would retain a bicemeral legislature, or whether Parliament would become effectively unicameral; and uncertain whether the referendum would become a part of the British Constitution, a proposal endorsed by the Conservative leader, A.J. Balfour, shortly before the December 1910 General Election. Moreover, until the secession of the 26 counties of the Irish Free State in 1922, it was possible to believe that Irish Home Rule might be the prelude to 'Home Rule All Round', transforming Britain into a quasi-federal

state. Most important of all, it was by no means implausible to
suppose that Britain would adopt the alternative-vote electoral system
or some system of proportional representation; and the issue
remained genuinely in doubt until 1918 when, in the Fourth Reform
Act, Parliament decided, almost by default, to retain the plurality
electoral system in single-member constituencies.

These three measures – the 1911 Parliament Act, the 1918
Representation of the People Act, and the Anglo-Irish Treaty of
1922 – served to remove constitutional issues from British politics
for almost fifty years. The Parliament Act not only put paid to
the possibility of referring legislation to the electorate; it also ensured
that there was no body other than the government of the day which
could make a judgment on the constitutional propriety of legislation.
The Parliament Act established an effectively unicameral system
of government in Britain. It was, Dicey claimed, 'the last and greatest
triumph of party government', and underlined the fact that party
government was 'not the accident or corruption, but, so to speak,
the very foundation of our constitutional system'.[5] What made Britain
unusual was that party government was henceforth to operate within
a political system which, unlike most democracies, contained nothing
to check the untrammelled power of the majority party.

Retention of the plurality system of election in the 1918 Representation of the People Act made possible Conservative hegemony in
the inter-war period, enabling the party to gain an overall majority
in the Commons in 1922 on only 38 per cent of the vote. The
vast extension of the franchise in 1918, together with the growth
of class feeling, contributed to the restoration of a two-party system,
but one in which Labour, not the Liberals, was the chief opponent
of the Conservatives. Labour took the view that the central issues
of politics were socio-economic, not constitutional; while the
Conservatives, in power for most of the time, were happy to accept
the status quo.

The removal of the vast majority of Irish MPs from the House
of Commons as a result of the Anglo-Irish Treaty made single-party
majority government more likely. Before 1918, any British Government needed around 100 more seats than the main opposition party
if it was to be assured of a working majority for a full Parliament
and avoid reliance on the 80-odd Irish Nationalists regularly returned
to the Commons after 1885. Four out of the eight elections held
between 1885 and December 1910 had led to hung parliaments in
which the government was dependent upon the Irish members.
Further, the Anglo-Irish Treaty also removed the constitutional issue
of Irish Home Rule from British politics, taking with it – so at
least it seemed for 50 years – both devolution and the Ulster question.

In the 1920s, the British party system was taking on the shape which it was to assume for over fifty years – a two-party system within which both parties emphasised the priority of socio-economic concerns. The Liberals, a party for whom constitutional questions formed the very stuff of political life, were replaced by Labour, a party whose political focus was directed at problems of economic management and social welfare. This new party system was buttressed by the growth of social solidarity and political consciousness amongst the working class. For the process leading to universal adult suffrage, slow as it was, preceded the embourgeoisement of the working class The existence of a wide suffrage combined with a politically conscious working class created the preconditions for a fairly rigid two-party system within which the Conservative and Labour Parties battled for control over terrain whose contours were primarily socio-economic, while constitutional issues were pushed off the map as a tiresome irrelevance. In opposition for much of the 1920s, 1930s, 1950s and 1980s, Labour's aim was nevertheless to capture the state, not to transform it; while the Conservatives dug themselves in around a defensive stockade, enjoying the supreme power bestowed on them by the Constitution, while assuming that the forces of radical change could be kept at bay for ever and ever. It was a high-risk strategy, but it worked.

Moreover, as Michael Steed has pointed out,[6] the very development of tightly organised mass parties had the consequence of fossilising the movement for constitutional change. For the parties succeeded in identifying all that was beneficent about democracy with their own dominance. One of the central concerns of constitutional reformers had been the extension of participation. Yet defenders of the party system could argue that the parties themselves were perfectly adequate channels of participation, and that reforms such as devolution, the referendum or primary elections were unnecessary. Sociology and ideology thus went hand in hand in underwriting the party system evolving in Britain in the 1920s; the parties were seen as being congruent both with social reality and with ideological attitudes.

III

It is hardly a coincidence, then, that the processes of social change which have produced embourgeoisement, have also stimulated the decline of ideological and class loyalties, the gradual breaking-down of the two-party system, and the return of constitutional issues to British politics. Indeed, since the late 1960s constitutional issues have formed a central part of the political agenda. In 1968, the civil rights movement in Northern Ireland erupted into violence and threatened the rule of the Ulster Unionists. As the Northern Ireland problem forced itself upon the attention of successive British governments, so they found themselves proposing constitutional innovations for that troubled province which they would not have dreamt of contemplating for the mainland. The year 1973 saw three constitutional reforms, consequent upon the abolition of the Northern Ireland Parliament. A border poll was held to display the allegiance of the province to the United Kingdom; a new legislature was proposed in the Northern Ireland Constitution Act which, departing significantly from the Westminster model of single-party majority government, was to be based upon the principle of power-sharing between the Unionist majority and the Nationalist minority. Further, the Assembly would be elected by the single transferable vote method of proportional representation, and the new district councils in Northern Ireland would also be elected by this method. It is hardly surprising that the Electoral Reform Society, which had been campaigning for the single transferable vote for nearly 90 years, called 1973, a 'Red Letter Year', and declared that:[7]

> The reform this Society seeks is no longer an academic matter, capable of being dismissed as the concern of a few enthusiasts; it is now something actually operating within the United Kingdom...The whole subject is topical as it has not been for half a century.

Changes in Northern Ireland, however, had comparatively little effect upon opinion in the rest of the United Kingdom for whom that province had, for many years, been seen as a rather peculiar entity subject to laws of its own and with no wider relevance. Yet the 1970s saw the introduction of another momentous issue into British politics, Britain's entry into the European Community, which not only had major constitutional implications, but also very considerable consequences for the political parties, since it was one of the issues which led to the split in the Labour Party and the secession of many on the Right wing to form the Social Democratic Party in 1981. Britain's entry into the Community was bound to pose problems for the theory of parliamentary sovereignty. Admittedly, the strains have not been as immediate or as obvious as might have been predicted; nevertheless, the central consequence of entry has been that decisions previously taken by the British Government are now taken by a body – the Council of Ministers – which is not and cannot be responsible to Parliament at Westminster. This transference of power from Britain to the institutions of the Community is underlined by the Single European Act of 1986, which makes a wider area of Community decision-making subject to qualified majority voting rather than unanimity. This will tend to shift decision-making power still further away from Britain, and also shift the balance of parliamentary responsibility from Westminster to the European Parliament. Britain's entry into the Community may not have caused any immediate constitutional revolution; but it was a change of major constitutional importance which led to a further constitutional innovation – the first nation-wide referendum, held in 1975, on the question of whether Britain should leave the Community or remain on the basis of the terms renegotiated by the Labour Government which had come to office in 1974.

Entry to the Community had yet another effect upon constitutional thinking in Britain. It exposed British politicians and lawyers to Continental political and legal systems, and showed them that the simple stereotypes which they had often used to disparage them were distortions of reality. In particular, direct elections to the European Parliament, first held in 1979, helped to keep the issue of proportional representation in the forefront of political debate. For supporters of proportional representation could claim that if, as turned out to be the case, Britain retained the single-member plurality system, it would prove to be the only member of the Community not employing one or other of the various systems of proportional representation for these elections. Not only would Britain be the odd man out, but the misrepresentation of British opinion would have a highly distorting effect upon the strength of the party groupings in the European Parliament. They also argued that MPs could support proportional representation for elections to the European Parliament without necessarily committing them-selves to proportional representation for elections to the House of Commons, since the European Parliament, unlike the Commons, was not required to sustain a government. The counter-argument employed by opponents – that proportional representation would lead to weak and/or unstable government – was therefore irrelevant.

Yet a third constitutional issue in addition to Northern Ireland and the European Community haunted Parliament in the 1970s – devolution. This too raised important constitutional questions re-lating to parliamentary sovereignty and federalism, issues which the 1974–9 Labour Governments sought, not wholly successfully, to avoid. Ministers faced the same question as had confronted Gladstone's Liberals in the 1880s and 1890s. Was it possible to provide for legislative devolution in only one part of a unitary state without causing intolerable anomalies in parliamentary representa-tion and in the distribution of financial resources? Was there a genu-ine half-way house between the unitary state and 'Home Rule All Round' or federalism? The problem was in some respects even more complex than it had been ninety years earlier, since the existence of a developed Welfare State and the requirements of a managed economy seemed to impose crucial limitations upon the extent to which power could be transferred from Westminster and Whitehall.

Like the Northern Ireland question and the European Community, devolution also involved a choice of electoral systems. In October 1973, the Report of the Royal Commission on the Constitution (Kilbrandon Commission) was published, and amongst its few unanimous recommendations was a proposal that any assemblies established in Scotland, Wales or the English regions, should be elected by the single transferable vote method of proportional representation. This recommendation was rejected, however, by the government which was prepared to accept the risk that, in a four-party political system in Scotland, the Scottish Nationalists might gain control of the Scottish Assembly, and claim a mandate for independence on a vote of 40 per cent or less. Fear of such an outcome was one of the factors inhibiting the Scottish electorate from giving whole-hearted endorsement to the devolution proposals in the referendum of March 1979.

The government found that devolution, like Britain's membership of the Community, was not an issue which could be satisfactorily resolved through normal parliamentary procedures, but needed popular endorsement by the electorate to gain legitimacy. Indeed, the devolution legislation would probably not have secured parliamentary approval at all had not the government been willing to commit itself to a referendum. So it was that the referendum on Britain's membership of the Community, justified by ministers in terms of the unique nature of the issue, was followed by referendums in Scotland and Wales four years later. A further innovation was the 40 per cent rule, a provision inserted in the Scotland and Wales Acts against the wishes of the government, which required that 40 per cent of the electorate, as well as a majority of those voting, cast a 'Yes' vote for the legislation to come into effect.[8]

IV

In the 1970s, then, three major problems – Northern Ireland, the European Community, and devolution – brought constitutional concerns back to the centre of politics. For a time, it seemed that British politics was actually dominated by constitutional issues. However, the period of constitutional ferment seemed to have ended with the defeat of the devolution proposals in the referendums held in March 1979, and the return of the Conservatives to office the following May. For the Conservative Party, under Mrs Thatcher, took the view that constitutional issues were a distraction from the real tasks facing government. Previous administrations, so it was argued, had spent too much time tinkering with the Constitution and reorganising the institutions of government. Mrs Thatcher's administration, by contrast, would focus its attention ruthlessly upon the socio-economic and cultural causes of Britain's long economic decline.

Yet, although her Government has, on the whole, stuck obstinately to its conviction of leaving constitutional issues alone, Mrs Thatcher has not been able entirely to exorcise the constitution. Evicted from one door, it soon returns by another. The problems of Northern Ireland, of course, remain to torment British governments, whether Labour or Conservative; while the gradual and seemingly inexorable transfer of powers to the European Community continued to pose difficult questions for those wedded to Britain's traditional constitutional arrangements.

In other areas also, new constitutional issues arose as a result of the policies of the Thatcher Government. In two areas in particular – trade union reform and the reform of local government – constitutional issues arose which the government would have preferred to have kept submerged. Coming to power in 1979, shortly after the so-called 'Winter of Discontent' in which a series of strikes had led to the closure of schools, the disruption and blocking of hospitals and even a refusal to bury the dead, it was inevitable that the Conservatives would seek to do away with some of the legal immunities which the trade unions had enjoyed since 1906, and to impose a new legal framework for the regulation of union affairs. The 1984 Trade Union Act was a part of this approach, and it provided, among other things, that unions should be required to test the opinion of their members every decade on whether they still wished to maintain a political fund from which, *inter alia*, affiliation payments were made to the Labour Party. This raised the whole question of the role of institutions – whether trades unions or companies – in the financing of political parties. On grounds of fairness, it seemed wrong to regulate trade union financing of the Labour Party, while leaving unregulated company financing of the Conservatives. Supporters of the Liberal/SDP Alliance claimed that a system in which the two major parties were financed by industry and the trade unions polarised politics and encouraged confrontational attitudes, as well as handicapping parties, such as the Liberals and the SDP, which did not enjoy close links with unions or companies. Some put forward the view that state aid to political parties was the only way to avoid undue reliance upon institutional interests. So what seemed at first sight an issue merely of trade union reform, began to pose questions about the relationship between organised interests and political parties, and indeed raised fundamental issues about the very nature of the British party system. These issues are, in essence, constitutional – although, like other constitutional issues, their resolution depends largely upon the future configuration of party politics.

The relationship between central and local government was another area in which, unexpectedly, constitutional issues arose. Relations between central government and local authorities, although regulated to a certain extent by statute, have always been based more upon shared understandings as to the proper role of the centre and of localities than upon precise legal regulations. These shared understandings were undermined when the Conservatives took office in 1979 – for two inter-connected reasons. The first was that the government was committed to a large reduction in public expenditure as part of its programme of containing inflation. This would inevitably fall heavily upon local authorities, which are responsible for a quarter of total public expenditure. Secondly, the Conservatives found that, in many urban authorities, power had passed from an older generation of Labour councillors to a new generation determined to implement genuinely socialist policies at local level, to make local government into a laboratory for the testing of socialism. This made them even more unwilling to heed government requests for restraint in public expenditure. It seemed that the consensual framework needed to sustain a partnership between the two levels of government no longer existed.

The Conservative Government decided to adopt drastic measures to deal with the problem. First, they intervened directly to curb the financial independence of local authorities. A series of legislative measures provided for the rigorous control of local government expenditure – whether financed from the block grant provided by central government, the Rate Support Grant, or from local government's own resources, primarily the rates. These measures culminated in the 1984 Rates Act empowering the Secretary of State for the Environment to impose maximum rate levels upon local authorities.

But the Conservatives took an even more direct step to deal with their political opponents in the Local Government Act 1985, abolishing the Greater London Council and the six metropolitan county councils, authorities for Britain's major conurbations established by a previous Conservative Government in the 1972 Local Government Act. These authorities had all been captured electorally by the Labour Party, and had formed a powerful focus of opposition to many of the government's social and economic policies.

The Conservatives' opponents accused them not only of undermining local autonomy, but also of breaking important conventions of the constitution. The Rates Act breached the principle that local authorities should be free to decide for themselves how much money they wished to raise locally. For, until 1984, it had been generally accepted that local authorities should be free to decide what level of rate to set, and to provide for services to meet the level of rates which they could raise. Governments, if they wished to limit local authority expenditure, did so through varying the level of central grant paid to local authorities, not by directly controlling the level of rates. The Rates Act, however, for the first time restricted the power of local authorities to set their own rates. This was a very different matter from central government restricting its *own* contribution to local authorities. That local authorities should be free to raise what money they required from those who elected them had hitherto been thought to be a cornerstone of local democracy in Britain. The abolition of the Greater London Council and the metropolitan authorities was also held to be a breach of constitutional convention because it undermined the right of local electors to have local services provided by directly elected local authorities. The 1985 Act did *not* replace the GLC and the Metropolitan Counties with a unitary system of local authorities, for comparatively few functions were devolved from the GLC and the Metropolitan Counties to the London Boroughs and Metropolitan Districts respectively. Most of their functions were transferred to London or county-wide bodies which were not directly elected; others were transferred directly to Whitehall. Thus, the upper tier of local government would remain but, instead of being directly elected, it would be administered through joint boards, committees, government 'quangos' (quasi-autonomous non-government organisations) and by the Minister. The unilateral abolition of elections to a tier of government was held by some to raise constitutional issues of great magnitude, and to set a dangerous precedent for any future administration seeking to abolish an elected body of which it disapproved.

The measures taken by the Conservatives had the consequence of calling into question traditional relationships between central government and local authorities, and made many ask whether there were any constitutional principles which ought to govern these relationships, and whether there was a need of constitutional protection for the values of local self-government. The various Royal Commissions and departmental committees established in the 1960s and 1970s to examine local government as a prelude to its reorganisation were required by their terms of reference rigorously to exclude constitutional questions. The consequence has been that central-local relations were governed by no discernible principles, but operated on a pragmatic and *ad hoc* basis. It is doubtful whether this can any longer be sustained. The major Opposition parties – Labour and the Liberal/SDP Alliance – have committed themselves to policies involving a restoration of local autonomy, and to Scottish devolution; they are also sympathetic to the establishment of a layer of regional authorities in England. And many believe that even a Conservative government would have to reconsider the basis of central-local relations, since the arrangements proposed in the Local Government Act of 1985 for the administration of London and the metropolitan authorities are, in the view of their critics, so ramshackle and unstable that they cannot possibly survive. But this re-examination of local government will, inevitably, involve the introduction of those very constitutional issues so rigorously excluded in the past.

The policies pursued by the Conservative Government have not only stimulated constitutional discussion on the financing of political parties and the role of local government. They have also given rise to a more general concern at the consequences of omnicompetent government. Lacking the checks and balances which exist in most democracies, Britain can easily approach the condition identified by Lord Hailsham as 'elective dictatorship'.[9] How, then, can the balance, at present so heavily tilted in the executive's favour, be redressed? Among the proposed remedies have been reform of the House of Lords so that, with a more rational composition, it can gain the authority to check the government of the day; a Bill of Rights – which in practice would mean incorporating the European Convention of Human Rights into British law; and a Freedom of Information Act providing for more open government. It is, however, fair to say that, although these reforms have been much discussed by opinion-formers and academics, they do not yet enjoy the popular salience of the major constitutional issues discussed earlier.

V

Northern Ireland, the European Community, devolution and central-local relations all involve questions of territorial politics in which local allegiances cut across party political loyalties. The history of the measures taken to deal with these issues shows how remarkably ill-attuned British party and parliamentary procedures are to issues of territorial politics. Britain remains a unitary state, but it contains a territorially heterogeneous population. The question is whether this unitary structure can be preserved when challenged by the development of a distinctive political consciousness in some of its component parts, such as Northern Ireland, Scotland, and possibly some of the English regions also. British politicians find it difficult to think in territorial terms; and the party structure, with the exception of the Scottish and Welsh nationalist parties and the Northern Ireland parties, is based mainly upon socio-economic rather than territorial cleavages. It is for this reason that territorial issues have placed such severe strain upon the cohesiveness of Britain's political parties. The European Community and devolution, in particular, were issues which split both parties, dividing allies while uniting those who were normally political opponents.

Part of the reason why British Governments have found it difficult to cope with territorial issues lies with the ideological heritage of Dicey, who was inclined to confuse the purely formal legal doctrine of the sovereignty of Parliament with the more controversial statement that Britain's political stability depended upon the existence of an omnicompetent Parliament. This entailed the absence of any competing legislative authorities, even if subordinate, which might challenge this omnicompetence. As a consequence, governments have been ideologically ill-equipped to deal with territorial problems whose resolution requires less an assertion of sovereignty than acceptance of the principle of power-sharing.

The return of territorial issues into British politics challenged the legislative dominance of Westminster, and required, so it seemed, something over and above the normal legislative procedures if they were to be resolved. Locke in his *Second Treatise of Government* declared (para. 141) that the power of Parliament was but a delegated power from the People, and that Parliament could not transfer its power of making laws without the approval of the People. So it is that Parliament has provided that Northern Ireland shall not cease to be a part of the United Kingdom without a border poll, and that the questions of Britain's membership of the European Community and of devolution could only be settled through a referendum. Legitimacy seemed to require, not just a positive vote by Parliament, but the endorsement of the People as well. Thus, to the question of where a constitutional reference point can be found in a political system with a sovereign Parliament, the British system can now answer – in the referendum. The electorate itself can be a democratic check upon the processes of representative government.

In Britain, the referendum has proved to be, as Dicey predicted, a method of securing *de facto* entrenchment in a country without a rigid constitution. It offers a means of drawing a distinction between ordinary laws and constitutional laws, such as is commonly drawn in countries with constitutions which can only be amended by a special procedure. Thus, if a government ever wished to deprive Northern Ireland of its membership of the United Kingdom, or to provide for legislative devolution, it would be difficult to do so without a referendum. The degree of entrenchment secured is, of course, greater if a hurdle in the form of a qualifying majority is imposed, such as the 40 per cent rule in the Scottish and Welsh referendums. This rule offers a graphic illustration of how it is possible to construct a barrier against fundamental change in a polity dominated by the principle of parliamentary sovereignty.

VI

The fundamental reason why constitutional issues have again become a part of the British political agenda is that the party system has found itself unable to accommodate them. It has become frozen.

British politics, more than that of most other democracies, is marked by the dominance of party, and more particularly by the dominance of the two major parties. Although political parties in Britain are not recognised in law, the law nevertheless helps the two major parties to retain their dominance. It does so in two ways. First, it provides for an electoral system – the plurality method of voting in single-member constituencies – which discriminates against third parties lacking concentrated class or geographical support. Thus, it reinforces the existence of a class-based party system, in which the central political cleavage is socio-economic. Secondly, Britain is quite unique amongst developed Western democracies in the extent to which the two major parties are financed from institutional sources – companies and trade unions. The bulk of the contributions made to the central organisations of the two major parties are the result of corporate rather than individual decisions, private donations, but not necessarily voluntary ones. It is difficult for a new party, not enjoying a privileged relationship with the trade union movement, as the Labour Party does, and unable to attract large company contributions, as the Conservatives do, to overcome this disadvantage. So the methods by which the parties are financed in Britain, like the electoral system, seem to reward those parties able to exploit one type of political cleavage – class conflict – at the expense of others.

The British political system, then, depends primarily upon the operation of party. In Britain, the parties not only control the game of politics; they also control the rules under which the game is played. This is perfectly acceptable when there is widespread agreement on what these rules should be, and when cohesive parties provide a rational framework for political debate based upon the real issues of the day. These preconditions have been met for much of the twentieth century, but it is questionable whether they are still met in the Britain of the 1980s. Until the Second World War, the British party system was given fluidity by a periodic process of realignment. Modern party politics began in Britain after the Second Reform Act in 1867. Yet, by the 1880s, realignment was beginning to occur. The right wing of the Liberal Party – the Whigs – were already finding that Gladstonian Radicalism was incompatible with a Whig interpretation of Liberalism, and they were beginning to move towards the Conservative Party, even before Gladstone's espousal of Irish Home Rule in 1885/6 hastened the process. The defection of Joseph Chamberlain in 1886 added a powerful element of populism to the Conservative Party, and the Unionist coalition ruled Britain almost continuously in the twenty years after 1886. In 1903, however, a new issue cut across the old politics – Tariff Reform, introduced suddenly and without warning by Chamberlain, the only politician in modern British history to split both major political parties. This caused defections from the Conservatives – an 1886 in reverse, although the numbers involved were much smaller. They did, however, include the young Winston Churchill, destined to be one of the radical social reformers in the 1905–15 Liberal Governments.

Meanwhile, the birth and development of the Labour Party which, over a period of 25 years, came to replace the Liberals as the main Opposition party on the left, introduced a further element of flexibility into the political system; while the splits within the Liberal Party which followed the formation of the Lloyd George coalition government in 1916 helped to ensure that Liberal values would be promoted in the Conservative and Labour Parties. In 1931, the formation of the National Government split the Labour and Liberal Parties, giving a new accretion of strength to the Conservatives, and enabling old battles on issues such as Free Trade and Empire to be settled peacefully.

Thus between 1880 and 1931, party alignments changed constantly in response to a changing political agenda. The realignment of 1931, however, was to prove the last for fifty years. The prime reason for this was ideological. Labour regarded the defection of MacDonald and his followers in 1931 as a unique betrayal, while the Conservatives benefited electorally from the disunity of their opponents, and were not disposed to throw away the advantage of party unity.

The end of realignment would not have mattered if there had been a real unity of feeling and purpose in the Conservative and Labour Parties. But instead the party system became frozen, emphasising the ritualistic issues of the past, while ensuring that others – the European Community in the 1950s, the role of sterling in the 1960s, the decentralisation of power in the 1970s, and above all the economic modernisation of Britain – were submerged in a directionless consensus. At the same time, many of the crucial lines of division in British politics were found to lie within the parties, not between them, and the real conflict often seemed to be found between warring intra-party factions, rather than in the more manufactured disagreement of the House of Commons and the hustings.

In the 1970s, however, it seemed that the parties were coming to take their rhetoric more seriously, and the 'adversary politics' thesis was put forward to show how the two-party system could be dysfunctional to the maintenance of Britain's position as an advanced industrial society.[10] In the immediate post-war period, the consensual aspects of British politics had seemed to discourage open debate on the real policy choices facing the country. In the 1970s, the party battle, which had hitherto appeared a sham fight, came alive. But, at the same time, support for the two major parties was seen to be waning. In the first eight elections after the Second World War, between 1945 and 1970, the average percentage of the vote gained by the winning party was 47.4; in the next four elections between February 1974 and 1983, the average percentage was only 40.7, a little over two-fifths of the vote. In the two general elections of 1974, no party succeeded in gaining as much as 40 per cent of the vote, while the Conservative landslide in 1983 was gained on 42.4 per cent of the vote, a lower percentage than was gained by any government with a comfortable majority since 1922, during another period of realignment. Indeed, the percentage of the vote gained by the Conservatives in 1983 was lower than that gained by the main Opposition party in *every* election between 1945 and 1974, except those of 1945 and 1966.

Pressures for party realignment were associated, as they had been in previous political crises in the twentieth century, with a programme of economic modernisation. It is striking that so many of those who have put the modernisation of the British economy at the forefront of their political programme – Joseph Chamberlain, Lloyd George, the Keynesian radicals of the inter-war years, and David Owen – have found themselves unable to work within the orthodox two-party system, and have been driven to seek new political combinations. They see the party system as an alienated superstructure, distorting and suppressing the real political choices which need to be made.

Thus, the final outcome of the constitutional debate in British politics depends crucially upon the vicissitudes of party politics. Dicey argued that one central weakness of Britain's party constitution was that constitutional change came to be muddled up with party considerations. The question of the best constitutional arrangement came to be mixed with other political questions, and above all, with the question of which party ought to be in government.[11] For the British Constitution is essentially a *political* constitution, one whose operation depends upon the strength of political factors and whose interpretation depends upon the will of its political leaders. If the two-party system reasserts itself, then constitutional change is unlikely. If, however, the party system remains in a state of flux, the constitutional conventions which are the product of the two-party system will no longer be sustainable. Coalition or minority government could come to replace single-party majority government as the norm, and British politics could again become what it was before 1867 – multi-party politics. A necessary condition of such an outcome is probably the introduction of proportional representation, something which would reinforce new political alignments. Proportional representation is, as it were, the key in the lock, the precondition for unfreezing the party system, and so making possible other constitutional reforms.

But the strength of the various political forces in Britain cannot be divorced from the processes of social change. For political parties reflect these processes, and are to some extent their product. The party system is in flux because British society is also in a state of flux. There has come to be a lack of congruence between the rules regulating the framework of party politics, and the social and economic patterns which in the past sustained it. It is impossible to foresee how Britain's institutions, its 'living Constitution' in Karl Llewellyn's phrase,[12] something amended not by the courts or Parliament, but in the last resort by the people themselves, will adapt itself to changing social conditions. In the words of Disraeli's Sidonia:[13]

> A political institution is a machine; the motive power is the national character [what political scientists today call political culture]. With that it rests whether the machine will benefit society, or destroy it. Society in this country is perplexed, almost paralysed; in time it will move and it will devise. How are the elements of the nation to be again blended together? In what spirit is that reorganisation to take place?
>
> 'To know that', replied Coningsby, 'would be to know everything.'

Notes and references

1. A.V. Dicey, Lectures on the Comparative Study of Constitutions, MS 323 LR 6 b 13. The manuscript of these lectures is to be found in the Codrington Library, All Souls College, Oxford, and I am grateful to the Librarian for allowing me to consult them.
2. A.V. Dicey, *Introduction to the Study of the Law of the Constitution*, 10th edn (Macmillan, 1959), p. 39.
3. Sidney Low, *The Governance of England* (T. Fisher Unwin, 1904), p. 12.

4. F.W. Maitland, 'The Crown as Corporation' in H.D. Hazeldine, G. Lapsley and P.H. Winfield (eds), *Selected Essays* (Cambridge University Press, 1936).
5. Dicey, Introduction to 8th edition of *Law of the Constitution* (Macmillan, 1915), p. ci.
6. Michael Steed, 'Participation through Western Democratic Institutions' in Geraint Parry (ed.), *Participation in Politics* (Manchester University Press, 1972).
7. *Representation* (Journal of the Electoral Reform Society), Vol. 13, No. 53, October, 1973, p. 54.
8. See Vernon Bogdanor, 'The Forty Per Cent Rule', *Parliamentary Affairs*, 1980; and, more generally, Vernon Bogdanor, *Devolution* (Oxford University Press, 1979).
9. Lord Hailsham, *The Dilemma of Democracy* (Collins, 1978).
10. S.E. Finer (ed.), *Adversary Politics and Electoral Reform* (Anthony Wigram, 1975).
11. Dicey, Lectures on the Comparative Study of Constitutions, *loc. cit.*
12. See, for example, Karl Llewellyn, 'The Constitution as an Institution', *Columbia Law Review*, Vol. XXXIV, January 1934.
13. Benjamin Disraeli, *Coningsby* Book IV, Chapter XIII.

5 The Constitution (1787) and modern American government
Richard Hodder-Williams

I

The making of the United States Constitution has been much described and explanations for its form have been much argued over. It is essential in the first place to sketch the historical context in which the delegates met at Philadelphia in 1787. In the period following the triumphant conclusion of the Revolutionary War against Britain, the various states which had thereby won their independence from the British Crown were governed according to their own separate constitutions; they also devised, in the Articles of Confederation, institutional arrangements intended to co-ordinate many of their activities. But the experience of these years was not an altogether happy one.

The immediate problems were essentially economic. Rivalry between states, difficulties with international trade, arguments over currency, concern for debtors, unreadiness on the part of several states to contribute to the running of the Confederation, and a general economic malaise worried many people and disappointed particularly those who had hoped for much from the expulsion of British rulers. The weakness of the Confederation and its legislative arm, the Continental Congress, was manifest; the rebellion of debtor farmers in Massachusetts, although no real threat to the state, hammered home the lack of power, whether military or civilian, of the Confederation. Several leading figures felt strongly that some form of action was needed; and so a small, self-generated convention took place in Annapolis, Maryland in September 1786 under Alexander Hamilton's prompting 'to consider how far a uniform system in [the states'] commercial relations may be necessary to their common interest and their permanent harmony'. It recommended a thorough investigation into the defects of the Confederation and the Continental Congress agreed to call a special convention in Philadelphia 'for the sole and express purpose of revising the Articles of Confederation'. The incentive behind the Convention was thus a set of particular exigences, economic crises and those political weaknesses of the Confederation which were widely thought to be their cause.[1]

The Convention was scheduled for 14 May, but it was not until 25 May that seven states could muster a quorum and the Convention could legally begin. The first business, although organisational, was not trivial. It involved establishing several procedural rules, three of which deserve comment. First, the delegates agreed that the unit for voting should, as in the Continental Congress, be the state, regardless of its wealth, size or delegate strength. This confirmed a central assumption of the day that the primary political reality was the independent existence of states. This assumption deeply affected the distribution of power later legitimated in the Constitution, provided the fuel for political conflict in the early part of the nineteenth century and ultimately the bloody civil war of 1861–4, and continues to provide one of the democratic paradoxes inherent in the United States political system. Even if, as Locke claimed and the Founding Fathers believed, governments derive their just powers from the consent of the governed, the precise geographical reach of government had still to be decided. For some, the rights of individuals were best protected by governments as locally based and locally accountable as possible; here the 'risky agent', in Landau's words,[2] was a national government. To others, only a strong central government could protect individuals from the overweaning power of local vested interests.[3] The American democratic political tradition began in the town meeting (or even Friends' Meeting House), expanded to the state legislatures and only then to a wider vision of a single union. One aspect of American limited government, then, is a geographic one, concerned as much with the physical space in which different governments may properly exercise their coercive power as with the balance between individual and societal rights.

The two other significant procedural points were an agreement that decisions, once taken, could be reconsidered and that there should be a rule of secrecy about the proceedings. The absolute essentials of good negotiations on complex questions had thus been wisely laid; they allowed the delegates to move cautiously towards a consensus, fearful neither of repudiation by those whom they might be thought to be representing nor of exploring possibilities of every kind. This tradition of negotiation and bargaining has largely endured in the domestic arena of politics to this day. But there was a price to be paid. In a country where considerable inequalities existed yet aspirations to political equality were strong, it was natural that the long silence became interpreted in some quarters as an elaborate plan by the fortunate to devise a system of government protecting the interests of the merchants and the wealthy against the poorer farmers, many of whom were debtors. This conspiratorial view, although incorrect as a description of the Convention's deliberations, contained an important element of truth: most of the Founding Fathers were nervous of an undiluted democracy.

The Constitution as it finally emerged was the product of many compromises. The initial informal agenda which structured the ensuing debate was not the Articles of Confederation but the constitutional plan presented by the Virginian delegation at the very beginning of the Convention.[4] James Madison, an early arrival, had profitably used the delay in getting the Convention under way in order to draft, with his colleagues, fresh constitutional proposals with a strong centralist bias and a dominant position for the larger states. Although this Virginia Plan had eloquent adherents, it struck two raw nerves: a widely held suspicion of any strong national government which might be akin to the recently removed British overrule and, second, the fear of the less populous and poorer states that their interests would be swept away by the larger and richer states. Nationalists argued with parochialists; the representatives of the strong states argued with the representatives of the weak states. Ultimately, a compromise was agreed upon which satisfied virtually all the delegates.[5] It contained four significant features.

First, it established the classic federal position of divided sovereignty.[6] The national government was to be granted enumerated powers to perform particular national functions thought necessary in the light of the weaknesses of the Continental Congress; the states were to retain responsibility for local matters. Furthermore, the states, large and small, were to be represented as equals in one chamber of the legislature, the Senate, while the population principle was to be reflected in the other chamber, the House of Representatives. In other respects, too, the separate independent existence of the states was recognised; the qualification for voting was left to the states, as was the selection of members to the electoral college which had the responsibility of electing the President. The separation of state and national authority was essential if the Convention was to agree on a new constitution, but its paper reality soon developed into something much more complex, more interactive. The clarity of a dual federalism, in which the exact reach of the state and national governments respectively was clear and mutually exclusive, became blurred over time as communications improved, political parties developed, the national government's tax base increased, popular demand for central intervention grew, and the focal point of American citizens shifted inexorably to Washington. The power of the national government and its involvement in state and local government operations is undeniable and some people even query whether the United States is any longer a federal system; but the federal principle remains, if not intact, still alive and tolerably well.[7] The laws that emanate from Baton Rouge and Sacramento are very different; the inhabitants of Louisiana and California live under different rules with different facilities. Which is better is another question and one to which I shall return later in this chapter.

Second, the new Constitution enshrined the principle of the separation of powers. It was Montesquieu who had erroneously seen this as the genius of the British constitution and it was Montesquieu to whose authority delegates often referred in the Convention. Four observations need to be made. First, although usually described as epitomising the separation of powers principle, the United States Constitution in fact demands interpenetration and interaction between the branches of government; the checks and balances demand this. Second, the primacy of the legislative branch is symbolised by the first article's attention and concern for Congress; the executive branch was consciously relegated to second place. Third, the separation of powers together with checks and balances obviously contributes greatly to the limitation of powers, but there was no overt mechanism in the Constitution for establishing authoritatively what was constitutionally permissible if the executive and legislative branches disagreed; subsequently the Supreme Court carved for itself the ultimate authority to pronounce on such occasions. Finally, just as the operation of federalism developed in response to the changing political environment, so too has the balance between the legislative, executive and judicial branches, and for many of the same reasons. The whole constitutional system is indeed like an organism adapting to the external environment. Sometimes its health has been in mortal danger, as in 1861–64, sometimes merely in trouble, as in 1963–73 perhaps; but it has shown a great capacity to survive.

Third, the new Constitution was an expression of the dominant ideological persuasion of the delegates, which might be characterised as doubtfully democratic. The colonies had long enjoyed a limited franchise and the catalyst which translated a wide range of complaints into insurrection against the colonial power in 1776 was the anger at being taxed by a parliament in which they had no representation. The ringing phrases of the Declaration of Independence expressed a widely held belief that the powers of government *did* rest on the consent of the governed. Yet the delegates at Philadelphia belonged to an economic as well as an intellectual élite; many were disturbed by the underlying anti-property and anti-establishment implications of Shays' rebellion; few, indeed, were so progressive, so utterly out of tune with their times, that they believed that the vote was an absolute right, even for men. The possibility of a limited franchise was consciously retained; election to both the Senate and the presidency was to be indirect, thus providing a filter between the feared irresponsibility of a propertyless mass and the highest offices in the land. The displaced tyranny of king and parliament was to be mitigated in future by the separation of powers and by federalism; the tyranny of the majority was to be mitigated by indirect elections on a limited franchise. In time, the undemocratic aspects of this defence against the possible excesses of democracy have all but been expunged. As the franchise was extended according to an egalitarian philosophy whose logical consequences could indeed be a tyranny of the majority, the Bill of Rights, originally devised precisely to protect individuals against the national government, came in the second half of the twentieth century to be used to constrain the tyranny of *state* majorities when popular prejudice was translated, through legislation, into discriminatory action against various groups such as blacks, and religious minorities like the Jehovah's Witnesses.[9]

Fourth, the compromises necessary to produce a Constitution at all resulted in two distinctive types of constitutional provision. Discussion during the Convention had been a mixture of principled generalisation and specific concern. When the Convention adjourned on 26 July, a Committee of Detail turned the agreed general propositions, augmented by existing constitutional provisions borrowed from the Articles of Confederaton and state constitutions, into a draft constitution. In performing this task the five-man committee was guided by two fundamental principles set down by Edmund Randolph. They deserve full repetition:[10]

> In the draught of a fundamental constitution, two things deserve attention: (1) To insert essential principles only, lest the operations of government should be clogged by rendering those provisions permanent and unalterable, which ought to be accommodated to times and events; and (2) To use simple and precise language, and general propositions, according to the example of the several constitutions of the several states; for the construction of a constitution necessarily differs from that of law.

This prescient appreciation and James Wilson's skill as a wordsmith produced a deceptively simple constitution, stronger on generalisation than specificity, open to interpretation, and flexible. However, although successful compromises may fudge some potentially divisive issues, they cannot fudge them all. So the United States Constitution also contains some clauses of great particularity without which acceptance in 1787 might well have been impossible.

Summarising the essential characteristics of the Constitution in this particular manner implicitly provides an explanation of its form. One interpretation, therefore, emphasises the practical experience of the delegates, the problems they wished to overcome and the practices of government they feared, and concludes, first, that there was in fact a broad consensus shared by virtually all those at Philadelphia and, second, that pragmatism prevailed in an orgy of rationality as the interests of the large states and the small states, of the nationalists and the parochialists, were cleverly balanced out in as classic a piece of negotiation as it is possible to imagine. A gloss on this interpretation adds a further dimension; the compromises, indeed the logically necessary outcomes of particular disparate but not mutually exclusive interests, were enhanced by the philosophical preferences of the Founding Fathers. Locke, Montesquieu, Paine and others clearly played a part; so educated a group of men, quintessentially Enlightenment men, had read widely and thought deeply about political ideas, as Thomas Jefferson's library richly illustrates. Yet these writers were really the coinage of the debates, a coinage which predated the Convention, a coinage, indeed, inseparable from the Revolutionary War and the inheritors of the former colonies.

This Whiggish interpretation has been challenged, most famously by Charles Beard, whose *Economic Interpretation of the Constitution* coloured for half a century its historiography.[11] Beard argued that the Constitution was essentially the political necessity for the preservation of economic advantage which the delegates sought to defend against the tyranny of the majority. The economic stresses which provided the primary incentive to rethink the Articles of Confederation lend some support to this view, as does the cautious embrace of simple democratic ideas such as a wide franchise. And yet, to an important extent much of Beard's thesis is trivially true; any gathering of articulate leaders in 1787 would have defended private property, would have been concerned with economic co-operation between the states, and would have had to compromise on the slave issue to establish a Union at all. But the disagreements within the Convention, the changes of mind, the place of principle for some, and the inexact match between affluence and support for the Constitution or economic disadvantage and opposition to the Constitution belie such an interpretation.[12] For its day it was unquestionably progressive and liberal; unsurprisingly it did the middle classes no harm.

Yet this is all slightly beside the point. The Constitution itself is, of course, a document of comparatively limited length, certainly a very much shorter document than, for instance, the Indian Constitution. But it should also be conceived as something considerably more than the formal document. Randolph's minute extolling the virtue of generality and, by implication, criticising the overspecification of powers was based upon the belief, surely correct, that a Constitution cannot provide authoritative and universally accepted solutions to every issue in the long life of a Republic. Since 1787, massive technological developments in transport, communications and manufacturing in the United States have been accompanied by changes in expectations and values. How, then, can the eighteenth-century document remain appropriate for the needs of ensuing generations? The answer is that, although the words remain virtually unaltered, their meanings and applications have changed dramatically. That is the secret of the Constitution's survival and success.

The vehicle for this continuous renewal is the Supreme Court. Whether its role as the final arbiter of the Constitution's meaning and its power to develop that meaning were intended by the Founding Fathers has been, and remains, a hotly debated issue. One school of thought envisages the Constitution as establishing in tablets of stone both the general principles and the specific policy assumptions of those who drafted and ratified it (and its amendments).[13] As Chief Justice Roger Taney wrote, the Constitution should 'speak out not only in the same words but in the same meaning for all time'.[14] There is a good case to be made for such a position, not least because the alternative – unelected and unaccountable Justices reading their own conceptions into the words of the Constitution – is difficult to defend in a political culture reflecting the simple assumptions of late twentieth-century democratic discourse and with a Constitution deriving its legitimacy ostensibly from 'We, the People' and containing means for its own emendation.

However, it is by no means clear that such a position is preferable to its alternative. The Committee of Detail, as we have observed, realised that flexibility was needed if the general principles of the Constitution and the Union itself were to survive. Chief Justice Marshall insisted that the Constitution was 'intended to endure for ages to come and consequently to be adapted to the various crises of human affairs'.[15] James Madison himself wrote in 1821 that '[a]s a guide in expounding and applying the provisions of the Constitution, the debates and incidental decisions of the Convention can have no authoritative character'.[16] The Founding Fathers had been brought up in the British tradition of a judicial power to interpret statutes and, more significantly, to apply incrementally an evolving conception of the common law.[17] In other words, although the Constitution ought to remain the fundamental basis to which disputes over the allocation of powers or the defence of individual rights should be referred, its meaning, like coral, could grow gradually in response to contemporary needs.

It is perhaps idealistic to portray the Supreme Court, in Woodrow Wilson's words, as a 'Continuous Convention' articulating the consensus of each age.[18] But there is a good deal of validity in the argument that the process of nominating Justices to the Court and the need for willing popular obedience or executive power to enforce the Court's judgments all contribute to the tendency for the Court to reflect the views of the dominant coalition of the day.[19] From time to time a majority of the Court is indeed manifestly out of step; but, just as legislative majorities soon realign, so do judicial majorities.

And it is simply untrue to categorise the United States system of government as merely majoritarian and hence logically antithetical to the principle of judicial supremacy. The Constitution is replete with checks on majorities; the Bill of Rights was designed precisely to prevent elected majorities doing certain things;[20] the federal principle consciously divides sovereignty. One may legitimately question whether the Justices always exercise their power wisely or consistently; but the exercise of that power, referred to in Philadelphia, alluded to in Hamilton's defence of the Constitution, boldly asserted in John Marshall's deceptively simply opinion in *Marbury v. Madison*, and reaffirmed countless times thereafter, is a reality.[21] Not only is it a reality; it is a necessity. The process of amending the Constitution has proved difficult and is, in any case, a crude and blunt method of achieving a nuanced development of a constitutional system. The Supreme Court, through the process of judicial review and the convention of judicial supremacy, fulfils the necessary function of adaptation.

Adaptation may be necessary; but its operationalisation is often contentious. Rules inevitably favour some people and groups over others; changing the rules will equally inevitably find both supporters and opponents. In the development of a society, some values take root more easily and deeply than others and their incorporation into the constitutional system occasions little resistance. Others face head-on more fundamental and cherished beliefs and explicitly challenge self-interested privileges; these occasion considerable resistance. And, because rules do affect the distribution of power and advantage, there are always groups eager to change those rules. Throughout the nation's history, then, political groups have attempted to use the Constitution or to amend it or to persuade a majority of the Supreme Court of their interpretation of its words in order to advance their political goals. The Constitution, if not always explicitly, is nevertheless implicitly involved in current political conflicts on a regular basis; sometimes the passion of the dispute is unmistakable, while at other times it is muted. But, even if the dominant impression of the United States constitutional system is one of stability and incremental adaptation, it should not be thought that critical voices have been, or are, absent.

II

The satisfaction felt by the delegates on 17 September at the completion of their handiwork hid both their inner doubts about some of the Constitution's specifics and also the strength of opposition which existed in some of the states. The preamble to the Constitution begins 'We, the People' and representatives of the People (or, at any rate, the enfranchised people) were to meet in the individual states to ratify the new constitution. It was, in fact, a perilously close-run thing. The quality of the arguments, most of which had been rehearsed in Philadelphia, was high, the quantity large.[22] The smaller states were generally keen to ratify; the more populous states, without whose accession the Union would be doomed, entertained more doubts. The campaigns, however, favoured the proponents of the new constitution; on 25 June 1788 Virginia voted to ratify by 89 to 79 and on 26 July New York voted to ratify by 30 to 27. Yet both states entered reservations, New York 'in the confident expectation' that amendments would be introduced.[23]

The anti-Federalists, as opponents of the Constitution were known, had some genuine points and genuine concerns.[24] The secrecy which had been so essential to the success of the Convention fuelled their belief that a small élite had consciously devised a new system of government tailored to its own élite interests at the expense of the 'small man'; the populist tradition in the United States, suspicious of the powerful and educated, socially conservative, and vocally independent thus started early. Assuming the worst, many sought and exaggerated the weaknesses of the Constitution. Two alleged failings in particular were picked upon, although they were in effect variations on the same theme.

First was the fear that the new central government would exercise too much power over the individual citizen. Presaged in some of the ratifying conventions and half-promised by several defenders of the new Constitution, establishing a Bill of Rights was the first major action taken by the first Congress of the United States of America. It was, in a way, the price to be paid for ratification. Proposed by Congress on 25 September 1789, the first ten amendments to the Constitution were formerly ratified on 15 December 1791 when Virginia became the eleventh state to endorse them. It was not until 1939, with the dominance of Hitler's Nazi Party in Germany, that Massachusetts and Connecticut in fact ratified, thus symbolising the enduring tension between adherents of efficient government (implicitly strong government) and weak government (implicitly more responsible to the popular will). Originally intended as a limitation on the national government, the Bill of Rights came, a century and a half later, to act as a limitation on state governments as well, a development which, as we shall see, was not universally applauded.

The second fear centred on the supposed dominance of the national government over the state governments. For all the additions, deletions, formulations and reformulations that were made in Philadelphia, the Constitution which emerged still bore the unmistakable marks of its origin in the Virginia Plan. Above all, it differed fundamentally from the Articles of Confederation (which, it will be recalled, it was supposed merely to amend) by granting the national government the right to coerce the individual states, even if only in a limited number of areas. The sovereignty of the several states, won in war, had been compromised in peace. The nature of the new compact was never resolved to everyone's satisfaction. Had the states given up their sovereignty to establish a more perfect union which had, in its turn, granted a portion of that sovereignty back to the states? Or had the states in effect loaned a portion of their sovereignty to the national government and were they, therefore, entitled to repossess that which they had loaned? Lincoln believed the former; the southern states defended the latter view. Ultimately it required a horrific four years of civil war to decide the issue, on the battlefield with steel rather than on the hustings with argument.

It was thus three-quarters of a century after the making of the Constitution before the precise nature of its innovating federal principle was defined. And even in the years since the end of the Civil War, there have always been some politicians and writers adhering to the view that ultimate sovereignty lay with the states. But by the beginning of the twentieth century the essential contours of the Constitution were all but universally accepted. The first ten amendments, the Bill of Rights, was till then more symbolic of aspirations than a genuine bulwark for individual rights generally and the thirteenth, fourteenth and fifteenth amendents, expressing the victors' conception of black citizenship after the Civil War, still failed to protect black rights in the states of the old Confederacy.[25] The Constitution, as Corwin has pointed out, by the twentieth century performed its dual function as a set of rules which governed political life and as a symbolic expression of the American people's aspirations.[26] It speaks volumes for the legitimacy granted to the Constitution itself that practice and aspiration did not always go hand in hand.

The 1930s provide an illuminating canvas on which to see the dissonance between politics and aspiration. Many writers of the time might have unthinkingly quoted Thomas Jefferson who had written in 1789 that '[t]he constitution ... is unquestionably the wisest ever yet presented to men'.[27] In a famous and much quoted article of the time, Max Lerner had suggested that the Constitution was 'totem and fetish' and was thought by Americans to possess 'supernatural Powers'.[28] Such metaphysical appreciation did indeed encapsulate one significant feature of the Constitution in American life. It was in the 1930s, after all, that a popular president, handsomely re-elected, found that his New Deal was declared by a majority of the Supreme Court to be impermissible under the Constitution and then responded by attempting not to amend the Constitution but to override the erring Justices whose interpretations displeased him.

It is important to pause a moment here. It is generally accepted that President Franklin Roosevelt's plan to 'pack' the Supreme Court in 1937 was a constitutional crisis.[29] The issue, however, was not presented in a form which questioned whether the Constitution was still appropriate for the crises of the depression; the issue became diffused into the propriety of Justices interpreting the venerated Constitution against the wishes of a popular majority (and lawyers working for the New Deal were well aware of the weakness of their position in constitutional terms)[30] and the propriety of a president offending the convention – it was no more – that there should be nine independent Justices of the Supreme Court removable only by an act of God or an act of will. The crisis, then, was not about the Constitution itself; it was about other, clearly more fallible, actors such as presidents and Justices of the Supreme Court. And it was also about constitutional conventions, the unenumerated but widely accepted assumptions within which the political game is played. The United States, as other countries also, has built up a set of unwritten rules, based neither on legislative fiat nor explicit judicial pronouncement, which carry as much force in the real world of politics as many a clause in the Constitution itself.

In the middle of the 1950s Pole could write that 'the people of the United States are united above all by their Constitution',[31] but over the next twenty years vocal groups challenged that Constitution's application to a range of social issues. When *Brown v Board of Education of Topeka*[32] outlawed the dual school system, southern politicians fought vigorously to prevent its application. Decisions followed which found that the recitation of prayers, reading of the Bible, or the saying of the Lord's prayer at the beginning of the school day were unconstitutional,[33] that the equal protection clause of the Fourteenth Amendment required constituencies in the states to be of equal size,[34] that a requirement to bus children across a school board's area to make a reality of integrated schools was consti-tutionally permissible,[35] that law enforcement officials were obliged to inform suspects of their rights and evidence improperly gained had to be excluded in its entirety from trials,[36] and that states could neither prevent, nor unduly constrain, women from choosing to have abortions in the early stages of pregancy.[37] All these decisions stimulated powerful currents of opposition to the Court and persuaded many to attempt 'reversal' of those decisions.

Because the Constitution *is*, in the last analysis, 'what the Judges say it is',[38] it is essential to distinguish between the Constitution itself and the contemporary application, or meaning, of it. Most Americans do not trouble themselves to make such a distinction, for few have much occasion to do so. But some, following the line of argument of Charles Beard (although not consciously in his intellectual footsteps), do not have positive attitudes towards the Constitution; intimately aware themselves of poverty, racial discrimination and political impotence, they sometimes blame their plight on the very Constitution the majority venerates.[39] Others, the legally educated above all, are still aware of the dichotomy but prefer, as a rule, to take the Constitution as a virtuous given and direct their criticisms to the Court. It is not the Constitution's fault, some of them would argue, that schoolchildren are forcibly bused, God is excluded from the classroom, law enforcement officials are constrained by technicalities favouring the criminal, the right to life is obliterated by a judicially created right to an abortion, and blacks or women can be given preferential treatment over white males. These are the fault of the Justices of the Supreme Court.

The authority granted to the Justices, and to judges more generally, is indeed exceptional. The United States is a litigious society.[40] This is not due to some national characteristic that encourages lawsuits but to a socially transmitted belief in the value and virtue of law in a society lacking a traditional ruling class or a deeply ingrained acceptance of common law innovations.[41] The Supreme Court has almost necessarily, therefore, been thrust into a position of political power; there is something organic about its assumption of constitutional authority unparallelled in other countries and unlikely to be replicated in the twentieth century. Historical accident, too, strengthened the reach of its power in recent decades. The acute tensions arising from racial discrimination in the United States in the 1950s were partly defused by the Supreme Court's decision in *Brown v Board of Education of Topeka* that single-race schools violated the equal protection clause of the Fourteenth Amendment; this decision, however, opened Pandora's Box as more and more of society's conflicts were brought to the Court for resolution and the equal protection clause was applied to a wider range of differentiating laws and regulations. Had race not fuelled the Court's activism in the 1950s, that activism might have been much less developed.[42]

Table 5.1 Count of proposed amendments to the Constitution, 1789–1985

	Number	%
1789–1889	1,736	17.37
1890–1934	1,713	16.14
1935–1944	499	4.99
1945–1954	506	5.06
1955–1964	1,463	14.63
1965–1974	2,702	27.02
1975–1985	1,372	13.72
Total	9,991	

Source:
Richard A. Davis, *Proposed Amendments to the Constitution . . .*, Congressional Research Service, Report No. 85–36 Gov, 1985.

A litigious society and an activist Court encouraged groups to see a judicial path towards their goals. Their opponents, failing to alter the jurisprudence of the highest bench, were thus forced into attempting to change the Constitution itself; for it is sometimes clear that this is the only practicable way of reversing the current meaning of the Constitution as pronounced by a majority of the Supreme Court. Most formal amendments are the culmination of several years' work by various interest groups which may, taken together, be thought of as social movements.[43] They have historically developed from small beginnings and become, in time, a new majority. This new political generation, as Stephen Schechter argues, accedes to power with a fresh agenda, part of which may necessitate constitutional changes.[44] Such was the case with the progressive movement at the turn of the century; such may be the case with the 'New Right' in the 1980s.[45] To overrule unliked decisions of the Supreme Court requires nothing less than amending the Constitution itself.

On four occasions in the past, a judgment of the Supreme Court has in fact been reversed by constitutional amendment, most recently in 1971,[46] and in several other instances Supreme Court decisions have been spurs to amendment attempts. Table 5.1 sets out the number of amendments proposed until the end of the ninety-eighth Congress. Although many are clearly intended only for publicity purposes to satisfy individual congressmen's political interests, the ebb and flow indicates a shifting level of satisfaction with the Constitution and current Supreme Court interpretations of it.

Over the whole period of the Constitution's life, apart from the period since 1955, the readiness of Congress to present Constitutional amendments to the people for ratification has been low; its parsimony is, indeed, remarkable. One reason for this is the symbolic authority of the Constitution, an authority which suggests, if not perfection, certainly the excellence of which Jefferson wrote and which sanctifies things done in its name. As Richard Trench has argued, the experts' commitment to the written Constitution as the sole source of power in the United States is so strong that, when confronted with major power centres not mentioned in the Constitution, they attempt to trace their origins to the Constitution by implication or inference.[47] The cult of the American Constitution,[48] as Clement Vose has written, is 'akin to the reliance on Biblical text of religious fundamentalism'.[49] For all its apparent imperfections, the Constitution must seem to be perfect and regular revisions, in the eyes of most politicians, would diminish that perfection unacceptably.

Explaining this symbolic authority is problematic. It lies in part in the reverence for law itself to which I have already referred, but it also lies somewhere in the unresolved dilemma of deciding what it is to be 'American', an identity much sought after and often disputed. The influx in the latter part of the nineteenth century of immigrants from non-Anglo-Saxon Europe – and Catholics to boot – was enriched by the gradual emancipation of black Americans and the more recent arrival of men and women from Asia and Spanish-speaking Central America. Shared language, shared history, shared religion, shared heroes no longer bound the people of America naturally into a nation. The melting pot needed some glue; the Parsonian sociologists' concern for coherence and stability sanctified that requirement. So the elementary schools had to play a consciously political socialising role and the oath of allegiance is still recited by the vast majority of young people in the country's schools. Such behaviour emphasises the concern to establish an American identity as did, in its more disquieting form, the uniquely American Un-American Activities Committee. Above all, however, the cement binding the disparate ethnic groups which make up American society became a veneration for the Constitution or, perhaps more accurately, a veneration for an idealised conception of the Constitution.

This veneration understandably has not been universally shared throughout the twentieth century. From about 1955 an increasing number of attempts were made to introduce constitutional amendments, as Table 5.1 indicates. Over half of all amendments introduced into the Congress have been introduced in the last thirty years. Again, the explanation for this is problematic. A high proportion of the changes proposed were intended to reverse decisions made by the Supreme Court. As governments generally began to increase their interference into people's lives, the claims for rights against governments also increased. A growing liberalism in élite values – on race, on access to political institutions, on justice – was transmitted through members of the Supreme Court into their decisions. The groups who lost out complained loudly; and one method of articulating these complaints was to introduce constitutional amendments. However, progress from introduction to hearings, let alone to Congressional authority to send them to the states for ratification, requires a consensus. The lack of a consensus to overrule the decision in many of the areas where passions have been roused is reflected in the minimal number of hearings actually held. These are set out in Table 5.2.

The decision whether to hold hearings on a proposed amendment or not is the major winnowing; yet only a proportion of those deemed worthy of a hearing reach the Congress for a vote, let alone get referred to the states for ratification. Twenty-six amendments have successfully travelled the full road; only seven amendments have been proposed by the Congress and have failed to be ratified.[50] Such a high success rate is a function of the seriousness with which leading politicians take amendment politics, the Constitutional requirement for special majorities in the Congress, and the intimately connected existence of a broad consensus in the country at large. The difficulty involved in amending the Constitution throws a special burden upon the Supreme Court to adapt the document to contemporary requirements, just as it provides ample opportunities for disgruntled public figures to express their opposition to some of its adaptive decisions as well as their feelings of disquiet at the failings of institutional rules producing outputs of which they disapprove.

Tables 5.2 and 5.3 illustrate well the priorities of these disaffected people. The social issues have indeed roused passions and these have encouraged some Congressmen to propose amendments to the Constitution. But other issues have also been salient. The method, and term of office, for president and vice-president have long been a favourite subject for prospective constitutional amendments. The conflicts caused by the Vietnam War and the concerns raised by the whole 'Watergate saga' gave an added impetus to those who wished to alter the existing practices. The enhanced status of the women's movement also provided a momentum to those who had, for many years, been seeking an Equal Rights Amendment. The number of proposed amendments is an indication of diffuse disquiet; more important are the occasions, and issues, on which hearings take place and, ultimately, votes are taken.

Table 5.3 brings into clear relief two points about the amendment process in the United States. First, it is difficult to gain majorities

Table 5.2:   Hearings on constitutional amendments, 1969–1984

Topic	Year	Chamber	Floor Debate	Floor Count
Election of President	1969	House	Yes	338–70
	1970	Senate	Yes	No
	1971	Senate	No	No
	1973	Senate	No	No
	1973	House	No	No
	1975	Senate	No	No
	1977	Senate	No	No
	1979	Senate	Yes	48–51
	1984	Senate	No	No
Vote for 18 year olds	1970	Senate	No	No
	1971	Senate	Yes	94–0
	1971	House	Yes	401–9
Equal Rights	1970	Senate	No	No
	1970	House	Yes	352–15
	1971	House	Yes	354–24
	1972	Senate	No	84–8
	1983	House	Yes	278–147
	1984	Senate	No	No
Representation of DC	1971	House	No	No
	1975	House	Yes	229–181
	1977	House	Yes	289–127
	1978	Senate	Yes	67–32
Busing	1972	House	No	No
	1979	House	Yes	209–216
Abortion	1974	Senate	No	No
	1975	Senate	No	No
	1976	House	No	No
	1981	Senate	No	No
	1983	Senate	Yes	49–50
School Prayer	1980	House	No	No
	1982	Senate	No	No
	1983	Senate	Yes	56–44
Balanced Budget	1975	Senate	No	No
	1979	Senate	No	No
	1980	Senate	No	No
	1980	House	No	No
	1981	Senate	Yes	69–31
	1982	House	Yes	236–187
	1984	Senate	No	No
Grand Juries	1976	Senate	No	No
	1977	House	No	No
Tenure of Congressmen	1978	Senate	No	No
	1979	Senate	No	No
Initiative	1977	Senate	No	No
Reconfirmation of Judges	1972	Senate	No	No
Affirmative Action	1981	Senate	No	No
Compensation for Congressmen	1983	Senate	No	No
Item Veto	1984	Senate	No	No
Legislative Veto	1984	Senate	No	No
English as Official Language	1984	Senate	No	No

unless there is a very broad consensus. Vanquished sections, almost by definition, are minorities and they rarely prevail in a political system demanding the building of majority coalitions; their resort to constitutional amendment is largely a cry of anguish from losers. Where change has come, it has tended to be either the clear expression of majority opinion or an extension of democratic rights which are implicitly part of the American ideal, even if not an explicit part of the Founding Fathers' vision. As Alan Grimes has summarised it:[51]

> What the people have done to the Constitution has been to make it a far more democratic document than the one they inherited from their ancestors. The amendments, in fact, constitute a formal record, in the fundamental law, of the growth of democracy in America. Although the amendments were written to meet the needs of specific historical situations, they present in their entirety a remarkably consistent democratic theme.

The successful amendments fall into only five comparatively busy periods.[52] The first twelve, ratified between 1791 and 1804, may be seen as the southern amendments, the victory of Virginia, as it were, over Massachusetts; only northern states failed to ratify them. The thirteenth to fifteenth amendments, ratified between 1865 and 1870, may be seen as the northern amendments and represent the consolidation of the northern victory in the Civil War. The sixteenth to nineteenth amendments, ratified between 1913 and 1920, may be seen as the western amendments, reflecting the populist and progressive power of the western states; apart from Utah, no western state failed to ratify any of these amendments, while many southern states and some Republican-dominated eastern states refused to endorse them. The fourth period, covering the repeal of Prohibition (1933), the re-arrangement of the dates on which elected federal officers take up office (1933) and the twenty-second (1951), a Republican *post facto* judgment on Franklin Roosevelt, are perhaps *sui generis*. The final period, the so-called urban or metropolitan amendments, ratified between 1961 and 1971, flow from a shift in the centre of political gravity for a period towards the Democratic urban constituency. Out of a 200-year history, action on amending the Constitution occupied only 35 years. Each period coincided with a shift in the balance of domestic power; each strengthened, as was intended, the dominant coalition of the day.

The failure of the Equal Rights Amendments illustrates much about the amendment procedure. Introduced first in 1923 by the Kansas Republican, Senator Charles Curtis (who was later to be vice-president under Herbert Hoover), it was not until 1972 that both the House of Representatives and the Senate approved such an amendment with the necessary two-thirds majorities. When the

Table 5.3   Subjects of proposed constitutional amendments 1971–84

SUBJECTS	92nd Congress Senate n	92nd Congress Senate %	92nd Congress House n	92nd Congress House %	93rd Congress Senate n	93rd Congress Senate %	93rd Congress House n	93rd Congress House %	94th Congress Senate n	94th Congress Senate %	94th Congress House n	94th Congress House %
Presidential Elections	13	(30.2)	49	(10.2)	4	(9.5)	43	(12.6)	3	(9.1)	27	(9.2)
Right to Vote	1	(2.3)	44	(9.1)	–		–		–		–	
Court Related	2	(4.6)	44	(9.1)	3	(7.1)	31	(9.1)	5	(15.2)	17	(5.8)
Equal Rights	6	(13.9)	96	(20.0)	–		–		–		–	
District of Columbia	1	(2.3)	11	(2.3)	1	(2.4)	8	(2.4)	1	(3.0)	13	(4.4)
Prayer in Public	3	(7.0)	74	(15.4)	8	(19.0)	36	(10.6)	4	(12.1)	31	(10.6)
Right to Life	–		1	(0.2)	2	(4.8)	44	(12.9)	8	(24.2)	69	(23.5)
Balanced Budget	–		12	(2.5)	2	(4.8)	25	(7.4)	3	(9.1)	29	(9.9)
Student Assignment	7	(16.3)	63	(13.1)	9	(21.4)	48	(14.1)	5	(15.2)	39	(13.3)
Foreign Policy	–		10	(2.1)	–		9	(2.6)	0	( )	4	(1.4)
Miscellaneous/Other	10	(23.3)	77	(16.0)	13	(31.0)	96	(28.2)	4	(12.1)	66	(22.5)
	43		481		42		340		33		293	

95th Congress				96th Congress				97th Congress				98th Congress				TOTALS	
Senate		House		Senate		House		Senate		House		Senate		House			
n	%	n	%	n	%	n	%	n	%	n	%	n	%	n	%	n	%
5	(14.3)	41	(12.1)	4	(10.8)	28	(11.0)	2	(5.5)	13	(7.2)	1	(3.2)	8	(6.2)	241	10.6
–		2	(0.6)	–		–		–		–		–		–		47	2.1
6	(17.1)	14	(4.1)	1	(2.7)	12	(4.7)	1	(2.8)	7	(3.9)	2	(6.4)	7	(5.4)	149	6.5
–		2	(0.6)	–		2	(0.8)	1	(2.8)	7	(3.9)	1	(3.2)	10	(7.7)	125	5.5
4	(11.4)	12	(3.6)	–		2	(0.8)	–	( )	1	(0.6)	–		–		54	2.4
2	(5.7)	24	(7.1)	1	(2.7)	17	(6.6)	2	(5.5)	10	(5.5)	3	(9.7)	8	(6.2)	223	9.8
5	(14.3)	63	(18.6)	2	(5.4)	35	(13.7)	5	(13.9)	21	(11.6)	7	(22.6)	11	(8.5)	273	12.0
6	(17.1)	72	(21.3)	21	(56.8)	80	(31.4)	12	(33.3)	64	(35.4)	5	(16.1)	27	(20.8)	356	15.6
1	(2.9)	27	(8.0)	–		16	(6.3)	–		11	(6.1)	–		5	(3.8)	231	10.2
–		1	(0.3)	–		3	(1.2)	–		2	(1.1)	–		1	(0.8)	30	1.3
6	(17.1)	80	(23.7)	7	(18.9)	60	(23.5)	12	(33.3)	50	(27.6)	12	(38.7)	53	(40.8)	546	24.0
35		338		37		255		36		181		31		130		2275	

seven-year period laid down within which ratification had to be completed ran out, the Congress extended the ratification period, but that, also, proved too short; the ERA officially died on 30 June 1983, three states short of the 38 needed for ratification.[53] Put simply, there was not a sufficient consensus to press the ERA to a successful conclusion. But that is an essentially tautological explanation. The failure to act (Utah in fact rejected the amendment while Idaho, Nebraska, Tennessee, Massachusetts and South Dakota rescinded their earlier approvals) occurred overwhelmingly among southern states and states which had also proved unsympathetic to the nineteenth amendment enfranchising women. The political culture of individual states, especially where fundamentalist Christian sects or the Mormon church were strong, proved particularly telling; so, too, did a changing environment in which the egalitarian liberalism of the mid-1960s waned and attraction to 'traditional conservative values' grew.[54] But the failure was ultimately a political failure, caused as much by the carefully planned political campaigns of anti-ERA groups and the religious Right as by a weakening belief in sexual equality. The opinion polls showed, if anything, an increasing level of popular support; but powerful interests managed, although late in the day, to mobilise sufficient political support to block ratification. The ERA was five years too late in its passing through Congress; it was also a classic example of the fact that amendment politics are indeed *politics*.

The failure of the ERA, which is concerned with rights, was less serious than the failure of the proposed District of Columbia Representation Amendment, which is about structure. Women's rights have been steadily, and in some ways dramatically, advanced by the Supreme Court's steady extension of the equal protection clause of the fourteenth amendment to outlaw practices which differentiate between men and women.[55] Starting with *Reed v Reed* in 1970, the Burger Court has used an intermediate level of review[56] to find a range of well established inequalities unconstitutional. Not all differentiation, to be sure, is discrimination; but the proposed ERA would not necessarily have outlawed all differentiation. William Rehnquist would have interpreted the loose phrase 'equality of rights' as narrowly if there had been an ERA as he has interpreted the 'equal protection of the law' clause narrowly; and William Brennan would have interpreted them both as broadly.

All the amendments so far considered originated from the Congress in response to popular pressures. But 'We, the People' are the source of the Constitution and a second route to constitutional amendment is provided under Article V.[57] State legislatures may petition Congress to call a Convention to amend the Constitution. Since this has never in fact occurred, the precise responsibility of Congress remains unclear as does the legitimate agenda of such a Convention. Legislators in Washington have been aware of this and some have tried to write into law the procedures and constraints on such a process; but they have failed to produce a law.[58] As a consequence, some senior politicians and commentators, such as Barry Goldwater, the late Howard Jarvis and George Will, have opposed the Convention method, even though their favourite cause, a balanced national budget, would be prejudiced. This goal, achieved already in most of the individual states, reflected not only an understandable alarm at the escalating size of the federal budget deficit but also a new fiscal orthodoxy that in part replaced the post-Keynesian liberalism of the 1960s. By the end of 1985, it only needed two more states to vote in favour of a Convention for one to be considered and the murky constitutional ramifications be publicly discussed. The closeness to achievement concentrated politicians' minds in a realisation that a balanced budget would have fundamental ramifications for a myriad of programmes which were admittedly politically painful to cut but which also provided the bottom line for a quasi-welfare system whose virtue they recognised in the abstract. On other occasions in the past, the votes for a Convention have nearly been reached; between 1893 and 1911, 31 out of the 32 states required called for a Convention for the direct election of Senators, while between 1906 and 1916, 27 of the 32 needed called for a Convention to consider the constitutionality of polygamy; between 1957 and 1969, 33 out of the required 34 states called for a Convention to consider negating the effects of the Supreme Court's decision requiring all state constituencies to be of equal size.[59] On only one of these occasions did Congress heed the call, on direct elections to the Senate which became the Seventeenth Amendment and probably pre-empted the Convention. It is little wonder, therefore, that those who wish to reverse the Supreme Court's interpretation of a Constitution turn most of their attention to the members of that Court.

Most of the political effort put into changing what the Constitution in practice means has been expended in recent years in attacks on the Justices of the Supreme Court. Those who wanted in the 1960s to 'Register Communists, not Guns' also wanted to 'Impeach Earl Warren' (as two bumper stickers succinctly put it); indeed, Gerald Ford, when he was still Congressman Ford, tried to start impeachment proceedings against the liberal Justice William Douglas. In the campaigns of 1968, the personal qualities and beliefs of Justices, and putative Justices, were a central theme. The Senate's refusal to confirm Abe Fortas as Earl Warren's successor in 1968 and its rejection of Clement E. Hainsworth and Harrold J. Carswell in 1970 both reflected the belief that control of nominations could lead to constitutional change.[60] This is in fact too oversimplified a view, but, notwithstanding the exceptions in recent years of Warren, Brennan and Blackmun, there is generally a close relationship between presidential preference and a nominee's jurisprudence on the Court.[61] Since attacking the Constitution itself is difficult, a vicarious attack on its interpreters is the natural alternative. The most obvious way to influence the interpretation of the Constitution in the longer run is to nominate new Justices with an approved judicial philosophy to the Supreme Court; Reagan's choice of the articulate and intellectually able Antonin Scalia is an obvious example of this strategy.

There are other indirect ways by which disaffected political groups challenge the current meaning of the Constitution. One is a Congressional path; this can involve either employing Article III, Section II.2 to circumscribe the appellate jurisdiction of the Supreme Court or utilising the amendment procedure to 'reverse' specific judgements of the Court. Although both have been tried, neither has advanced much in the last decade. A second path is the interest group litigating path, by which carefully selected cases, well briefed, provide the vehicles for persuading a majority of the Court to depart from past precedents. The National Association for the Advancement of Coloured Peoples is the classic example;[62] but many others, including many conservative groups, are now deeply involved in using the judicial supremacy of the Supreme Court to 'legislate' where Congress has failed.[63] This path is associated with private interest groups, but it should not be forgotten that administrations, too, attempt to advance parts of their agenda along this route.[64] This was true of the Kennedy administration in its desire to reduce the gross disparities in the size of electoral districts.[65] It is also true of the Reagan administration, although it has embarked upon the more difficult task of reversing constitutional principles only recently enunciated. Unable to translate executive power into its desired social changes, the administration is forced to attempt to influence the judicial branch, either through personnel change or by persuasion in actual litigation of its choice.[66]

Amending the Constitution, whether through the formal process or informally through judicial interpretation, is a matter of power. As Schechter has pointed out, the battle over Prohibition reflected the socio-religious dimension of the Populist-Progressive movement's attempts to break the concentration of political power in the boss-dominated legislatures of the eastern states, pitting the urban (often Catholic) voters of the East against Protestant (and eventually Progressive) voters of the South and West. The battle for the Nineteenth Amendment (Women's Suffrage) reflected the growing strength of the Progressive Movement, producing a coalition of bipartisan western support and Progressive eastern support over the opposition of the southern Democrats and eastern Republicans.[67] Power is needed to be successful; and enhanced power is the purpose of the effort. It is no accident that the periods of formal amendment activity coincided with fundamental shifts in the aggregate support of political tendencies in the United States. And shifts in Supreme Court jurisprudence likewise have followed shifts in the dominant coalition in Washington. Contemporary America is finely balanced between competing political forces, a partisan dealignment having failed to give birth to a partisan realignment. Consequently, the United States is likely to go through a period of transient majorities, unstable and unpredictable.[68] One sign of this is the widespread antipathy to many interpretations of the Constitution but no consensus on how, or in what form, to alter the current position. The Court's jurisprudence thus becomes one of the many battlegrounds in a system noticeable for its multiple points of political access, and the noise exaggerates both the forces that lie behind the demands for change and the likelihood of that change. Power has not yet decisively shifted.

III

Constitutions provide the rules of the political game; they necessarily also entrench disparities of power and influence. Liberal democracy is not a neutral philosophy (although it may well be able to embrace a good deal more variety than other philosophies); it establishes values which enhance the chances of some and hinder the chances of others.[69] Constitutions, furthermore, if they are to survive, adapt to their changing environment and reflect over time shifts in the political forces of the states to which they refer. The United States Constitution exemplifies both these propositions. The growth into a world superpower and the changing assumptions about government have all contributed to an evolution of the Constitution from a set of rules appropriate to the American colonies at the end of the eighteenth century to a set of rules not inappropriate for a world power at the end of the twentieth century.

The adaptation of the United States Constitution through the Supreme Court's reinterpretation of that document is perhaps unique; certainly the range of issues, essentially claims to rights, on which it has spoken authoritatively is extraordinary. The Court's power is unmistakable and now assured; indeed political actors attempt to *use* the Court's authority to advance their own agendas.

It would be wrong, however, to assume that the only adaptive forces were the formal and informal processes of amendment to which I have called attention. Franklin Delano Roosevelt was in principle correct when, in his inaugural address of 1933, he said: 'Our Constitution is so simple and practical that it is possible always to meet extraordinary needs by changes in emphasis and arrangement without loss of essential form.'[70] He sought at the time to expand the power of the national governent. Although the Supreme Court checked that claim in the short run, in the longer term the assumption of executive branch leadership and an enhanced regulative role for the Congress became so widely accepted that those expectations shifted the balance of constitutional power away from the states towards Washington. The political forces which normally alter the effective, as opposed to the formal, distribution of power in any state have been at work in the United States as well.

Nevertheless, however admirably the Supreme Court's adaptive role may be judged, there remain some aspects of the Constitution which generate debate and disquiet and for which no easy solutions are at hand. Take, first, that fundamental liberal paradox created by a democratic ethos embracing both majoritarian assumptions and concern for minorities. On the one hand, any government whose legitimacy depends upon the consent of the governed inexorably depends upon majorities for that legitimacy; on the other hand, a Constitution which protects individuals from the full rigours of governmental powers provides a mechanism by which majorities may be thwarted. Even this paradox contains within itself a further problem; for it fails to define from which people appropriate majorities should be drawn in order to legitimate policies in different issue areas. Federalism presupposes that the nation is not the geographical unit appropriate for all issue areas. The evolving American Constitution has resolved none of these difficulties, although it has shifted the boundaries between the powers of government and the rights of the individual, between the reach of national government and the preserve of state authority. The liberal dilemma remains unresolved.

A second area of concern continues to revolve around the nature of American federalism itself. Although some of the Founding Fathers might well be surprised at the extent to which the national government predominates in many areas of domestic concern, they would surely have appreciated the enduring popular suspicion of Washington which helped both Jimmy Carter and Ronald Reagan towards the White House. They would be content with the surviving, if weakened, belief in the virtue of diversity and the necessity for different priorities in different state capitals. That the definition of obscenity in Oklahoma was not parallelled in Los Angeles would cause neither suprise nor concern. Above all, the continuing reality of the sovereign individual as the basic building block for a liberal society would encourage them. Despite a growing tendency to interpret equality, and the equal protection clause of the Fourteenth Amendment, as warranting equality of outcome throughout the Union, the survival of a robust belief in what Seymour Martin Lipset called equalitarianism[71] would warm their hearts. Equalitarianism provides the ideological justification for inequalities, which the Supreme Court's decisions in *Reynolds* and *Gideon* have only partly dented.[72] The liberal society, adapted to the requirements of the twentieth century, survives.

But equalitarianism in 1987 has different consequences from equalitarianism in 1787. Modern capitalism with its expensive high technology, the logic of large combines, the end of the expanding frontier, the rise of intellectual over physical skills, all have encouraged a degree of cumulative inequality uncommon two hundred years ago. With political power increasingly dependent upon access to air time and consequently money, the myth of a political class reflecting the social and economic concerns of their electors inexorably weakens. Yet it is still *simpliste* to deduce from the portfolios of President Reagan's cabinet that only the very rich prevail; the calculus of consent demands a real attention to the representative principle.

Some scholars might argue that the affluent and powerful, through a 'mobilisation of bias' and control over so much of the nation's public ideology, have thwarted the original ideals of the Founding Fathers. Such an argument overlooks not only the truncated concept of democracy which prevailed in the original states of the Union but also the fundamental changes in American society over the last fifty years. More than Roosevelt's New Deal even, the Supreme Court's fleshing out of the bones of the Bill of Rights has brought to the underprivileged advances both substantive and symbolic. The eradication of state-sponsored racial discrimination, the growth in suspect rights, the developing principle of sexual equality, a hesitant advance in environmental concern, all have been real victories for the less powerful and established powers. For some, it has all gone too far and disabled America;[73] yet not all unpopular minorities prevail, as homosexuals found early in 1986, when the Supreme Court decided that sodomy between consenting adults was not protected from state regulation under the Constitution.

Concern with the way the Constitution operates is not confined entirely to those who object to specific developments sanctioned by the Supreme Court. There is also disquiet at a systemic level, expressed not only by those with vested interests involved. The link between the governors and the governed, for example, on which academics and ex-politicians have had a good deal to say, has generated an important debate. Representatives, it has been argued, are forced by their relentless attention to parochial matters and their electors' presumed needs to emphasise local demands and the search for electoral financial contributions at the expense of a national interest.[74]

This worry extends into the process by which American presidents are selected and elected. The number of Constitutional Amendments on this subject is only one sign of the concern. The Congress itself has attempted to set limits on financial expenditures, but these attempts have in part run foul of the First Amendment's developed 'right to communicate'.[75] The parties, particularly the Democratic Party, have altered their rules governing the selection of candidates, with unintended and, to many, unfortunate consequences.[76] But many people remain unsatisfied, believing that the extension of primaries, by reducing the influence of professional politicians and exaggerating the significance of mediagenic candidates gaining early victories, has systematically built into the electoral process conditions which militate against the "best" candidates competing for the presidency. This last belief would not surprise Lord Bryce entirely, even though the reasons why great men do not get elected president have changed.[77]

There is another, more fundamental concern. When Harold Laski claimed that federalism was 'obsolescent',[78] he was asserting the socialist's belief in the need for central government dominance if a planned economy and egalitarian outputs were to be achieved. Of course, these arguments fall on deaf ears in the United States. But, from Roosevelt's presidency onwards, presidents in particular have chafed at the limitations upon their office set by the federal division of sovereignty, the separation of powers, and the Bill of Rights. In the 1960s, seduced by John Kennedy's vitality, many observers sought in the presidency the leadership which the parochial culture of Congress and the federal divison of powers denied. But the 'imperial presidency' it spawned and the calamities of Vietnam and Watergate dulled the attraction of a strong president.[79] As the 1960s and 1970s recede from the nation's collective conscience, more people have become attracted to the idea of a strong president, even if, in the same breath, they mouth the great populist belief in the danger of strong national government.

Strong presidents are seen as essential for efficient government. So, too, are disciplined, 'responsible' parties. That was a concern of academics in the 1950s;[80] it resurfaced in the later 1970s.[81] What worried thoughtful observers was the central problem of a governmental system of divided powers: where did accountability lie? Responsible national parties, strong presidents and centralised authority would provide both efficiency and accountability. In the early 1980s, Lloyd Cutler, fresh from service under President Carter, called for debate on what he saw as a structural fault in the American constitutional system which prevented the production of a national programme directly accountable to the people.[82] Others, too, have questioned the virtue of the central principles of the American Constitution at the end of the twentieth century.[83]

These concerns are real enough; and there is no doubt that divided powers do provide challenges to American politicians which are not easy to manage. But the call for efficiency can blot out the demand for limitations on potential tyranny.[84] And it is this demand which remains a core value in the American political culture, shared by populists and many neo-conservatives alike. It is also its attraction to foreigners. Despite the extraordinary difficulty involved in making such a system work at all, necessitating, as it does, a great readiness to bargain and compromise and a deep conviction that politics is not a zero-sum game, the American model has been considered by constitution-makers elsewhere. The federal principle, adapted and refined, was proposed as a solution to many states' problems after the Second World War.[85] In many it survived. More recently, the architects of the second Nigerian Republic imported the American federal model complete with separation of powers; although it failed (essentially because the culture necessary to underpin such a system was absent), it is still considered by some scholars as the most appropriate model for Nigeria.[86]

Despite the very real concerns expressed about the Constitutional system and the social and economic practices protected by it, there is little likelihood of major changes in the foreseeable future. Those who have specific complaints about specific interpretations will still find it difficult to mobilise the requisite majorities in the two houses of Congress either to introduce constitutional amendments or to limit the Court's jurisdiction by statute. They may fare better after 1988 should President Reagan's successor nominate conservative jurists to replace retiring liberals. Those who have broader, systematic concerns will likewise find the United States political system more suited to incremental drift than radical change. Intellectuals may seem to carry more weight in the United States than in, say, Great Britain, but they operate in a system which is highly political and which is designed more as a brake on change than as an accelerator for innovation. In times of crisis, short-lived majorities can shift the system briefly out of its normal pace, as happened after the 1932 election and again in the 1960s. The Watergate saga of the early 1970s generated much angst about the system but by the end of the decade the prevailing view increasingly came to be, in the words of one book on Vietnam, that 'the system worked'.[87] Tocqueville's prescient observation that any issue which divides the American people ultimately reaches the Supreme Court for judgment remains true. But the passionate political conflicts which are inevitably played out in the judicial branch with the coinage of constitutional precedent and Founding Fathers' intention should not deceive the casual onlooker into thinking that the Constitution itself is under challenge. It is not.

Notes and references

1. The literature on the Constitutional Convention is vast. Three easily accessible books are Jack N. Rakove, *The Beginnings of National Politics: an interpretive history of the Continental Congress* (New York: Alfred Knopf, 1979); Clinton Rossiter, *1787: the Grand Convention* (New York: Macmillan, 1966); Catherine Drinker Bowen, *Miracle at Philadelphia: The Story of the Constitutional Convention, May to September 1787* (Boston: Little, Brown, 1966).

2. Martin Landau, 'Federalism, Redundancy and System Reliability' in Daniel J. Elazar (ed.), *The Federal Party* (New Brunswick: Transaction, 1974), p. 187.

3. Robert D. Thomas, 'Cities as Partners in the Federal System', *Political Science Quarterly*, 10, 1986, pp. 49–64.

4. A useful collection of relevant documents, including the Virginia Plan, is Winton V. Solberg (ed.), *The Federal Convention and the Formation of the American States* (Indianapolis: Bobbs-Merrill, 1958).

5. Only three of those still present on Monday 17 September refused to sign: Randolph, Mason and Gerry. Thirty-eight of the fifty-five delegates involved at some stage in drawing up the Constitution were there and signed; Dickenson, exhausted, had left at the weekend asking Read to sign on his behalf.

6. Although the meaning of 'federalism' has been much debated, I think it best to take the United States system of 1787 as an 'ideal type' and contemporary federalisms as variations, developed to meet different conditions and needs. See K.C. Wheare, *Federal Government*, 4th edn (London: Oxford University Press, 1963).

7. On the classic form of 'dual federalism' see M.J.C. Vile, *The Structure of American Federalism* (London: Oxford University Press, 1965). For modern variants, see Michael D. Reagan and John G. Sanzone, *The New Federalism*, 2nd edn (New York: Oxford University Press, 1981).

8. Alexis de Tocqueville, *Democracy in America*, 1835 and 1840 (Oxford: World's Classics, 1946).

9. See Henry J. Abraham, *Freedom and the Court: civil rights and liberties in the United States*, 2nd edn (New York: Oxford University Press, 1972), pp. 29–88.

10. Cited in Rossiter, *1787*, pp. 201–2.

11. Charles Beard, *An Economic Interpretation of the Constitution of the United States* (New York: Macmillan, 1913).

12. Robert E. Brown, *Charles Beard and the Constitution: a critical analysis of 'An Economic Interpretation of the Constitution'* (Princeton: Princeton University Press, 1956); Forrest McDonald, *We, the People* (Chicago: University of Chicago Press, 1958).

13. A classic exposition of this view is Raoul Berger, *Government by Judiciary:*

the transformation of the Fourteenth Amendment (Cambridge, Mass.: Harvard University Press, 1977).

14. *Dred Scott v Sandford*, 19 *How.* 393 (1857) or 60 US 691 (1857) at 709.

15. *McCulloch v Maryland*, 4 *Wheaton* 316 (1819) at 415.

16. James Madison to Thomas Ritchie, 15 September 1821, cited in H. Jefferson Powell, 'The Original Understanding of Original Intent', *Harvard Law Review*, 98, 1984–5, p. 936.

17. Powell, 'The Original Understanding', pp. 885–945.

18. Woodrow Wilson, *Congressional Government* (Princeton: Princeton University Press, 1895).

19. Robert A. Dahl, 'Decision-making in a Democracy: the role of the Supreme Court as a national policy maker', *Journal of Public Law*, 6, 1957, pp. 279–95. There has been a considerable debate on Dahl's thesis and several refinements have been made to it: yet its basic thrust seems to me still broadly correct. David Adamany, 'Legitimacy, realigning elections and the Supreme Court', *Wisconsin Law Review*, 1973, pp. 790–846; Richard Funston, 'The Supreme Court and critical elections', *American Political Science Review* 69, 1975, pp. 795–811; Jonathan D. Casper, 'The Supreme Court and national policy making', *American Political Science Review*, 70, 1976, pp. 50–63; Paul Allen Beck, 'Critical elections and the Supreme Court: putting the cart after the horse', *American Political Science Review*, 70, 1976, pp. 930–32; Bradley Canon and S.S. Ulmer, 'The Supreme Court and Critical elections: a dissent', *American Political Science Review*, 70, 1976, pp. 1215–21.

20. See Robert Jackson's opinion in *West Virginia State Board of Education v. Barnette*, 319 US 624 (1943) at 638: 'The very purpose of a Bill of Rights was to withdraw certain subjects from the vicissitudes of political controversy, to place them beyond the reach of majorities and officials and to establish them as legal principles to be applied by the Courts. One's right to life, liberty, and property, to free speech, a free press, freedom of worship and assembly, and other fundamental rights may not be submitted to the vote; they depend on the outcome of no elections.'

21. See, for instance, Alexander Hamilton *et al.*, *The Federalist* (London: Dent, Everyman's Library, 1911, 1971), letter 80; *Marbury v Madison* 1 Cr. 137 (1803).

22. The most distinguished of all were *The Federalist*, papers written by Alexander Hamilton, John Jay and James Madison. Although often cited, even by Supreme Court Justices, as the authentic commentary on the Constitution, they were, of course, the defence's brief and accordingly partisan. For the Debates and other writings of the time, see: Max Farrand (ed.), *The Records of the Federal Convention of 1787* (New Haven: Yale University Press, 4 vols, 1937); Jonathan Elliott (ed.), *The Debates in the Several State Conventions on the Adoption of the Federal Constitution* (Philadelphia: J.P. Lipincott, 5 vols, 1787–88 (Brooklyn: 1888; reprinted New York: De Capo, 1968).

23. Cited in J.R. Pole, 'The Making of the Constitution' in H.C. Allen and C.P. Hill (eds), *British Essays in American History* (New York: St Martin's Press, 1957), p. 20.

24. See the classic work by Herbert Storing and Murray Dry (eds), *The Complete Anti-Federalist* (Chicago: University of Chicago Press, 7 vols, 1982) and Herbert Storing, *The Abridged Anti-Federalist* (Chicago: University of Chicago Press, 1985).

25. C. Van Woodward, *The Strange Career of Jim Crow* (New York: Oxford Univesity Press, 3rd edn, 1974).

26. E. Corwin, 'The Constitution as Instrument and Symbol', *American Political Science Review*, 30, 1936, pp. 1071–85.

27. Thomas Jefferson to David Humphrey, 18 March 1789. It is perhaps proper to point out that not all Jefferson's comments on the Constitution were so laudatory.

28. Max Lerner, 'Constitutions and Court as Symbol', *Yale Law Journal*, 46, 1945–46, p. 1294.
29. Robert H. Jackson, *The Struggle for Judicial Supremacy* (New York: Knopf, 1941); Leonard Baker, *Back to Back: the duel between FDR and the Supreme Court* (New York: Macmillan, 1967).
30. See Peter Irons, *The New Deal Lawyers* (Princeton: Princeton University Press, 1983).
31. Pole, 'The Making of the Constitution', p. 18.
32. *Brown v Board of Education of Topeka, Kansas*, 347 US 483 (1954); 349 US 294 (1955).
33. *Engel v Vitale*, 370 US 421 (1962); *Abington School District v Schempp*, 374 US 203 (1963).
34. *Reynolds v Sims*, 377 US 533 (1964).
35. *Swann v Charlotte-Mecklenburg Board of Education*, 402 US 1 (1971).
36. *Miranda v Arizona*, 384 US 436 (1966).
37. *Roe v Wade*, 410 US 113 (1973); *City of Akron v Akron Center for Reproductive Health*, 103 SCt 2481 (1983).
38. Charles Evans Hughes, *The Supreme Court of the United States* (New York: University of Columbia Press, 1928).
39. Larry R. Baas, 'The Constitution as Symbol: patterns of meaning', *American Politics Quarterly*, 8, 1980, pp. 237–56.
40. Jethro K. Lieberman, *The Litigious Society* (New York: Basic Books, 1981).
41. The United States inherited the common law from Britain and there is still, outside Louisiana with its French traditions, an American common law. But it plays a much less significant role than the judge-made law based upon constitutional exegesis.
42. I am indebted to Geoffrey Marshall for this point.
43. Clement E. Vose, *Constitutional Change: amendment politics and Supreme Court litigation since 1900* (Lexington: D.C. Heath, 1972).
44. Stephen L. Schechter, 'Amending the United States Constitution: a new generation on trial' in Keith G. Banting and Richard Simeon, *The Politics of Constitutional Change in Industrial Nations: redesigning the state* (London: Macmillan, 1986), pp. 160–202.
45. See generally on the 'New Right', Gillian Peele, *Revival and Reaction: the Right in contemporary America* (Oxford: Clarendon Press, 1984).
46. The 11th Amendment reversed *Chisholm v Georgia* (1793), the 14th *Dred Scott v Sandford* (1857), the 16th *Pollock v Farmers' Loan and Trust Co.* (1895) and the 26th *Oregon v Mitchell* (1970).
47. Richard Trench, 'A Chancy Business, this Constitution', *Yale Review*, 69, 1980, pp. 342–56.
48. The phrase originated in Ralph Gabriel, *Course of American Democratic Thought*, 2nd edn, (New York: Ronald Press Co., 1956).
49. Vose, *Constitutional Change*, p. 344.
50. For the details, see Schechter, 'Amending the United States Constitution', p. 169.
51. Alan Grimes, *Democracy and the Amendments to the Constitution* (Lexington, D.C. Heath, 1978), p. xi.
52. *Ibid.*
53. See Janet K. Boles, *The Politics of the Equal Rights Amendment: conflict and decision process* (New York: Longman, 1979).
54. Some of the evidence for this can be found in the following articles: Val Burris, 'Who opposed the ERA? an analysis of the social bases of antifemininsm', *Social Science Quarterly*, 64, 1983, pp. 305–17; Janet K. Boles, 'Systemic Factors underlying Legislative responses to Women Suffrage and the Equal Rights Amendment', *Women and Politics*, 2, 1982, pp. 5–22; Ethel B. Jones, 'ERA Voting: labor force attachment, marriage and religion', *Journal of Legal Studies*, 12, 1983, pp. 157–68.

55. Richard Hodder-Williams, 'The Supreme Court, the Constitution, and Women's Rights', *Teaching Politics*, 16, 1987, pp. 80–92.
56. *Reed v Reed*, 404 US 71 (1971); Ruth Bader Ginsburg, 'The Burger Court's Grapplings with Sex Discrimination' in V. Blasi (ed.), *The Burger Court: the counter-revolution that wasn't* (New Haven: Yale University Press, 1983), pp. 132–56.
57. See Bill Gangush, 'Principles Governing the Interpretation and Exercise of Article V Powers', *Western Political Quarterly*, 35, 1982, pp. 212–21; C. Hermann Pritchett, 'Congress and Article V Conventions', *Western Political Quarterly*, 35, 1982, pp. 222–7; Charles Black, 'Amending the Constitution: a letter to a congressman', *Yale Law Journal*, 82, 1972, pp. 189–215.
58. See, however, Sam Ervin, 'Proposed legislation to implement the Convention Method of Amending the Constitution', *Michigan Law Review*, 1968.
59. Schechter, 'Amending the United States Constitution', p. 183.
60. Richard Harris, *Decision* (New York: Dutton, 1971); Robert Shogun, *A Question of Judgement* (Indianapolis: Bobbs-Merrill, 1972).
61. Robert Scigliano, *The Supreme Court and the Presidency* (New York: Free Press, 1971).
62. See, particularly, the writings of Clement E. Vose, such as *Caucasians Only* (Berkeley: University of California Press, 1959); and Richard Kluger, *Simple Justice* (New York: Knopf, 1976).
63. Lee Epstein, *Conservatives in Court* (Knoxville: University of Tennessee Press, 1985).
64. Allan Wolle, *The Presidency and Black Civil Rights: Eisenhower to Nixon* (Cranbury: Associated Universities Press, 1971); R. Huston (ed.), *Roles of the Attorney-General of the United States* (Washington: American Enterprise Institute, 1968).
65. Victor Navasky, *Kennedy Justice* (New York: Atheneum, 1971).
66. See, for example, Randolph D. Moss, 'Participation and Department of Justice School Desegregation Decrees', *Yale Law Journal*, 95, 1985–6, pp. 1811–35.
67. Schechter, 'Amending the United States Constitution', pp. 187–88.
68. Byron E. Shafer, *The Changing Structure of American Politics* (Oxford: Clarendon Press, 1986).
69. C.B. Macpherson, *The Real World of Democracy* (Oxford: Clarendon Press, 1966).
70. Cited in Arthur M. Schlesinger jr, 'Roosevelt and the Courts', *Society*, 24, November/December 1986, p. 53.
71. Seymour Martin Lipset, *The First New Nation* (London: Heinemann, 1964).
72. *Reynolds v Sims*, 377 US 533 (1964), mandated equally weighted votes; *Gideon v Wainwright*, 372 US 335 (1963), required states to provide lawyers in cases where a custodial sentence was possible.
73. Richard E. Morgan, *Disabling America: the 'rights industry' in our time* (New York: Basic Books, 1984).
74. Elizabeth Drew, *Politics and Money* (New York: Collies, 1983).
75. *Buckley v Valeo*, 424 US 1 (1976); *Federal Election Commission v National Conservative Political Action Committee*, 105 S.Ct 1459 (1985).
76. James Ceaser, *Reforming the Reforms* (Cambridge, Mass.: Ballinger, 1982), Nelson W. Polsby, *Consequences of Party Reform* (Oxford: Oxford University Press, 1983).
77. James Bryce, 'Why great Men are not chosen Presidents', in his *The American Commonwealth*, 3rd edn (London: Macmillan, 1893), pp. 78–85.
78. Cited in F.J. Carnell, 'Political implications of federalism in New States', in Ursula K. Hicks (ed.), *Federalism and Economic Growth* (London: Allen & Unwin, 1961), p. 18.
79. Arthur M. Schlesinger, jr, *The Imperial Presidency* (Boston: Houghton Mifflin, 1973).

80. 'Towards a more responsible Two-Party system: a report of the Committee on Political Parties', *American Political Science Review*, 44, 1950, Supplement.
81. For example, Gerald Pomper, 'Towards a more responsible Two-Party System? What, again?', *Journal of Politics*, 33, 1971, pp. 916–40.
82. Lloyd N. Cutler, 'To form a government', *Foreign Affairs*, 59, 1980–1, pp. 126–43.
83. See, for example, James L Sundquist, *Constitutional Reform and Effective Government* (Washington: Brookings Institution, 1986); Donald L. Robinson (ed.), *Reforming American Government: the bicentennial papers of the Committee on the Constitutional System* (Boulder: Westview, 1985).
84. Arthur S. Miller, 'Separation of Powers: does it still work?', *Political Quarterly*, 48, 1977, pp. 54–64.
85. Carnell, 'Political implications of federalism', pp. 16–59.
86. Larry Diamond, 'Issues in the design of a Third Nigerian Republic', *African Affairs*, 86, 1987, pp. 209–26.
87. Leslie H. Gelb (with Robert K. Betts), *The Irony of Vietnam: the system worked* (Washington: Brookings Institution, 1979).

6   Constitutional politics in Australia (1900)*
Campbell Sharman

Few countries can have had a more dramatic transition from a period in which constitutional issues were of minor and sporadic concern in national politics, to one where they were the subject of intense political debate. As such, the dismissal of the Whitlam Government in 1975 and the deadlock between the two houses of the national Parliament which preceded it, represent a major discontinuity in the political visibility of constitutional issues in Australia.

To the extent that the events of 1975 raised questions about the role of the head of state and the place of bicameralism in a British derived parliamentary system, 1975 also marked a major shift in the style and subject matter of constitutional debate at the national level. As a federation, Australia had long familiarity with constitutional politics in the form of disagreements over the division of powers between the two levels of government – commonwealth and state. Since 1975, however, the overwhelming concern has been with those constitutional issues that relate to the structure of the commonwealth government itself and in particular, the relationship that should exist between a British-style parliamentary executive based on a partisan majority in the lower house, and such institutions as the Senate and the Governor-General as head of state.

This shift has corresponded with an increased awareness of the hybrid nature of Australia's constitutional structure and the duality of its constitutional tradition. Part has been derived from the British parliamentary tradition which, when coupled with the modern mass party, concentrates power in a parliamentary executive. But part can also be traced to aspects of its colonial experience and to the federal form of government adopted by Australia in 1901, both of which have made for the dispersal of power among governmental institutions and the establishment of constitutional rules which check

*   I wish to acknowledge the helpful comments of Robert Dowse, Martyn Forrest, Jeremy Moon, Gordon Reid, and Chris Ulyatt on earlier drafts of this paper, and to thank the University of Western Australia for enabling me to attend the Conference at which this paper was first presented.

the power of the executive. This ambivalence not only provided the underpinning for the constitutional crisis of 1975 but can also be seen as a distinguishing characteristic of the Australian form of government.[1] A similar point has been made in a comparative context by Lijphart using the notions of majoritarian and consensus democracy.[2] The former is characterised by the adoption of structures which concentrate power for the exercise of collective choice in the name of the majority, the latter by structures which make for the dispersal of power and require mutual accommodation between institutions for the operation of government. Using a variety of indices, Lijphart's analysis can be employed to show that Australia is very much in the middle, drawing on institutions from both democratic traditions.[3]

The point need not be laboured, but this theme echoes one of the fundamental problems of constitutional design; on the one hand, to give adequate power to governments for them to execute the collective choice of citizens, yet on the other, to constrain governments so that power is used only for agreed-upon ends and in prescribed forms.[4] In a compromise between these conflicting goals, much of recent British constitutionalism has been underpinned by a tendency to stress coherent government action at the expense of constitutional limits, while a compromise in the opposite direction has long been held to characterise the constitutional tradition of the United States. Australia has borrowed heavily from the former and haphazardly from the latter, with a corresponding mixture of incongruous elements enshrined within its governmental structure.

Australia is of interest both because of this mixed constitutional tradition and because of recent changes in the relative importance of the constituent elements and in the nature of constitutional politics. Part of the pressure for these changes has resulted from domestic political events, but the country has also shared in the pervasive disenchantment with the role and effectiveness of government that has characterised the recent political history of most liberal democracies. While much of what follows is a commentary on the idiosyncrasies of Australian constitutional politics, this should be seen as but another manifestation of the perennial adaptation required to operate a system of popular constitutional government in a context of changing political values.

Constitutional development

Although the circumstances of European settlement in Australia varied from colony to colony, all six were established over a period of seventy years around the first half of the nineteenth century and shared similar constitutional histories.[5] By 1860, all colonies except

Western Australia had secured substantial political independence from Britain and ran their affairs under a system of British-style parliamentary government. Executive power was exercised by a Governor in the name of the Crown, but on the advice of a cabinet which depended for its continuance in office on the support of a majority in the lower house of a bicameral parliament. Colonial constitutions made little mention of the way in which executive power was to be made accountable to the popularly elected lower house, these matters being regulated by procedures adopted from current British practice. They did, however, establish upper houses, a majority of which were elected and all of which had considerable powers.

By the turn of the century, all six Australian states had established traditions of parliamentary self-government based on the British model. They had also acquired a familiarity with constitutional disputes resulting from disagreements between the two houses of bicameral parliaments.[6] Since the upper houses had been designed to reflect the views of the propertied and more conservative sections of the state communities as a check to the wide franchise of the lower houses, such disputes were not uncommon. Governments based on majorities in the lower house might find that important elements of their legislative programmes were thwarted by hostile majorities in an upper house whose powers were constitutionally enshrined and which, in many cases, could not be amended without cumbersome procedures which produced both delay and political risk. As a result, the deliberations during the 1890s that led to federation in 1901 were held between politicians who were familiar both with British-style parliamentary government and with the checks provided by politically and constitutionally autonomous upper houses. In other words, strong bicameralism and constitutional limits on the power of a parliamentary executive are long-standing elements of Australia's constitutional tradition.[7]

Federation reinforced this duality in Australia's constitutional experience. British-style parliamentary government was taken as the pre-eminent operating principle for the design of the new commonwealth government although, as before, many of the critical details relating to the operation of executive government were not specified in the constitution.[8] Limiting elements were also included, not least of which was the federal division of powers itself. Specified powers were granted to the national government and a judicial body, the High Court, was to arbitrate in cases where the legislative or executive competence of the commonwealth government was in dispute. Another constraint was the entrenchment of the commonwealth Constitution by a procedure that required the reference of proposed constitutional changes to a popular referendum.[9] Yet another was the provision of a bicameral parliament whose upper house, the Senate, was designed to represent the six state political communities through the popular election of an equal number of senators from each state despite wide variations in state populations.[10] The Senate was endowed with broadly similar powers to those of the lower house, the House of Representatives, and procedures were provided for the resolution of deadlocks between the houses only by reference to the electorate and, if necessary, a subsequent joint sitting of the two houses.[11]

In the event, the potential for major collision between a parliamentary executive based on a majority in the lower house, and a hostile majority in the Senate were only partially fulfilled for the first seventy years of federation. There were occasions when different partisan majorities controlled the House of Representatives and the Senate, and twice during this period the deadlock provisions of the Constitution were invoked.[12] But these events, while of high political controversy at the time, did not raise major constitutional issues. In a similar fashion, the procedural independence of the Senate in the discharge of its parliamentary functions did not give rise to constitutional politics in the style of 1975.[13]

In large part, the quiescence of the Senate over this period can be explained by the rise of the modern mass party. By 1910 the growth of the Australian Labor Party at the national level had precipitated the emergence of a party system characterised by programmatic politics and the existence of disciplined blocks of parliamentary representatives.[14] This, when coupled with the voting procedures initially adopted for the Senate, had the result of reducing the opportunities for the Senate to act as a politically autonomous chamber except on those few occasions when there were differing partisan majorities in each house. There was not, in other words, the establishment of a pattern of politically autonomous behaviour on the part of the Senate in its dealings with the executive and its supporting majority in the House of Representatives.

The growth of mass parties also had the familiar effect of subordinating the legislative role of the House of Representatives to the wishes of the executive so that, in Lijphart's terms,[15] a majoritarian strand of democracy was well established in the style of parliamentary government adopted by the national government.

As a consequence of these developments, constitutional politics at the national level came to be equated with aspects of the constitutional structure other than the internal operation of the commonwealth government. For the first seventy-five years of federation, they became synonymous with disputes over the interpretation of federalism and the appropriate role of the new national government. To the extent that constitutional politics can be taken to mean those aspects of the Constitution, dispute over which becomes sufficiently intense to spill into the public political arena, then constitutional politics had an even more specific meaning. It became identified with the sporadic attempts by the national government to amend the commonwealth Constitution and the consequent recourse to the popular referendum.

Federalism and constitutional change
The limited nature of the powers granted to the new commonwealth government reflected the circumstances of federation. Although such issues as defence and immigration played a part, together with a rising nationalist sentiment, it was largely economic and commercial considerations that provided the impetus for a form of union between the six Australian states in the 1890s.[16] Given the geographic dispersal of the states around the periphery of a continent, the strong tradition of self government in these political communities, and the fact that it was state politicians who negotiated the form of union, only a federal association was broadly acceptable. The new national government was to have responsibility only for those matters specifically granted it by the commonwealth Constitution and these were overwhelmingly matters concerning international affairs and interstate trade and commerce. Jurisdiction over the great bulk of activities that affect the daily lives of citizens, from the ownership and use of property, health and education, to the police and the administration of justice, were all to remain with the states.[17]

From early in its history, the commonwealth chafed at these constitutional constraints and sought to enlarge the ambit of its powers. Some of the pressure for change stemmed from alterations in the structure of Australian society and its economy, alterations that were accelerated by the effects of war, depression and technological change. Other pressures can be traced to changing expectation of the scope and purpose of government on the part of the electorate. But much of the drive for expanded powers originated simply from the ambitions of successive commonwealth governments to become involved in a broader range of political activities.

The procedure for amending the commonwealth Constitution requires initiation from the national government itself so that the rate and extent of change might appear to depend principally on the preferences of the government of the day. In the event, the large majority of proposals put to the people at constitutional referendums have been defeated, particularly those that have sought to transfer significant new powers to the commonwealth government.[18]

This lack of success at constitutional change has led some commentators to argue that Australians are especially conservative about constitutional matters, or demonstrate a singular obtuseness when it comes to assessing the benefits of constitutional change.[19]

On closer examination, such conclusions are open to serious doubt. Most proposals for change have been prompted by the need to cope with immediate political problems on the part of the central government and not from any broadly based consensus on the need for constitutional adaptation. Accordingly, the failure of most referendum proposals to gain the required support should be seen not as a wholesale rejection of constitutional change but as a rebuff to the often self-serving attempts by Canberra to remove political uncertainty or embarrassment through constitutional engineering. This has resulted in most referendum campaigns being concerned much more with partisan assessments of the political gains and losses generated by proposed changes on the part of a range of interest groups, state governments and opposition parties, than with arguments over constitutional structure.[20] There is some irony in the fact that the commonwealth's monopoly of the initiation procedures for amending the national Constitution may encourage a partisan bias in proposals for change with a consequent increase in the likelihood of defeat in the subsequent referendum.

This difficulty in achieving changes to the formal allocation of jurisdiction under the commonwealth Constitution has not limited the ability of the commonwealth to become involved in a wide range of activities. Part of this has resulted from interpretation of the Constitution by the High Court which, especially in the last thirty years, has tended to give a broad reading to commonwealth powers, particularly those touching on interstate trade and, more recently, on external affairs.[21] But the flexibility achieved through judicial interpretation of the Constitution has been a minor factor when compared with the use the commonwealth has made of its superior access to taxation revenue. The greater revenue-raising potential that it has had since federation, has been used as a mechanism to buy influence in areas of state concern. Financial transfers and conditional grants to the states, together with the network of intergovernmental relations which such arrangements engender, have meant that the commonwealth is now involved in many areas of predominantly state administration.[22]

These developments and the growth of commonwealth government influence undoubtedly add an important element of the federal division of powers under the commonwealth Constitution, but their importance is easily overstated. The fact that formal constitutional change has been so difficult to accomplish has meant that the states continue as powerful entities in the federal system and reflect the situation that the state political communities remain as the multiple centres of gravity of the Australian political and governmental system.[23]

The changing constitutional agenda

Until 1975, then, constitutional politics at the national level had been equated with the clash between the central government and the states over the scope of the commonwealth government's powers. Such clashes had been particularly acute during periods when the Labor Party held office in Canberra. Many of that party's more ambitious goals of planning and social engineering were incompatible with a federal division of powers[24] to the extent that, by the end of the 1940s, the party had experienced a series of defeats in its attempts to increase the scope of commonwealth power by constitutional amendment.

After twenty-three years in opposition, a Labor government came to power in 1972 with far-reaching plans for social change in many areas of state administrative responsibility.[25] While it embarked on a desultory attempt at altering the division of powers to give the commonwealth legislative power over prices and wages in 1973,[26] the main thrust of the Whitlam Government's policy initiatives was to affect priorities in areas outside commonwealth jurisdiction not by constitutional change but by accelerating the use of financial inducements and administrative arrangements to shape state policies. The political success of this strategy was mixed but its broader goals of avoiding both constitutional challenge to its policies and the need to initiate formal change to the constitution were largely achieved. Whatever difficulties the Whitlam Government was to have with the Constitution, problems of the federal division of powers were not among them.

The seeds of change in the nature of constitutional politics had, however, been sown in 1948. At that time the then Labor Government had amended the procedures for the election of Senators so that they were chosen under a system of proportional representation using the single-transferable-vote method. The reasons for this change related to long-standing difficulties with previous electoral arrangements, the fact that these would be exacerbated by a proposed enlargement of both houses of the commonwealth Parliament, and tactical considerations which are reputed to have led some members of the Labor Party to believe that it would be in the long-term interest of the party to adopt such a system. There is no evidence from the public debate at the time to suggest that thought was given to any changes in the role of the Senate that might result from the adoption of proportional representation.

The initial experience with the new electoral system confirmed the forecasts of those who expected little change except that the pattern of representation in the Senate much more closely mirrored the pattern of electoral support of the existing parties in the six state electoral districts. The quota for regular elections for half of the Senate was 17 per cent, a threshold which was seen as being sufficiently high to limit representation to the two major party groupings – the Australian Labor Party on the one hand, and Liberal and National Parties on the other – and preserve the Senate as a chamber usually subordinate to the wishes of the government of the day.

These expectations were confounded in the mid-1950s by the rise of the Democratic Labor Party which led to a series of changes of great significance to the Senate. By 1955, the potential for proportional representation to reduce the discrimination against the representation of smaller parties had been fulfilled and, by 1967, the government had lost its majority in the Senate. After the 1970 Senate election, the balance of power was held by a number of Democratic Labor Party and independent Senators and institutional change followed swiftly. From tentative beginnings when government legislation was occasionally held up or amended, the Senate moved with growing self-confidence to establish a comprehensive committee system and to question government policies across a wide range of topics. The election of the Whitlam Government in 1972 corresponded with the consolidation of the Senate as a chamber exercising its considerable powers independently of the wishes of the government.[27]

These developments were viewed with considerable misgiving by the two largest parties, although each when in opposition was only too willing to exploit these changes. There was much talk about the breakdown of coherent government but there was also a rival theme pointing out the virtues of a vigorous and independent Senate in providing an effective check to the over-concentration of power in the executive. These issues were raised both in the general context of debates over the role of parliament and in discussions relating to particular Senate inquiries or legislation before the Senate. Only as the term of the Whitlam Government progressed were there signs that a major constitutional issue was at stake.

The constitutional politics of 1975

If the growing political assertiveness of the Senate provides much of the background to the events of 1974 and 1975, a further element was the high level of partisan hostility between the two major political groupings. The reasons for this can be traced to the scope and rate of change proposed by the Whitlam Government, and to an opposition resentful at losing office. As time passed, the government became increasingly frustrated in achieving its goals by major changes in the domestic and international economies, by growing hostility to its policies on the part of state governments and the Senate, and by an increasingly determined opposition bent on exploiting the government's mistakes and its growing electoral unpopularity.[28]

In these circumstances, the Senate became a major forum for embarrassing the government by blocking and amending legislation and, by 1974, the opposition and minor parties were threatening to use their majority in the Senate to refuse to authorise government expenditure as a way of forcing the government to the polls. Early in 1974, the government anticipated this challenge and itself brought on an election using the deadlock provisions in the Constitution to dissolve both the House of Representatives and the whole of the Senate (that is, a double dissolution election).[29] At the same time, it submitted to the electorate four proposals for constitutional change.

These referendum questions represented a significant shift in the constitutional concerns of the national government. One of them had federal overtones in the sense that it was intended to increase the ability of commonwealth government to become involved with local government, but the remaining three were concerned with matters of representation and the process of constitutional change.[30] Of greatest significance was a proposal to ensure that elections for the Senate would always occur at the same time as those for the House of Representatives. Existing arrangements gave the Senate a fixed term so that, while the House of Representatives could be dissolved at a time chosen by the government of the day, the sequence of elections for the Senate had to follow a much more constrained timetable. This had meant that the three Senate elections preceding 1974 had not been held at the same time as elections for the House of Representatives. The result had been to give the electorate a choice at Senate elections much like that of a by-election; a chance to express dissatisfaction without defeating the government of the day, a situation favouring the representation of opposition and minor parties. Accordingly, a constitutional amendment requiring simultaneous elections of both houses was seen as a way both of giving the government greater flexibility in the timing of elections and of increasing the probability that the Senate would have a similar majority to that of the government in the lower house. The rising autonomy of the Senate was thus to be checked by an attempt to increase the chance that the government would have a partisan majority in the Senate.

All four referendum proposals were defeated even though the government was returned with a reduced majority in the House of Representatives. In the Senate, a variety of factors combined to leave the chamber evenly balanced between the two major party groupings. This set the scene for the series of events that led to the constitutional crisis of November 1975.

After the 1974 election, as well as being concerned with rapidly deterioriating political and economic circumstances, the government had to contend with three major challenges to previous constitutional practice. The first dealt with the filling of casual Senate vacancies. Such vacancies were filled at the discretion of the government of the state in which the vacancy had occurred until a new senator was chosen at the next election for the Senate or the House of Representatives. It had been the practice since the introduction of proportional representation in 1949 for state governments to fill vacancies with senators of the same political party as the Senator who had died or resigned, in order to maintain party strength in the Senate.[31] This practice was breached by the state governments of New South Wales and Queensland whose hostility to the government in Canberra led them to replace two Labor Senators with two non-Labor ones. Although this did not appear to be the result of any concerted plan by the opposition at the national level, the result was to give the Liberal and National Parties a majority in the Senate.

With control of the Senate, and with the Whitlam Government in political disarray and facing major economic problems and electoral unpopularity, the opposition parties in the Senate moved to block the flow of funds to the government for expenditure on key areas of administration. This second challenge to past practice led to fierce argument about the merits of such action. The government claimed that the Senate action was a breach of the fundamental conventions of British-style parliamentary government, while the opposition pointed to the explicit wording of the commonwealth Constitution which granted such powers to the Senate and argued, in its turn, that the conventions of parliamentary government required a government to resign and face an election if it was denied finance by the parliament. Deadlock resulted and political tension increased; neither side appeared willing to compromise and the government was faced with the prospect of running out of funds.

After some four weeks of this stand-off, the Governor-General made the most unexpected breach of past practice by dismissing Whitlam and his government. The grounds were that Whitlam would not give suitable advice to the Governor-General for solving the deadlock between the two houses of parliament and the consequent exhaustion of government funds.[32] The Governor-General initiated a double dissolution election at which the Labor Party was defeated in a landslide after a campaign of great acrimony and controversy over the actions of the Governor-General. The Labor Party argued that his actions had been a fundamental breach of the principles of British-style parliamentary government, while the Liberal and national Parties contended that the Governor-General had acted in the national interest by permitting the people to decide on the issues that precipitated the parliamentary deadlock. The constitutional structure of the commonwealth government had moved to the centre of the political stage and the definition of constitutional politics had been fundamentally changed.

Constitutional politics 1975–83

A large literature has been precipitated by these events[33] but it is not the intention of this chapter to discuss either the fine detail or the merits of the actions of the various participants. Rather, it examines the broad constitutional issues and the way in which the governmental system responded to the changes in the constitutional rules of the game.

It has been argued above that, before 1975, constitutional politics at the national level could be largely equated with disputes over the limits imposed on the commonwealth government by federation and the machinery for constitutional change. Within the operation of the commonwealth government, however, executive dominance of the parliamentary process had been greatly strengthened by the rise of the disciplined mass party. Executive dominance in this context is used to mean the certainty that the government of the day could control parliamentary procedures and through this the rest of the commonwealth governmental process. Constitutional politics, in other words, had to do with the context of commonwealth government action, not with its internal operations.

From this perspective, the critical characteristic of the events of 1975 was that they represented a major attack on executive dominance by indicating the existence of three new areas of constitutional uncertainty; first, the uncertainty over the filling of casual vacancies in the Senate and hence the predictability of the partisan composition of the Senate; second, the Senate's use of its powers not just to block and amend government legislation and to inquire into matters independently of the government, but to wrest the initiative from the government over the timing of elections; and third, the Governor-General's action which struck at the monopoly of the political executive to manipulate the formal machinery of government. In all three cases, initiative was lost by the government of the day; to the states, to the Senate, and to the Governor-General. It is clear that governments see uncertainty as a threat. Accordingly, the response of governments after 1975 was to marshall a strong drive to reduce these areas of uncertainty by amending the Constitution where possible or by using other means to achieve the same end.

This process, which lasted for some ten years after 1975, involved a number of paradoxes. The first was that the general problem of the limits of executive power was treated by the national government as though it were new to Australia, even though it had been long familiar to those state governments whose constitutional structure included strong bicameralism. The second was that the uncertainty generated by the events of 1975 resulted from the use of powers expressly stated in the commonwealth Constitution, that is, the government was complaining about the breaching of practices whereby certain constitutional powers were not used or were used only in accordance with the preference of the government of the day. The final paradox was that much of the clamour for constitutional reform was concerned with putting the clock back to re-establish constitutional practices taken for granted before 1975 and, in the case of the Senate, before 1967.

In the short term, perspectives on constitutional change were strongly affected by partisan factors since the Labor Party had been the loser and the Liberal and National Parties the beneficiaries of the changes to the constitutional rules. But it became clear that the two major party groupings had common interest in reasserting the dominance of the executive branch. The Liberal Party in particular, although secure in its large majority in the House of Representatives after 1975 and a similar coalition majority in the Senate, knew that its Senate majority was likely to be lost in subsequent elections and that it would then be vulnerable to similar uncertainties to those that had afflicted the former Labor government. Accordingly, preparations were made for constitutional change on a number of fronts.

The issue that generated the least controversy was the question of the filling of casual Senate vacancies. No commonwealth politician wanted to leave that discretion to the states and there was wide support at the national level for the proposal that it should be the relevant party machine that had the final say in the choice of replacement.[34] The replacement senator would also take over the whole of the term left vacant, adding yet further certainty to the partisan composition of the Senate. A referendum proposal to this effect was put to the people in 1977 and was carried with bipartisan support at the national level together with two other minor amendments, one extending the referendum franchise to the residents of the Northern Territory and the Australian Capital Territory, the other fixing the retirement age of commonwealth judges at seventy.

A fourth question was also put in 1977 concerning simultaneous elections for the Senate and the House of Representatives. This failed as it had done in 1974, notwithstanding the fact that its former opponents when in opposition were now its supporters when in government.[35] The Senate, in other words, remained a problem for the executive. Even if the simultaneous election amendment had passed over the objections of the residents of the smaller states,[36] the chamber would have remained as a powerful upper house with the potential of limiting the discretion of the executive.

This problem was exacerbated by the fact that the commonwealth Constitution had provided for a double dissolution election only in the event that legislation had been twice blocked by the Senate over a period of three months, and it did not provide for a sudden withdrawal of funds from the government as had occurred in 1975. Only the stockpile of previously blocked legislation had given the Governor-General the option of calling a double dissolution election, otherwise he would have been able to coerce only the House of Representatives and half the Senate to the polls. This situation meant that the Senate might, if its timing was right, be able to force a government and its House of Representatives majority to an election while the Senate itself avoided any test of its electoral popularity and, hence, the legitimacy of its actions.

Two solutions were proposed. The first, strongly supported by the Labor Party, was to amend the Constitution by removing the power of the Senate to block money bills or, at the least, those bills which did no more than provide the government with funds for the regular operation of its administration.[37] Given the hostility of the non-Labor parties to a direct diminution of the Senate's powers, and the even stronger opposition from the residents of the smaller states to any alteration of the Senate, this proposal was doomed to be seen as highly partisan and certain to be defeated at a referendum. The Liberal Party had a rival solution which involved giving consitutional recognition to what had happened in November 1975. The Constitution would be amended to provide that, once the Senate had blocked the government's supply of funds, there would be an automatic and immediate double dissolution election.[38] The Labor Party was highly critical of this proposal but there was little corresponding enthusiasm on the part of the Fraser Government in Canberra. While the rhetoric was to its liking, it shrank from the prospect of entrenching the Senate's power over the executive. No such constitutional amendment was put to the people during the life of the Fraser Government.

The third source of uncertainty manifested in 1975 was the role of the Governor-General. The unilateral actions of Sir John Kerr in dismissing the Whitlam Government while it still had a majority in the lower house, touched on one of the most sensitive and critical areas of British-style parliamentary government, that of the relationship between the popularly elected component of government and the formal machinery of executive power.

In the immediate aftermath of November 1975, there was some talk in Labor ranks of abolishing the existing office of Governor-General and of making Australia a republic. While some of these' proposals raised matters of constitutional interest, they tended to ignore the central problem; whether monarchy or republic, what should be the relationship between the head of state and the head of government?[39] No party chose a solution which involved spelling out the relationship as a constitutional amendment. The explanation for this can be found in the far-reaching consequences of any attempt to reduce the relationship to a series of statements of formal constitutional rules. To begin with, it would involve stipulating the role of the Prime Minister and the Cabinet, neither of which are mentioned directly in the commonwealth Constitution. Secondly, it would require the specification of the practices regulating the relationship between both the Prime Minister and the Governor-General and between the Prime Minister and the rest of the ministry. Finally, it would touch on the vexed question of what reserve powers, if any, the head of state might have in times of emergency, a matter that is always one of great difficulty and controversy. In sum, any such proposals would have the twin disadvantages of being specific about a range of sensitive matters which it usually suited the executive to keep vague, and of enabling the possibility of constitutional challenge in an area which, if it remained one of custom alone, was the exclusive concern of the executive.

As a consequence, this area of constitutional uncertainty has fallen outside any agenda for constitutional reform, with perhaps two exceptions. There have been successful attempts to reduce the relationship between the Governor-General and the political executive to a list of constitutional practices which have secured broad political support.[40] There has also been a continuing, if minor, interest both in the nature of executive power in Australia and in the possibility of moving towards a more consistently republican form of government.[41] Although not of direct constitutional significance, it can also be observed that Sir John Kerr's actions in November 1975 have led subsequent governments to make the selection of Governors-

General (and of state Governors) a matter that warrants a great deal of attention; there has been a marked change in the calibre of appointees, in the status and political visibility of the office, and in the care with which governments view their relationship with the representative of the Crown.

Constitutional politics since 1983

By the time the Fraser Government fell in 1983, constitutional matters had ceased to be a major political concern. The issue of casual vacancies in the Senate had been resolved by constitutional amendment, the issue of the role of the Governor-General was seen as being too difficult to resolve, and only the Senate remained as a thorn in the side of the government. The Fraser Government had tried to reduce the probability of deadlocks by the simultaneous election proposal in 1977 but the failure of this amendment marked the end of any attempts by the Liberal and National Parties to achieve formal constitutional change. The 1977 election also saw the rise of a new party, the Australian Democrats which, by the 1980 election, had secured the balance of power in the Senate and returned the relationship between the two houses of the common-wealth Parliament to what it had been between 1967 and 1975. Fraser liked this situation as little as had Whitlam before him but it was not a problem for which he had any constitutional solutions.

The return of a Labor government under Hawke in 1983 marked a revival in the political visibility of constitutional issues. While wishing to distance itself from any association with the political and constitutional problems of the Whitlam Government, the new Labor administration was anxious to deal with the problems of a hostile Senate and to examine any changes to the Constitution that might limit the ability of a Governor-General to precipitate an election at a time not of the government's choosing. Under the direction of its energetic Attorney-General, Senator Gareth Evans, the government investigated the possibility of putting a number of constitutional amendments to the people.[42] The matter of simultaneous elections for both the House of Representatives and the Senate was revived yet again as a means of reducing the probability of hostile Senate majorities. But there was also examination of both lengthening the term between House of Representatives elections from three to four years, and of introducing fixed terms for this house. The latter proposal was prompted by the government's wish to preclude such dissolutions of the commonwealth Parliament as had been precipitated by the Governor-General in 1975. In the event, and after the realisation that both these proposals raised significant ancillary problems, neither of these amendments was submitted to the referendum.

As well as these post-1975 style constitutional issues, there was a revival of constitutional politics of the more traditional kind, the struggle of the commonwealth government to increase the scope of its jurisdiction. Part of this was a manifestation of a trend of judicial decision in the High Court favouring the increase of commonwealth jurisdiction, dramatically illustrated by the Court's decision in a case prompted by the Hawke Government to stop the construction of a dam in the Tasmanian wilderness.[43] Part can also be traced to a broad concern with the issue of human rights on the part of various groups in the community including sections of the Labor Party.[44] Holders of such views tended to assume that the commonwealth was the appropriate level of government to implement such policies, even though the issues dealt with were predominantly in areas of state administration. There was, however, a marked aversion to putting such issues to the test of a referendum and the commonwealth government was happier to trust to the trend of High Court interpretation than to try for direct public endorsement.

In spite of an initial enthusiasm for constitutional amendment, only two matters were eventually put to a referendum in 1984; first a proposal for simultaneous elections (although with a changed name), and secondly, a proposal for the interchange of powers between state and commonwealth governments. The latter was seen as having some appeal to the states since both they and the commonwealth government could bargain over the allocation of jurisdiction to the exclusion of any necessity for popular ratification. Both proposals failed, and the Hawke Government, although returned, felt that it had lost face. Senator Evans was replaced as Attorney-General and constitutional issues were given a low priority as was any matter which was likely to generate hostility between the commonwealth and the states.

In the meantime the Hawke Government had initiated changes to commonwealth electoral laws that were likely to achieve a long-term diminution of the independent role that the Senate had acquired since 1967. If changes to the electoral laws in 1949 had been a major cause of the rise of the political power of the Senate, then altering those electoral laws might help to reduce that power. The changes were complex but their longer-term result was to make it less likely that minor party and independent candidates would be able to secure representation in the Senate and, if represented, would be less likely to hold the balance of power.[45] If this prediction is correct, the 1984 changes to the electoral laws will have achieved much the same result as that intended by the proposals to amend the Constitution to require simultaneous elections for the Senate and the House of Representatives.

To that extent, the executive will have partially succeeded in its efforts to resume the dominance that it had over the parliamentary process before the 1960s. Even if successful, this electoral engineering will not remove the potential for the Senate to challenge the executive. Indeed, one effect of the changes will make it likely that governments always face a deadlocked Senate, a situation marginally better, from the executive's point of view, than one where small parties and independents hold the balance of power and use an opposition majority in the Senate to further goals that challenge those of the government of the day. The Hawke Government has shown itself willing to accept a greater chance of deadlock in the Senate as the price for reducing the discretion that minor party and independent Senators have over the actions of the Senate.

It appears that commonwealth governments may have reluctantly become resigned to the persistence of a Senate that favours consensus politics rather than the majoritarian politics favoured by a parliamentary-based executive. If this is true, constitutional politics will have returned, in many respects, to a pre-1975 condition. The commonwealth Constitution will become an issue only sporadically and the trigger for its political salience will be a clash between the various elements of Australia's federal system.

The Constitutional Convention

The permutations of constitutional politics that the sections above have described, can be traced in the life of an institution that has persisted from the early 1970s until the mid-1980s, the Australian Constitutional Convention. This body had its beginnings during a period of considerable tension between the states and the commonwealth in the late 1960s. The states were dissatisfied with their access to commonwealth collected funds and dismayed by the trend of decisions in the High Court and the unsympathetic view of the Gorton Government in Canberra. Representatives from all state Parliaments were invited by the Victoria Government to participate in a convention to discuss changes to the commonwealth Constitution.

By the time the Convention had its first meeting in 1973,[46] representatives of the commonwealth Parliament, local government and the territories had become involved and the recent election of the Whitlam Government had made major changes to the agenda. Representing as it did the partisan composition of seven Parliaments, the Convention rapidly became a sounding board for current political concerns, with the views of commonwealth and state politicians being cross-cut by differing partisan loyalties and philosophies. While there was discussion of such matters as the place of the Senate in the constitutional framework of the commonwealth, the bulk of the Convention was taken up with matters which related to the division of powers in the federation. When the Convention met again in September 1975 the debate was coloured by the high political tension between Labor and non-Labor at that time, and the subsequent meeting in 1976 was overshadowed by the events of November 1975 as was, to a lesser extent, the Convention which met in 1978.

While useful work was being done by the standing committees of the Convention during this period, the polarisation that had occurred as a result of the constitutional crisis meant that plenary sessions of the Convention could achieve little. When, after a five-year interval, the Convention met in 1983 and again in 1985, there was growing bipartisan support for a number of constitutional proposals. Some of these, building on the work of the standing committees, raised precisely the kind of issues that had precipitated the setting up of the Convention in the first place; such matters as federal finance, the selection of High Court judges, and limitations to the ambit of the external affairs power of the commonwealth.[47] But by this time, the national government had become disillusioned with constitutional change and saw it as a growing political liability. It was in no mood to sponsor amendments that might limit its own powers and it felt, moreover, that the agenda for constitutional change was slipping from its control and passing to the states. Instead of providing an avenue for the possible reduction of uncertainty for the commonwealth government, constitutional change was becoming a source of uncertainty.

The commonwealth tried to wind up the Convention and thereby remove an authoritative forum for constitutional debate which had been putting increasing pressure on the national government to initiate constitutional amendments that were at odds with its own priorities. It also moved to downgrade the quality and significance of debate on constitutional amendment by setting up a Constitutional Commission.[48] This new body made up of a number of notables appointed by the commonwealth government was to seek submissions from interested groups in the community and make recommendations for constitutional change. A more effective way to indicate a government's disenchantment with serious attempts at constitutional amendment would be hard to imagine.

Perspectives on constitutional politics in Australia
In examining the constitutional process in any country it is easy

to ignore the broader trends and overstress the idiosyncratic features, particularly if they are as dramatic as those of 1975. Since the 1970s Australia, together with other Western democracies, has experienced a growing disenchantment with the ability of governments to ameliorate the social and economic conditions of their citizens. Post-war optimism about the beneficial effects of government intervention has given way to a more qualified assessment of the proper role of the state. A corresponding change has occurred in attitudes to the components of government, and the executive branch, which was the great beneficiary of the growth of government intervention since 1945, has come under increasing scrutiny. There has been an interest in strengthening the role of the legislature,[49] together with a range of mechanisms for making the executive responsive to the preferences of citizens both as voters and as consumers of government services. There has, in short, been an increasing concern with limiting the mode, if not the scope, of government action.

In parliamentary systems such as Australia, one of the forms this trend has taken has been that of challenging the majoritarian assumption that the parliamentary executive can be equated with the will of the people. These developments were dramatised in Australia by the crisis of 1975 but this was a symptom not a cause. Given the two strands of Australian constitutionalism, 1975 can be seen as a violent demonstration of a shift in their relative importance and as a factor that greatly accelerated the growth of interest in constitutional structures at both state and national levels. As well as the commonwealth responses examined above, the events of 1975 combined with local factors to prompt debate over state constitutional arrangements, particularly in those states with upper houses. South Australia had already begun this process before 1975, but it was soon to be joined by New South Wales, Tasmania, Victoria and Western Australia in examining, at varying levels of political intensity, the nature and place of bicameralism in each political system.[50]

This general interest in constitutional politics in Australia is now beginning to wane not simply because some change has been accomplished, but for a more fundamental reason. This can be found in the ambiguity of the notion of constitutional politics itself. On the one hand, it can be equated with disputes over the appropriateness of constitutional arrangements and, as such, constitutional politics amounts to a direct attack on the legitimacy of governmental structures. The short-term response to the events of 1975 was the generation of constitutional politics in this sense, focusing on the legitimacy of the actions of the Senate and the Governor-General.

But constitutional politics can also be seen as disputes between governmental agencies, agreement between which is a pre-requisite for government action. As such, it is both inevitable and desirable since it flows from a constitutional structure designed to limit power by dividing it amongst competing agencies after the manner of the United States. It has been argued here that Australia has always had the potential for such constitutional politics partly because of its history of strong bicameralism and partly because of its federal structure since 1901.

This view of constitutional politics is at odds with other aspects of the Australian tradition. The inheritance of British-style parliamentary government gives little scope for constitutional politics in this sense and the crisis of 1975 can thus be seen as being as much a collision between two views of the proper scope of constitutional politics as it was between political ideologies. From the perspective of the parliamentary executive, 1975 generated a crisis in legitimacy and required responses at that level. Once constitutional politics ceased to address the uncertainties generated in 1975 and became an examination of structures for the limitation of the mode of exercise of government power, governments have had an interest in suppressing constitutional debate. The majoritarian and consensus strands of democracy differ not only in the mechanisms through which popular control of government is exercised but also in their definitions of constitutional politics.

From this perspective, the constitutional turmoil of 1975 has served to focus attention both on Australia's governmental structure and on the assumptions that underpin it. While there has been a rise and fall in the visibility of constitutional issues and in their importance as major topics of political debate, there has not been a return to a period of constitutional indifference. There is now a greater awareness of the constitutional structure and the competing elements within it. Such matters as the reserve powers of the Governor-General and the role of the Executive Council are no longer regarded with official indifference and there is broad acceptance of the need to be more explicit about government procedures.[51] Governments are now aware of long-standing areas of ambiguity; this does not mean that solutions will be found, but there is an appreciation of the nature of the problem.

There have been similar effects on commentary on the operations of government. The neglect of the formal machinery of state by political scientists has passed and it is no longer possible to avoid discussion of the rival elements within Australian constitutionalism. In sum, the events of 1975 have acted as a catalyst for broadening the scope of constitutional politics. Rival assessments of Australia's mixed constitutional tradition will continue, but at least the nature of the incongruity is better understood.

Notes and references

1. See, for example, Richard Lucy, *The Australian Form of Government* (Melbourne: Macmillan, 1985).
2. Arend Lijphart, *Democracies: Patterns of Majoritarian and Consensus Government in Twenty-one Countries* (New Haven: Yale University Press, 1984).
3. *Ibid.*, chapter 13.
4. Charles H. McIlwain, *Constitutionalism: Ancient and Modern*, Revised edn (Ithaca, NY: Cornell University Press, 1947).
5. See R.D. Lumb, *The Constitutions of the Australian States*, 4th edn (Brisbane: University of Queensland Press, 1977); and W.G. McMinn, *A Constitutional History of Australia* (Melbourne: Oxford University Press, 1979).
6. For a brief survey, see Joan Rydon 'Upper houses – the Australian Experience' in G.S. Reid (ed.), *The Role of Upper Houses Today: Proceedings of the Fourth Annual Workshop of the Australasian Study of Parliament Group* (Hobart: University of Tasmania, 1983).
7. R.D. Lumb, *Australian Constitutionalism* (Sydney: Butterworths, 1983).
8. A survey of the principal features of the constitutional arrangements of the commonwealth can be found in Colin Howard, *Australia's Constitution: What It Means and How It Works*, revised edn (Melbourne: Penguin, 1985).
9. *The Commonwealth of Australia Constitution Act*, section 128. Note that, to be successful, a constitutional amendment must secure the support of a majority of the whole electorate and majorities in a majority of states (that is, in four of six states).
10. It was intended as a states' house: see Campbell Sharman, 'The Australian Senate as a states house', *Politics* 12(2), November 1977, pp. 64–75.
11. *Constitution*, section 57.
12. There have been double dissolution elections in 1914, 1951 1974, 1975, 1983 and 1987. Only once, in 1974, has the full deadlock procedure been invoked including a joint sitting of both houses.
13. The relationship between the Senate and the House of Representatives was subject to considerable variations during this period, some of which are mentioned in J.R. Odgers, *Australian Senate Practice*, 5th edn (Canberra: Australian Government Publishing Service, 1976). A full description will be available in the study produced by G.S. Reid for the Parliamentary Bicentenary Publications Project to be published by Melbourne University Press in 1988.
14. See generally, Dean Jaensch, *The Australian Party System* (Sydney: Allen and Unwin, 1983). For a more detailed treatment, see P. Loveday, A.W. Martin and R.S. Parker (eds), *The Emergence of the Australian Party System* (Sydney: Hale and Iremonger, 1977).
15. Lijphart, *Democracies*.
16. For a range of views on the reasons for federation, see L.F. Crisp, *Australian National Government*, 5th edn (Melbourne: Longman Cheshire, 1983), chapter 1; Gordon Greenwood, *The Future of Australian Federalism: A Commentary on the Working of the Constitution* (Melbourne: Melbourne University Press, 1946), chapter 2; and Ronald Norris, 'Towards a federal union' in Bruce W. Hodgins, Don Wright and W.H. Heik (eds), *Federalism in Canada and Australia: The Early Years* (Canberra: Australian National University Press, 1978). Note also J.A. La Nauze, *The Making of the Australian Constitution* (Melbourne: Melbourne University Press, 1972).
17. The main grants of power to the commonwealth are set out in Section 51 of the *Constitution*: see Howard, *Australia's Constitution*.
18. For a list and categorisation of referendum proposals, see John McMillan, Gareth Evans and Haddon Storey, *Australia's Constitution: Time for Change?* (Sydney: Allen and Unwin, 1983), chapter 2.
19. See Don Aitkin, 'Australia' in David Butler and Austin Ranney (eds),

Referendums: A Comparative Study of Practice and Theory (Washington: American Enterprise Institute, 1978); and Crisp, *Australian National Government*, chapter 2.

20. See Campbell Sharman and Janette Stuart, 'Patterns of state voting in national referendums', *Politics*, 16, 1981, pp. 261–70.

21. For a brief review, see John Brasden, 'Judicial review and the changing federal balance of power' in Dennis Woodward, Andrew Parkin and John Summers (eds), *Government, Politics and Power in Australia*, 3rd edn (Melbourne: Longman Cheshire, 1985). Note also Brian Galligan, *Politics of the High Court: A Study of the Judicial Branch of Government in Australia* (Brisbane: University of Queensland Press, 1986).

22. There is a large literature on this aspect of Australia's federal process: for an authoritative survey note R.L. Matthews, 'The commonwealth–state financial contract' in Jennifer Aldred and John Wilkes (eds), *A Fractured Federation? Australia in the 1980s* (Sydney: Allen and Unwin, 1983).

23. See Campbell Sharman, 'The commonwealth, the states, and federalism' in Woodward *et al.*, *Government, Politics and Power in Australia*.

24. Brian Galligan, 'Federalism's ideological dimension and the Australian Labor Party', *Australian Quarterly*, 53, 1981, pp. 128–40.

25. See generally Allan Patience and Brian Head (eds), *From Whitlam to Fraser: Reform and Reaction in Australian Politics* (Melbourne: Oxford University Press, 1979).

26. Joan Rydon, 'The Prices and incomes referendum of 1973: the pattern of failure', *Politics*, 9, 1974, pp. 22–30.

27. There is now a substantial literature on the evolution of the Senate but note in particular, Hugh V. Emy, *The Politics of Australian Democracy: Fundamentals in Dispute*, 2nd edn (Melbourne: Macmillan, 1978), pp. 189–245; Lucy, *The Australian Form of Government*, pp. 199–232; Gordon S. Reid, 'The trinitarian struggle: parliamentary executive relationships' in Henry Mayer and Helen Nelson (eds), *Australian Politics: A Fifth Reader* (Melbourne: Cheshire, 1973); and Donald V. Smiley, *An Elected Senate for Canada? Clues from the Australian Experience* (Kingston, Ontario: Institute of Intergovernmental Relations, Queen's University, 1985).

28. The events of 1975 have generated a very large literature and almost all the standard texts on Australian politics make reference to the constitutional crisis and its background. Note, however, Paul Kelly, *The Unmaking of Gough* (Sydney: Angus and Robertson, 1976); Howard R. Penniman (ed.), *Australia at the Polls: The National Elections of 1975* (Washington: American Enterprise Institute, 1977); Geoffrey Sawer, *Federation Under Strain: Australia 1972–1975* (Melbourne: Melbourne University Press, 1977).

29. C.J. Lloyd and G.S. Reid, *Out of the Wilderness: the Return of Labor* (Melbourne: Cassell, 1974), Part II.

30. For a discussion of those proposals, see Joan Rydon, 'Constitutional change and referendums', *Politics*, 12(2), November 1977, pp. 96–103.

31. Note Joan Rydon, 'Casual vacancies in the Australian Senate', *Politics*, 11, 1976, pp. 195–204.

32. Sawer, *Federation Under Strain*, chapter 8.

33. For a range of predominantly legal perspectives, note Gareth Evans (ed.), *Labor and the Constitution 1972–1975: The Whitlam Years in Australian Government* (Melbourne: Heinemann, 1977).

34. For details of the procedure, see section 15 of the *Constitution*.

35. For a survey of the campaign, note Denis Strangman, 'Two defeated referendum proposals, 1967 and 1977' in Richard Lucy (ed.), *The Pieces of Politics*, 2nd edn (Melbourne: Macmillan, 1979).

36. The residents of the smaller states have demonstrated a consistent hostility to any changes to the Senate: see Sharman, 'The Senate as a states house'.

37. See the speech by Whitlam, Australian Constitutional Convention, *Proceedings* (Hobart, 27–29 October 1976), pp. 98–104. The platform of the party also provided for the Senate having no more than delaying power for any bill: see Australian Labor Party, *Platform, Constitution and Rules* (1982).

38. This was the so-called Court proposal, named after its proposer Sir Charles Court, premier of Western Australia: see Australian Constitutional Convention, *Proceedings* (Hobart, 27–29 October 1976), pp. 104–7.

39. For an exception to this generalisation, see David Solomon, *Elect the Governor General!* (Melbourne: Nelson, 1976).

40. See resolution 5 adopted by the Australian Constitutional Convention in 1983: Australian Constitutional Convention, *Proceedings* (Adelaide, 26–29 April 1983), pp. 295–6.

41. George Winterton, *Parliament, the Executive and the Governor-General* (Melbourne: Melbourne University Press, 1983) and *Monarchy to Republic: Australian Republican Government* (Melbourne: Oxford University Press, 1986).

42. See Campbell Sharman, 'Referendum puffery', *Australian Quarterly*, 56, 1984, pp. 20–29; but note Peter Ford, 'Referendums and the public interest: a reply to Campbell Sharman', *Australian Quarterly*, 56, 1984, pp. 256–64.

43. The Franklin Dam case, *Commonwealth v. Tasmania*, 46 ALR 625. For brief comments on this and related cases, see Geoffrey Sawer, 'The external affairs power of the commonwealth and the Koowarta case', *Australian Quarterly*, 54, 1982, pp. 428–34; Colin Howard, 'The external affairs power of the commonwealth', *Current Affairs Bulletin*, 60, September 1983, pp. 16–24; and note Galligan, *Politics of the High Court*.

44. For the general flavour of this approach, see McMillan *et al.*, *Australia's Constitution: Time for Change?*.

45. For a detailed analysis, see Campbell Sharman, 'The Senate, small parties and the balance of power', *Politics*, 21(2), November 1986, pp. 20–31.

46. The Convention met in Sydney in 1973; its subsequent meetings have taken place in Melbourne (1975), Hobart (1976), Perth (1978), Adelaide (1983), and Brisbane (1985). The proceedings of the Convention have been published, together with reports of its standing committees.

47. See Australian Constitutional Convention, *Proceedings*, Vol. II, Standing Committee Reports (Brisbane, 29 July–1 August 1985). For a brief review of the work of the Commission, see Howard, *Australia's Constitution*, pp. 145–49.

48. For comments on these developments note Parliament of Victoria, Legal and Constitutional Committee, *Second Report on the Australian Constitutional Convention – An Assessment of the 1985 Brisbane Plenary Session; The Convention Generally and its Future* (March 1986).

49. See, for example, Norman J. Ornstein (ed.), *The Role of the Legislature in Western Democracies* (Washington: America Enterprise Institute, 1981).

50. See, for example, Western Australia, Royal Commission into Parliamentary Deadlocks, *Report*, Perth, 1984–5.

51. See, for example, the commonwealth's publication, *Federal Executive Council Handbook* (Canberra: Australian Government Publishing Service, 1983). Perhaps the recent move to tie up all loose ends affecting residual links between Britain and the component parts of the federation in the Australia Act is also an example of this.

7 The politics of the Indian Constitution (1950)*
W.H. Morris-Jones

Cobblers stick to their lasts. The political scientist will readily show how constitutions, both formal and working, are shaped by politics. The constitutional lawyer for his part will know how constitutional frames exert a moulding influence on political practice. Each regularly sees the truth which the other may sometimes miss. But in constitutional politics the interacting processes are universal. A living constitution is inescapably an expression of a country's experience, sometimes over a long period, always of a proximate past. A significant constitution is engaged, directly or indirectly, in acting upon, and reacting to, the wider political arena of the society. India stands as no exception; its Constitution is both living and significant. It may be added that precisely by not being an exception in that respect (which entails having not only a real Constitution but also a great deal of real, that is, free and open, politics) India may well make itself something of an exception in another context, that of the category of 'new states' or 'developing countries'.

The status of the Indian Constitution in the political life of the country is nevertheless not easily susceptible of precise definition. It has been said recently and in a striking phrase that the Constitution 'deserves to be considered the rule-book of the Indian political game' and that 'Granville Austin's authoritative account of the framing of the Constitution, *The Indian Constitution: Cornerstone of a Nation*, does not seem grandiloquently titled'.[1] This does not of course entail that the Constitution occupies a position of any salience in popular minds. The term 'man in the street' needs adjustment for India: taken literally, he is outnumbered four to one by the man in the village lane. A substantial proportion of urban dwellers would have some conception of the Constitution, whereas this would hold of few, if any, of the genuine inhabitants of villages. As regards political debate, Parliament and State Assemblies are familiar enough with

* This paper has benefited not only from conference comments but more especially from observations and additional information most generously furnished by Dr Rajeev Dhavan of Brunel University and the Indian Law Institute.

the country's fundamental law, but only of one general election, that of 1977, could it be claimed that the Constitution was a matter for inclusion in hustings speeches, and even then only in cities or large towns. On the other hand, it is scarcely to be pretended that the normal course of politics in any country causes constitutional questions as such to be prominent with the voting public. Such questions are of intense concern, in India and elsewhere, to given interest groups at particular times and to very particular interests – such as constitutional lawyers and civil rights activists – at any time.

Indian 'constitutional politics' has passed through three stages. During roughly the first two decades the Constitution was, one could say, undergoing testing trial runs; from these it emerged somewhat altered but upright and in one piece. During the 1970s it encountered what can only be described as a crisis phase during which it seemed for a while as if steps were being taken for it to be overthrown and replaced; that did not quite happen but it was still radically assaulted and substantially knocked out of its original shape. The third phase has witnessed a partial restoration marked by untidy uncertainties and unresolved problems, along with signs of new strains.

This chapter sets out the overall development according to that chronology but with a brief preface on the debates which determined the forming of the Constitution in the years before 1950. However, it may be as well at once to indicate the four substantive sets of issues around which, in shifting proportions, constitutional politics has been concentrated throughout the whole period of the country's independent history. Since, in the first place, India is almost inescapably some kind of federal polity, relations between the Union and the States are prominently on any agenda of framework formation and maintenance. The remaining three sets of issues all stem, at least in form, from the presence of a doctrine of fundamental rights. Thus, a second set of issues relate to the tension between individual freedoms and governmental powers for use in the cause of order and state security. Individual rights, this time of property, are engaged in the third set of issues where their conflict is with aspirations of social justice and development. Finally, rights of equality have to be reconciled with policies which call for positive discrimination in favour of disadvantaged sections of society.

In examining how the Constitution has come under strain and become an element in political contention as well as how far the difficulties have been overcome, we shall certainly have to look at pressures stemming from social and political change. At the same time there is a tale of constitutional law to be told. In this the political powers in government and parliament are no doubt prominent, especially when they amend the Constitution. But the judges too, notably those of the Supreme Court, have leading roles to play. Indeed it will emerge that a large, albeit mostly underlying, theme of India's constitutional politics is the search for an accommodation between judicial review and executive power exercised through parliamentary sovereignty. This search, which has arisen largely in relation to the issues of fundamental rights and the parliamentary power of constitutional amendment, surfaces at times as a confrontation over the directions of constitutional development between the men on the bench and the men in government. We shall also see how in the most recent years it may be proper to discern developments which, so far from relegating constitutional matters to insignificance, may perhaps be said to herald a new constitutionalism.

The making, 1947–50

There is no difficulty in describing the making of the Constitution as an autochthonous process, at least in formal terms: it was hammered out by a Constituent Assembly which, when it was not doubling as a provisional parliament, worked hard in committees and 165 days of full sessions over a period of three years (1947–9). The 300 members were not a perfectly representative body – for apart from nominated persons from princely states, the rest were indirectly elected by provincial assemblies based on about one-third of full adult franchise – but they contained a full range of ideological views. Autochthony, however, does not entail a blank slate; the founding fathers had their various predilections and preoccupations, therefore preferences for certain models rather than others.

The model closest to hand was the constitution under which the country was being governed at the time. This was none other than the British-made Government of India Act of 1935; in the rush of the partitioned independence in 1947 it proved possible to amend this huge document – only a decade earlier a 'slave constitution' and 'charter of bondage' in nationalist eyes – sufficiently for it to serve as the constitution of the new Dominion, pending the framing of a framework for the Republic. An element of schizophrenia persisted: the model was one to be escaped from – but oh! so cautiously. Above all, there was no escape from two of its main features: it provided for parliamentary government and for a federal structure.[2]

Although there was no deep cleavage in the Assembly on the basic principle of parliamentary-cabinet government, dissent was interestingly present and some of its few voices still echo from time to time. One that does not is the plea made at the time, by representatives of the Muslim minority remaining in India, for Swiss-style composite executives to secure them from political exclusion. More durable has been the hankering after the alternative of executive presidency. The winning case against this was essentially based on experience and familiarity, but the presidential case in terms of strong and stable government and a focus for national unity can still be heard when the centre seems to be feeble or fissiparous tendencies are threatening or when the prospect of the end of Congress dominance lets in uneasy visions of governance, especially at the level of the States, being placed at the mercy of shifting alliances of several unstable parties.[3]

The seemingly persistent Indian (specifically Hindu, more generally Asian?) fear of chaos if the centre does not hold[4] was again in evidence on the matter of federalism. There were some voices favouring an essentially unitary state with no autonomy nonsense; a strong centre was what the Muslims would have prevented but now the curse of Pakistan could at least yield the blessing of a powerfully unitary India. The great majority of members were more realistic and also in any case closely identified with some distinctive linguistic and cultural region of the country. Moreover, many of them had experience as provincial politicians and looked forward to resuming careers at that level, only with greater powers. Their enthusiasm towards autonomy had to be checked by the national leadership which was already coming to realise that in Centre–State relations the Centre had to have the major say and the last word. Hence the carefully drawn up lists of Central, State and Concurrent subjects (the Centre to prevail in disputes on the Concurrent), Central financial dominance and above all (see below) Central emergency powers to take over the State administrations. Even with Congress the only party in sight of power at any level, State-based Congressmen in the Assembly found this medicine rather unpalatable, but took it.[5] They also accepted, with surprising readiness, that whereas amendment of the Constitution required two-thirds majorities, and even ratification by half the States, in matters of States' powers, the judiciary and the election of the President, nothing more than a simple parliamentary majority was required to make, break or merge a State. They were no doubt influenced by a sense that the units at 1950 were likely to be quite temporary.

To follow a model left behind by imperial rule was useful but hardly an exhilarating experience for nationalists newly in power. It was therefore with unanimous exuberance that they espoused a thoroughly un-British feature: a charter of fundamental rights. This in fact had a solid Indian pedigree: as early as 1895 nationalists had framed a Constitution of India Bill which listed certain basic rights and these were enlarged (from study of the Irish Constitution of 1921) and regularly reiterated up to independence. Now at last they would march along a Franco-American path; more to the point, they would seize what they felt they had been denied and at the same time allay the fears of minorities. Accordingly, rhetoric on rights soared in the Assembly: 'the silent, immaculate premise of our outlook', 'to safeguard the liberty of the human spirit', 'inalienable', 'inherent', 'our pact with the civilised world'. The draftsmen could not fail to follow, at least some of the way. Thus the fundamental rights are placed early on as Chapter III; they are listed comprehensively as rights (in this order) to equality, freedom, against exploitation, to freedom of religion, cultural and educational rights, property and constitutional remedies; they are stated boldly in such terms as 'all citizens shall have the right to freedom of speech and expression', 'no person shall be deprived of his life or personal liberty except according to procedure established by law'; above all, they are backed by two general provisions that laws inconsistent with the rights shall be void and that the right of access is guaranteed to the Supreme Court which is empowered to enforce the rights.

However, there were two sets of members who were less than happy about these rights. One set, few but vocal, felt that eighteenth-century rights were good but not enough. Men by now had rights to free education, adequate standards of living and social justice. Nehru's sympathy notwithstanding, it was difficult to see how the Constitution could guarantee what no Indian government in the foreseeable future could provide. The Irish Constitution supplied the way out: placed next to Fundamental Rights are a set of fifteen Directive Principles of State Policy. These are slightly more than laudable aspirations, perhaps points of leverage for placing pressure on governments – but expressly non-justiciable.

The other set of uneasy members were the country's leaders, members of the Assembly but already engaged in the daily conduct of the business of government. They readily saw that individual rights without limits and with judicial protection could prove obstructive to the two paramount tasks confronting the rulers: dealing with unrest amounting to insurrection and paving the way to agricultural reform. These would respectively require curbs on rights of freedom and property. These were provided: property could be compulsorily acquired on payment of compensation – indeed pending land reform measures were expressly safeguarded from property rights litigation – and freedom could be abridged to permit preventive detention. Such limitations on rights in fact became very extensive: nothing was to prevent laws 'imposing reasonable restrictions on the exercise of the right in the interests of' – public order, morality and other desirable but flexible objectives. One critic at the time protested that a microscope would be needed 'to discover the free-doms whenever it suits the state to deny them'. The judges were soon to use their microscopes.

Such built-in qualifications to rights, coupled with the fact that the rights appeared to be in no way specially 'entrenched' – requiring only the standard amendment procedure of a two-thirds majority of votes and a majority of the membership of the two houses of parliament[6] – left some rights enthusiasts disillusioned. For them, and for those who hoped for greater States autonomy, there was worse to come. Did the leaders of the young nation, who had for years suffered from and protested against the periods of repression (which alternated with phases of guarded collaboration) under British rule, secretly harbour anxieties that perhaps after all India might at times need to dispense with liberal ways and have a Raj with reserve powers that could reach out with a heavy hand? In any event what emerged was a constitution within the Constitution, called 'Part XVIII Emergency Provisions'. Three types of emergency were envisaged: a threat to security by war or external aggression or internal disturbance; a threat to financial stability; a situation in which the government of a State cannot be carried on according to the Constitution. The third 'constitutional' type entails the suspension (for up to six months but up to three years if Parliament agrees) of the federal system with regard to the State(s) concerned: the State government and legislature are replaced either by President's Rule or Governor's Rule, in any case by central government command. The security type of emergency which is extendable without limit by Parliament also removes federalism by allowing the centre to ignore the federal distribution of powers and of finances and to issue directions to State governments. Moreover, in both types fundamental rights are suspended, as is the right to move any court for their enforcement. Finally, emergencies are declared 'if the President is satisfied that a situation has arisen . . . ' but his satisfaction cannot be questioned in any court.

When the three years of debating were over and the Constitution adopted, it was clear that if the government failed to govern it would not be for lack of constitutional powers. Equally, it would have seemed likely that even if the Congress party was going to be domi-nant, opposition could come from within and obstacles could come from the courts.

Encounters of the first phase, 1950–66
The government of the new republic had to meet the judges before they met the electorate (in 1952). The higher judiciary (in the States' High Courts and above all in the Supreme Court) enjoyed at the

outset very considerable status and respect[7] and it showed its confidence at once when it was called upon to deal with cases brought by members of the public claiming that their new fundamental rights were being infringed by government legislation. The first Chief Justice roundly declared at the inception of the Supreme Court that it was 'established to safeguard the fundamental rights and liberties of the people';[8] it has indeed spent a good deal of its time seeing how, and how far, it could do that.

On property rights (Art 19(1) f and g, (5) and (6) and Art 31) the government beat the Supreme Court to it. When the centre found that States' legislation to abolish *zamindari* (intermediary landed) interests in accordance with Congress promises was being declared unconstitutional by some High Courts and while appeals were pending with the Supreme Court, it achieved the First Amendment (1951). This provided that such legislation could not be held void on account of inconsistency with fundamental rights and, to make doubly sure, went on to place 13 Acts of various States in a new (9th) Schedule of the Constitution as retrospectively validated notwithstanding any abridgment of rights or any court decision.[9] This still left other kinds of property which could by law be acquisitioned with compensation. Such legislation was at once challenged on the ground that the compensation was unfairly inadequate. The Court ruled that while the legislature could lay down the principles for determining compensation, it still had to be real compensation, i.e., a just equivalent. The 4th Amendment (1955) removed adequacy of compensation from adjudication. The task of reconciling the property rights of some with the Directive Principles of State Policy (Art 39(b)) which exhort the state to direct its policy towards distribution of 'the material resources of the community ... to subserve the common good' was never going to be a simple matter – once those in the Constituent Assembly who wished directive principles to have precedence over rights had been defeated.[10]

But freedom rights (Arts 19(1) a to e and 21) made property rights seem comparatively simple. A promptly passed Preventive Detention Act came before the Supreme Court in *Gopalan's Case* (1950) when the Court had to determine its validity in view of Art 21 stating that 'no person shall be deprived of his life or personal liberty except according to procedure established by law'. The Court by majority decided that 'law' here meant simply an Act duly passed by Parliament, that no element of 'natural law' or 'due process' entered, in effect therefore that fundamental rights could not prevail against the legislature. A minority of one judge strongly disagreed and even the majority was uneasy. In a series of subsequent cases, the Court sought somewhat to recover ground by asserting firmly that it was for the Court to determine whether restrictions on rights were (as required by Art 19) 'reasonable' and by *obiter dicta* which went so far as to suggest that fundamental rights properly enjoyed a 'transcendental position'. Freedom of speech and expression was also examined at an early stage in *Romesh Thappar's Case* (1950); when the Court decided that this freedom included propagation and circulation and that state security was not so endangered as to warrant curtailment of the right, the Constitution was amended to extend to threats to public order. Later the Court decided that restrictions imposed in the interests of public order had to have a 'proximate connection with public order, not one far-fetched, hypothetical, problematical or too remote' (*Ram Mohan Lohia's Case*, 1960). The Court also held that a right of orderly demonstration had to be regarded as entailed in freedom of speech and assembly, finding a government service rule void on that account (*Kameshwar Prasad's Case*, 1962).[11]

The rights to equality are formulated (Arts 14–16) in terms of equality before the law, equal protection of the laws and absence of discrimination on grounds only of religion, race, caste, or place of birth. The Court has been willing to accept that legislation, e.g. to set up special courts for particular purposes, must often distinguish and classify persons to be brought within the scope of the laws but in doing so it must not be arbitrary and the distinctions must be reasonable. However, the application of this principle appeared erratic, even to the Court itself, which then, exceptionally, set out the principles of interpretation it would follow. Since the Constitution itself expressly permits discrimination of a positive kind in favour of disadvantaged groups, the Court has readily accepted such measures but it has struck down some discriminatory rules, e.g. of educational institutions, which are either unwarrantedly exclusive or inappropriately concessionary. In 1962 the Court not only struck down but described as 'a fraud on the Constitution' the Karnataka Government's reservation of 68 per cent of places in certain higher education for those from the 'backward classes'.[12]

The Emergency proclaimed in 1962 did of course entail the suspension of fundamental rights. For that reason its extension for five years and to all parts of the country, even 1500 miles away from the Chinese border, has been described as 'almost ludicrous . . . an excessive and irresponsible exercise of executive power'.[13] The Court was obliged to reject petitions solely because the right to move the Court had been lost. Even the Attorney-General could not deny that certain Defence of India Rules (made under the Act of that name in that period) were invalid because not in conformity with the Constitution's own provisions regarding preventive detention.

The 'political' cases decided by the Court have naturally involved the government but there were also encounters with legislatures. Most of these concerned parliamentary privilege and arose from the Constitution's provision that Union Parliament and State Assemblies could define their own privileges but until they did so they would be those of the UK House of Commons. This meant that they could commit judges for contempt. And this is what one State Assembly did when two judges of the High Court dared to admit a petition from a citizen who had himself been placed in prison for contempt of the Assembly. On a reference to the Supreme Court, the Assembly claimed that the Courts had no jurisdiction. But the Supreme Court decided that Indian legislatures could not derive from the distant court-like attributes of the House of Commons powers that would brush aside the Indian Constitution's establishment of judicial scrutiny and fundamental rights.

The first two decades of independent India thus saw a new Constitution framed and tested in tussles largely between the judiciary and government. But of course the same years also witnessed a more general exploration: all institutions were 'finding their way about in the new world, taking stock of themselves in relation to others – parliament to cabinet, Congress to other political parties, centre to states, civil servants to politicians, politicians to voters'. Some of these explorations, as well as new ventures in policy, had significance for the Constitution and the manner of its functioning. Two are worth some mention: both relate primarily to the federal aspect; each represented somewhat opposite pressures on the framework.

As already noted, the units with which the Indian Union was launched were clearly provisional, if only because the absorption of the host of princely states was a highly complex operation which called for piecemeal treatment that was incomplete in 1950. The Constitution was obliged to place the units in three classes: 'A' the nine former provinces of British India, 'B' the eight substantial former princely states or new unions of such states, 'C' the ten smaller central administered areas. The princely factor apart, there was a further reason why this could not last. It had been Congress doctrine since 1920 that units should correspond not to the accidents of British conquests but to the main large linguistic communities of which the nation was formed. Even the British had made concessions to this view when they created Sind and Orissa in 1936; it was not to be easily dodged by a post-independence government. On the other hand, tearing up and re-drawing the internal boundaries of India was not to be lightly undertaken. A one-man commission reporting in 1948 was firmly hostile to the idea, which was condemned as likely to cause administrative chaos, new unhappy minorities and loss of national coherence. The consequent resentment caused Congress to make its own high-level examination; its report was unenthusiastic about wholesale change but hedged with regard to one insistent demand, thus inviting others to be equally insistent. By 1956 a States Reorganisation Commission had been set up, reported, and its findings were embodied in an Act which substantially altered the map and produced 16 States.[14] It is fairly certain that this matter, if not attended to, would not have gone away but become an angrily running sore, a focal point for anti-centre agitation. However, it was a case of solving one problem to create a second: the new units were more contendedly coherent but just for that reason more self-consciously proud. Moreover by now the inherited all-India leadership of great anti-imperial campaigns was disappearing and elections with adult franchise were uncovering deeper layers of social soil from which more parochial new politicians were sturdily growing. On the whole this could mean no more than that the centre would have to be ready for more robust bargaining methods on the part of the States; weak units are not a necessary condition for strong centres. It was unfortunate that all this coincided with another language issue. The Constitution had distinguished between the (fourteen) 'languages of India' and the 'official language' for governmental use and declared that the latter would be the Hindi of Northern India, with the proviso that English could continue to be used until 1965. When in 1958 a Commision found that the Constitution's formula could not sensibly be varied, new pride in regional languages took a blow, especially in the Tamil South where anti-Hindi feelings briefly took on separatist hues. Nehru quickly conceded that there should be no fixed time limit for English to continue as an associate official language. But he soon afterwards revealed the depth of central anxieties by seeking through Constitutional amendment to outlaw secessionist demands and by making much of the establishment of a National Integration Council. (The latter, it should be added, was occasioned by excesses not solely of linguistic zeal but also of communal, mainly Hindu-Muslim, antagonism.)

If in the eyes of the (older) national leadership the federal balance was being at least somewhat threatened by the rise of the regions, during the same period those men rising in the regions were not less aware of threats to the balance from the growth of the centre. This growth could be measured in terms of size of central bureaucracy, expansion of government into public corporations and government companies and the enlargement of economic and social controls by legislation or executive orders. It will be sufficient here to focus on one central institution, the Planning Commission. This was set up in the same year as the Constitution was inaugurated; it was ignored by the Constitution (and indeed was not even the creation of law) but its effects on the federal aspects of the Constitution were marked during the Commission's heyday and may have survived its later decline. Briefly, financial relations between centre and States as set out in the Constitution no longer accurately reflect the pattern of those relations in practice.[15] The former lays down in detail the sources of revenue for States and centre, distinguishes between revenue to be collected and retained by States and revenue to be collected by the centre for distribution to the States, and prescribes an independent Finance Commission which lays down the State-wise distribution of shared revenue and also the principles for the making of central grants-in-aid. But all this has been overtaken by the rise of a constitutionally unenvisaged system of matching grants which have become the major element in federal developmental finance. This introduced alongside the allocative constitutional federalism an extra-constitutional market-place federalism which might be co-operative but also combative by turns, certainly always hard bargaining. The Commission was in a position to determine national priorities but the States were nevertheless the chief instruments for implementation. States' fears and complaints notwithstanding, there was probably not so much central dictation as there was State supplication; each State no doubt had its own priorities, perhaps mainly shaped by political constraints, but it was in competition with others and could expect to win the biggest grants if it went furthest to meet central preferences. Individual States' lobbies at Delhi became continuous, while the grand forum of the National Development Council (Planning Commission plus all States' Chief Ministers) afforded a chance to display a States' united front – but also for the Prime Minister to exhort and reprimand. Nehru was the Commission's creator and sustainer; with his death, it began to languish – but the mechanisms of federal bargaining remain, though now less obviously concentrated.

The Constitution in crisis, 1966–77

Reference has been made above to the Emergency provisions as being 'a Constitution within the Constitution'.[16] During the eighteen months of Mrs Gandhi's Emergency (1975–57) the inner constitution came out with a vengeance. Proclaimed, literally, overnight – even the cabinet learnt of it only in the morning – leading opposition politicians including MPs were arrested fast in large numbers; in all, during the period over 100,000 people were locked away without trial; a severe press censorship was imposed, independent news agencies taken over and the reporting of critical speeches even in

Parliament blocked. An authoritarian, and in parts of Northern India a highly repressive, regime affected the general public mainly by removing the police and the petty official from any effective account-ability and restraint.[17]

The proximate factor which triggered off India's first 'internal disturbance' Emergency was rather adventitious: in a belated action the Allahabad High Court found the Prime Minister guilty of trivial technical offences against election laws and had unseated her and barred her for six years from electoral contest; the Supreme Court had granted only a conditional stay order allowing her to continue as Prime Minister pending appeal. This was humiliating and awkward but by no means desperate – even for Mrs Gandhi there were several alternative courses – let alone 'an internal disturbance threatening the security of India'. Less immediate was the fact that the States of Bihar and Gujarat had witnessed widespread agitation, which in turn was a response to an economic crisis which brought inflation and shortages, and a political crisis for the governing Con-gress which had rapidly lost cohesion and support since its 1971–72 victories and had lately suffered electoral reverses in Gujarat.

The agitations which were presented as the justification for the 'internal disturbances' Emergency had in fact seemed to be past their peak when they were revived by Mrs Gandhi's overheated reaction to the Allahabad decision. Her strident mobilisation on the streets of arranged crowds of supporters during the two weeks between the Allahabad judgment and the Emergency Proclamation relate both to her personalised style and to the state of the Congress Party. It has to be recalled that following the deaths of Prime Minister Nehru and Shastri in rapid succession (1964 and 1966), the contest for power in the party opened up rifts which were at once ideological, generational and of organisational style. The outcome was a dispirited performance in the 1967 elections: the dramatic loss of its massive parliamentary majority (reduced from 228 to 48) owed less to the strength of other parties than to the collapse of solidarity in Congress. The bitter struggle continued for two years until the formal split was completed in 1969. For the purposes of our subject in this chapter the relevance of the Congress crisis is that the process of its resolution in the years 1966–71 entailed the simultaneous salience of two political tendencies with profound constitutional conse-quences: Mrs Gandhi's difficult path towards the conquest of power in Congress followed a route characterised by a posture of populist leftism and a steady concentration of power around her central governmental office. The Emergency was the outcome of this parti-cular pairing. But the impact of the two tendencies on constitutional matters and on the status of the judiciary as guardian and interpreter of the fundamental law was already evident in the immediately preceding years.

Perhaps the first shot in the constitutional war was fired by the Supreme Court – though whether this was an unintended effect of legal reasoning or had in it features of a pre-emptive strike is not clear. In the 1967 *Golak Nath* case it ruled by a 6 to 5 majority that Parliament was 'barred from using its constituent authority to amend fundamental rights protecting the liberties of the citizens'.[18] This surprising stand was greeted by parliamentary indignation; Mrs Gandhi with a thin parliamentary majority was at first characteristically cautious but later, after her success in the 1971 elections, not averse to confrontation. By then at her side as a Minister was a good Marxist, Cambridge-trained lawyer, Mohan Kumaramangalam. In the space of a few months the 24th, 25th and 26th Amendments were passed. The 24th was directly aimed at *Golak Nath*: 'Notwithstanding anything in this Constitution, Parliament may in the exercise of its constituent power amend by way of addition, variation or repeal any provision of this Constitution . . . Nothing in Article 13 [the general statement of Fundamental Rights including 'The State shall not make any law which takes or abridges the rights conferred by this Part'] shall apply to any amendment made under this Article.' The 25th was concerned once and for all to put a stop to judicial impediments to acquisition of property by the state. It sought to do this by eliminating in particular the word 'compensation' and using instead 'amount', but also by making a general assertion that 'no law giving effect to the policy of the state towards securing [those directive principles of state policy which urge 'distribution of ownership and control of material resources . . . to subserve the common good' and avoidance of 'concentration of wealth and means of production to the common detriment'] shall be deemed void on the ground that it is inconsistent with [the relevant fundamental rights provisions]'. The 26th quite simply unfurled the radical banner: all recognition, privileges and privy purses hitherto given to the former princely rulers were terminated.

The Supreme Court was not silenced but perhaps it had in 1971 'read the election returns'. It met the challenge in the landmark *Kesavananda* case in 1973 and did so 'in a delicately balanced and inherently complex response'.[19] Even oversimplifying the complexities, it has to be said that the judgment, once again by the narrowest margin (7 to 6), contrived at once to retreat and advance from *Golak Nath*. It retreated from the limited but adamant position that fundamental rights provisions could not be amended but it advanced to a broader (though ill-defined, perhaps deliberately) position that no part of the Constitution could be amended in such a manner as to alter the 'basic structure and framework' of the Constitution. Above all, the Court was seemingly determined to preserve its own role, as guardian. Thus the 24th Amendment was upheld and Parliament could indeed amend fundamental rights – but not anyhow, not so as to spoil the Constitution; judicial review must remain and it will be for the Court to determine whether an amendment damages the Constitution in its 'basic structure' or 'essential features'. The 25th Amendment was partly acknowledged: certain Directive Principles might properly be allowed in given areas of state endeavour to override some fundamental rights – but only subject to judicial review which would safeguard the 'essential features'. The Court failed to offer any precise definition or full list of these 'features' but indicated that the federal system, free elections and of course, judicial review itself would be among them. The definition would no doubt develop as the Court did its work. The Court allowed that 'amount' could take the place of 'compensation' but it would have to be an amount that was not 'arbitrary' or 'illusory'. Finally, there was nothing to be done for the princes and their purses; the 26th Amendment was upheld.

The proclamation of the Emergency on 26 June 1975 put the ball safely back on the government's side of the net; the Prime Minister could and did return it fast, hard and often. The initial steps were by Ordinances: these effected total censorship on 26 June and tightened the existing Defence of India Rules and Maintenance of Internal Security Act to secure that grounds no longer needed to be given for preventive detention without trial. In a second phase Ordinances were, if appropriate, converted into Acts by a depleted and thoroughly tamed Parliament.[20] But, at a third level, confrontation with the judiciary was not to be avoided. Within weeks, in early August, the 38th and 39th Amendments were passed by Parliament. The 38th was a blanket exclusion of any judicial inquiry into the legitimacy of the Proclamation – 'the satisfaction of the President shall be final and conclusive and shall not be questioned in any court on any ground' – and reaffirmed that Fundamental Rights could not be held to restrict any state action. The 39th was a remarkable example of constitutional change for a very particular purpose: since Mrs Gandhi's election case was still before the Supreme Court on appeal, this amendment helpfully removed matters relating to the election of the Prime Minister from any questioning or review by any court and, making doubly sure, repealed the provisions of the Act under which Mrs Gandhi had been convicted; some trace of embarrassment was revealed in the touching coupling of the office of Speaker with that of the Prime Minister and the inclusion of parallel provisions for President and Vice-President. The Supreme

Court should have been cowed and crippled. It was not, or not entirely: it caved in as regards preventive detention, it allowed the retrospective deletion of the electoral offences, but it dug its heels in on judicial review by reaffirming the inviolability of *Kesavananda*'s 'essential features' ground and striking down the parts of the 39th Amendment which would remove elections from their purview.[21]

If the judges showed a certain courage in the midst of their fears, there was some ground for these latter. Towards the end of 1975 a curious anonymous document titled 'A fresh look at our Constitution: some suggestions' began to circulate in, and leak from, higher quarters in Delhi, almost certainly a kite-flying exercise with blessings from the top. It envisaged a fundamental change to a Gaullist-style regime: a directly elected presidential executive which would avoid involvement in 'fruitless debate and discussion in Parliament';[22] a partially non-parliamentary cabinet; most noteworthy, the management of the whole judiciary to be placed in the hands of a Judicial Council nominated and headed by the President and dominated by non-judicial members. The ambitious plan was quietly abandoned but a Congress committee was set up to make proposals and these were presented to Parliament in September 1976. These formed the basis for an amendent virtually to end all amendments, the 42nd. A surviving member of the 1947 Constituent Assembly described it as 'neither amending or mending but simply ending the Constitution'.[23] Extending to 59 clauses, the Amendment strengthened the executive in a variety of ways but above all constituted a grand assault on the judiciary: 'there shall be no limitation whatever on the constituent power of parliament to amend' was the reply to *Kesavananda*; more sweepingly than the 25th, it subordinated Fundamental Rights to parliamentary legislation seeking to give effect to any of the Directive Principles; it curtailed the judiciary's scope for restraint through the issue of writs. It was in force by the end of 1976. It endured about a year only, for three months after its birth Mrs Gandhi's Congress was thoroughly rejected at the polls and a government pledged to its removal was in power.

Before turning to the post-Emergency period a word has to be said on an additional executive line of attack on the judiciary. Soon after her 1971 election triumph, Mrs Gandhi launched the doctrine of a 'committed bureaucracy': what was required of government servants was not impartiality and neutrality in the business of administration but a sense of devoted commitment to the forward-looking economic and social policies of the government. Mohan Kumaramangalam eagerly extended this idea to the judges: government needed help from judges with 'the most suitable philosophy and outlook', from 'a committed judiciary'.[24] One way of securing the right judges was to make a break with the established seniority rules in order to push forward the 'progressives'. A dramatic intervention of this kind took place in 1973 when no less than three judges of the Supreme Court were passed over in order to appoint the more suitable fourth as Chief Justice.[25] Another route towards at least influencing the judges it has to put up with was found in the transfer of judges. By convention the Constitution's provision that the President may transfer a judge from one High Court to another 'after consultation with the Chief Justice' meant that the Chief Justice's advice would be followed. But the practice has tended to vary from this; even worse perhaps is the informal evidence of pressures to give greater satisfaction or face punitive transfer.[26]

Partial restoration and new strains, 1977–86
Many of the Members of Parliament who had blithely extended the term of the body by a year were not present when the new Parliament was elected and met in March 1977. It is difficult to know whether they or Mrs Gandhi were the more surprised. India's first non-Congress parliament and government arrived because Congress was electorally annihilated in most of Northern India. It really did seem as if, in the areas of maximum Emergency impact, revulsion against authoritarian rule was not confined to lawyers and liberals; as if the slum-dwellers who were ignorant of the Constitution recognised that they had no redress when Sanjay Gandhi's bulldozers flattened their shacks; as if those villagers who encountered compulsory sterilisation required no lessons in fundamental rights.

The Janata coalition lasted less than three years – anti-Congress was not enough to hold it together – but some of its good intentions were carried out. The Emergency was ended, censorship dismantled, DIR and MISA repealed, all political detainees released – all quite promptly. It then tackled the 42nd Amendment. Some of its features were removed by the 43rd Amendment; for example, no longer would it be possible to use the catch-all term 'anti-national' to ban opposition groups. But its core was to be dealt with by a separate Bill: in this the 38th and 39th Amendments were removed, Fundamental Rights could not be suspended and an internal Emergency would require not mere 'disturbance' but 'armed rebellion'. These and other changes went into the 45th Amendment Act as passed. But on the way the Congress majority in the Upper House was able to delay and thus remove two important proposals: the Act omits to protect Fundamental Rights against a law claiming to implement Directive Principles and it omits to protect the 'essential features'. What Janata failed to complete owing to internal divisions and Congress obstruction, the Supreme Court attended to: in

Minerva Mills (1980) it re-asserted *Kesavananda* against the 42nd Amendment; judicial review is applicable to constitutional amendments and it is for the Court to examine whether laws claiming to implement Directive Principles contravene Fundamental Rights.[27]

Otherwise, too, the Janata performance was partial. Desai, the new Prime Minister, deliberately restored the seniority rule even though the new Chief Justice had been 'helpful' to the government during the Emergency. Also he sought advisory opinions from the Court on two matters. He was told that he would be justified in calling for elections (not held since 1972) in nine States where Congress ruled as if the national elections had not demonstrated its lack of support. (Mrs Gandhi on her own return in 1980 was quick to point to the precedent.) He was also advised that legislation would be in order to set up special courts to try Mrs Gandhi, Sanjay and others for abuse of powers, etc., during the Emergency. This latter move failed; legislation was slow, courts were cautious while watching Janata's growing difficulties, and they dismissed all cases when Mrs Gandhi came back in 1980.[28]

Meanwhile the working Constitution has been undergoing new strains from political developments. The most salient of these relates to federalism. The ideological thrust, if that is not too positive a term, of Janata was decentralisation and rural (including agro-industrial) development. The noble vision faded before it achieved any significant realisation. Mrs Gandhi's triumphant return brought with it no distinctive ideology – even the 'progressive' flavouring of the 1970s was absent. Instead there was the familiar absorption with political manipulation above all in relations with States and a rather unprecedented prominence given to strident nationalism and fears of disintegration. The two were perhaps connected, the latter a necessary corrective to failure on the former. Mrs Gandhi showed herself to be consistently less comfortable in bargaining contractual relations with Chief Ministers of States than in the search for submissive subordinates. Three kinds of outcomes ensued: sometimes her preferred nominees were unable to secure support and a succession of resignations produced instability; less often they were able to survive and misgovern; in five States anti-Centre feelings rose to bring new regionalist formations to power (in Andhra and Karnataka) or to produce crisis conditions (in Assam, Kashmir and Punjab). This was an unhappy legacy to pass on to her son, but on this front at least he has displayed a more relaxed and less distrustful approach to the States.[29]

However, the rise of regionalism relates to another feature, another sad legacy to Rajiv Gandhi with which he has found it more difficult to deal: the institutional decay of the Congress Party. This began with the split of 1969 and has not been effectively checked; once a comprehensively articulated (though very imperfectly functioning) set of organs not only at the Centre (All-India Congress Committee, Working Committee, Parliamentary Board, Parliamentary Party) but also at State and lower levels, the party has degenerated to a personalised rally machine populated by opportunists. This has come about not solely as a consequence of Mrs Gandhi's leadership style but also as the result of the de-linking of central and State parliamentary elections. With effect from 1971, the separation in time of these two operations has allowed the national elections to be conducted by highly expensive leader-focused publicity campaigns producing emotional 'wave' results across the country, while State elections continue to be run on the customary basis of complex calculations in terms of a mixture including policy issues, community and caste alignments, local personalities and pressure groupings. This fracturing of the electoral operation has aggravated Congress disinstitutionalisation and increased the distance between the two sides of the federal relationship. One outcome is that even in States where regionalism has not created its own parties, the State-level Congress has become 'regionalised'. The appointment of the Sarkaria Commission to review Centre-State relations was no doubt prompted immediately by the Punjab crisis but its task was properly made general. There has in fact built up a level of frustration in the States which can probably only find relief through a constitutional change in the direction of greater autonomy.[30] There will no doubt be anxiety and nervousness at the Centre at such a prospect, for alarmist spectres of national integration have always been easily conjured up in India. With calm central leadership, however, it is to be hoped that some moderate and well-considered alteration in the terms of the federal compact will be seen as no threat but a reinforcement of national coherence.

If the federal relations are the most salient of pressures on the constitutional system, they are not the most serious; they are essentially manageable for the basic reason that every part of India has a profoundly vested interest in India's unity. Altogether more intractable and depressing is a quite different consequence of the institutional decay of the dominant party and indeed, with it, other parties and therefore the party system.[31] It can be labelled in several ways because it is a multi-faceted phenomenon. It is a prevalence of disorder and an increase in crime; it is angry protest against social evils; it is a new form of political participation; it is here and there, from time to time, a state of war with an absence of either law or justice. Catching the headlines and attracting even a little international attention are such incidents as 'dowry deaths' in the capital city and frenzied riots between mobs of antagonistic communities. Less noticed but still adequately reported in local newspapers and certain weeklies are frequent mass killings in rural areas, usually carried out by gangs of thugs, with police tolerance or collaboration, at the behest of better-off farmers against trouble-some landless labourers.[32]

There are many profound social factors at work: social groups have risen unevenly and all aspirations are high; older forms of social constraint have weakened; certain abysmally deprived social layers are no longer willing passively to suffer. There are also more proximate causes of which the Emergency legacy of uncontrolled violence and unaccountable police is surely one. But beyond these is the absence of channels for settling or at least de-fusing conflicts. Precisely this was one of the key functions of the institution of party in India: all parties to some extent, Congress *par excellence*, were aggregators and reconcilers of interests – and they are now scarcely on the scene in that capacity. On the scene instead are a host of *ad hoc*, largely local, non-party protest organisations attract-ing leadership from political activists who themselves would earlier have been party workers. Moreover, the outcome of these bloody confrontations in remote rural areas is seldom that anyone is brought to justice or even to trial. If the authorities describe the victims as 'Naxalites' the worst can be feared, for this is now a term which is loosely applied and gives licence to announce that someone was 'shot while resisting arrest' or 'shot when trying to escape'.[33] One must hope that Rajiv Gandhi's declared aim of 'leading India into the 21st century' will somehow come to include attention to social horrors as well as to computer technology.

In a society such as India's where political freedom – some would say to the point of chaos – is valued, the closing of outlets just when pressures are increasing can only lead to the emergence of fresh channels. In this respect there are some positive signs which have to be read alongside the negative aspects just mentioned above. The rise of articulate and influential non-party organisations to take the place of moribund parties is indeed one example. But their signifi-cance would be less were it not for their ability to enlist more estab-lished institutions as aides. The two most important institutions available in this connection are the press and, more surprisingly, the judges, especially of the Supreme Court. There is a sense in which the three very diverse entities constitute a mutually supportive three-pronged standing 'Opposition' – in no sense as a new opposi-tion party, rather as a continuing substitute mechanism attempting to do what parties, both 'opposition' and from within the governing party, previously did: increase the accountability of those in office by drawing attention to unsatisfied demands and acts of misgovernment.

The press scarcely found it practicable to be heroic during the Emergency but that memory has stirred it to new levels of responsibility as independent investigator and critic. In this the Supreme Court has been supportive, strongly striking down governmental attempts to interfere with the press (often through detailed controls over newsprint and advertisements), already in *Sakal Newspapers* (1961) and *Bennett Coleman* (1972) but most notably in the *Indian Express Case* (1986).

But the Court has been forging new instrumentalities of its own. In a context which has seen a veritable explosion of its writ jurisdiction – some of it arising from its own responsiveness and that of the bar to new 'public interest litigation' from the non-party civil rights and protest organisations – it has been innovative on its own account in two main directions. First, in its development of legal rules, it has both relaxed its restrictive view of *locus standi* and moved perceptibly through its heightened stress on 'reasonableness' towards an approximation to 'due process', most strikingly in *Maneka Gandhi* (1978) and subsequently. Secondly and most interestingly, the Court has become an active creator of its own business. It has invented what has been dubbed 'epistolary jurisdiction' – the conversion of letters addressed to it into writ petitions; it has started ordering commissions of inquiry into matters brought to light in cases, for example, as to the conditions of migrant labourers building the Asiad Stadium; unprecedentedly it has begun to take a lively interest in matters of prisoners' rights and prison reform; it has asked district judges to monitor and report to it on the implementation of certain of its decisions. One is bound to say that all this 'new constitutionalism' may be a complex reaction to the Emergency years: complex because it is not only a flexing of previously bound judicial muscle; it may also, strangely, be a stirring of social conscience on behalf of the oppressed, those for whom Mrs Gandhi liked to claim her anti-poverty programmes *and* her Emergency were supposed to help.[34]

★   ★   ★

The attempt to make sense of the Indian experience should have shown that the guiding conception inspiring this volume is amply justified: neither the political life nor the constitution of a country can be understood without the other. Attention to constitutions is neither 'old hat' nor the exclusive business of the constitutional lawyers. At the same time this does not entail an attitude of disregard towards, say, political sociology. The study of politics is inescapably multi-disciplinary. In an article already referred to above,[35] Henry Hart made reference to Huntington's work on political development and decay and spoke of the need for 'a bridge between an interpretation of the Indian constitution under immediate stress and the development or decay of the system over decades'. In setting out on that task, he remarks wistfully that 'anyone who tries building such a bridge is on his own', but he went ahead most usefully. The present conclusion may be taken as an annotated comment on that attempt.

A Constitution is a framework relating political institutions, and as such therefore itself a high form of institutionalisation. Democratic constitutionalism is at once a guarantee and a regulator of political participation. Huntington formulated three general propositions: when social mobilisation outstrips economic development, social frustration will ensue; when social frustration exceeds social mobility opportunities, political participation will increase; if political participation grows faster than political institutionalisation, the result is political instability. Hart suggests that social frustration and political participation have been evidently increasing in India, albeit patchily. He believes, however, that India's achievement has been to avoid grave instability by increasing institutionalisation at the same time and he instances regular elections and the development of *panchayati raj*, the extension through democratic decentralisation of choice and accountability down to village level. However, he also recognises that there is a discernible tendency for 'one stage of extension of institutionalised participation to preclude the next'. In other words, the locally newly powerful come to 'stand like rocks against such redistributive programmes as ceilings on land holdings, minimum farm wages or preferential credit to the poor ... Here is a vast pool of frustrated villagers who might, if they became participant, act outside the locally entrenched institutions.'[36]

The Indian Constitution has been largely freed from the illiberal features of the Emergency period. Its guardians have been able largely to discard these fears of a decade ago. They are said also to have become 'people oriented' in their outlook.[37] What remains is to make the Constitution's protection available where it is most needed and to proceed to the restoration of accountability of the political process to the citizen body – including those who are still in the throes of discovering that they are members of it.

To return to the opening paragraph of this chapter: one purpose has been to shorten the distance between constitutional lawyers and students of politics. In pursuing this aim it may seem to some that too much attention has been given to the role of the higher judiciary.

But perhaps enough has been said to show that if that view would have had some force in the earlier years of the new republic, it is no longer tenable. For a variety of reasons – including faults of commission and omission by the government – the Constitution and the Supreme Court have arrived at a place of political centrality. This will of course be less readily appreciated in Britain than in North America or Australia.

Notes and references

1. Henry Hart, 'The Indian Constitution: Political Development and Decay', *Asian Survey*, 20, 4, April 1980, p. 429. Austin's book was published in London in 1966.
2. This is of course an over-simplification. Since the 1935 Act did not contemplate a transfer of power to a sovereign Indian parliament but preserved powers in the Viceroy and London, it would be appropriate to say that it envisaged quasi-parliamentary government. As to federal provisions, these were present in the Act but never in fact implemented; they were dependent on the inclusion of the princely states which had not been effected when 1939 put an end to British constitutional constructions. However, the Indian Constitution of 1950 certainly follows the 1935 Act in being comprehensive and detailed, a manual as well as a declaration. This naturally means that it is not confined to institutions of the Centre but spells out also those of the States. The Austin book already referred to is the best study of the deliberations of the Indian founding fathers sketched in this section. The main themes were summarised in my *Government and Politics of India* (3rd edn, London: Hutchinson, 1971), pp. 78–85.
3. The Indian President was intended to be a constitutional head of state and the practice since 1950 has sustained this position. Even the exercise on one occasion of some discretion regarding selection of a Prime Minister is compatible with this. It should however be noted that the 'constitutional head of state' at State level, the Governor, is not quite on the same model. Appointed by the President (in effect, therefore, the Prime Minister's nominee) his relations with his Chief Minister may be heavily influenced by the centre. It would have been altogether different if the framers had stuck to their original intention to have Governors chosen by popular election.
4. See Lucian and Mary W. Pye, *Asian Power and Politics: the cultural dimensions of authority* (Cambridge, Mass., Harvard University Press, 1985).
5. There were also some seriously dedicated Gandhians in the Assembly who made pleas for radical decentralisation, a 'Ram Rajya' or genuinely Indian kingdom of God, with power bestowed upwards from thriving 'village republics'. This was slapped down sharply by Dr Ambedkar, chief draftsman and an untouchable, who referred to 'false sentimentality' and asked: 'What is the village but a sink of localism, a den of ignorance . . . ?' Nevertheless, there remained to the end some unease that the Constitution had 'no manifest relation to the fundamental spirit of India': 'we wanted the music of *veena* or *sitar* . . . we have the music of an English band'.
6. The phrase 'requiring only' must not be taken to imply that the Constituent Assembly considered that they were making amendments easy – though they certainly thought that the Constitution would need constant readjustment to changing needs. Nor is it implied that the special majorities are negligible obstacles, though in practice they have, by virtue of large (usually Congress) majorities, been available throughout the 36 years except only for 1967–71 and (in respect of the Upper House) for 1977–80.
   The Constitution has been amended 55 times in those years. It is doubtful,

however, that this has had any ill effect on the extent of respect for the Constitution. The relevant public understands quite well the reasons for change. The very length (22 Parts, comprising nearly 400 Articles plus 10 Schedules) and detail of the document invites 'adjustment' amendments. An examination of the first 42 amendments reveals that no less than 15 were occasioned simply by changes in the status or boundaries of the States or other constituent units and no less than 14 were concerned with minor and virtually routine adjustments. 11 can be identified as significant responses to interpretations of the document made in Supreme Court judgments.

7. Respect for the courts of law was high even before independence. It owed something to the perception of judges as being somewhat independent of the main government machine, something also to the dignity accorded in indigenous traditions to servants of the laws. But additionally, judges are recruited from the Bar, the first profession open to the educated Indian. India's first generations of political leaders were heavily drawn from such lawyers. If, as the Constitution-makers were agreed, the Supreme Court was to be even greater than the Federal Court which it replaced, it would be indeed an apex institution. Today its general status remains high. However, as the judges have become at times associated with particular positions identified as more or less political, degrees of respect no doubt vary to some extent according to political attitudes.

8. Quoted in M.C. Setalvad, *The Indian Constitution, 1950–1965*, (Bombay: University of Bombay Press, 1967), p. 168. The author points out that India cannot refer to an equivalent of the US 'Marshall Court' (if only for the reason that Indian Chief Justices change so frequently – 17 in the first 36 years) and its Supreme Court cannot pretend to the same level of achievement as the US body. Twenty years on, the former statement remains true but as regards the second one may wonder whether, allowing for different durations, comparisons would be so absurd. It has been claimed that 'the jurisdiction and powers of [the Indian Supreme Court] . . . are wider than those exercised by the highest court of any country in the Commonwealth or by the Supreme Court of the US'. Setalvad gives a lucid account of key cases of the period and has been followed here. The more typical detailed legal commentary treatment is found in several works; one of the best is H.M. Seervai, *Constitutional Law of India*, 3rd edn Vols 1 and 2 (Bombay: N.M. Tripathi, 1984).

9. In 1977 the number of Acts listed in the 9th Schedule was 188, 101 of which were inserted during Mrs Gandhi's Emergency period of 18 months.

10. It will be convenient to make clear here that although property rights matters are not discussed in the later sections of this chapter, such cases did persist even after the 1st and 4th Amendments. Just as *Bela Banerjee's* case (1954) prompted the 4th Amendment in the following year, so the Court's interpretation of 'estate' in a trio of cases during 1962–4 led to the 17th Amendment (1964) and its pursuit of the doctrine of 'eminent domain' in the shape of compensation that was at least not 'illusory' (*in Vajravelu's case*, 1965, and above all in *R.C. Cooper's case*, 1970, also known as *The Bank Nationalisation case*) led to the intentionally sweeping 24th and 25th Amendments of 1971. See R. Dhavan, *The Supreme Court of India* (Bombay: N.M. Tripathi, 1977), especially Ch. 3; also H.C.L. Merrillat, *Land and the Constitution in India* (New York: Columbia University Press, 1970). Along this road of conflict the Court's interest moves from the strict issues of property rights towards a concern about the constitutionality of amendments which impair fundamental rights. It should be noted that in a symbolic gesture of socialist enthusiasm the Janata Party by the 44th Amendment (1978) eliminated some of the provisions (Art 19(1)f and Art 31), securing the inviolability of the right to property. The change has proved rather cosmetic; property cases may use, for example, Art. 14.

11. On the whole the Court's position was much more respectful to government legislation on freedom rights than on property rights. This is no doubt related

to the pressures from propertied litigants as well as to the relatively modest number of political arrests and preventive detentions in the first two decades. As indicated below, the scale of the latter changed during the 1975–7 emergency period, while the Court felt better able to develop its grounds for scrutiny when that emergency was ended. It then moved from what had been a cautious inspection of procedures towards a stouter defence against unreasonable use of state power against individuals.

12. A masterly study deals comprehensively with this vast and complex field of reservations and the problems of positive discrimination: Marc Galanter, *Competing Equalities* (Los Angeles: University of California Press, 1984). Briefer essays are contributed by R. Hardgrave and M. Galanter to R. Dhavan *et al. Judges and the Judicial Power* (Bombay: N.M. Tripathi, 1985). The '68%' case referred to here is *Balaji* (1963). Originally the Supreme Court had felt obliged to strike down special quotas for the deprived as being hostile to the equality rights but they then accepted a constitutional amendment which sanctioned such provisions. In *Balaji* they took the view that special quotas should be neither so excessive as to damage society's general interests nor based solely on caste without regard to income criteria. In *Thomas* (1975) the Court appeared to move from such a classic compromise position to lean further towards positive discrimination. Court jurisdiction is a blunt tool for difficult social reform; it is in use largely because state governments have made it a dangerous vote-catching game, while the central government has been unable to formulate an all-India policy. Meanwhile in the streets ferocious riots can take place on the issues, as when in 1986 upper caste engineering and medical students exploded at an increased reserved college quota for the 'backwards'.

13. Setalvad, *op. cit.* p. 221.

14. 'Union territories' remained as smaller, residual, more centrally-dependent areas. The 1956 measure left some unsettled matters and there were further divisions into States in 1960 (Bombay becoming Gujarat and Maharashtra), 1963 (Nagaland being broken off from Assam), 1966 (Punjab into Punjab and Haryana and Himachal Pradesh) and further spawnings from Assam up to a total of 23 in 1986. The 1956 Act provided two intended checks on linguistic chauvinism: Five Zonal Councils (unrecognised in the Constitution) for the settlement of regional inter-State disputes and a Commissioner for Linguistic Minorities.

15. A rather fuller account is given in Morris-Jones, *op. cit.* pp. 108–14 and more particularly pp. 150–53.

16. Henry Hart (*loc. cit.* p. 434) puts it well: 'India appears to have two constitutions pieced together in one document. One gives power to a few leaders in Delhi to control the country through coercion of its politically active stratum. The other makes all citizens voters and empowers them to choose and reject their rulers. The tension is severe.' One cannot agree that coercion has been limited to activists but the article remains one of the most thoughtful and important on the politics of the Constitution.

17. One of the fullest studies of the Emergency is Henry Hart (ed.), *Indira Gandhi's India* (Boulder, Col.: Westview Press, 1976). Article treatments include L. and S. Rudolph, 'To the brink and back', *Asian Survey*, 18, 4, April, 1978, and W.H. Morris-Jones, 'Creeping but Uneasy Authoritarianism', *Government and Opposition*, 12, 1, Winter 1977.

18. L. and S. Rudolph, 'Judicial Review versus Parliamentary Sovereignty: the Struggle over Stateness in India', *Journal of Commonwealth and Comparative Politics*, XIX, 3 November 1981. In this section I am greatly indebted to this penetrating discussion of a central constitutional theme. Formally, the case was concerned with property rights: land reform legislation imposing a ceiling on land holdings was being challenged by petitioners whose inheritance was being denied to them. However, the arguments developed by the time the case reached the Supreme Court were focused on the 17th Amendment and more broadly

on whether there were limits on the amending power itself. The decision was suprising because the Court had previously adhered to the view that parliament's amending power was unlimited. This was the clear and unanimous judgment in *Shankari Prasad* (1951) and it had been sustained even after the 17th Amendment in *Sajjan Singh* (1965); on the latter occasion, however, there were two dissenting judges who found genuine incompatibilities between certain clauses in the fundamental rights chapter and others in the amendment articles. An exhaustive examination both of *Golak Nath* and its successor case, *Kesavananda* (1973) (discussed below) is in R. Dhavan, *The Supreme Court and Parliamentary Sovereignty* (New Delhi: Sterling, 1977). There are some constitutional lawyers who find the legal reasoning of the majority in *Golak Nath* to be 'absurd'; Dr Dhavan has said that the decision was 'unsound, using dubious techniques . . . more of a political testament than a jurisprudential verdict' (p. 410).

19. U. Baxi, *The Indian Supreme Court and Politics* (Lucknow: Eastern Book Company, 1980), p. 22.

20. One member, Prof. Mavalankar, son of Parliament's first Speaker, was notably neither arrested nor completely silenced; he managed to secure a limited clandestine distribution of his unreported speeches.

21. Baxi suggests that the Court did well not to 'commit self-immolation' but instead to 'endeavour to survive, seeking to play a role as a centre of some kind of political opposition at a little more opportune time' (*op. cit.* p. 193). Justice Khanna gave the solitary dissenting opinion on the *habeas corpus* (preventive detention) issue; Baxi (*op. cit.* p. 84) says that his 'moral vision and personal courage . . . earned him a place among the immortals'.

22. Quoted in Rudolphs' 'Judicial Review', p. 241.

23. Quoted in M. Henderson, 'Setting India's Democratic House in Order: Constitutional Amendments', *Asian Survey*, 19, 10, October 1979. More sober language is used by Dr Dhavan in his account of the steps which culminated in the Amendment: it was 'clearly beyond a mere repair job' (*The Amendment*, 1978, p. 5).

24. Quoted in Henderson, *loc. cit.* p. 951. Kumaramangalam's views are conveniently brought together in his *Judicial Appointments*, (New Delhi: Oxford and IBH Publishing Co., 1973)

25. See K. Nayar (ed.), *The Supersession of Judges* (New Delhi, Indian Book Co., 1973). Of course, judges are not safely to be judged so simply; they may be 'progressive' on some points but not on others. Chief Justice Ray had given satisfaction with some of his opinions before his elevation; he tried to give more as Chief Justice (seeking on the government's behalf to undertake a general review of *Kesavananda* – but failing through lack of cooperation from his brothers); but when it came to the 39th Amendment he joined the others in invalidating its core. The 1973 supersession in favour of Ray was the first but also the last. It followed very soon after *Kesavananda* had no doubt angered Mrs Gandhi. That it was not repeated by Mrs Gandhi (or other Prime Ministers) subsequently may be connected with the difficulty of placing judges in precise and constant positions on a political spectrum.

26. Some discussion of this matter is available in Baxi, *op. cit.* pp. 200–5, 219–21. To the surprise and dismay of many members of the bench and bar, the Supreme Court in *The Transfer of Judges* case (1982) failed to challenge alleged government interference. In the post-Emergency climate, however, the recommendations of the Chief Justice will carry some weight.

27. Henry Hart (*loc. cit.* p. 448) points out an interesting might-have-been of the Janata failure. One proposal which failed to secure the two-thirds majority in the Upper House was the radical one that any amendment affecting the essential features of the Constitution – specifically 'impairing the secular or democratic character of the Constitution or abridging the rights of the citizen or compromis-

ing the independence of the judiciary' – would require submission to a popular nationwide referendum.

28. On one problem arising in the difficult days of changing governments in 1980 the Supreme Court found a neat way of presenting the issue and of shelving its responsibility. It took together the *Baroda Dynamite* case brought by Congress during the Emergency against Janata supporters and the *Bansi Lal* case lodged by Janata against a Congress Minister, and then sanctioned the withdrawal of both cases by the petitioners. (Rudolphs' 'Judicial Review', pp. 246–7. The authors ask: 'is it then all right . . . to commit crimes, provided they are politically motivated?')

29. Mrs Gandhi's last year in power witnessed perhaps the most grotesque misuse of President's Rule in attempts, mainly unsuccessful, to secure subservient State governments. Space has not permitted any discussion of this particular device for imposing from the Centre periods of emergency rule in a State (mentioned earlier in setting out the Constitution's Emergency Provisions). Suffice it then to say that this power, virtually to suspend the federal parliamentary Constitution, has been extensively used: on 9 occasions during the 17 Nehru and Shastri years, 1950–67, on 27 occasions in the first 9 years of Mrs Gandhi, 1967–76. (The figure for the 8 years of Janata and Mrs Gandhi's second period, 1976–84, is 35. But this is misleading, for 18 of these cases were special: President's Rule was imposed on 9 States in 1977 as part of compelling them to hold elections and Mrs Gandhi returned the compliment to the 9 in 1980.) The device has been used to overcome situations of genuine multi-party instability and of defection-induced uncertainties, but also to bring down opposition party governments and States' Chief Ministers who proved unacceptable to the central government. Full studies are available in S.R. Maheshwari, *President's Rule in India* (New Delhi: Macmillan, 1977), B.D. Dua, *Presidential Rule in India, 1950–1974* (New Delhi: S. Chand, 1979) and R. Dhavan, *President's Rule in the States* (New Delhi: Indian Law Institute, 1979). Of several articles, that of Douglas Verney, 'The limits of political manipulation', *Journal of Commonwealth and Comparative Politics*, XXIV, 2, November 1986, is of exceptional interest and value because it relates the device to wider constitutional issues.

30. States will no doubt press for some financial adjustments and some means of curbing Central penetration into areas of activity located within the States' list of subjects. There have been occasions in the past when States have protested at the deployment in their areas and without their consent of the Central Reserve Police and Border Security Force; on the other hand, the value of these bodies has been apparent in recent crises beyond the power of local police. The examination of federal relations by the Administrative Reforms Commission in the late 1960s concluded that adjustments in administrative practice would suffice and constitutional change was not required. But that was before the regionalising consequences of Congress collapse and central government's poor political management had appeared.

The Sarkaria Commission will have to consider how far they can go towards meeting demands already formulated by two of the States with the most ambitious aspirations for increased autonomy. As early as 1969 the non-Congress DMK Government of Tamil Nadu appointed a Centre-State Relations Inquiry Committee (Rajamannar) which reported two years later. The Communist West Bengal Government followed with its *Document on Centre-State Relations* in 1977. Their common case is for a substantial set of constitutional amendments designed to achieve a more truly federal system. Summaries and full references to both documents are usefully provided by Dr Alice Jacob of the Indian Law Institute in 'New pressures on Indian Federalism' in R. Dhavan and A. Jacob (eds), *Indian Constitution: Trends and Issues* (N.M. Tripathi, 1978), a volume which contains a wide range of articles on the main issues of constitutional debate discussed here. While the selection of articles and the tone of some of them reflect the uncomfortable proximity in time to the Emergency period, they do suggest that there could indeed be room for a major review of certain constitutional dilemmas. However, a more likely outcome is piecemeal political and judicial adjustment.

It may be worth remarking (in that last connection) that India's experience is something of an oddity in the context of federal constitutions in that the role of the courts with regard to federal relations has been by no means prominent. It would seem that this may owe something to the absence of any awkward 'commerce clause', to the very detailed allocation of subjects between Centre and States and to the extensive list of concurrent subjects. Conflict has instead tended to be handled politically by virtue of the position of the Congress Party in power at the Centre and in most of the States for most of the time – and also by the capacity of the Centre to impose President's Rule on State governments perceived as being obstructive or merely unpalatable (see note 29).

31. One important aspect of the dominant party system was that almost all parties fashioned themselves to some degree on Congress. As Congress has fallen apart as a really cohesive interacting structure – Rajiv Gandhi's attempts to revive internal elections notwithstanding – so other parties have also suffered; they were mostly less well organised and have therefore had less far to fall.

While it does not seriously detract from the view taken here of party decay, mention should be made of one bold move by Rajiv Gandhi's government which in principle works in the opposite direction. In the unsettled period of the late 1960s there was some public dismay at the widespread practice of party defections among politicians of several parties in most State legislatures and there was much talk of legislating against this. On coming to power, the new Prime Minister took early action to secure, with general approval, the passage of the 52nd Amendment Act 1985. This defines defection as either giving up membership of the party for which the member was elected or disobeying (without condonement) the voting direction of that party. For this the penalty is immediate disqualification from membership of the House. Exemption from this outcome is, however, allowed if a member's defection is consequent upon a party split (not less than one-third of the original party representation) or a party merger (not less than two-thirds of the original party). So far as is known no case of defection has arisen since the law was passed. The outward coherence and discipline of legislature parties is thus no doubt improved. But party factionalism appears to remain rife and internal party organisations are largely inoperative.

32. A glance at the files of *Economic and Political Weekly* or even at the more glossy *India Today* (e.g, an excellent summary review in the issue of 31 December 1986) will provide ample sickening evidence. Paul Brass has written effectively on the matter with special reference to conditions in adjacent eastern UP, in 'National Power and local politics', *Modern Asian Studies*, 18, 1, 1984. As regards the role of the police, a sober but alarming assessment of that service, based on privileged access in 1978 and 1980 and study of the Indian police over many years, is found in David H. Bayley, 'Police and Political Order in India', *Asian Survey*, XXIII, 4, April 1983. He ascribes the 'decline in the rule of law' in large part to police involvement, especially during the Emergency, in partisan politics: 'they are preoccupied with it, penetrated by it and now participate individually and collectively in it'.

33. It is not always a great improvement if that does not happen. In a case that, exceptionally, found its way to the Supreme Court, that Court found it advisable specifically to direct that certain young appellants labelled as 'ideological teenagers' should 'not be treated with any tinge of brutality – a caveat which has become necessary when we remember that they are treated as "Naxalites"'' (Baxi, *op. cit.* p. 237.)

34. On these developments see U. Baxi's contribution to R. Dhavan *et al.* (eds), *Judges and the Judicial Power* (1985).
35. Henry Hart, *loc. cit.*
36. *Ibid.* p. 441.
37. Baxi, *Indian Supreme Court*, p. 246.

8 Canada's new Constitution (1982): Some lessons in constitutional engineering
Geoffrey Marshall

Of all constitutions based on a parliamentary framework Canada's Constitution surely offers the richest mine of materials for the political scientist and the constitution maker. It teaches a number of lessons about the mechanics of constitution making and it raises questions about almost every major problem of constitutional government – including the federal distribution of powers; judicial review; Parliamentary and state sovereignty; and the constitutional relationship of law and convention. For Britain, Canada has an additional and particular interest in that its constitutional history has helped to elucidate the role of the Crown and the character of the Commonwealth relationship.

The political background: prelude to 1982
The crisis over Canada's Constitution that enveloped both Britain and Canada from 1980 to 1982 had its origins in an event remote in time, namely, the attempt of the Imperial Parliament in 1931 to bring the law of the Commonwealth into line with the political reality of Commonwealth independence and to acknowledge the equal status of the then Dominions with the United Kingdom. The Imperial Conferences of 1926 and 1930 had recognised the status of Canada, Australia, South Africa, New Zealand, Newfoundland and the Irish Free State as independent freely associated nation states no longer subject to the Imperial sovereignty of the British Parliament. In 1931 the Statute of Westminster translated – or did its best to translate – that equality of status into terms of strict law. In both Canada and Australia there were difficulties deriving from the federal status of the respective constitutions. Neither country wished its federal Parliament to receive the entire gift of sovereign power from the United Kingdom that would have entitled the central government to exercise an unrestricted power of constitutional amendment. So restrictions were written into the Statute of Westminster. In Canada's case these resulted in the British

Parliament being left – somewhat reluctantly – with the power to change Canada's basic constitutional instrument (the British North America Act of 1867), until such time as the provincial and federal authorities were able to negotiate to their mutual satisfaction a procedure for constitutional amendment that would satisfy their potentially conflicting interests. At that time (to use the language of the 1970s) power over the constitution could be 'patriated' – that is, an agreed final amendment of the British North America Act could be procured from the Westminster Parliament giving Canada a native and legally autonomous constitution. Frustratingly the time was continuously unripe. Some limited powers of amendment were transferred to the federal Parliament in 1949 but despite repeated federal-provincial conferences, internal differences, and in particular the reservations of the province of Quebec, prevented any agreed approach to Westminster.

In 1980 a referendum in Quebec on a proposal for semi-independence of the province (or 'sovereignty-association') was held and defeated. In the course of the campaign the federal government gave undertakings that defeat of the referendum proposals would be followed by constitutional changes to meet Quebec's aspirations. Further federal-provincial conferences were initiated but no agreement could be reached on a mechanism for constitutional change.

Towards the end of 1980 Pierre Trudeau's Liberal Government declared that in the absence of agreement it would take steps unilaterally to bring about a patriation of the Constitution, together with a charter of rights. A resolution was prepared for debate in the federal Parliament and transmission to Westminster, approving an address to the Queen requesting her to lay before the United Kingdom Parliament a Bill, enclosed with the Address, to bring about the necessary amendments to the British North America Act, so as to enact a new Constitution Act and to put an end to the British Parliament's authority to legislate for Canada. The proposed legislation was submitted to a Special Joint Committee of the Canadian Senate and House of Commons and finally approved in April 1981.

The procedure of submission to Westminster was interrupted, however, by events both in Canada and the United Kingdom. Eight of the ten provinces were opposed to the federal government's proposals and three of them (Manitoba, Quebec and Newfoundland) began legal proceedings in the provincial appeal courts to seek rulings that the approach to the British Parliament by the federal government and Parliament, and the enactment of a new constitution without the consent of the provinces, would be contrary to law or to the conventions of the Canadian constitution. In Britain a

Select Committee of the House of Commons (the Foreign and Commonwealth Affairs Committee) began hearings into the role of the United Kingdom Parliament and the propriety of its acting at the request of the Canadian federal authorities. The Trudeau Government, for its part, maintained that the British Parliament was not entitled to go behind the request for legislation, and that any refusal to act would be derogatory to Canada's status and to the comity of the Commonwealth. The particular proposals constituted a package that must be passed into law without question. There must, Prime Minister Trudeau said, be no sniffing of the package. The British Parliament must hold its nose if necessary and do its duty.

Despite this injunction and an apparent commitment of Mrs Thatcher and her predecessors to attempt to procure the necessary legislation, the Foreign Affairs Committee concluded that it would not be in accordance with constitutional propriety for the British Parliament to enact the proposed Canada Act without the substantial support of the Canadian provinces. That view was dramatically supported in Canada when three provincial court decisions were appealed to the Supreme Court of Canada. In September 1981 the Court held that a substantial degree of provincial support was by convention necessary, and that though the federal government could lawfully proceed with its request, such unilateral action would be a breach of the constitutional practice of Canada.[1]

The decision of the Supreme Court compelled the Trudeau Government to begin fresh consultations with the provinces. By November 1981 federal concessions had secured the agreement of nine of the ten provinces. Quebec continued to resist the constitutional settlement and engaged unsuccessfully in further court action to establish the right of veto. The agreement of the nine provinces and the federal government was embodied in a resolution that was passed by the Canadian Senate and House of Commons in December 1981 and enacted by the United Kingdom Parliament in March 1982. So Canada finally got and patriated its Constitution. The Constitution Act is contained in the Canada Act 1982 which terminates the authority of the UK Parliament to legislate for Canada. It came into force on 17 April 1982, the date having been proclaimed in Ottawa by Elizabeth II, Queen of Canada.

Having, finding and making a constitution
Until 17 April 1982 Canada, like the United Kingdom, had no instrument that in terms of strict law could be called its constitution. The preamble to the British North America Act of 1867 admittedly said that it should have a 'Constitution similar in principle to that

of the United Kingdom' but that Act did not in its terms – unlike many more recent statutes providing for the affairs of new Commonwealth states – enact detailed provisions for responsible government, or for the mode of exercise of executive powers. Nor, for that matter, does the Constitution Act of 1982. So Canada's Constitution is still in part a non-documentary one with some of its important central principles resting on convention. The Constitution Act of 1982 has, however, created a legal entity entitled 'the Constitution of Canada' which is to be the supreme law of the land and which has an entrenched status alterable only by the special amendment procedures laid down in the Act itself, unless the Act or the Constitution to which it refers provides otherwise. Finding the Constitution is not, however, a simple matter, since it includes much more than the Constitution Act. In the first place it includes the Canada Act (an Act of the United Kingdom Parliament) in which the Constitution Act is contained. Secondly (by reason of Section 52(2) of the Constitution Act), it includes the series of Acts formerly known as the British North America Acts 1867–1975 (now confusingly renamed Constitution Acts) and a number of other Acts and orders listed in the schedule to the Act. These include the Alberta and Saskatchewan Acts of 1905, the Canada (Ontario Boundary) Act of 1889, the Manitoba Act of 1870 and other territorial Orders in Council. Other important statutes which might be thought to be of constitutional importance are not included (e.g. the Supreme Court Act, and the 1960 Bill of Rights).

There are some warnings here for any future exercise in Great Britain aimed at the establishment of a written or documentary constitution. The Canada Act is not a model to be followed, and its uncertainties underline the magnitude of the exercise involved in attempting to formalise an existing body of statutory and non-statutory rules.

Distributing legislative powers: constitutional hard labour

The existing distribution of legislative authority between the federal Parliament and the provinces was not directly affected by the Constitution Act 1982 (except in respect of a new provincial power to make laws in relation to non-renewable natural resources inserted as s. 92A of the 1867 British North America Act (now the Constitution Act 1867)). The federal division of powers still rests on the provisions of that Act, as amended, and the new regime has done nothing to ease the difficulties of the world's most complex system of federal distribution, which remains as an awe-inspiring example of what is to be avoided by any modern draftsman allocating legislative powers. The more complex history of intergovernmental disputes in Canada as compared with the United States reflects the existence in ss. 91 and 92 of the 1867 Act of exclusive lists of provincial and federal legislative powers. It stems also from the palpably vague and overlapping character of some major items in each list, together with a persistent uncertainty as to whether the federal peace, order and good government power provides any additional or residual power over and above what is allocated to the federal Parliament in the specific heads of power enumerated in s. 91. Major difficulties flow from the division of powers of economic and social regulation between the federal 'Trade and Commerce' head and the provincial 'Property and Civil Rights in the Province' head, together with the equally fissiparous division of authority over criminal law and the administration of justice.

Recent constitutional litigation has shown no lessening of the impact of these difficulties. A particular problem, given exclusive lists and an uncertain residual power, is the classification of new subjects requiring regulation, such as narcotics, television, atomic energy or inflation. The Anti-Inflation Act of 1975 was upheld as a subject falling within the peace, order and good government power of the federal Parliament[2] partly in response to the notion that an economic emergency may operate to alter the distribution for the time being of power between federal and provincial legislatures. In *Labatt Brewers* v *A.G. Canada*[3] in 1979, however, federal standards for beer enacted under the federal Food and Drugs legislation were held not to fall within the power to regulate trade and commerce. Attempts to impose national standards in new areas, even if designed to have general application, may impermissibly entrench on the provincial property and civil rights jurisdiction (as did the federal attempt to regulate dishonest business practices by civil remedies, rejected in *MacDonald* v *Vapor Canada*).[4]

Federal jurisdiction over criminal law raises philosophical as well as practical difficulties. What is the power to enact criminal law? If any act at all can be made criminal, then the federal authority has an infinitely expansible weapon of economic regulation. In 1951 the Privy Council disallowed a federal law prohibiting the manufacture, import or sale of margarine as not falling within the Criminal law power;[5] and in 1981 the Supreme Court of Canada struck down a provision in the Federal Criminal Code prohibiting driving whilst having a suspended provincial driving licence.[6]

Federalism, it is traditionally admitted, means legalism, and anyone in doubt of the truth of that proposition need only consult the recent history of Canada's federal division of powers.

In one respect, however, the Constitution Act of 1982 has potentially affected the federal-provincial balance. That at least was the view of a majority of the Supreme Court in the *Patriation Reference* case in 1981. There it was argued for the government that the new Constitution Act was not a matter to which the provinces had by convention or law a right to object since it did not affect the balance or distribution of authority between federal and provincial Parliaments in any way. The court rejected that argument, however, on the ground that the Constitution Act contained a new Bill of Rights. Although the limitations imposed by the new Charter of Rights admittedly applied equally to the federal and provincial legislatures, that in itself was a relative re-adjustment of their positions since the pre-existing Bill of Rights of 1960 was a federal statute that applied only to federal legislation. The new Charter would therefore potentially narrow the provincial legislative powers that had been previously unrestricted (except by the allocation of jurisdiction in the BNA Act). In the United States the Federal Bill of Rights has had a striking impact on state legislative authority and is believed by the states to have been a potent factor in altering the balance of the federal system. That feeling may soon exist in Canada. Certainly the Charter of Rights and Freedoms has already had a significant impact on what were hitherto perceived as important areas of provincial autonomy.

Patriation: constitutional amendment and the new balance of power

In one way the result of the constitutional struggle of 1980–82 over the repatriation of the constitution has been to strengthen the authority and autonomy of the provinces. Indeed Canada is now a legal federation in a way in which it was not before 1982. In its argument before the Supreme Court in the Reference Case of 1981 the federal government argued that there was no support in Canadian law for the belief that provincial consent was required for amendments to the Constitution (submitted to the Westminster Parliament) even when they affected the federal structure. The federal government alone was responsible for securing constitutional amendments until such time as an all-Canadian amendment procedure had been devised. In this respect, they said, the Canadian political system departed from the federal model. The decision of the Supreme Court[7] in effect confirmed this view as a legal proposition. There was no legal bar to the unilateral federal submission of amendments to the BNA Acts to the United Kingdom Parliament or to the authority of the United Kingdom Parliament to amend the constitution of Canada. Thus before 1982 the federal government could legally have procured the abolition of all the provincial governments, or turned Canada into a unitary state. It would of course (as the Court held) have been a violation of Canadian constitutional practice to submit unilateral amendment proposals affecting the provinces, but the provinces were in no way protected from such action except by a debatable convention and the possible unwillingness of the United Kingdom Parliament to acquiesce in a breach of Canadian constitutional practice.

Since 1982, by contrast, provincial authority is buttressed by legal guarantees and the bargain struck with the Trudeau Government in the federal-provincial agreement of 5 November 1981 has put the provinces in an unprecedentedly strong position in relation to constitutional amendment. The general constitutional amending procedure requires the assents of the Federal Parliament and of two-thirds of the provinces representing 50 per cent of the population. In effect, seven of the ten provinces must agree to an amendment and the seven must in practice include at least one of Ontario or Quebec. In addition s.38(3) of the Constitution provides that an amendment that derogates from the legislative powers or rights or privileges of the legislature or government of a province shall not have effect in any province that passes a resolution of dissent. (This opting out must take place before the issue of the proclamation of the amendment.) On top of that there are financial compensatory provisions for opting out of any amendments that transfer provincial powers over education or cultural matters to the Federal Parliament. Finally there are a number of matters that can only be amended by unanimous provincial agreement (including an amendment of the amendment procedures).

The loser in the new balance of forces was clearly Quebec, whose government did not agree to the constitutional settlement. In the pre-1982 situation Quebec had in effect – though not legally – a veto on constitutional amendment. That veto no longer exists. Moreover, Quebec has lost what it takes to be important aspects of its autonomy in relation to French language and education rights through the operation of the Federal Charter of Rights and Freedoms. Quebec shares, on the other hand, the major privilege gained by the provinces of having the right to override the application of the Charter of Rights to its own legislation in relation to a number of the Charter's major provisions (though not those relating to language rights).

Canada's new amendment procedure has not attracted universal enthusiasm from Canadian commentators. On the contrary, it has been criticised for eliminating popular participation in the amendment process such as often occurs elsewhere through referendum requirements, and also for perpetuating a government and leadership-dominated process of a kind that turned the 1982 constitutional bargaining into something that looked 'more like labour management negotiations than the drafting of a constitutional amendment'.[8]

Legislative override: a Canadian invention

The device now known as the legislative override has been described as 'the uniquely Canadian contribution to the theory of constitutionalism'.[9] Its origins are not easily discoverable but it appeared, possibly for the first time, in the Canadian Bill of Rights of 1960, a federal statute that applied only to federal legislation (and has incidentally not been repealed by the new Constitution Act and so still places restrictions on the federal government not identical with those of the new Charter of Rights and Freedoms). The 1960 Bill of Rights provided that every law of Canada should be construed and applied so as not to infringe the rights and freedoms set out in the Act 'unless it is expressly declared by an Act of the Parliament of Canada that it shall operate notwithstanding the Canadian Bill of Rights'. In other words, Parliament might in any Act passed subsequently to the 1960 Bill of Rights oust its operation in relation to that particular legislation. Similar ousting clauses were also incorporated in the Quebec Charter of Rights and Freedoms of 1975 and in the Alberta provincial Bill of Rights of 1972. In fact, only one federal statute passed since 1960 has incorporated this device. An ousting provision, though of a limited kind, was inserted in 1970 to protect from challenge some of the provisions of the Public Order (Temporary Measures) Act, passed to deal with the threat of insurrection and terrorism in Quebec.

The significance of the parliamentary ouster or legislative override is that it sidesteps at least some of the objections often made to Bill of Rights legislation in the name of parliamentary sovereignty. It introduces the notion of an 'unentrenched' Bill of Rights that acknowledges rather than repudiates the supremacy of the legislative body that enacts it. It has therefore been of considerable interest to Bill of Rights advocates in other parts of the Commonwealth, and all the draft Bills proposed in the United Kingdom have incorporated a provision directly modelled on the Canadian example. The Bill commended by a majority of the House of Lords Select Committee on the Bill of Rights in 1978 to incorporate the European Convention of Human Rights provided that 'in every case of conflict between any enactment subsequent to the passing of this Act and the provisions of the said Convention the said Convention shall prevail unless subsequent enactment shall explicitly state otherwise'.

The incorporation of the legislative override in the Canadian Charter of 1982 can be regarded in different ways. Some have seen it as an acceptable compromise between the new world of the Charter and Canada's tradition of parliamentary supremacy. Others see it as a questionable and unprincipled surrender that undermines the human rights principle.[10] Certainly the override clause was not a part of the Charter as originally drafted. It was introduced in the federal-provincial negotiations in November 1981 as part of the price paid for the patriation package after the government's set-back in the Supreme Court. In order to meet provincial misgivings about a loss of legislative autonomy Section 33 of the Charter enacts that either the Federal Parliament or the legislature of a province may expressly declare in a federal or provincial Act that the Act or any provision of it 'shall operate notwithstanding a provision included in section 2 or sections 7–15 of the Charter'. This means that the override is a limited one with important exceptions. It cannot be used to override the Charter guarantees in relation to voting rights ('Democratic Rights'), freedom of movement and job establishment ('Mobility Rights')[11] or the guarantees relating to the use of the English and French languages (Language Rights) or the provision that the rights in the Charter are guaranteed equally to male and female persons. In addition, an override provision ceases to have effect after five years, though it may be re-enacted.

The political uses of the override clause in the Charter may be far-reaching, and the threat to use Section 33 could be a bargaining counter in provincial disputes with the federal government. In 1982 the legislature of Quebec enacted a measure entitled 'An Act Respecting the Constitution Act 1982'. The Act attached an override clause to every Act passed by the National Assembly of Quebec before 17 April 1972 and began the practice (that recently ceased with a change of government) of attaching a similar clause to each Act passed after April 1982. The first attempt at blanket legislation was plainly inconsistent with the Charter and has been so held. It is also the case that Quebec cannot use the override clause to protect all the provisions relating to language, education[12] and business regulation that were contained in the Province's official language legislation. (Some of them relating to the language of the courts and legislature have also been found inconsistent with the requirements of Section 133 of the British North America Act 1867 that have been held to require legislation to be enacted in both languages.)[13]

The relation of the override clause to the general declaration in section 1 of the Charter which provides that restrictions on Charter rights have to be demonstrably justified raises a question of general interest about the limitation of rights. The Section 1 limitation clause is similar to that to be found in the European Human Rights Declaration and in the Bills of Rights of many Commonwealth countries.

It states that the Charter guarantees the rights and freedoms set out in it 'subject only to such reasonable limits prescribed by law as can be demonstrably justified in a free and democratic society'. It is possible to argue that restricting the Charter rights by an override provision is a legislative act that must also be shown to be a reasonable limitation that is demonstrably justified.[14] But it seems unlikely that this view will be upheld by the courts. It was certainly not the intention of those who drafted the Charter and who put in the override clause in order to protect provincial legislation from judicial review. The limitations on rights that have to be justified under section 1 are presumably any limitations imposed by the federal and provincial legislatures under the powers allocated to them under sections 91 and 92 of the BNA (Constitution) Act 1867 as amended. The limitations or denial of rights that may be involved in an overriding of the Charter provisions is authorised and its limits defined by the Charter itself in section 33. If an override power is validly exercised as provided by that section it must be assumed to take the legislation that embodies the override outside the guarantees of the Charter altogether, so that it has to be neither reasonable nor justified. Over a certain area, in other words, legislative supremacy as to the substance of legislation is preserved.

A matter of large significance in relation to override clauses which enact that repeals or modifications of earlier statutes must embody a particular form of words, is whether such clauses can be regarded as 'manner and form provisions' that will bind future legislative action. The override provision in the Charter does not help to settle that question, since it was not a condition imposed on themselves by Canadian legislatures but one imposed on them by a legislative body exercising superior authority (the United Kingdom Parliament); so that there is no doubt that future legislative action that ignored it would be held invalid. The override clause in the 1960 Federal Bill of Rights, however, was self-imposed and some Canadian authorities have treated it as a manner and form provision.[15] The conclusion that a particular form of words would be so treated by the courts[16] would be an important one for the general theory of constitutional entrenchment and parliamentary sovereignty.

The Charter and judicial review
Since Canada's system of government is a parliamentary regime similar in principle (save for its federal elements) to that of the United Kingdom, the introduction into it of an entrenched Bill of Rights is an apter model than that provided by the United States for predicting the effect of incorporating a declaration of rights into British law. The House of Lords Select Committee in 1978 remarked

that 'there are no more than a few marginal situations where a Bill
of Rights might bestow a remedy where present law does not do
so'.[17] Canada's experience suggests that that prediction is wide of
the mark. A very large number of cases arising out of the application
of the Charter are now pending before provincial courts and a significant number have reached the Supreme Court. Under the 1960
Canadian Bill of Rights the courts seemed reluctant to hold legislative
measures invalid (only one provision in a federal statute was found
inconsistent with the Bill of Rights in twenty years).[18] Unlike the
Bill, however, the Charter clearly provides that 'any law that is
inconsistent with the provisions of the Constitution is to the extent
of the inconsistency of no force or effect'. Canada's judiciary,
therefore, finds itself in a new situation.

A number of the Charter's provisions have already come under
judicial consideration at the Provincial Appeal and Supreme Court
level including Section 2 (Freedom of expression);[19] section 6
(mobility rights and establishment);[20] section 8 (search and seizure);[21]
and section 23 (language rights).[22] In some of these cases legislative
provisions have been held inoperative for inconsistency with the
Charter.

Some general lessons can be learned from the problems experienced in applying the Charter, and from its uncertainty of
phraseology. The question, for example, whether rights guaranteed
to citizens are against governmental or legislative acts only, or against
other private persons, is an important one that is not clearly settled
in the Charter and different views have been expressed.[23] Section
32 states that the Charter applies to the Parliament and Government[24]
of Canada and to the legislature and government of each province
with respect to the matters falling within their authority. The section
does not state clearly (as it might have done) that application of
the Charter is solely to governmental and legislative acts, but
principle and the legislative history of the Charter suggest that it
was not intended to extend to the private sector.

Secondly, there are some difficult problems arising from the
general limitation clause in section 1, which provides that the Charter
rights are subject to 'such reasonable limits prescribed by law as
can be demonstrably justified in a free and democratic society'. The
handling of this provision by the Supreme Court suggests that
constitution-makers have some lessons to learn about the drafting
of such clauses. In at least one case[25] the Supreme Court seems
to have distinguished between legislation that 'limits' a Charter right
but which can then be justified under the second part of the limitation
clause, and legislation that 'collides' with, or is inconsistent with,
or, if valid, would amount to changing, the Charter right. But it

seems doubtful whether the negation or denial or amendment of a right can be clearly distinguished from limitation or modification of its scope. So, unless further explained, this approach to the Charter guarantees seems question-begging and lacking in coherence.

Patriation and sovereignty

The process by which Canada has acquired its new Constitution has helped to clarify some difficult questions about the theory of imperial sovereignty and the history of its redistribution. The process of dividing imperial sovereignty began with the Statute of Westminster in 1931. Under this Statute the Dominions in theory retained a legal, umbilical cord to the Imperial Parliament, which could legislate for them at their request and consent. Indeed, it was at the request and consent of Canada that Westminster enacted the Canada Act of 1982. Some Canadian writers have argued that Canada's independent statehood made that legislation unnecessary and that it was not by virtue of the legal authority of the British Parliament that the Constitution was patriated.[26] If that was the case, they argue, Canada's Constitution is not securely founded on an independent (or autochthonous)[27] legal basis.

The first theory, however, is inconsistent with the views expressed by the Supreme Court of Canada in 1981. It was clearly accepted by them that the United Kingdom Parliament had in 1981 full legal authority to legislate for Canada and it is noteworthy that (unlike Ireland in 1922) no attempt was made to produce a parallel constituent enactment in Canada. The United Kingdom Parliament, however, in the Canada Act of 1982 declared that no future Act of the Parliament of the United Kingdom should extend to Canada as part of its law, thus proposing to do what Dicey in *The Law of the Constitution* said no sovereign legislative body could do, namely make a partial abdication of its powers. If patriation is a reality Dicey's proposition can finally be regarded as indefensible.

The Crown

The constitutional change of 1982 displayed some differences between the legal and conventional roles of the Crown. Until 1982 petitions to Westminster to amend the BNA Act were forwarded from Canada in the name of Her Majesty's humble and obedient subjects. Some believed that by convention Her Majesty's subjects in Canada were addressing the Queen of Canada, not the Queen of the United Kingdom. But the Queen of Canada could not lay the petition before Parliament nor, legally play any part in its enactment. Who then issued the proclamation in Ottawa in April 1982 that brought the Act into force? By convention at least it was the Queen of Canada (acting perhaps on behalf of Elizabeth II of the United Kingdom).

Canada, for the immediate future at least, has retained the monarchy, though there have been suggestions that the Crown might at some point be replaced by a Canadian Head of State. That would require a constitutional amendment and by s. 41 of the Constitution any amendment affecting 'the office of the Queen' would require the unanimous consent of all the provinces. If the Governor-General were to be substituted for the Queen as Head of State some method of election or appointment would need to be provided and it might be thought expedient at that point to attempt some codification of the rules that affect the exercise of the existing prerogative powers of the Crown which at present rest on conventions clarified partly in Britain and partly in Canada. This might (as in Australia) prove difficult. It would be no easier in Britain.

Convention and law

Canada's recent experiences have also taught us some lessons about the part played in constitutional change by law and convention, and about the relation between them. In the two advisory opinions delivered by the Supreme Court of Canada in 1982 the nature of constitutional conventions and the mode of their establishment was considered at some length. They were said to rest upon three elements: precedent, principle and the political beliefs of the actors involved. In the second reference in which Quebec asserted the claim that convention had established its right to a veto on constitutional amendment[28] the Court gave a crucial importance to the third factor. In the first case the Court concluded that conventions, however firm politically, were not enforceable in the courts, but that this raised a justiciable question of fact (under the relevant Canadian legislation that authorises provincial and federal governments to seek advisory opinions from the courts).

Is there a possible model for British legislation here invoking judicial arbitration for disputed questions of constitutional convention, of which there may be many in the near future? Judicial answers to non-legal questions would not of course be legally binding, but they might carry weight, as it is hoped do the conclusions of Royal Commissions or Committees of Inquiry with judicial chairmen. If the conventions of the British Constitution are ever codified, some such panel of arbitrators or moderators may be needed. Can politicians be trusted to referee the governmental game?

Notes and references

1. *Reference Re Amendment of the Constitution of Canada* (1982) 125 DLR (3d) 1.
2. *Re Anti Inflation Act* [1976] 2 S.C.R. 373.
3. [1980]1 S.C.R. 914.
4. [1977]2 S.C.R. 134.
5. *Canadian Federation of Agriculture* v *A.G. Quebec* [1951] AC 179. Cf. the problem of characterising powers of cinema censorship in *Nova Scotia Board of Censors* v *McNeil* [1978] 2 S.C.R. 662.
6. Boggs v The Queen (1981) 2 S.C.R. 373.
7. *Reference Re Amendment of the Constitution of Canada* (1982) 125 DLR (3d)1.
8. Peter Hogg, *Constitutional Law of Canada* (1985), p. 76. See also Stephen A. Scott, 'Pussycat, Pussycat; or Patriation and the New Constitutional Amendment Processes' 20 *University of Western Ontario Law Review*, 247, 1982.
9. S. la Selva, 'Reflections on the Charter's Notwithstanding Clause', 63 *Dalhousie Review*, 383.
10. An ingenious suggestion has been made that provincial attempts to override the Charter could be frustrated by federal executive action to remove the authority of the Governor-General and the provincial Lieutenant-Governors to assent to Bills containing override provisions. See S.A. Scott, 'Entrenchment by Executive Action: a Partial Solution to "Legislative Override" ', 4 *Supreme Court Law Review* 303, 1982.
11. The French version – 'Liberté de circulation et d'établissement' – is better, though each sounds rather more like the regulation of traffic than the protection of civil liberty.
12. See *A.G. Quebec* v. *Quebec Protestant School Bds.* [1984] 2 S.C.R. 66 (restriction of access to English-speaking schools held invalid as inconsistent with the Charter).
13. *A.G. Quebec* v. *Blaikie* 1979 S.C.R. 1016. Manitoba also had an Official Language Act, passed in 1890, which has been held inconsistent with the BNA Act's bilingual guarantees (*A.G. Manitoba* v *Forest* [1979] 2 S.C.R. 32). Since all of Manitoba's statutes had been passed in English all the laws of Manitoba were in principle invalid but, pending their translation into French, Manitoba has been saved from constitutional dissolution by the Supreme Court's invocation of the principle of necessity (*Reference re Language Rights under the Manitoba Act, 1870* [1985] 1 S.C.R. 347. See also *Bilodeau* v *Attorney-General of Manitoba* (1986) 27 D.L.R. (4th) 39).
14. See Brian Slattery, 'Override Clauses under Section 33 (1983)', 61 *Canadian Bar Review* 391.
15. See Walter Tarnopolsky, *The Canadian Bill of Rights*, 2nd edn (1975), p. 143. In *Manuel* v *Attorney General* [1982] 3 All ER 822 the (UK) Court of Appeal was prepared to assume that Section 4 of the Statute of Westminster (requiring a recitation of the request and consent of a Dominion to British legislation) might be binding upon the British Parliament.
16. *In Re Singh and Minister of Employment and Immigration* (1985) 17 D.L.R. (4th) 422. Beetz J. held a section of the Immigration Act 1976 inoperative although enacted *subsequently* to the Federal Bill of Rights on the ground that it was inconsistent with the Bill of Rights and did not contain any ousting clause (at 441–2).
17. HL 176 (1978), p. 33.
18. In *R.* v *Drybones* [1970] S.C.R. 282 a section of the Indian Act was held to be inoperative as infringing the equality guarantees in the 1960 Act.
19. *Re Ontario Film and Video Appreciation Society* (1984) 45 O.R. (2d) 80.
20. *Law Society of Upper Canada v. Skapinker* [1984] 1 S.C.R. 357.
21. *Hunter* v *Southam* [1984] 2 S.C.R. 145.

22. *A.G. (Quebec)* v *Quebec Protestant School Boards* [1984] 2 S.C.R. 66.
23. See D. Gibson, 'The Charter of Rights and the Private Sector (1982)', 12 *Manitoba Law Journal* 213; Yves de Montigny, 'Section 32 and Equality Rights' in A.F. Bayefsky, *Equality Rights and the Canadian Charter of Rights and Freedoms* (1985); P.W. Hogg, *Constitutional Law of Canada*, 2nd edn (1985), p. 674.
24. Including acts done under prerogative powers. See *R.* v. *Operation Dismantle*, 3 DLR (4th) 193.
25. *AG Quebec* v. *Quebec Protestant School Boards* [1984] 2 S.C.R. 66.
26. See Brian Slattery, 'The Independence of Canada', (1983) 5 *Supreme Court Law Review*, 369. Cf. Peter W. Hogg, 'Patriation of the Canadian Constitution: Has it been Achieved?' *Queen's Law Journal*, 123, 1982.
27. A term invented by Sir Kenneth Wheare (see *The Constitutional Structure of the Commonwealth* (London: Oxford University Press, 1960), chap. IV).
28. *Re Attorney-General of Quebec and Attorney-General of Canada* (1982), 140 DLR (3d), 385.

  Although Quebec's attempt to assert its constitutional veto failed in 1982, a meeting of all the provincial and Federal first ministers in June 1987 has reached a new constitutional Accord. Under it Quebec has been offered guarantees on a number of issues including immigration and the nomination of members to the Senate and Supreme Court. An Amendment to the Constitution Act is to be proposed giving effect to these changes and providing that the Constitution of Canada shall be interpreted in a manner consistent with the recognition that Quebec constitutes within Canada a distinct society and that the existence of French-speaking Canadians in Quebec and elsewhere in Canada constitutes a fundamental characteristic of Canada.

  What difference this provision will make to the interpretation of the Constitution Act is a question to which, for the time being, no obvious answer presents itself.

PART C
THE REACTIVE
CONSTITUTIONS

9   Japan (1947): Forty years of the post-war Constitution*
Lawrence W. Beer

Modern Japan has experienced two constitutional revolutions, one from the latter half of the nineteenth century until 1945, and the other since 1945. By 'constitutional revolution' is meant a long process in which a fundamental shift takes place in constitutional values diffused throughout society by means of law, administrative actions, judicial decisions, and education, both formal and informal.

Previous to these modern constitutional revolutions, neo-Confucianism, already well known and understood in 1600, was adapted to produce what might be called the Tokugawa constitutional revolution.[1] In contrast to this, the two modern constitutional revolutions were not precipitated by the maturing of internal forces over a long period. They were assimilative reactions to Western legal traditions. As a result, contemporary Japanese law blends traditional elements with European (especially German) civil law and legal theory, and Anglo-American common law traditions.

This chapter analyses (i) prewar and present Japanese constitutionalism and the revision debate; (ii) legal culture, embracing the legal system and values, as related to such issues as freedom of expression; and (iii) some problems pending in Japanese constitutional law.

The two modern constitutional revolutions

Pre-1945 concepts of constitutionalism and law affect legal interpretation and debate today. Many leading judges, prosecutors, legal scholars and lawyers have had to straddle mentally two constitutional eras, and received much of their formative training and experience under the pre-1945 legal system. The Meiji constitutional revolution (1868–1945)[2] institutionalised the system against which much of the post-1945 constitutional system has been a reaction, but also laid the foundation for aspects of the post-1945 revolution.

Study of the law, administrative practice and police developments affecting freedom of expression between 1868 and 1945 suggests

* This chapter is a substantial revision of my 'Constitutional Revolution in Japanese Law, Society and Politics', *Modern Asian Studies*, Vol. 16, No. 1, 1982, pp. 33–67.

that most parts of a thorough system for restraining free speech had fallen into place by 1913 after piecemeal development, and that enforcement of the Peace Preservation Law of 1925 and subsequent related law brought a final touch of unusual sophistication to the pre-1945 system of control, for which the military were not as responsible as sometimes assumed.[3] Neither the legal system nor traditional culture seems to have honoured individual rights, as these came to be understood in Japanese law under Western influence.

Rights and freedoms were quite new concepts in Meiji Japan. However, the absence in Japan of a long and coherent tradition of liberalism does not imply that the Meiji constitutional revolution did not vastly expand pre-existing group tendencies to assertion for and against policies in accord with their sense of justice and self-interest.[4] In general, the maintenance of civil liberties in a country does not depend on explicit emphasis in law or society upon rights and freedoms, as understood in the law and intellectual traditions of the West, but on: (i) a mixture of institutionalised values which taken together favour liberty; (ii) the existence of competitive, as opposed to authoritarian politics; (iii) actual expression of agreement or dissent on substantive issues along with the possibility of dissent with impunity; (iv) such a balance of social and political forces that those favouring rights outweigh those opposed.[5] The sociological interplay of such factors in Japan from the 1860s until the 1930s resulted in a growing awareness of individual legal rights, as understood today in Japanese and Western law, among many scholars, officials and other citizens at the same time that a modern system of political repression was being refined and increasingly enforced in service to the Emperor.

The constitutional system of Japan today, reflecting a quite different interplay of factors, stresses enforcement of individual rights. The present widespread acceptance of the constitution in Japan rests in part on a continuing reaction against a prewar system that failed in the mind-numbing defeat of the Second World War. It does not seem probable that Japan would soon have become a constitutional democracy without the shock of losing the Pacific War and without massive Occupation support for Japan's liberal forces.[6] Modern political systems which are systematically authoritarian, whether left or right in orientation and however inefficient in the light of abstract goals, appear much simpler to maintain as regimes than constitutional democracies. Japan's authoritarian apparatus, by comparative standards, was efficient in its methods of political control during the militarist period, and not likely to evolve along more liberal lines.

The widespread, deep, and genuine loyalty to the emperor-nation of that earlier era is not much discussed in public today. The rejection now of major military power under the pacifist provisions of Article 9[7] and the denial of power to the Emperor under Chapter I[8] of the Constitution seem intimately linked in the Japanese mind to the utter national failure resulting from total and militant loyalty to the Emperor. Just as pre-war children were programmatically indoctrinated in *kokutai* ideology, so post-war children have been conditioned systematically to believe in freedom ever since the first student was required to memorise the new constitution during the Occupation (1945–52).[9] The shock of those who had believed unquestionably in the invincibility of the nation under the Emperor, although profound, is difficult to convey to today's Japanese youth.

Closely associated in the collective memory of the 'militarist period' is its severe limitation of freedom of thought, freedom of expression, and other individual rights. The radical post-war rejection by the overwhelming majority of the pre-war military-bureaucratic system, which is seen as having misused the imperial institution for its own ends, explains in part why efforts to alter notably the status of Japan's Self-Defence Forces, *or* the Emperor, *or* individual rights have been perceived by many liberal and leftist Japanese as an attempt to rip apart the entire fair fabric of the 1947 Constitution, and not simply as an attempt to modify one of its elements. Whether or not this perception represents a persuasive assessment of relationships, the three parts are commonly seen as crucial and inseparable; no other components of the new constitutional structure arouse such noteworthy emotion. More power to the Emperor would mean, it is thought, more power to the military which would mean expanded police powers and less democratic freedom; and conversely, strict limitation of imperial and military functions in government is necessary to assure the maintenance and development of constitutional rights. In sum, the term 'Peace Constitution' is used in Japan as a reference to the anti-militarist provisions of the constitution, its guarantee of individual rights, and imperial powerlessness.

The revision controversy
The Constitution of Japan has not been amended even once, as the constitutional revolution of post-war Japan has continued to take root. As it has been applied, it seems sufficiently flexible to remove any pressing need for amendment. The Meiji Constitution was never amended, unless the establishment of the present constitution is viewed technically as a constitutional amendment.[10] The aspects of perception described above seem a critical factor underlying the seriousness of academic, legal and political debate on questions of constitutional interpretation and revision over the past thirty-five years. A litmus test

applied to scholars and politicians, as well as to laws and judicial decisions on many issues is how they relate to the tripartite revision issue. So thoroughly integrated into political and legal rhetoric is this constitutional sensitivity that court cases concerning a wide range of subjects – for example, history textbook certification, academic freedom, demonstrations, the rating of teachers, and the Japan–United States Security Treaty – have evoked references to all aspects of the tripartite image of Emperor, military, and individual rights.

Once the Allied Occupation ended in 1952, the revision controversy gathered momentum and reached a peak during the mid- and late-1950s following the formation of the Liberal-Democratic Party (LDP) and the Japan Socialist Party (JSP) by coalitions of smaller parties. Some powerful LDP leaders wanted revision precisely to strengthen the positions of the Emperor and the military and to limit individual rights; but this does not mean that there was a widespread desire in the LDP for a return to the political system of the wartime period from the Manchurian Incident (1931) till late 1945, during which period bureaucrats and militarists decisively replaced elected party politicians as top leaders of the government.[11]

At least six factors seem to have rendered improbable any constitutional revision in the near future, assuming no severe economic upheaval:

(1) The Security Treaty Crisis of 1960 seems to have been more of a community rite affirming consensual democracy than an anti-treaty or revolutionary struggle.[12] It was the largest mass involvement in Japanese history,[13] and it may well have suggested to LDP leaders such as Prime Minister Ikeda Hayato that an effort at major constitutional change, whether needed or not, would awaken organised opposition on a much grander scale than that of 1960.

(2) The Sunagawa Decision of the Supreme Court[14] spoke of Japan's natural right of self-defence and held Japan's Co-operation and Security Treaty with the United States to be constitutional under Article 9. This decision may have reduced the revisionists' sense of urgency about revision for the sake of Japan's military security. The present Security Treaty of 1960 was similarly upheld by the Supreme Court on 2 April 1969.[15] Two other aspects of Japan's politics tend to support Article 9's anti-militarism and Article 66.2, a constitutional requirement that 'the Prime Minister and other Ministers of State must be civilians'. First, over 80 per cent of the Japanese people support Article 9 and the Security Treaty; 57 per cent favour maintaining the Self-Defence Forces at present levels, while only 19 per cent support an increase in military strength; and very few Japanese exhibit a sense of external military threat.[16] Most feel there are greater internal than external threats to the

system, and even internal threats are minimal. Second, Article 9 has operated in such a way that the military has been removed from the political drama, and, barring an unforeseeable crisis, this has negated the possibility of a military *coup d'état* in Japan. If Japan had a conventional constitution, without Article 9, a strong military, whatever its political alignments, would have at its disposal the instruments of coercion which, Japanese history suggests, it would not be reticent to use politically.

(3) The issuance in 1964, under the leadership of Professor Takayanagi Kenzō, of a non-committal final report by the Commission on the Constitution (1957–64; *Kempō Chōsakai*) also discouraged further revision efforts, at least for some time. No recommendations for amendment were made after six years of hearings, study and debate.[17] From its inception, many critics viewed the Commission as a revisionist tool; if such was the original intent of the LDP, it was frustrated. Many scholars and politicians refused to participate in or support the Commission's activities. Whether their participation would have added even greater force to the Commission's final refusal to recommend changes is a moot point. In any case, many opponents of the Commission were actively involved in parallel study groups, which included Commission members, during the long debate over every important and technical provision of the Constitution of Japan. In its function, this debate may be viewed as a Japanese-style *constitutional convention*, with long consultations at home and abroad, and widespread debates in pursuit of national consensus. Japan had had no opportunity for such a 'convention' under the Occupation.

(4) In the late 1940s and early 1950s, food, clothing, and other basic needs were the preoccupations of most, leaving a small minority to debate ideologies and constitutional ideas. The post-war revolution of thought had a slow start. By far the most frequently cited reason in 1979 for Japan's peace since the Second World War was 'the personally experienced misery of war,'[18] and popular support for the 'peace constitution' is perhaps equally attributable to that experience, at least initially. The fact is that popular assimilation and support for the Constitution have grown, and militate strongly against revision. This has been primarily the result of education, accumulating experience of the operation of the Constitution, prosperity, the absence of any appealing alternative, the work of the Commission on the Constitution, and the long-term absence of a perceived external military threat.

(5) The LDP lost in the late 1960s and 1970s the overwhelming parliamentary power necessary to revise the constitution. This, and factional differences within the LDP render revision very unlikely.

Inside and outside the political parties, Japan has many power centres, groups organised along relatively non-authoritarian, quasi-familial lines. A few such centres seem dominant – such as the ruling political party, the Ministries (especially the Finance Ministry), the judiciary, mass media combines, and industry federations – with lesser interest groups or domains filling out the system. In general, loyalty to the small face-to-face group is primary,[19] and it is quite common for such groups or factions to be in competition with, or at best indifferent to, the others. But they can also freely enter into alliances of mutual benefit, usually for limited periods and for particular purposes. This often happens, for example, among factions of the LDP, and this capacity for making and breaking alliances makes the system dynamic and highly organised. But a consensus within the LDP to revise the Constitution is certainly not readily foreseeable, and co-operation with other political parties is much more unlikely. The distribution of seats in the Diet remains fairly stable, the LDP's capacity to retain control of the Diet being primarily due to the absence of an alternative appealing to the voters. Even after atypical LDP landslide victories in 1980 and 1986 the LDP's numbers[20] were short of the two-thirds majority required to amend the Constitution.[21]

(6) Also militating against constitutional revision is the institutionalisation of the Constitution of Japan through law and judicial decisions. The district, high and Supreme Courts of Japan have been much too diverse in their ideological leanings and interpretive methods to allow blanket characterisations of judicial performance since 1947 with respect to constitutional law. But the net cumulative effect of their work in millions of cases, civil, criminal and administrative, has significantly strengthened the roots of rule of law democracy in Japanese soil.[22] In addition, family courts, Civil Liberties Commissioners, and Local Administrative Counsellors have also brought the law of the Constitution to bear in resolving millions of disputes in a quiet atmosphere.[23] District courts more often than appellate courts[24] have stressed civil liberties in their findings; but even the now conservative Supreme Court has notably nurtured freedom and procedural rights of the accused[25] while allowing creeping restraints on the rights of public employees, on and off the job.[26] (Other examples are discussed later.) The courts are restrained by an insufficiency of judges, jurisprudence that is sometimes self-restrictive, and other factors touched on later. In general, the courts have guarded jealously their tradition since the Meiji period[27] of judicial independence in deciding individual cases; they have also upheld their institutional prerogatives in dealing with the Diet and administrators.

Legal professionals as well as politicians, ranging from rightists to moderate liberals to democratic socialists to those who view Marxists as rank conservatives, seem cautious about the intentions of their political foes on the revision issue. It is more a debate among élites who would speak on behalf of the citizenry than an issue like economics or education preoccupying the public in general. Many Japanese of otherwise differing views would like the revision controversy to cool down sufficiently to allow a complete rewriting of the Constitution of Japan into appropriate Japanese language without changing the intent of any important provision. That may of course be an impossible dream; but the present translation into Japanese of some parts originally in English is not adequate, and may be an unnecessary reminder of the document's Occupation-period origins.[28]

Some anti-revisionists maintain the LDP policies and the decisions of conservative courts have already revised the Constitution in fact, if not formally, in pursuit of a 'reverse course' preference for the pre-war order.[29] Surely, in Japan as in past and present democratic law and politics the world over, one can find much evidence of an abiding preference for anti-democratic policies and judicial decisions at both the official and private levels of society; but the contention that substantive constitutional revision has occurred seems a doubtful political judgment and an oversimplification of the tasks of courts in Japan, unless by 'revision' one really means 'interpretation' which one finds needlessly restrictive. Moreover, the problems in interpreting the Article 9 'no war clause' are unprecedented in world judicial history; they cannot be solved or whisked away by too facile a use of 'political question' doctrine, the view in law that courts have no right to decide certain politically sensitive issues such as those affecting national security.[30]

Japan's power centres criticise each other for wrong-headedness regarding the constitution, and in doing so they manifest the competitive politics essential to the maintenance of liberties. Anti-revisionists retain sensitivity to the repressive past and show awareness that democracy is a vulnerable system of law and government always in some respects in tension with its professed ideals. By 1986, survey research indicated that the Constitution and the courts, along with the quality mass media (especially the major national newspapers) had become the most respected national institutions, as both élites and the general public grew confident in their democracy.

Japan's constitutional theory
The Constitution of Japan is now the most authoritative reference

point for public values in Japan and is, as Edward Seidensticker has noted, 'among the Sacred Books of the East.'[31] The constitution's theoretical thrust is based on natural law suppositions and on the attribution of intrinsic value to the individual person. So many formal philosophies and ideologies co-exist in Japan's political and intellectual worlds that it is hard to discern any agreed-upon general theory underpinning Japanese constitutional democracy. Among the pillars and struts of Japanese thought are traditional ideas drawn from Buddhism, Confucianism and Shinto, as well as theories related to Christianity and Marxism; but how they relate to each other, if at all, is elusive.[32] But it is clear that customary law has had a powerful influence. Though generally unwritten, these rules are partially expressed in such documents as company rules.[33] A sophisticated system of rules with effective sanctions governs *oyabun-kobun* (quasi-parental-filial) group structures[34] and gives specificity to such motive forces as *amae* (reciprocal dependency[35] and loyalty. Nagao Ryūichi suggests that a better understanding of the enigmatic urge to absolute loyalty – not simply to loyalty – may be a key to understanding the history of Japanese social and political ideas.[36]

Every five years the Institute of Statistical Mathematics in Tokyo conducts comprehensive surveys of Japanese national character. The results indicate that there has been no appreciable modification of a clear Japanese preference for traditional values since 1953. Among the possible approaches to clarifying the principles underpinning or at variance with the Constitution is analysis of the reasons given by voters for their voting preferences. An attitude study of 1,500 Tokyo voters w made in 1978 by a team of Japanese scholars.[37] Analysis indicated that ideology and party preference were relatively unimportant. The single most important determinant of political choice (the key factor to 29 per cent of voters, and a major factor to 53 per cent)[38] was the image of the candidate as expressing and supporting traditional values and what might be termed 'the good Japanese way' of doing things. But a most striking contrast to this preference for traditionalism in the personal style of candidates is found in the analysis of the positive elements in the images which voters entertained of liberalism, capitalism, socialism, and communism: the most likely to succeed were candidates, ideologies, and parties presenting an image of flexibility, modernity, conservatism, and economic egalitarianism somehow combined. For maximum legitimacy, a leader was seen as combining great respect for traditional values and modes of human interaction with concern for constitutional freedoms and economic policies promoting equality. Forty-two per cent of the voters studied considered themselves entirely unaffected by political ideologies such as the four above;

only 1 per cent consider socialism-communism preferable in general to liberalism-capitalism, but only 10 per cent rate the latter pairing preferable to the former.

Along with the strong support for Article 9 pacifism (*not* a general philosophy of pacifism) referred to earlier, values such as hierarchy, equality, groupism, freedom and loyalty form at least part of the structure of operative constitutional theory in Japan. Replacing in some measure and without much emotion their earlier loyalty to the Emperor, perhaps the generality of Japanese now share a loyalty to the Constitution, not as a formal document, but as a summation of preferred values and guidelines for public action. What the Constitution rejects seems as important as the rights it guarantees, but the whole structure rests on a recognition of the equal dignity of each individual. As the late constitutional lawyer Miyazawa Toshiyoshi once expressed it, while contrasting pre-war and post-war Japan, 'Every day I enjoy breathing freedom again.'

Constitutional culture and law

The core new element in post-1945 Japanese constitutionalism is legally protected freedom and individual rights, based primarily on the Preamble and Chapter III (Articles 10 to 40) of the Constitution.[39] Japan would very likely be a well-organised (some might say, over-organised) nation under almost any imaginable governmental system; but much was added to order by the present constitutional revolution. The Preamble proclaims that 'sovereign power resides with the people', and Article 13 that 'all of the people shall be respected as individuals'. This abstract latter provision has been invoked by the courts as the textual basis for both establishing and limiting certain constitutional rights. The individual person has replaced the Emperor as the highest public value. The Emperor is a 'symbol of the State and of the unity of the people' (Article 1); and 'he shall not have powers related to government' (Article 4). This is the first time the powers of the Emperor have ever been legally limited, although historically he seldom, and, since 1868, almost never, actually exercised any political powers. Although continuities do exist which link present and pre-war institutions, significant changes have been made in their organisation and function.[40] The Cabinet has no military membership and is collectively responsible to the Diet (Article 66). Constitutional rights, although in fact sometimes subordinate to informal in-group pressures and bureaucratic presumptions, are more freely exercised than in pre-war Japan, vastly expanded in scope, usually honoured by the police and prosecutors, and justiciable or conciliable in public tribunals.[41]

The mass media serve more adequately than before as a quasi-constitutional Fourth Estate, a power centre relatively independent of any political party or Ministry, without which Japanese democracy might crumble.[42] The Diet is the 'highest organ of State power' (Article 41) except for the ruling political party, yet subject to judicial review (Article 81) of the constitutionality of its official acts.[43] The court system, supervised by the Supreme Court, is judicially and administratively independent. Finally, the status of women has improved markedly, in both fact and law.[44]

The Supreme Court and lower courts have the 'power to determine the constitutionality of any law, order, regulation or official act';[45] but like most court systems, they exercise this power against other branches of government only rarely. They are further restrained by predominantly civil law perceptions of the judicial role in government, a role of democratic deference to the elected parliament.[46] The technical effect on future law of a judgment of unconstitutionality is still debated, but a 'conclusion in a decision of a superior court shall bind courts below in respect of the case concerned', and not in general.[47] For example, if a legal provision is held unconstitutional by the Supreme Court, it is nevertheless possible that the same or other courts may rule differently in other cases on the same issue, and it is possible that the Diet will not pass remedial legislation to remove the offending provision. A judgment of unconstitutionality does not necessarily trigger among lawyers, legal scholars, mass media leaders or politicians the requisite sustained pressure on the Diet to take legislative action to support such a judgment.[48] If the judicial decision is that an official action is invalid, no court doctrine has resolved the scholarly debate on whether some legal provision enables a court to order an administrative agency to take remedial action.[49] Article 37 of the Constitution guarantees the accused in a criminal case 'the right to a speedy and public trial'; but some political cases have languished in the courts for years. Widely spaced trial sessions characterise Japan's civil law system, courts have been used at times as political forums, causing additional delays, and judges are generally meticulous in moving slowly towards a decision. These factors occasionally constitute a systematic obstacle to quick justice.

The conviction rate in Japan is extremely high, at over 99 per cent. But over the years criminological reasons rather than insufficient evidence have led prosecutors not to prosecute around 40 per cent of serious violations of the Criminal Code. A lay Prosecution Review Commission regularly reviews a prosecutor's determinations on whether or not to file charges; these organs recommend a change or indictment or a reinvestigation of the case about

10 per cent of the time, and such recommendations are accepted by the Chief of the District Public Prosecutor's Office in 30 per cent of the cases.[50] 'In Japan in 1971 less than 4 per cent of persons convicted were given a jail sentence and almost two-thirds of those were suspended. Over 96 per cent of persons convicted of a crime were punished only with a fine', usually a small fine. That year, 44.7 per cent of the convicted went to prison in the United States and for much longer periods than the Japanese sentenced. Criminal justice in Japan is generally not severe.

Freedom of expression is a *sine qua non* of any constitutional democracy. A review of the status of freedom of expression will thus be a particularly useful way of conveying reasonably reliable perspectives on the state of Japan's democratic law. Issues to be touched on include the freedom to demonstrate, mass media freedom, privacy, obscenity, and textbook certification.

The law of demonstrations

In any assessment of the strength of freedom, we need to study judicial decisions, which are the backbone of the law on liberty; but especially where values differ from Western ones, we need to understand the society in order to comprehend how law is perceived and how it functions. For example, the Japanese commitment to groupism instead of to individualism has not, and does not, prevent people from resorting to the law to protect their rights and interests.[51] Nor has it been an obstacle to the people's support for freedom of expression.[52] But it has affected the forms that these take.

There is a strong sense of *group* right rather than individual right in public contexts, analogous to an individualist sense of right in the West. Largely due to this, privately and freely organised demonstrations have been very frequent in post-war Japan. Freedom of association and freedom of assembly have been central aspects of freedom of expression in Japan, and contrast sharply with the pre-war suppression of these freedoms. Highly vocal but non-violent group dissent or advocacy by groups seems more fully accepted public behaviour in Japan than in the United States.[53] Even peaceful marches sometimes arouse considerable public ire in the United States, as they did during the civil rights and anti-war movements of the 1960s and 1970s.[54]

A number of agencies and laws regulate demonstrations in Japan,[55] but the most important are the local 'public safety ordinances' (*kōan jōrei*) and 'public safety commissions' (*kōan iinkai*) of prefectures or cities.[56] The key constitutional provision on freedom of expression is Article 21:

Freedom of assembly and association as well as speech, press, and all other forms of expression are guaranteed.

2. No censorship shall be maintained, nor shall the secrecy of any means of communication be violated.

Basic Supreme Court doctrine on demonstrations and other 'collective activities' was laid down in the landmark Tokyo Ordinance Decision in 1960,[57] which held that local authorities are obliged under public safety ordinances to grant permits with 'maximum respect for freedom of expression'. Denial of a permit is legitimate only when a collective activity 'will directly endanger the maintenance of the public peace' and thus contravene 'the public welfare' (*kōkyō' no fukushi*).

Later judicial decisions have followed and refined *Tokyo* doctrine.[58] Although the 'public welfare' was defined early (1950) by the Supreme Court as 'the maintenance of order and respect for the fundamental human rights of the individual',[59] for many years the judicial use of the term evoked unease and protest from many constitutional lawyers and opposition politicians. 'Public welfare' reminded them of terms used during the ultra-nationalist period to urge all to forget their own interests and revere the Emperor.[60]

One of the most significant developments in constitutional law since 1947 may be the decreased use, especially in the lower courts, of abstract formulations of public welfare doctrine, and increased specificity since 1965.[61] The courts have honed more concrete criteria for determining what the public welfare is in each class of cases. These technical developments are in some cases due more to changes in judicial education, the influence of legal scholars, and accumulated judicial experience under the 1947 Constitution than to liberalism. For example, *Tokyo* doctrine, which was handed down in the aftermath of the 1960 Security Treaty Crisis, de-emphasised the place where demonstrations are held. In fact, *Tokyo* upholds the right of authorities to regulate mass demonstrations 'in any place whatsoever', contending that debate on such matters as place is 'completely profitless'. But a 1970 Supreme Court decision hinged upon the meaning of 'public place' (*kōkyō no basho*) in the Hiroshima prefectural ordinance. It was defined by the judges as 'a place which in reality is generally open and can be used and entered freely by unspecified persons'.[62] The ordinance requires a permit only for a demonstration which is to take place in a public place. The accused were public employees who staged a demonstration outside the prefectural capitol building without obtaining a permit. They contended that the ordinance did not apply, since the location of the demonstration was not a public place; the judges disagreed, and they lost their case.

Vigorous exercise of the freedom to demonstrate by groups representing local and national interests will probably continue little affected by adverse court decisions. Most public group actions in Japan are orderly and peaceful, and are often attended with colourful pageantry and a festival spirit, a healthy blend of seriousness and play. Convictions for illegal collective activities are usually for physical obstruction or violence which would be held illegal in most or all of the world's other democratic courts; and as noted earlier, Japan's courts are quite lenient in sentencing. On the other hand, the Supreme Court has been criticised when it has overturned acquittals handed down by both a trial court and an appellate court; this it did about twenty times between 1974 and 1979 in civil liberties cases. Restriction of the political activities of public employees to voting alone deserves special mention. In the late 1960s, the Supreme Court recognised that different degrees of restraint were appropriate to a management-level official in a Ministry and a janitor in the public monopoly tobacco corporation.[63] But from 1973 on decisions of the Supreme Court affected adversely the political freedom of public employees. The privatisation of businesses such as the tobacco industry in the mid-1980s brought many out from under this restrictive law.

In the famous *Sarufutsu* Case,[64] a postal employee was convicted for putting up six political posters on a public bulletin board during his leisure hours. The issues still debated include the proper delineation of limits on the rights of teachers, postal workers, telecommunications workers, and transportation workers to strike or to engage in political activities, and whether administrative discipline (most common), criminal penalties or no punishment should be applied for related violations of the laws governing public employees.

Some aspects of freedom for the mass media

Along with group activism, freedom of the press is particularly close to the core of Japanese democracy, because the mass media may represent the only power centres that are effectively organised, separate from the government, linked with important people and groups, especially in Tokyo and Osaka, and whose influences spread throughout the nation.

Japan's print and broadcast media are mammoth in scale, technologically impressive, and socially pervasive.[65] Daily newspapers with nationwide circulation like the *Asahi Shinbun*, *Mainichi Shinbun*, *Yomiuri Shinbun*, and *Nihon Keizai Shinbun* print over fifty million copies each day, about 20 per cent of which are distributed in Tokyo. The newspaper's political roles are complex, although the major papers do not endorse political candidates. For example, the press helped to sustain the crisis atmosphere for a time during the 1960 Security Treaty Crisis, they moderated the tension in most cases during the nationwide University Crisis of 1968–69, they massively publicised the Lockheed scandals and trials during the 1970s after disclosures were made in the United States, and they have played a major role in activating, publicising and supporting the consensus against pollution since 1970. The principal organisation for news-papers, television and radio is the *Nihon Shinbun Kyōkai* (Japan Newspaper Editors and Publishers Association), which at times when a need is felt can form a cohesive power centre by alliance among its leaders in the face of external threat. For example, during the Hakata Station Film Controversy of 1969, the media united to oppose a court order for evidence to be presented (TV film of a student-police confrontation) in the alleged absence of other or better evi-dence. The Supreme Court upheld the courts' prerogatives after months of well-organised media resistance.

The University of Missouri world survey of press freedom rates Japan highly, but has noted industry centralisation and self-regulation as problems. On the latter score, the *'kisha kurabu'* (reporters' clubs) attached to politicians or agencies may be men-tioned. Reporters from competing papers do not so much compete for news as form a coherent group which may determine when and what news is suitable for release to their respective papers. Stable ties can develop between a 'reliable source' and a press club; the wishes of both the club and the source may heavily influence what a reporter decides to convey to the public. (Foreign correspondents were not allowed at all until the mid-1980s.) There is some merit in the system, because secrecy-loving officials would probably obstruct access to information more substantially, if the cordial relations of mutual trust with the press did not exist. On the other hand, this system of agency-media and reporter–reporter relations too effectively limits the freedom of informaton, and is one reason why news of such affairs as the Lockheed scandals derived first from foreign sources rather than from Japanese investigative journalism. The right of access to information (*akusesuken*) and the individual's right to know have been major themes studied by specialists such as Itō Masami, Shimizu Hideo, Okudaira Yasuhiro, and Horibe Masao.

In the *Nishiyama* Decision of 1978,[66] the Supreme Court made its first ruling on the relationships between state secrets and news-gatherings. While attached to the Foreign Ministry, Nishiyama Takichi, a reporter for the *Mainichi Shinbun*, gained access to secret cables on the negotiation of terms for the reversion of Okinawa to Japan. Nishiyama had received this information from Hasumi

Kikuko, a girl friend working in the Ministry. At a Diet committee meeting on 27 March 1972, a Socialist (JSP) member made the contents of the cables, received somehow from Nishiyama, a part of his attack on government policies. The documents contradicted the government's earlier assurances that no secret agreements had been made with the U.S. The Supreme Court held: (i) that the courts have the authority to determine what constitutes a state secret under the National Public Employees Law (and what, for example, is merely a political secret); (ii) that the government's secrecy regarding international negotiations in this case was appropriate; (iii) that the government's failure to bring the full facts before the Diet did not conflict with the constitutional order or constitute illegal secrecy; and (iv) that although free newsgathering and reporting are of special importance to the people's democratic right to know and freedom of expression generally, Nishiyama violated the legal prohibition against inducing divulgence of official secrets by a public employee in his ethically questionable relationship with Hasumi, a married woman.

In conjunction with closer operational military co-operation with the United States in the 1980s, the LDP Government repeatedly brought to the Diet a disputed anti-espionage bill, the first in post-war Japan. Among other concerns, opponents think a strong freedom of information act should precede a security law which might exacerbate the government's penchant for secrecy regarding consumer product safety as well as political affairs.

The right of privacy has been another noteworthy issue in recent law. Expanded press freedom since 1945 has occasioned an increase in journalistic excursions into the private lives of political leaders, other public figures, and ordinary citizens (unknown but for a cruel *exposé*).[67] The former have served the people's right to know about and criticise the famous and the powerful. According to a survey, both well-known and unknown victims of defamation and violation of privacy more often suffer in silence and 'go to bed weeping' (*nakineiri suru*) than assert their legal rights as individuals. The consensus among scholars seems to be that there have been too few legal charges lodged by victims. Where any redress has been sought, the more common solution has been a conciliatory out-of-court settlement with public and private apologies and monetary compensation by publishers.

Courts and scholars alike have strongly supported the rights to privacy (*puraibashii*) and good name, but there seems to have been a low demand for the legal protection of these rights at least until the 1970s. In sharp contrast to official secrecy, the right of privacy seems to have been less honoured in group-oriented Japan than the right of families, occupational groups or other groups or communities to know about the affairs of their members, and to impose sanctions for deviance. For example, the institution of ostracism from the community (*mura hachibu*) for non-conformity is a persistent problem, according to Japan's Civil Liberties Bureau.[68] On the other hand, if one values the positive aspects of the strong Japanese sense of community, one must hope that a stress on privacy rights will not unduly disturb it.

The constitutional right of privacy was first established in Japan not by a law, but by a 1964 Tokyo district court decision against Mishima Yukio in a case involving his novel *Utage no Ato* (*After the Banquet*).[69] The novel, serialised in *Chūō Kōron* in 1961, dealt in thinly veiled fashion with marital affairs of Arita Hachirō, a Socialist (JSP) politician and unsuccessful gubernatorial candidate in the 1960 Tokyo elections. Arita sued Mishima, who was ordered to pay a substantial amount in damages. The emergence of the right of privacy is an example of the considerable influence of Japanese legal scholars on some areas of the law, the fruitful interaction of campus and court, and the importation of a legal concept from American law into Japanese legal discourse.

The constitutional basis for the privacy right is found in the sentence, 'All the people shall be respected as individuals' in Article 13, while code law provision is detected in Articles 709 and 710 of the Civil Code, under which a person is bound to make compensation for intentional or negligent violation of the right of another, whether 'injury was to the person, liberty, or reputation of another or to his property rights'. Among other noteworthy privacy cases are the following:

(1)   A 1969 Supreme Court decision held that, as an aspect of the right of privacy, one has the right not to be photographed against one's will during an illegal demonstration unless the photography was necessary to a criminal investigation.[70]

(2)   A 1969 Tokyo high court decision in the Kato Case required a weekly magazine to pay remuneration and to apologise publicly in a national newspaper, on grounds of damage to good name and privacy rights.[71] The magazine at issue claimed that two famous TV and film personalities cohabited before marriage, which was denied.

(3)   In 1970, an injunction to ban the showing of an art film on the grounds of privacy violation was denied.[72] The film dealt with the early amorous and political affairs of an elderly feminist politician, Kamichika Ichiko; but she herself had publicised her private life on a number of prior occasions, thus negating

in the court's view the confidentiality factor necessary for a valid claim of privacy violation.

(4) The 1977 *Kawabata* Case was settled out of court with public apologies for lack of circumspection. The bereaved family of the late Nobel Prize-winning novelist, Kawabata Yasunari, sued the publisher and author of a novel which suggested that Kawabata's 1972 suicide was linked to indiscreet relations with the family maid, apparently an outcast *burakumin*.[73]

The increase in civil defamation suits in the early 1970s exemplifies the utility of analysing the side effects of specific legal changes.[74] An important but unintended and unforeseen by-product of legal change in one issue area influenced the effects and applications of law in another. Prior to 1970, very few civil defamation suits had been brought to court compared, for example, to German and French experience under similar defamation laws.[75] In the early 1970s, the success of groups and individuals bringing civil suits against companies for injury or illness caused by pollution was thoroughly publicised. As a result, popular awareness of the possibility of effective court action against newspapers and other media enterprises for civil defamation rose dramatically and so did the number of successful suits.[76]

The obscenity question is another media-related issue affected by the second modern constitutional revolution. Under Article 175 of the Criminal Code, various laws regulating the media, the police laws, obscenity regulation, public security maintenance and thought control were sometimes linked in the Japanese official mind before 1945.[77] Today, such connections are seen by few officials and citizens. Since the Occupation period, Japan has been again rather tolerant, producing large numbers of erotic books, pictures, magazines, comic books, advertisements, TV broadcasts, motion pictures and tape recordings.[78]

Two of the major Supreme Court decisions on obscenity, both concerning translations of foreign works are: the 1957 *Lady Chatterley's Lover* Case[79] and the 1969 *de Sade* Case.[80] Article 175 provides penalties for 'a person who distributes or sells an obscene writing, picture or other object or who publicly displays the same . . .'[81] In *Chatterley* the Supreme Court held that twelve obscene passages at issue infected D.H. Lawrence's entire work with obscenity, and defined obscenity as follows:[82] 'In order for a writing to be obscene, it is required that it wantonly arouse and stimulate sexual desire, offend the normal sense of shame, and run counter to proper concepts of sexual morality.'

The *Chatterley* decision has continued to draw criticism from liberal scholars for arrogating to the courts 'a clinical role' in case society's moral views become lax. In *de Sade*, the court generally followed *Chatterley* doctrine, but seemed to some analysts to stress artistry and intellectual values more than *Chatterley* in the following passage:[83]

> There may be cases where the artistry and intellectual content of work may diminish and moderate the sexual stimulus caused by its portrayal of sex to a degree less than that which is the object of punishment in the Criminal Code, so as to negate obscenity . . . .

Dissenting opinions denied the obscenity of the partial translation of de Sade's *In Praise of Vice* either because of its artistic and intellectual content, or because its sadistic repulsiveness reduced its erotic appeal to insignificance. Majority doctrine is regarded by commentators as somewhat restrictive.[84]

While providing binding guidelines for official Japan, judicial decisions do not give much hint of the systems for purveying and regulating obscenity in Japan. Critical to freedom of erotica are public agencies and private regulatory agencies connected with different industries. For example, the major motion picture producer-distributors abide by decisions of their own Motion Picture Ethics Committee (*Eiga Rinrikitei Kanri Iinkai*, or *Eirin*) in applying the industry's code of ethics and their understanding of what is legally permissible.[85] The film *Kuroi Yuki* (*Black Snow*) was shown with the approval of *Eirin*, but was held obscene by the Tokyo high court in 1969.[86] For some years after that, the courts did not accept *Eirin*'s view as a basis for immunity from prosecution. *Black Snow* depicted the life of prostitutes in the environs of an American base. The accused were acquitted on the grounds that until this judicial decision, they could assume reasonably that if *Eirin* approved of a work, it was indeed legal. On the other hand, the Tokyo district court held in the 1978 Nikkatsu Romantic Sex Film Case[87] that *Eirin* was an instrument for determining what is in accord with prevailing community standards, and acquitted the Nikkatsu company of obscenity charges based on *Eirin* approval of its films. However, scores of 'eroductions' appear annually, unregulated by *Eirin* and rarely restricted by officials.

The Customs Bureau censors imported printed material, films and pictures,[88] particularly those brought in for commercial purposes, with the assistance of a committee of citizens of 'learning and experience'.[89] The constitutionality of this system has long been questioned by scholars, and by some judges. In 1984, the Supreme Court, with four dissenting, upheld the law's ban on 'materials such as books which would harm the social order and morals' as not constituting censorship but an acceptable part of revenue collection procedures. Opening such items arriving in the mails is constitutionally permissible because they are not letters. Dissenters quarrelled with the law's vague wording and called for rigorous clarity (e.g. 'obscene publications and pictures') where free speech and thought may be affected.[90]

Frank and undisguised pornographic writings with the traditional designation of *shunpon* (literally, springtime books), can be found in specialised shops and do not often generate widespread concern. Weekly pulp magazines, poster advertisements, pornography vending machines, and lewd comic books for children present the most noteworthy problems today. Their content is often strongly erotic and presents a degraded image of humanity, especially women.

About 60 per cent of Japan's popular magazine sales take place in news-stands in railway stations, where concession privileges are controlled by the private Railroad Benefit Association (*Tetsudō Kōsaikai*).[91] The RBA can forbid the sale of a magazine or a particular issue of a magazine which its officials feel might be obscene. Among other sanctions, should police seize a magazine under obscenity law, the RBA may ban the next three issues from all its news-stands.

Local systems for regulating reading materials outside railway stations vary. For example, the private but powerful Tokyo Newspaper Sellers Commission (*Tokyoto Shinbun Sokubai Iinkai*)[92] determines the permissibility of distributing certain magazines to member news-stands and bookstores, and makes periodic spot checks to assure compliance with its policies. If objectionable material is found, a review committee considers the case and may issue a warning. Three warnings in a single year or one police seizure of a magazine may bring suspension of the seller's franchise. In addition, the Publications Ethics Council (*Shuppan Rinri Kyōgikai*) has been the publishing industry's main self-regulatory agency since 1963; but it does not appear very vigorous and it is helpless *vis-à-vis* 'outsiders', who do not belong to the Magazine Publishers Association (*Zasshi Kyōkai*) or other industry organisations.[93]

The above and other private-sector systems of restraint combine in a complex web; they are supplemented by 39 local youth protection ordinances.[94] Ordinances such as Tokyo's encourage primary reliance upon self-regulatory systems. The Tokyo Governor may give warnings which, if not heeded, are followed by an order to stamp 'unfit for youth' on the cover of offending publications. In some cases, a dozen or more official cautions or warnings have been given before any other enforcement action was taken against pornography affecting children.[95] In 1979, parental and offical concern focused on pornography vending machines within easy access of young children, and on objectionable TV advertisements and films shown during children's usual viewing hours.[96] Efforts to solve the latter problem have been led by local TV branches of the Federation of Commercial Broadcasting Labour Unions (*Minpō Rōren*).[97]

As in other areas of regulation, so in restraining obscenity, particularly on behalf of children, Japanese regulatory authority is spread around among many public and private agencies, while the courts and interested scholars debate rather abstract definitions. The picture that emerges is not one of clear or simple leniency or restrictiveness, but relations between law and society resembling in complexity a *kanji* ideograph of 25 strokes. As William Spinrad notes in his sociology of civil liberties, formalised and just legal structures are essential to freedom but are 'never a carbon-copy reflection of the libertarian or anti-libertarian attitudes of politicians or any general public consensus'.[98] This applies to Japan.[99]

Government certification of pre-collegiate textbooks has been another object of controversy for many years, in part in reaction to the very stringent controls of pre-war days. In the complicated processes of writing, publishing, local selection, and marketing of such textbooks may be found unintended restrictions on freedom which may be more important than censorship,[100] and these problems are further complicated by the polarisation of debate on some educational issues along rigid political lines. The textbook certification process takes place within the Ministry of Education. The *Ienaga Textbook Review* Cases significantly challenged administrative review criteria and processes with respect to textbooks, but also dramatised the continuing sensitivity of many Japanese to anything faintly reminiscent of the thought control exercised by the pre-war government. Professor Ienaga Saburo brought two suits, in 1965 and 1967, against the Ministry of Education for requiring him to make changes in the manuscript of his revised high school history text under the Ministry's textbook certification system. Both cases[101] were appealed to the Supreme Court, one against a 1975 high court ruling that the Ministry had failed to adhere to its own criteria in assessing Ienaga's book. In 1982, the Supreme Court upheld Ienaga's contested right as author to seek reversal in the Ministry's disapproval of the controversial passages, but avoided most substantive questions to concentrate on subtle legal technicalities which it directed the lower court to decide.[102]

Among the issues raised by the Ienaga cases are freedom of expression, academic freedom, the educational rights of parents, children and the state, and the question of whether the controversies themselves are among the great constitutional cases of modern Japan (a view this writer shares) or exclusively matters of administrative and civil law. A key point of contention was whether Ienaga's book was unfairly critical of the imperial family in discussing the mythological and historical origins of the Emperor system, so as to imply, to some, authoritarian unconcern for the people. The relevant passages are of less interest to Japanese schoolchildren than tonight's TV programmes; but the length of the Ienaga controversy and the intensity of feeling supporting Ienaga well illustrate the concern of Japanese intellectual élites, if not necessarily the generality of citizens, about possible reversion to reverence for the Emperor and an overturning of the post-war constitutional revolution. The treatment accorded pre-1945 history, domestic and international, in many school textbooks does gloss over a great many unpleasant facts, and Ienaga is joined by China, Korea and other countries in complaining about this tendency.[103] Ienaga's special concern is understandable, as he was a principal co-author of the first official history text for the compulsory grades in post-war Japan.[104] Moreover, official systems for restricting freedom of thought and expression in pre-war Japan were realistically seen as coercive measures secondary to and supplementary to the desired natural effects of a modern public education system permeated with the imperial orthodoxy over a period of decades.

Problems and prospects

Japan in the mid-1980s is in a constitutional era when moderate concern about reversion to the pre-war system or at least excessive militarisation continues, but has receded into the background for many working-age people.[105] Among pending constitutional issues are: refinements of freedom of information and privacy rights; the ban on election canvassing; limits on the freedom of expression of public employees; poverty, in the light of Article 25 guarantees of minimum standards of living; capital punishment; unreviewed internal rules and processes of regulatory agencies which affect individual rights; the extent of expanding environmental rights; discrimination against *burakumin* (traditional outcasts), women, Okinawans, and resident aliens; and serious malapportionment of seats in the Diet.

In substance, if not directly, the Supreme Court in 1982 concurred with the Sapporo high court in upholding the constitutionality of the Self-Defence Forces in the *Naganuma* Case.[106] The long debate on this case helped to refine and clarify positions on this unique issue. Article 9's pacifist provisions continue to be meaningful in law and politics as a unique symbol of self-restraint on military power and the constitutional order under the 'Peace Constitution', and need to be understood by Japan's allies. Whether a similar confluence of history, internal law and politics, and geopolitics will enable pacifism to occur in another nation-state remains to be seen.

Discrimination is a significant constitutional and human problem in Japan, although it does not receive much attention from scholars and is of interest to relatively few lawyers, politicians and citizens. The Civil Liberties Bureau works imaginatively to combat discrimination through educational means and the Civil Liberties Commissioner system.[107] Some social discrimination against the million Okinawans is likely to continue. The *burakumin*, numbering something over 1.5 million by government estimates and 2.5 million according to the Burakumin Liberation Movement, have been helped, as Japanese citizens, by remedial discrimination in the 1970s which has provided them with educational and other aid.[108] However, resident aliens, legal and illegal, have had less recourse under Japanese law, and are not eligible for aid from the Civil Liberties Commissioners.[109] Most notable are roughly 650,000 Koreans, 50,000 Chinese, and a few thousand refugees from Indochina since 1975.[110] A noteworthy advance in the mid-1980s was the long-called-for move towards simplification of alien registration procedures and documents, and limitation of finger-printing requirements, an irritating symbol of discrimination particularly to Korean residents (c. 650,000 due to pre-1945 Japanese colonialism). For the above and for women, employment discrimination is the most discussed problem. Japan ratified the United Nations convention against sex discrimination in the 1980s, after passage of laws intended to enhance the rights of working women. *Burakumin* and aliens suffer at times from private restraints on their choice of a marriage partner, but recent law has made possible regular appointments for foreign scholars at public universities.[111]

Rules of the LDP for the selection of the party president (and, as a consequence, the Prime Minister) were revised and used for the first time in late 1978, something comparable to a primary election system, though not preliminary, as in the United States, to a popular election for public office, but to a run-off election for party leadership. This was a major innovation, as previously the electors were limited to the parliamentary party, plus prefectural party leaders. Votes were cast by registered LDP members throughout the country in November 1978, and Ōhira Masayoshi received perhaps the highest total (more than 550,000 votes) ever received in an election by a single aspirant to the premiership.[112] Ōhira became party president, when the second-ranking vote-getter (of four candidates), Fukuda Takeo, declined to participate in a run-off election. This system has encouraged broader popular participation in LDP politics.

The malapportionment of seats in the House of Representatives and the less powerful House of Councillors under the Public Office Election Law is an unresolved constitutional problem which the political parties have chosen not to solve by legislative action. In 1976, the Supreme Court held unconstitutional the distribution of lower house seats in 1972.[113] The *degree* of malapportionment was against requirements for equality under the law and universal adult suffrage, and against the prohibition on discrimination against any particular candidates for public office.[114] (Candidates, for example, who must get twice as many votes as candidates in another district in order to be elected are suffering a form of discrimination.) But the court invalidated neither the election nor the subsequent actions of the malapportioned Diet, as requested by the plaintiffs. In 1975 the Diet added twenty seats, bringing the total to 511;[115] but the apportionment at each general election since has been challenged in court as in violation of Article 14 equality requirements.[116] Some LDP leaders have expressed their disagreement with 'one-man-one-vote' thinking and the repeated challenges; but some opposition politicians have also seen a threat to their political positions in reform. In 1985, the apportionment caused discrepancies in the effective weight of a vote, depending on election district, ranging up to 5.12 to 1 in the lower house and about 6 to 1 in the upper house, with 1 representing the minimum weight.[117] The interplay of the Supreme Court and the Diet on the malapportionment issue continued to merit close attention in the latter 1980s.

After a number of high court holdings in favour of voter claims, the Supreme Court in 1983[118] by appeal to a technicality narrowly avoided finding lower house apportionment unconstitutional (by an 8–7 vote), and warned the Diet to remedy the situation. In a strongly worded judgment in July 1985, the same court[119] declared a district's malapportionment constitutionally intolerable for exceeding a 3–1 value discrepancy when compared to other districts, but stopped short of nullifying the election on a technical interpretation. Finally, in May 1986 the recalcitrant Diet added eight seats in the House of Representatives to eight election districts while subtracting seven seats from other constituencies and promising further reform after the impending elections.[120] With this election law revision, the worst imbalance fell below the Supreme Court's guideline to 2.99 to 1 in a Kanagawa district. The consensus of constitutional lawyers and many judges is that anything over a 2 to 1 discrepancy should not be countenanced under the Constitution.[121] It seems that only an automated system tied to periodic census reports will solve the problem and unravel Japan's convoluted apportionment politics.

On balance, despite political and judicial problems, the second

modern constitutional revolution of Japan is likely to be guarded
with vigilance by substantial forces in the public and private sectors.
In Bonn, Matsuyama Yukio, international journalist with the *Asahi
Shinbun*, put well the hopes of many Japanese:[122]

> We want to be peaceful, and we want to remind you that Japan is next
> to none in her love of freedom, after having enjoyed its sweetness in
> these recent years. And we will not have it taken away by any government
> of any form. I still remember being deeply impressed with President
> Kennedy's remarks on his visit to the Berlin Wall, when he said, *'Ich
> bin ein Berliner'*. He meant, of course, that he was a free man, dedicated
> to liberty. And I still remember being deeply impressed by Martin Luther
> King, when he raised a vision for all mankind and said, 'I have a dream.'
> For man to be free and at peace with his neighbours. *I* have a dream
> that the day will come when I shall be able to say to the world at large,
> *'Ich bin ein Japaner'*. And the world will know that such is a man who
> tries to keep his liberty through peaceful means.

I share those hopes for Japan, and believe that constitutional
democracy will probably continue without further constitutional
revolution, barring a severe economic dislocation, the resurgence
of extreme nationalism, or a holocaust. The reasons for optimism
in 1986 are that competing constitutional structures and certain
values of Japanese law and society give substance to such hopes,
and that the balance of political forces for and against stable Japanese-
style democracy seems more likely to weigh increasingly on the side
of responsible freedom.

Notes and references

1. David M. Earl, *Emperor and Nation in Japan* (Seattle: University of Washington
   Press, 1964); John Fairbank *et al.*, *A History of East Asian Civilization – East
   Asia: The Great Tradition* (Boston: Houghton Mifflin, 1960); and Dan Fenno
   Henderson, *Conciliation and Japanese Law: Tokugawa and Modern*, 2 vols
   (Seattle: University of Washington Press, 1965), vol. I.
2. Lawrence Ward Beer, *Freedom of Expression in Japan: A Study in Comparative
   Law, Politics, and Society* (Tokyo and New York: Kodansha International–Harper
   & Row, 1985), hereafter cited as Beer, *Freedom*, pp. 37–38, 45–85. For a concise
   historical analysis of rights in the West, see Richard P. Claude, 'The Classical
   Model of Human Rights Development' in Richard P. Claude (ed.), *Comparative
   Human Rights* (Baltimore: Johns Hopkins University Press, 1976), pp. 6–50.
3. Yasuhiro Okudaira, *Political Censorship in Japan, 1931–1945*(Philadelphia:
   University of Pennsylvania Law School Library, 1962), esp. pp. 1–50.
4. Probably the most valuable compilation of detailed studies and official trial
   records of group political actions in Japan from the 1860s till the Pacific War
   is *Seiji saiban shiroku*, 5 vols (Daiichi Hōki, 1969–70), ed. Daiichi Hōki Publishing
   Co. An additional five volumes on recent decades were published in 1980.
   These studies amply illustrate preferences for group, as opposed to individual,
   assertiveness, and for other traditional values (referred to below) which antedated
   but are not integrated with Western legal ideas of justice.
5. William Spinrad, *Civil Liberties* (Chicago: Quadrangle Books, 1970), pp. 5–26,

292–306. On the historical and social contexts of constitutionalism in Japan, see Beer, *Freedom*, chapters 2 and 3.

6. See *Legal Reforms in Japan during the Allied Occupation*, special reprint volume, *Washington Law Review*, 1977.

7. 'Article 9. Aspiring sincerely to an international peace based on justice and order, the Japanese people forever renounce war as a sovereign right of the nation and the threat or use of force as a means of settling international disputes.
   '2. In order to accomplish the aim of the preceding paragraph, land, sea, and air forces, as well as other war potential, will never be maintained. The right of belligerency of the state will not be recognized.' *The Constitution of Japan*, in Itoh and Beer, *The Constitutional Case Law of Japan* (Seattle: University of Washington Press, 1978), p. 258.

8. 'Article 4. The Emperor shall perform only such acts in matters of state as are provided for in this Constitution and he shall not have powers related to government.' *Ibid.*, p. 257.

9. Beer, *Freedom*, chapter 7; Ronald Suleski, 'A New Generation of Japanese Intellectuals', *Japan Foundation Newsletter*, 6, No. 4, October–November, 1978, pp. 10–12.

10. The Constitution of Japan was promulgated on 3 November 1946, and went into effect on 3 May 1947. The amendment provision in The Constitution of the Empire of Japan was as follows: 'Article 73. When it has become necessary in future to amend the provisions of the present Constitution, a project to the effect shall be submitted to the Imperial Diet by Imperial Order.
    '2. In the above case, neither House can open the debate, unless not less than two-thirds of the whole number of Members are present, and no amendment can be passed, unless a majority of not less than two-thirds of the Members present is obtained.' Hideo Tanaka and M. Smith (eds) *Japanese Legal System*, (Tokyo: University of Tokyo Press, 1976) p. 23.

11. On the history of the revision controversy, see Haruhiro Fukui, 'The Liberal Democratic Party and Constitutional Revision', in David Sissons (ed.), *Papers on Modern Japan* (Canberra: Australian University Press, 1968), and 'Twenty Years of Revisionism,' in Dan Fenno Henderson (ed.), *The Constitution of Japan: Its First Twenty Years* (Seattle: University of Washington Press, 1969), pp. 41–70; and Reinhard Neumann, 'The Inaba Affair, Constitution Day and Constitutional Revision,' *Law in Japan: An Annual*, Vol. 9, 1976, pp. 129–43.

12. Max Gluckman's distinction between 'rituals of rebellion' and 'revolution' may apply to the 1960 Security Treaty Crisis and to some aspects of the University Crisis of 1969. Revolution seeks to overthrow the whole existing order, while ritual rebellion, which may be a luxury limited to societies like Japan with a stable established order, reaffirm the system in venting tensions between leaders and led and between viewpoints. In this connection, see Max Gluckman, *Custom and Conflict in Africa* and *Politics, Law and Ritual in Tribal Society*; and Takeo Doi (John Bester, trans.), *Anatomy of Dependence* (Tokyo: Kodansha International, 1973).

13. On the Security-Treaty Crisis, see George R. Packard III, *Protest in Tokyo: The Security Treaty Crisis of 1960* (Princeton: Princeton University Press, 1966); Richard Rabinowitz, 'Law and the Social Process in Japan,' *The Transactions of the Asiatic Society of Japan*, Third Series, Vol. 10, 1968: 54–71; John M. Maki, *Government and Politics in Japan* (New York: Praeger Publishers, 1962); Robert Scalapino and Junnosuke Masumi, *Parties and Politics in Contemporary Japan* (Berkeley and Los Angeles: University of California Press, 1962).

14. *Japan v. Sakata*, 23 *Keishū* 3225 (Sup. Ct., Grand Bench, December 16, 1959). For a translation, see John M. Maki (ed.), *Court and Constitution in Japan* (Seattle: University of Washington Press, 1964), pp. 298–361.

15. *Japan v. Sakane et al.*, 13 *Keishū* (No. 5) 685 (Sup. Ct., Grand Bench, April

2, 1969). A translation appears in Itoh and Beer, *Constitutional Case Law of Japan*, pp. 103–30.

16. *Asahi Shimbun*, 1 November 1978 and 1 January 1979; Lawrence W. Beer, 'Japan's Constitutional System and Its Judicial Interpretation', *Law in Japan*, Vol. 17, 1984, hereafter cited as Beer, 'Constitution', pp. 11–13, 22–23.

17. Kenzō Takayanagi (John Maki, trans.), 'The Conceptual Background of the Constitutional Revision Debate in the Constitution Investigation Commission,' *Law in Japan: An Annual*, Vol. I, 1967, pp. 1–24; Robert E. Ward, 'The Commission on the Constitution in the Prospects of Constitutional Change in Japan,' *Journal of Asian Studies*, Vol. 24, 1965, pp. 401–30; John M. Maki, *Japan's Commission on the Constitution: Its Final Report* (Seattle: University of Washington, 1980).

18. *Asahi Shimbun*, 1 November 1979 and 1 January 1979.

19. Such loyalty is especially emphasised among white collar workers. See Thomas Rohlen, *For Harmony and Strength, Japanese White-Collar Organization in Anthropological Perspective* (Berkeley: University of California Press, 1974).

20. The distribution of seats in both Houses of the Diet in July 1986 was as below. For perspective, statistics after prior lower house and upper house elections are included.

Party	House of Representatives				House of Councillors		
	1979	*1980*	*1983*	*1986*	*1980*	*1983*	*1986*
Liberal Democratic Party	253	286	250	309	135	137	143
Japan Socialist Party	107	107	112	86	47	44	41
Kōmeitō	58	34	58	56	27	27	24
Democratic Socialist Party	36	33	38	26	12	12	12
Japan Communist Party	41	29	26	26	12	14	16
New Liberal Club	4	12	8	(5)*	2	3	(2)*
United Social Democrats	2	3	3	4	2		1
Independents & Others	10	7	16	5	15	12	15†
TOTALS	511	511	511	512	252	252°	252

*The New Liberal Club rejoined the LDP after the July 1986 elections
†Includes one vacancy   ° Includes three vacancies
Sources: Asahi Shimbun, 23, 26 June 1980; *Mainichi Shimbun*, 8 July 1986, Yomiuri Shimbun, 28 June 1983.

21. *The Constitution of Japan*, Article 96:
Amendments to this Constitution shall be initiated by the Diet, through a concurring vote of two thirds or more of all the members of each House and shall thereupon be submitted to the people for ratification, which shall require the affirmative vote of a majority of all votes cast thereon, at a special referendum or at such election as the Diet shall specify.
2. Amendments when so ratified shall immediately be promulgated, by the Emperor in the name of the people, as an integral part of this Constitution.
(Itoh and Beer, *Constitutional Case Law of Japan*, p. 268.)

22. Hiroshi Itoh, *Constitutional Interpretation in Japan, 1947–1980* (New York: Marcus Weiner, 1987); and Beer, *Freedom*, chapter 4. Annually, *Hōsō Jihō* (*Hōsōkai*) publishes authoritative statistical reports on cases dealt with by the courts, and *Hōritsu Jihō* (Nihon Hyōronsha) carries reviews of both constitutional case law and constitutional studies (*kenpōgaku*). By the end of 1981, the Supreme Court had 'taken cognizance of 203,963 cases, out of which, 1,049 cases were referred to the Grand Bench [by petty benches], and in 263 cases the Court declared a law, order, regulation or official act unconstitutional', *Justice in Japan* (Tokyo: Supreme Court of Japan, 1982), p. 19.

23. Family courts, summary courts, and various modes of lay participation in dispute

resolution are briefly described in *Justice in Japan*. pp. 14–17, 23–26. Concerning the Civil Liberties Bureau and Commissioners, see Lawrence W. Beer, *Human Rights Commissioners (Jinken Yogo Iin) and Lay Protection of Human Rights in Japan*, Occasional Paper No. 31, October 1985, International Ombudsman Institute, Alberta, Canada.

24. Concerning Japan's court system and judges, see Itoh and Beer, *Constitutional Case Law of Japan*, pp. 7–21, 250–55; and, on barriers to civil litigation, John Owen Haley, 'The Myth of the Reluctant Litigant,' *Journal of Japanese Studies*, summer, 1978, pp. 359–90. In Japanese, Wada Hideo, *Saikō saibansho ron* (Nihon Hyōronsha, 1970), and *Saikō saibansho* (Hōgaku seminah-Nihon Hyōronsha, 1977).

25. For example, *Abe* v. *Japan, 20 Keishū* (No. 6) 537 (Sup. Ct., Second Petty Bench, 1 July 1966), translated in Itoh and Beer, *Constitutional Case Law of Japan*, p. 167–68

26. See, for example, *Japan* v. *Ozawa, 28 Keishū* (No. 9) 393 (Supreme Court, Grand Bench, 6 November 1974; for comments and other cases on this issue, see Beer, *Freedom*, chapter 6.

27. The Otsu Case (1891) and the Meiji Constitution established judicial independence for the first time in Japan. As Kenzō Takayanagi notes: 'In a sense, the Otsu Incident and its legacy contradict the basic thesis advanced by the Western scholars interviewed by Kaneko: the inclusion in the Constitution of an institution quite foreign to the Japanese scene provided the foundation on which a tradition of judicial independence very quickly emerged.' Takayanagi, *op. cit.* See also Marc Galanter, 'The Displacement of Traditional Law in Modern India,' *Journal of Social Issues, 24,* 1968, pp. 65–91.

28. See Tanaka (ed.), *Japanese Legal System*, pp. 642–85, and works cited therein.

29. A good presentation of these views is Neumann, 'The Inaba Affair, Constitution Day and Constitutional Revision,' *op. cit.*

30. Hiroshi Itoh, 'Judicial Decision-making in the Japanese Supreme Court,' *Law in Japan: An Annual*, 3, 1969, pp. 128–61; Kisaburo Yokota, 'Political Questions and Judicial Review,' Henderson (ed.), *Constitution of Japan*, pp. 141–66; Hideo Wada, 'Decisions under Article 9 of the Constitution: The *Sunakawa, Eniwa, Naganuma* Decisions,' *Law in Japan: An Annual, 9*, 1976, pp. 117–28; 'Recent Developments,' *ibid.*, p. 153; Robert L. Seymour, 'Japan's Self-Defense: The Naganuma Case and Its Implications', *Pacific Affairs*, Vol. 47, 1974–75, p. 421; and Kenneth M. Tagawa, 'Justiciability and Judicial Power in Japan', PhD. dissertation, University of Colorado, 1979.

31. Edward Seidensticker, 'Japan After Vietnam,' *Commentary*, September, 1976, p. 56.

32. Gino Piovesana, *Recent Japanese Philosophical Thought* (Tokyo: Enderle Bookstore, 1961); Charles A. Moore (ed.), *The Japanese Mind* (Honolulu: East-West Center Press, 1968); Miyazawa Toshiyoshi, *Kenpō* (Yūhikaku, 1962).

33. Carl Steenstrup, 'The Company Code,' *Asian Law Forum*, Vol. 1, 1976, pp. 21–25; Frank Upham, *Law and Social Change in Postwar Japan* (Cambridge: Harvard University Press, 1987).

34. Chie Nakane, *Japanese Society* (Berkeley and Los Angeles, University of California Press, 1970); Beer, *Freedom*, chapter 3.

35. The term 'reciprocal dependency' is taken from Douglas D. Mitchell, *Amae: The Expression of Reciprocal Dependency Needs in Japanese Politics and Law* (Boulder, Colorado: Westview Press, 1976). Mitchell seems to this writer to present Takeo Doi's important views on dependency more systematically and more clearly than Doi himself. See also Takeo Doi, *Anatomy of Dependence*.

36. Ryūichi Nagao, in a review of R. Minear, *Japanese Tradition and Western Law* (Cambridge, Mass.: Harvard University Press, 1970), in *Law in Japan: An Annual, 5*, 1972, p. 224. For current views, see *Jurisuto*, no. 884, 3 May, 1987.

37. Hayashi Chikio *et al.*, *Nipponjin no kokuminsei* (Shiseido, 1970); and Hayashi

Chikio, 'Seiji ishiki no seitai', *Asahi Shinbun*, 16 December 1978, p. 4. See also the comprehensive survey report in *Asahi Shinbun*, 1 January 1979, pp. 1, 10–13.

The term 'feudal,' often used pejoratively to criticise traditional aspects of modern Japan, is usually applied to factors such as the family system which predated feudalism by centuries and which made Japanese feudalism different from other feudalisms such as those of Western Europe. See F. Joüon des Longrais, *L'est et l'ouest, institutions du Japon et de l'occident comparées* (Paris and Tokyo, 1958). This writer does not share a uniformly negative view of Japanese-style 'feudalism' as it functions today.

38. Hayashi, 'Seiji ishiki no seitai.' Only a small percentage (*c.* 20%) of Japanese expressed much trust in politicians in late 1978 compared, for example, to tax officials (*c.* 45%), judges, teachers, police, doctors, newspapers, and weather forecasters, among whom the last in the ascending order were the most trusted. *Asahi Shinbun*, 22 October 1978 and 1 January 1979. See James Marshall, *Japan's Successor Generation: Their values and attitudes* (Washington DC: Office of Research, USIA, 1985).

39. *The Constitution of Japan*, Article 97 in the 'Supreme Law' chapter of the Constitution reads: 'The fundamental human rights by this Constitution guaranteed to the people of Japan are fruits of the age-old struggle of man to be free; they have survived the many exacting tests for durability and are conferred upon this and future generations in trust, to be held for all time inviolate.'

40. On the severe limitations on the Emperor's political role as an individual in the Tokugawa period (1600–1868), see Herschel Webb, *The Japanese Imperial Institution in the Tokugawa Period* (New York, Columbia University Press, 1968), and for the period 1868–1946, see David A. Titus, *Palace and Politics in Prewar Japan* (New York, Columbia University Press, 1974), and *Modern Asian Studies*, 14, 4, 1980, p. 529.

41. On the prosecutors, see B.J. George, Jr., 'Discretionary Authority of Public Prosecutors in Japan,' *Law in Japan*, Vol. 17, 1984, p. 42; on the police, see David H. Bayley, *Forces of Order: Police Behaviour in Japan and the United States* (Berkeley: University of California Press, 1976).

Takayanagi Kenzō noted that pre-war debates on constitutionality involved political rhetoric, but rarely justiciable rights; n. 32 above. 'Conciliable rights' is meant to express the prevalent style of dispute resolution, involving a third-party status bearer (informal or official) pursuing compromise and formal harmony. On Japanese right consciousness, see Beer, *Freedom*, chapter 3.

42. Discussions since 1978 with Itō Masami and Shimizu Hideo. They consider press freedom more critical to democracy in Japan than in most countries.

43. *The Constitution of Japan*, 'Article 91. The Supreme Court is the court of last resort with power to determine the constitutionality of any law, order, regulation or official act.' Itoh and Beer, *Constitutional Case Law of Japan*, p. 266. Lower courts, by judicial decision and Article 76, also have the power of judicial review.

44. Laurence W. Beer and C.G. Weeramantry, 'Human Rights in Japan: Some Protections and Problems,' *Universal Human Rights*, No. 3, 1979, p. 1; Beer, 'Constitution,' pp. 14–15.

45. Article 81 of the *Constitution of Japan*. Article 76 is also critical: 'The whole judicial power is vested in a Supreme Court and in such inferior courts as are established by law.

'2. No extraordinary tribunal shall be established, nor shall any organ or agency of the Executive be given final judicial power.

'All judges shall be independent in the exercise of their conscience and shall be bound only by this Constitution and the laws.' Itoh and Beer, *Constitutional Case Law of Japan*, p. 265.

For a study of the pre-war administrative court system, to which paragraph

2 of Article 76 is in part a reaction, see Hideo Wada, 'The Administrative Court under the Meiji Constitution,' *Law in Japan: An Annual*, 10, 1977, pp. 1–64.

46. For comparative perspectives, see Beer (ed.), *Constitutionalism in Asia*; Ivo Duchacek, 'Constitutions: Adapting to Change', *Power Maps: Comparative Politics of Constitutions* (Santa Barbara: ABC Clio Press, 1973), pp. 210–32; Claud, *Comparative Human Rights*, David H. Bayley, *Public Liberties in the New States* (Chicago: Rand McNally & Co., 1964). On judicial roles in civil law systems, see John Henry Merryman, *The Civil Law Tradition* (Stanford: Stanford University Press, 1969); Rudolf B. Schlesinger, 'Common Law and Civil Law: A Historical Comparison,' *Comparative Law*, 2nd edition (Brooklyn: Foundation Press, 1959), pp. 179–98.

47. Article 4, Court Organisation Law, Law No. 59 of 16, April 1947. See Itoh and Beer, *Constitutional Case Law of Japan*, pp. 7–11, 251–55; on the effect of an unconstitutional judgment, Ukai in Beer, *Constitutionalism in Asia*; Itoh, *op. cit.*

48. Discussions with judges, Tokyo, 1978–9.

49. Haley, 'Myth of the Reluctant Litigant,' pp. 387–90; Itoh, *op. cit.*

50. Conversation with Matsuo Kōya, specialist in criminal procedure law, 1979; B.J. George, Jr., 'Discretionary Authority of Public Prosecutors', pp. 64–65; Bayley, *Forces of Order*, pp. 141–44. Civil liberties lawyers say police brutality is less a problem than prolonged interrogation. Author's discussions, in Japan 1987.

51. Kahei Rokumoto, 'Problems and Methodology of Study of Civil Disputes,' pt 1, *Law in Japan: An Annual*, 5, 1972, pp. 97–114; Upham, *op. cit.*

52. Beer, *Freedom*, contains extended discussion of issues and cases mentioned in the remainder of this chapter.

53. On the other hand, *individual* dissent and post-consensus dissent from the views of one's in-group seem notably limited in Japan. However, pre-consensus debate within one's group is relatively uninhibited (except by the seniority order of presentation), as is expression of group disagreement with government policies or the opinions of 'outsiders' of whatever kind. See Beer, *ibid.* chapters 3 and 12.

54. See Bayley, *Forces of Order*, pp. 172–83; Beer, *Freedom*, chapter 5.

55. Freedom of assembly can be regulated under Article 7 of *Dōrō Kōtsūhō* (Law 105 of 1960), Article 19 of *Densenbyō yobōhō* (Law 36 of 1897), Articles 5 and 7, *Hakai katsudō bōshihō* (Law 240 of 1952), Articles 106 and 107, *Keihō*, and Article 4 of Ministry of Welfare Order No. 19 of 1949 (*Official Gazette*, No. 938); and by public safety ordinances.

56. On public safety ordinances and their use, see Beer, *Freedom*, chapter 5.

57. *Japan v. Itō*, 14 *Keishū* 1243 (Sup. Ct., Grand Bench, 20 July 1960). For a translation and the ordinance in question, see Maki (ed.), *Court and Constitution in Japan*, pp. 84–116.

58. The Supreme Court can and does on occasion reverse its own precedent. For examples, see Cases 7 and 24 in Itoh and Beer, *Constitutional Case Law of Japan*.

59. *Japan v. Sugino*, 4 *Keishū* 2012, 1014 (Sup. Ct., Grand Bench, 1950).

60. See Miyazawa Toshiyoshi, *Nihonkoku kenpō* (Nihon Hyōronsha, 1963), p. 205; and Yamamoto Keiichi, 'Kōkyō no fukushi'' in Tanaka Jirō (ed.), *Nihonkoku kenpō taikei*, Vol. 8 (Yūhikaku, 1961), p. 16. On legal theories in Japan on the public welfare, see Satō Isao, *Kenpō Kenkyū Nyūmon*, 3 vols (Nihon Hyōronsha, 1966), 2: 25–117:

61. Ashibe Nobuyoshi *et al.*, 'Kenpō hanrei no zonen', *Jurisuto*, special issue (3 May 1977), pp. 452, 453, and Itō Masami, 'Kenpō kaishaku to rieki kōryōron', p. 200, on the increased judicial use of an interests-balancing approach.

62. See *Asahi Shinbun*, 17 July 1970 (Sup. Ct., Petty Bench, 16 July 1970); conversations with Justice Irie Toshio, January 1971.

63. See, for example, *Japan* v. *Sakane et al.*, above n. 15, and *Toyama et al. v. Japan*, 20 Keishū (No. 8), 901 (Sup. Ct. Grand Bench, 25 October 1966), in Itoh and Beer, *Constitutional Case Law of Japan*, pp. 85–130. See also *Rōdō to jinken* (Hōgaku seminah-Nihon Hyōronsha, 1978) and Beer, *Freedom*, chapter 6.

64. *Japan* v. *Ozawa, 28 Keishū* (No. 9), 393 (Sup. Ct., Grand Bench, 6 November 1974).

65. On the courts and media, see Beer, *Freedom*, chapters 7–10.

66. *Nishiyama* v. *Japan, Hanrei Jihō* 887 (11 July 1978): 14–41 (Sup. Ct., First Petty Bench, 31 May 1978); Ronald G. Brown, 'Government Secrecy and the "People's Right to Know" in Japan: Implications of the *Nishiyama* Case,' *Law in Japan: An Annual*, 10, 1977, pp. 112–39; and Beer, *Freedom*, chapter 8. See also the final report of the Secrecy and Disclosure Subcommittee, Senate Select Committee on Intelligence, October 1978, U.S. Senate.

67. Beer, *Freedom*, chapter 9. On rights of the person in the United States, see Don R. Pember, *Privacy and the Press* (Seattle: University of Washington Press, 1972); and Arthur R. Miller, *The Assault on Privacy* (Ann Arbor, University of Michigan Press, 1971).

68. Conversation with Onizuka Kentarō, Head, Civil Liberties Bureau, Justice Ministry, October 1978. See Beer and Weeramantry, 'Human Rights in Japan', p. 13. *Mura hachibu*, ostracism from the village, was the prototype of this powerful sanction, but for the Tokugawa period, *machi hachibu* (ostracism from commercial districts of towns and cities) was also common. See *Nihon Keizai Jiten* (Nihon Hyōronsha, 1943), p. 1844. Today *mura hachibu* is the official catch-all term for illegal ostracism. In the cities, *mura hachibu* may even include ostracism of a housewife in a modern apartment complex by other women living there.

69. *Arita* v. *Mishima*, 15 *Kakyū Minshū* (No. 9) 2317 (Tokyo district court, 28 September 1964). For Donald Keene's translation of the novel at issue see Yukio Mishima, *After the Banquet* (New York: Alfred A. Knopf, 1963). On private enforcement of rights, see Hideo Tanaka and Akio Takeuchi, 'The Role of Private Persons in the Enforcement of Law: A Comparative Study of Japanese and American Law', *Law in Japan: An Annual*, 7, 1974, pp. 34–50. The Civil Code provisions are:

    'Article 709. A person who violates intentionally or negligently the right of another is bound to make compensation for damage arising therefrom.

    'Article 710. A person who is liable in compensation for damages in accordance with the provisions of the preceding Article shall make compensation therefore even in respect of a nonpecuniary damage, irrespective of whether such injury was to the person, liberty or reputation of another or to his property rights.'

    A theory which would directly apply such constitutional guarantees as good name and privacy without reference to code provisions seems to have little support. See Ukai in Beer, *Constitutionalism in Asia*, p. 122; and more generally Beer, *Freedom*, chapter 9.

70. *Hasegawa* v. *Japan*, 23 *Keishū* 1625 (Sup. Ct., Grand Bench, 24 December 1969). For a translation, see Itoh and Beer, *Constitutional Case Law of Japan*, pp. 178–82. Similar specification of the public welfare as what is necessary for criminal justice is used by the same court in *Kaneko* v. *Japan*, 23 *Keishū* 1490 (Sup. Ct. Grand Bench, 26 November 1969), translated in *ibid.* pp. 246–50.

71. *Katō* v. *Shūkan Jitsuwa, Hanrei Jihō* 537 (1968), 28 (Tokyo district court, 25 November 1968), and *Shūkan Jitsuwa* v. *Katō, Juristo* 449 (1970), 128 (Tokyo high court, 25 December 1969).

72. '*Eros + Gyakusatsu*' Case, *Kamichika* v. *Art Theatre Guild, Jurisuto* 449 (1970), 21 (Tokyo district court, 14 March 1970), and 23 *Kōminshū* (No. 2), 1172

(Tokyo high court, 13 April 1970). See also *Asahi Shinbun*, 13 and 14 April (morning and evening edns).

73. *Kawabata v. Chikuma Shobo et al.*, Tokyo district court, 1977. See *Japan Times Weekly Edition*, 27 August 1977. *Burakumin* are still discriminated against socially, despite laws to the contrary, as noted in the concluding section of this chapter.

74. See the statistics for both civil and criminal defamation in annual reports in *Hōsō Jihō (Hōsōkai)*; Beer, *Freedom*, chapter 9.

75. For example, at least until the 1970s, on a *per capita* basis France and Germany had roughly 200 times as many defamation suits and ten times more convictions than Japan. See K. Igarashi and H. Tamiya, *Meiyo to puraibashii* (1968), pp. 74–78; *Jurisuto* 332 (1965), 60; and *Jurisuto* 653 (1970).

76. Conversations with Judge Mutō Shunkō, Legal Training and Research Institute, in July 1973 and December 1978. The sharp rise in civil defamation suits peaked in 1973 and thereafter levelled off.

77. The term '*waisetsu*' (obscenity) and punishment of its 'public display or sale' first appeared in Article 259 of the Criminal Code of 1880. Article 175 of the 1907 revised Criminal Code remains today the primary legal provision for restraint of obscenity, amended only in 1947 by the addition of imprisonment to fines as possible penalties. See Beer, *Freedom*, chapter 10.

78. Ibid., which presents the historical perspective.

79. *Itō et al. v. Japan*, 11 *Keishū* (No. 3) 997 (Sup. Ct., Grand Bench, 13 March 1957); a translation is in Maki, *Court and Constitution in Japan*, pp. 3–37.

80. *Ishii et al. v. Japan*, 23 *Keishū* (No. 10) 1239 (Sup. Ct., Grand Bench, 15 October 1969); all opinions are translated in Itoh and Beer, *Constitutional Case Law of Japan*, pp. 183–217.

81. Ministry of Justice, Japan, *Criminal Statutes* (n.d.), Vol. 1, p.39.

82. See Maki, *Court and Constitution in Japan*, p. 7.

83. Itoh and Beer, *Constitutional Case Law of Japan*, p. 184. See also Beer, *Freedom*, chapter 10.

84. Itō Masami and Shimizu Hideo (eds), *Masu komi hōrei yōran* (Gendai Jānarizumu Shuppankai, 1966); Shimizu, *Hō to masu koyūnikēshon*; Okudaira, *Hyōgen no jiyū towa nanika*.

85. Discussions with Itō Masami, a member of *Eirin*, August 1979. Concerning *Eirin*, see Masu Komi Rinri Kondankai (ed.), *Masu komi no shakai sekinin* (Nihon Shinbun Kyōkai, 1966), hereafter cited as *Sekinin*. On Japan's film industry see also J.I. Anderson and D. Richie, *The Japanese Film: Art and Industry* (New York: Grove Press, 1960).

86. *Japan v. Murakami et al.*, *Hanrei Jihō* 571 (11 November 1969), 19 (Tokyo high court, 17 September 1969).

87. *Japan v. Nikkatsu Co.*, *Hanrei Jihō* 897 (11 October 1978), 39–53 (Tokyo district court, 23 June 1978); *Asahi Shinbun*, 23 (evening edn), 24 June 1978. 'Black Snow' was also a Nikkatsu film. In the 1970s Nikkatsu turned out a series of sexually explicit films allegedly to help clear up debts due to legal fees in an earlier case, and due to the depression of Japan's film industry. *Japan Times*, 4 November 1977; *Asahi Shinbun*, 28 January (evening edn), 11 February, 25 May and 21 June 1972; and Fujiki Hideo, 'Eirin jiken o meguru hōritsu mondai', *Jurisuto* 504 (1 May 1972), p. 56. For 'Poruno sangyō toshite no Nihon eiga', see *Asahi Jānaru* (28 April 1972), p. 38; also *Jurisuto*, special issue (10 December 1970).

88. This is done under the Customs Standards Law (*Kanzei teiritsu hō*), Law 54 of 11 April 1911, Article 11, which is in Itō and Shimizu, *Masu komi hōrei yōran*, p. 75.

89. For examples of seizures at airports, see *Asahi Shinbun*, 17 January 1979.

90. *Matsue v. Japan*, 38 *Minshū* (No. 12) 1308 (Sup. Ct., G.B., 12 December 1984).

91. *Sekinin*, pp. 51–75. (This book, available only at the offices of the Nihon Shinbun

204   *Constitutions in Democratic Politics*

Kyōkai, remains a principal source of information on private regulatory systems.) In addition to the criminal and customs law provisions already mentioned, obscenity is also regulated under *Kōgyō hō* (Law 137 of 10 July, 1948) *Fuzoku eigyō torishimari hō, Kankyō eisei hō, Denpa hō, Hōsō hō*, and local youth protection ordinances.

92. *Sekinin*, pp. 273, 64.

93. *Asahi Shinbun*, 22 January 1979, an interview with Nunokawa Kakuzaemon, President, Publication Ethics Council, and member, Tokyo Youth Protection Council.

94. *Sekinin*, p. 208; and *Nihon Keizai Shinbun*, 12 July 1978.

95. *Nihon Keizai Shinbun*, 12 July 1978. For example, amidst widespread parental and public concern, pornography vending machines in Saitama Prefecture increased from 887 in August 1977 to 2,116 on 31 July 1978. After a great many warnings, police seized two machines in October 1978. *Asahi Shinbun*, 10 October 1978.

96. For example, occasionally imported Western films restricted to adult-oriented theatres in the United States are shown on commercial television in Japan. See also *Asahi Shinbun*, 22 and 23 September and 12 December (evening edn), 1978.

97. *Ibid.*

98. Spinrad, *Civil Liberties*, pp. 5–26, 292–306. On the law and experience of the United States, see *The Report of the Commission on Obscenity and Pornography* (New York: Bantam Books, 1970), especially pp. 346–422.

99. For related opinion poll data, see *Asahi Shinbun*, 3 January 1979, p. 7.

100. Beer, *Freedom*, chapter 7.

101. *Ienaga* v. *Ministry of Education, Hanrei Jihō* 604 (1970), p. 35 (Tokyo district court 17 July 1970); and *Ienaga* v. *Ministry of Education, Hanrei Jihō*, special issue (15 October 1974) and *Jurisuto* 569 (1974), p. 14 (Tokyo district court, 16 July 1974).

102. *Ministry of Education* v. *Ienaga, Hanrei Jihō* 800 (1976), p. 19 (Tokyo high court, 20 December 1975); *Japan* v. *Ienaga, Hanrei Jihō* (No. 1040), p. 3 (Sup. Ct., G.B. 8 April 1982).

103. Private discussions with Japanese textbook authors at various times during the 1970s; Beer, *Freedom*, chapter 7.

104. Ministry of Education (ed.), *Kuni no ayumi* (October 1946). For a recent expression of Ienaga's views, see *Rekishi no naka no kenpō* (Tokyo Daigaku Shuppankai, 1977), 2 vols. Ienaga sees the issues in broad constitutional and political terms, as part of efforts on behalf of Article 9 and against constitutional revision. Correspondence with the author, 10 December 1978.

105. See *Asahi Shinbun*, 1 January 1979, pp. 1, 9–13. Survey results therein indicate middle-class preoccupation, not with large political questions, especially those of the past, but with work, inflation, children's education and other immediate problems.

106. *Ono et al.* v. *Ministry of Agriculture, Forestry and Fisheries*, 36 *Minshu* 1679 (Sup. Ct., G.B. 9 September 1982); Beer, *Constitution*, pp. 22–23.

107. Beer and Weeramantry, 'Human Rights in Japan; and n. 23 above.

108. *Tōkei Nenkan* (Ōkurashō Insatsukyoku, 1977), p. 26; and Frank K. Upham, *op. cit.*

109. Discussions with Onizuka Kentarō (Head, Civil Liberties Bureau), Nakadaira Kenkichi (attorney), Sasahara Keisuke (attorney), and Andō Isamu (Head, Asian Relations Centre, Sophia University, Tokyo) in 1978 and 1979.

110. Japan came under some international pressure in 1978 and 1979 to allow some refugees to reside in Japan. However, as of July 1979, only 12 South-East Asian refugees had been given visas for a year or so of residence. In the 1980s, the conditions improved and numbers increased very gradually.

111. Sources cited in n. 109 above; *Asahi Shinbun*, 21 January 1979; Joyce C.

Lebra *et al.* (eds), *Women in Changing Japan* (Boulder: Westview Press, 1976); see n. 114 below.

112. The LDP rules provide that one electoral point is assigned to a prefectural party chapter for every 1,000 party members. The two national party candidates with the most votes in each prefecture divide the points in proportion to the number of votes each receives in the 'primary'. No other candidates are allotted electoral points. The voting for the four candidates in the 1978 primary election was as follows: Ohira Masayoshi 550,891 (748 points); Fukuda Takeo, 472,503 (638); Nakasone Yasuhiro, 197,957 (93); Komoto Toshio, 88,917 (46). *Asahi Shinbun*, morning and evening edns, 27 and 28 November and 8 December 1978. After the first round in a primary with more than two candidates in which no one has received a majority of the points, the top two vote-getters compete in a run-off election. See also Minoru Shimizu, 'LDP Reform Movement Retrogresses', *The Japan Times*, 24 May 1979.

113. *Kurokawa* v. *Chiba Prefecture Election Commission*, 30 Minshū 223 (Sup. Ct., Grand Bench, 14 April 1976). See 'Recent Developments', *Law in Japan: An Annual*, 9, 1976, pp. 151–52.

114. *Constitution of Japan*:
    'Article 14. All the people are equal under the law and there shall be no discrimination in political, economic or social relations because of race, creed, sex, social status or family origin . . . '
    'Article 15. The people have the inalienable right to choose their public officials and to dismiss them.
    '2. All public officials are servants of the whole community and not of any group thereof.
    '3. Universal adult suffrage is guaranteed with regard to the election of public officials.
    '4. In all elections, secrecy of the ballot shall not be violated. A voter shall not be answerable, publicly or privately for the choice he has made.'
    'Article 44. The qualifications of members of both Houses and their electors shall be fixed by law. However, there shall be no discrimination because of race, creed, sex, social status, family origin, education, property or income.' Itoh and Beer, *Constitutional Case Law of Japan*, pp. 258–59, 261.

115. Law 63 of 1975 added twenty seats to the House of Representatives, and created new election districts in Tokyo, Chiba, Saitama, and Kanagawa, areas severely afflicted with malapportionment.

116. *Hanrei Jihō* 902 (21 November 1978), pp. 24–34 (Tokyo high court, 11 September 1978); *Koshiyama* v. *Election Commission, Hanrei Jihō* 902 (21 November 1978), pp. 34–51 (Tokyo high court, 13 September 1978).

117. Beer, 'Constitution', pp. 36–39; *Yomiuri Shimbun*, 9 May 1986.

118. *Tokyo Election Commission* v. *Koshiyama*, 37 Minshū 1243 (Sup. Ct., 7 November 1983).

119. *Kaneo et al.* v. *Hiroshima Election Commission, Hanrei Jihō* (No. 1163)3 (11 November 1985) (Sup. Ct., G.B. 17 July 1985). The Supreme Court first held unconstitutional the apportionment of seats in a local assembly (Tokyo) on 17 May 1984. *Japan Times*, 2 June 1984, and again in 1987. The 1986 promise of further reform had not been kept a year later.

120. *Yomiuri Shimbun*, 9 and 23 May 1986; *Mainichi Shimbun*, 22, 23 May 1986.

121. Tomatsu Hidenori, '*Shūgiin teisū ikenhanketsu no igi to teiseian*', *Hōgaku Kyōshitsu*, No. 64, January 1986.

122. Yukio Matsuyama, 'What Has Been Changing in Japanese Politics and What Not?" unpublished speech, Trilateral Commission, Bonn, West Germany, 23 October 1977, pp. 9–10.

Italy (1948): Condemned by its constitution?
David Hine

The 1948 Constitution: theory and practice[1]
At the centre of Italy's Republican Constitution is a classic parliamentary form of government, with a cabinet responsible to (and in practice drawn from) Parliament, and a head of state (President of the Republic) occupying a largely ceremonial position. Parliament is divided into two houses, both elected for five-year terms, and endowed with identical powers, and the political executive (Prime Minister, a cabinet of just under 30, and a further 50 junior ministers) must maintain the confidence of both houses. In sharp contrast to the Fifth French Republic, which at least initially was grafted on to a party system very similar to that in Italy, no part of the executive branch enjoys the prestige and legitimacy of separate and direct election, and hence the government's power over the politically diversified majority coalition which must support it is correspondingly reduced.

On paper, the 1948 Constitution's promulgation brought into being one of the most liberal constitutional texts to be found in Europe. It was infused with a complex series of checks and balances which, at least in principle, imposed significant restrictions on governments, and dispersed power across a wide range of institutions. It placed parliament squarely at the centre of the political system, and provided few of the mechanisms (restrictions on parliament's power to legislate; limits on its ability to bring down the government; priority passage for government legislation etc.) which, in some other constitutions, were intended to concentrate power in the executive. It allowed for an element of direct democracy, in the form of an abrogative referendum (i.e. one allowing repeal of existing legislation by popular initiative). It established a forum in which various types of economic interest group could participate – albeit in an advisory capacity – in the formation of economic and social policy. Power was also devolved territorially, with a system of regional governments endowed with substantial legislative and administrative authority. Finally, the Constitution guaranteed judicial independence through the High Council of the Judiciary, a body placed between the judicial class and the Ministry of Justice, and it established the principle of judicial review via a Constitutional Court. This was grafted on to a Council of State and a Court of Accounts, which acted as checks on the legal probity of the government.

Bolstering this dispersal of power were practices which, while not part of the formal constitution, nevertheless eventually became part of the *acquis constitutionnel*. One was the strict proportionalism of the electoral system, which was highly permissive, and did nothing to mould the fragmented, dispersed party system into a manageable range of parliamentary groups. Another was the excessive legalism underlying the actions of the executive. The nature of legislation and the attitudes prevalent among the administrative class created an environment in which scope for executive autonomy or discretion was limited, generalised framework legislation creating such discretion was rare, and the administration itself was subject to a tangled mass of complex legal controls.

If this was the theory of the Constitution promulgated in 1948, the practice during the early years of the Republic was rather different. To understand why, it is necessary to consider the party system on which the constitutional edifice was constructed. The system was a fragmented, polarised one, marked by deep cleavages of class, religion, and ideology. The Communist Party very quickly established a dominant position on the left, while the Christian Democrat Party emerged as the strongest party of the centre-right. Between the two, and protected by the permissiveness of proportional representation, were the Socialist Party, the Social Democrats (a splinter group from the latter, protesting at its pro-Communist sympathies), and the Republicans, while on the right were the Liberals (inheritors of the pre-Fascist Liberal tradition), and the neo-Fascist MSI, unashamed heirs to Italy's inglorious interwar years.

Putting together stable coalitions in such a system was inevitably a difficult task. The central position of the Christian Democrats dictated that they formed the pivot of any government, and indeed this has remained the basic rule of the system ever since 1945, even when, as recently, their party has not held the premiership itself. However, since the Christian Democrats have never held a workable parliamentary majority, the key question has been that of which parties they will work with. And, given the presence of an untouchable neo-Facist fringe, and the very limited size of both the Republicans and Liberals, it has always been necessary to draft at least one of the three main parties of the left into the coalition. Thus, at the risk of some simplification, it may be said that post-war Italy has had three main types of coalition: 'Centrist', when only the Social

Democrats are drafted in; 'Centre-Left' when the Socialists join in too; and a 'Grand Coalition' (labelled 'Tripartite' in the 1940s, and the 'Historic Compromise' in the 1970s) when the Communists themselves have to be co-opted.

How the constitution has actually operated has been closely related to which of these three coalition solutions operates. The liberal system of checks and balances described above was the result of a revulsion against Mussolini's authoritarianism and, within the Christian Democrats and the smaller lay parties of the centre, of a fear of the intentions of the Communist Party. It also reflected the liberal participatory spirit of the Resistance, the broad-based anti-Fascist unity of which was the inspiration for the Tripartite coalitions (those including Communists) of the immediate post-war years. In the spring of 1947, however, this unity was shattered. It had lasted long enough to leave its mark on the paper constitution, but not long enough to underwrite its enactment. On the contrary, the tense, confrontational atmosphere of the Cold War – presided over by Centrist governments excluding both Communists *and* Socialists – proved a far more hostile environment for participatory liberalism, and many of the constitution's provisions were still-born, or got off to a very slow start. Once in power, and with the radicals isolated, Christian Democracy and its minor lay allies were far less anxious to protect the rights of minorities and oppositions than they had been before the 1948 election results were known. It took almost a decade to get the Constitutional Court operating, even longer to move very far towards a genuinely independent judiciary, and over twenty years to establish the referendum provisions and a comprehensive network of regional government. The administrative system remained closed and unresponsive, the government parties enjoyed privileged control of the media, and basic civil rights were not always well protected.

Gradually, however, from the mid-1950s onwards, Italian democracy began to mature. The impact of the Cold War on domestic politics became less intense, and critics of the political system could begin to make themselves heard without immediately being branded as fellow-travellers. There was a gradual turnover in the ranks of the judiciary, and even to a degree in the civil service. Within the ruling Centrist coalition, the Social Democrats and Republicans, and some progressive Christian Democrats, began to exercise more influence. And at the beginning of the 1960s, Centrism finally became unworkable, and the political centre of gravity within the coalition shifted markedly to the left with the Socialist Party joining a new Centre-Left government, and the Liberals being ousted.

Over the decade from the mid-1950s to the mid-1960s, these changes had an important impact on constitutional practice. Power began to shift away from the central executive, and the system of checks and balances orginally envisaged became more of a reality. Civil rights were better protected; the judiciary became more independent; and devolved tiers of government were given rather more freedom of manoeuvre. Moreover, the loosening of the ties binding the ruling national coalition, combined with the widening of the range of parties considered eligible to participate in it, had the effect of enhancing the influence of Parliament over the executive.

This last process was given a further important boost by the political changes of the late 1960s. The Socialist Party was by this time the pivotal party in the system, exercising influence disproportionate to its modest electoral support, and it began, at both national and local levels, to re-establish a working relationship with the Communists, while still retaining a place in the ruling Centre-Left coalition. The eventual result of this ambiguity in party alliances was of course the Historic Compromise of the later 1970s – a coalition which ironically proved extremely distasteful to the Socialists – but even before this, the political context ushered in after 1969 had important constitutional consequences.

It created within parliament an environment in which the boundary between government and opposition became very indistinct, and in which majorities could vary significantly in composition from one issue to another. It also made the passing of major legislation extremely difficult unless it enjoyed wide inter-party support. These changes tilted the balance of power further away from the executive. Indeed, as the frequency of cabinet crises in the 1970s indicates, they made it increasingly difficult for coalition governments to survive at all, let alone govern. Such practices were in fact semi-institutionalised in the shape of new rules of parliamentary procedure adopted in 1971. These rules took the crucial power over the timetable out of the hands of the presiding officers of the two chambers, and placed it under the control of an all-party committee of party-group leaders, who were enjoined to operate on the principle of unanimity.

The late 1960s and the 1970s also saw other changes taking constitutional practice back in the direction envisaged by the constitutional drafters. First, the full edifice of the system of regional government was gradually put into place. While not as radical as many had hoped, it wrested control over certain areas of the administrative machine from the central executive and placed it in the hands of local politicians. During the 1970s, in fact, there was a significant transfer of power from the Christian Democrat Party to the Communists, as the latter, in alliance with the Socialists, gradually extended their grip over local government in at least the northern two-thirds of the peninsula. Moreover, regionalisation weakened the hold of the prefect, and hence of the central government, over sub-regional tiers of administration – principally the municipalities – which now passed under the supervision of the regions. And it greatly complicated the process of coalition- and parliamentary-bargaining at national level, because issues and alliances at regional level were frequently thrown on to the national bargaining table.

A second constitutional complexity which developed in the 1970s was the use of the referendum. This was introduced almost by default, since none of the main parties had really wanted it, when civil divorce was put on the statute book in 1970. It was essentially a sop to the Catholics who thought, wrongly, that they could exploit the device to repeal the new law. Although no government-backed legislation has actually been repealed through the seven referendums held to date, the submission of a thorny issue to public judgment has proved to be a device which can be exploited by opposition parties to divide and embarrass the parties of the ruling coalition.

Finally, in the wake of the upsurge in labour militancy during the so-called Hot Autumn of 1969, the Centre-Left coalition passed a major reform of the labour laws, known as the *Statuto dei Lavoratori*, which greatly enhanced the power of organised labour, both in the workplace and in its relationship with government. It thereby considerably amplified those generalised sections of Title III, Part I, of the Constitution dealing with the rights of organised labour. As in the case of the regional reforms, this change, set against the background of an increasingly powerful Communist Party, added to the complexities of government decision-making because the additional power it gave to the labour movement could be harnessed by the Communists in the parliamentary arena as well.

The contemporary constitutional debate

By the latter half of the 1970s, then, the political context in which the Italian Constitution operated had changed substantially from the early years of the Republic, and the process of fleshing out its component parts with detailed enabling legislation and established convention was virtually complete. These changes occurred against a background of increasing concern about what was labelled, with none too much conceptual precision, the 'crisis of governability'. This alleged crisis had many of the same symptoms as in other Western democracies during the 1970s: enhanced distributional conflict between employers, wage earners, and welfare beneficiaries; higher inflation and higher unemployment; severe problems of budgetary management; a more volatile electorate; less cohesive parties; and increased political violence.

However, in Italy a satisfactory political response to this perceived crisis seemed even more remote than elsewhere precisely because there had never been a strong, *dirigiste* style in government. Indeed in the 1970s constitutional and political developments seemed to be making such a style even less achievable than ever. The immobilism of the party system, principally the consequence of the size and role of the Communist Party, pre-empted the alternation in power which could bring a new party and programme to government. Yet at the same time the much increased frequency of cabinet crises indicated the inability of those actually in power to give stability and purpose to the existing coalition formula. This was confirmed most clearly in the stalemate of 1976, when the only government which could be formed at all was one based on a parliamentary coalition so wide as to be almost meaningless.[2]

It was thus inevitable that attention should increasingly turn to constitutional reform as a possible solution to the governability problem, and that the inhibitions which had previously prevented politicians (other than those on the far right) from calling the Constitution into question should gradually drop away. The debate which followed began in a cautious, low-key fashion, limited to academic circles and one or two interested political leaders. Gradually, however, it has widened out as parties and indeed parliament have devoted more attention to institutional issues, and all political leaders have felt obliged to define their position in the debate. It has also widened in scope. What follows is a brief summary of some of the main themes in the three areas of prime concern: Parliament; the executive; and the parties and the electoral system. However, it should be remembered that beyond the core relationship between executive and legislature lie a variety of other issues which have been sucked into the debate, including concern over the public administration, the judiciary, local government, and the legal and constitutional aspects of macro-economic management.

Parliament[3]
The Italian Parliament has been criticised on a number of counts. First, it is alleged that its version of bicameralism, under which both houses enjoy equal powers, is cumbersome and time-consuming. It is difficult to deny the force of this criticism. There are many good reasons for having a second chamber, but exact repetition of all tasks by a second chamber identical, or nearly so, in composition to the first, and unable to claim any representative legitimacy distinct from it, can hardly be counted as one of them. In fact, the main effect of the Italian version of bicameralism is to slow down the legislative process, since obstructionist tactics which fail in one house

can be repeated in the other, and the many minor amendments to legislation passed in the second chamber entail a time-consuming series of exchanges between the two houses. The safeguarding role of a second chamber (which in Italy, in any case, could well fail against serious constitutional abuse, given the identity of composition between the two branches) would not be seriously impaired if one branch were given ultimate legislative superiority, and the other given the prominent role in scrutiny and investigative functions, which latter are at present performed very inadequately.

Secondly, parliament produces a mass of what has been labelled 'micro-sectional' legislation, the importance and scope of which is very limited, and covers matters which would frequently be subject to administrative discretion in other political systems. The backlog of this type of legislation chokes the parliamentary timetable, and limits the scope for satisfactory performance of other functions (controlling and scrutinising the executive), and for examining major legislative projects. It also forces the majority to adopt expedients such as the provision to allow committees to act *in sede legislativa* (i.e. without the need for reference back to the whole chamber for the full legislative procedure). This necessitates the co-operation of the opposition, which can if it wishes prevent such a procedure being used, and in turn gives the opposition parties some influence over not only the parliamentary timetable but also the substance of much government legislation.

This influence is enhanced by rules of procedure that put a premium on wide inter-party agreement over the shape of the parliamentary timetable, which must normally be agreed unanimously by a committee of party-group leaders. It is further increased by the provision for secret voting in a wide range of circumstances – a measure originally devised to limit the potentially excessive power of the strong party apparatus and the party whip. This provision, which would be damaging enough to cohesive one-party governments, can have devastating effects in Italy's broad-based coalitions, where each party is itself highly factionalised. Opposition parties can frequently exploit policy dissension in the ranks of the majority, or the career ambitions of government backbenchers hoping for ministerial office in the next administration, by calling for a secret vote, and highlighting the divisions in a supposedly united majority. The first Craxi cabinet (August 1983 to June 1986), which was widely regarded as a cohesive and business-like government, was in fact defeated no less than 163 times in secret parliamentary votes.

On occasions the secret vote has actually brought governments down. This has happened twice during the 1980s in the special circumstances of the vote on the conversion into law of decrees (*decreti leggi*) issued under Article 77 of the Constitution on the government's own authority, but requiring parliamentary approval within 60 days. Frequently, when trying to force a particular measure through, governments have made it an issue of confidence, but by an ironic twist of the regulations of the Chamber of Deputies, on bills of only one article (the case with most decrees) the confidence vote (an 'open' one) must be followed by a substantive vote actually converting the decree into law, and this latter vote may be a secret one.[4] Dissident government backbenchers are thus able to call their leaders' bluff, and if the collapse of confidence is serious enough, the government may be humiliated into resigning, as happened in June 1986 over the issue of local government finance.

Lest it be thought that the conversion into law of decrees is a small matter, it should be pointed out that their incidence has increased greatly in the last decade, and they have become perhaps the major mechanism by which governments get measures through parliament.[5] In so doing they have become a further target for criticism of the workings of parliament in that their frequency disrupts the planning of the parliamentary timetable, and deprives parliament itself of the opportunity to oversee the entire range of government policy in a particular sector. Strictly speaking, such criticism should be levelled at government rather than parliament (as indeed frequently happens), but it is clear that one important reason why governments feel obliged to resort to rule by decree is precisely that they are unable to get their programme through parliament, or even get parts of it considered, without forcing it on to the agenda via the *decreto-legge*. The absence of priority for government legislation (other than the opportunity to supplicate before the relevant chamber to have it declared urgent), and of any limit on private members bills, the sheer volume of legislation to be considered, the absence of government control over the timetable, and the procedural (as well as electoral) incentives to indiscipline within the government majority, all leave harassed governments with what they perceive to be no alternative but resort to this device.

Naturally, what has been discussed in this brief overview concerns essentially those aspects of the operation of parliament which are determined by constitutional factors, whether through the Constitution itself or through the parliamentary regulations which the Constitution empowers each chamber to draw up. There are, however, other aspects of the Italian Parliament – most notably the nature and quality of the parliamentary class itself, and the relationship between parliamentary parties and parties and groups outside parliament – which have also come in for scrutiny and criticism, but which, except in the section below dealing with the electoral system, are not examined here.

The executive[6]

With the executive as with parliament, it is difficult to separate those aspects of its operation attributable to cultural and sociological factors from those which stem from strictly legal or constitutional factors. The lack of collegiality, cohesion, and stability in Italian government is legendary, and has already been alluded to. A major cause of these shortcomings obviously lies in the nature of the party system, and in the electoral relationship between parties and voters. However, there are also some interesting legal dimensions to these problems – particularly in relation to the role of the Prime Minister – which should not be ignored.

As with heads of government elsewhere, the potential importance of the Prime Minister lies above all in the capacity to give strategic purpose and direction to the work of a large and disparate group of ministers and their administrative teams. However, the debate on prime-ministerial power has traditionally never reached the levels of intensity attained in some other countries for the obvious reason that that power has rarely appeared to extend to the point where it creates an over-mighty chief executive, dominating policy-making in a highly personalised way, and overriding the checks and balances inherent in the collegial nature of collective cabinet responsibility. Rather, the debate on the Prime Minister has focused on the inadequacy of the powers – both formal/legal and political – which he enjoys. Article 95 of the Constitution describes these powers as follows:

> The President of the Council (i.e. the Prime Minister) conducts, and is responsible for, the general policy of the government. He maintains unity in general political and administrative policy, and promotes and co-ordinates the activities of the Ministers.
> Ministers are jointly responsible for the decisions of the Cabinet as a whole, and individually for those of their own particular departments.
> The law establishes regulations concerning the Presidency of the Council of Ministers, and establishes the number, responsibilities and organisation of the various Ministries.

To date, however, no such law has been established, and the relationships between the Prime Minister and his Cabinet have been left almost entirely to the evolution of custom and practice. Precisely how far the Prime Minister speaks for his Cabinet; how much discretion he enjoys in selecting his Cabinet; how far he can curb the public statements of his ministers (especially when they are speaking on subjects outside the remit of their own departments); how far he can refer back to cabinet, block, or indeed, in pursuit of general policy, impose decisions taken within individual ministries; how far he can impose his own solutions in the event of inter-departmental conflict; how far he can allocate special responsibilities to individual ministers, or establish an inner cabinet to deal with urgent or immediate business; all these relationships have remained ambiguous.

Admittedly, such matters are frequently the product of variables considered too intangible to be regulated by legal or constitutional rules. In Britain where the Prime Minister is usually able to silence, switch, or disregard Cabinet ministers as he or she chooses, restructure the Cabinet Office, create new cabinet committees at will, transfer functions between ministries, decide what appears on the Cabinet agenda and so forth, the law as such does little more than define the Prime Minister's salary and pension. But while in Britain there is a presumption (deriving from the conventions which have grown up around strong majoritarian party government) that the Prime Minister *has* such powers, in Italy the presumption is that the Prime Minister can do none of these things. It is in fact precisely because Italy's form of party government has normally worked *against* the Prime Minister that there is an active school of thought arguing that legal regulation is needed to tip the balance back in his favour.

The technical support which the Prime Minister receives is also poor. There is no Cabinet secretariat as such. The Prime Minister's office houses a number of specialised functional agencies which have found a home there for no particularly clear reason, and which have been of some marginal use to the Prime Minister in his central political role.[7] But the absence of a firmly institutionalised Cabinet secretariat is a serious matter, and is only partly offset by the relative stability of the personnel of the Prime Minister's personal *cabinet*, which serves as the substitute for a secretariat proper. Between them, the Under-Secretary of State (i.e. junior minister) in the Prime Minister's Office and the *chef de cabinet* occupy a position somewhat akin to the Secretary to the Cabinet in Britain, but their main role focuses on the Cabinet's relationship with Parliament, rather than on the Prime Minister's relationship with ministers and departments. Nor is there anything similar to a 'Think Tank' like the (former) British Central Policy Review Staff. If Mrs Thatcher found she could manage better without such a body, it was because she had other ways of controlling her Cabinet; her Italian counterpart does not have this underlying political strength, and, it may be argued, needs all the assistance he can obtain from such bodies.

The electoral system and the political parties
The main criticism levelled against the Italian electoral system is naturally its extreme proportionality. The threshold for representation in the lower house is effectively a little over 1 per cent of the national vote (considerably lower for parties with territorial concentration of support). The system is therefore highly permissive;

new parties can establish themselves with relative ease (i.e. they at least take root, even if they do not generally grow), and, without a threshold, existing small parties, even those in decline, take a long time to die off, because their voters have few fears about wasting their vote, and are thus under less pressure to desert to the closest alternative. As a result, the Italian Parliament is normally blessed with at least eight national parties.

In itself, this may or may not be a bad thing, but when combined with the absence of pressures, once a government has been formed, to maintain coalition discipline, it has two adverse consequences. First, it prevents governments (which must invariably be based upon parliamentary coalitions of at least three parties) from taking decisive action, and frequently brings them down if they become too activist. Secondly, it may lead to a major change in the composition of a government (or the majority coalition on which it is based) between elections, and therefore without any electoral ratification. This is quite rare; it happened only in the late 1940s and the early 1960s. But even if this drastic rupture of the democratic link between electoral choice and government formation has not occurred for 25 years, the fact that, in advance of elections, parties feel under little obligation to state clearly their prospective alliance partners, has the effect of making any alliances which *are* formed extremely brittle. And it releases parties from any strong sense of obligation to the voters to stick to alliances when disagreements arise. Naturally, this is in a sense a failure on the part of voters as well as parties, since although there is clear evidence of a *general* public dissatisfaction with coalition instability, voters seem relatively unwilling to punish their parties for provoking that instability – partly, one suspects, because they are so used to such behaviour, and partly because they are unable to determine who has been responsible for the stoppage of play!

A further consequence of the presence of numerous small parties is their ability to defend particular sectional interests. The fear of even quite modest electoral losses to parties prepared to mount a staunch rearguard defensive action may inhibit the larger parties from doing what in a wider perspective may be highly desirable.

A final quirk of the electoral system, much condemned but never yet rectified, is the so-called 'preference vote': the mechanism by which voters (but only the fairly small minority that actually exercises this right effectively) are able to cast preferences for particular candidates on their party's list, thus determining which are actually elected. This procedure has been much discussed in the literature, and its detailed operation need not be considered here. Its effects, however, are profoundly deleterious to party cohesion, and ultimately also to coalition stability, since factional alliances act as 'extra' parties in parliament. The preference vote is also exceedingly damaging to the tone and morality of public life, for one of the most common mechanisms used to win votes is the exploitation of public resources for patronage purposes.

Party cohesion, and the more general question of the inner workings of political parties, is a further area where critics of the Italian constitutional framework have focused their attention. Here, the main criticism is the almost complete absence of legal regulation. Parties are mentioned in electoral law, and are recognised (and in the minimal sense of the requirement to produce and publish annual accounts, are regulated) by the law governing the public finance of political parties. Beyond this, however, they are entirely free. Yet the Italian state is a party state *par excellence*, and parties are central to every aspect of public life. Party nomination is essential for a vast range of public sector appointments, right down to very menial occupations; parties control enormous tracts of the credit and financial system; parties have a major stake in the media, and so on. Ultimately, at both local and national level, decisions about such issues are determined in *party* decision-taking bodies. Yet the individuals who man these bodies get appointed to them, and remain on them, by processes which vary considerably from party to party, are generally hidden from public view, and not infrequently appear to be decidedly detrimental to what might be taken to be the public interest. To reply, in the face of these problems, that such party bodies only get to dispose of public resources if they actually win public (legally regulated) elections in the first place, and that if the electorate is dissatisfied with a party's internal workings, it has the option of not voting for it, may, in the Italian context, be disingenuous. The system is so complex, the normal mechanism of electoral rewards and punishments so limited, the scope for small or unpopular parties to wield power so considerable, that a general *electoral* penalty against corrupt or undemocratic party practices may be seen as inadequate, and more detailed controls as correspondingly necessary.

Other constitutional issues

The issues considered so far are the central ones in the main constitutional debate on governability. There are, however, many other aspects of the working of Italian institutions which have given rise to controversy, but which cannot be examined in detail here, and which, in any case, are less clearly the product of concerns to strengthen the purposiveness and cohesion of central government. (On occasions, indeed, the original concern may work in quite the opposite direction.)

Some of these are clearly *constitutional* problems: the role of the President of the Republic, his term of office, his prerogatives etc; the structure and powers of the three main devolved tiers of government, and the protection of their financial autonomy; the relationship between the judiciary and the political class. Others are in a grey area, which, to British eyes, might not appear to be primarily a constitutional one. There are several examples. One is the reform of the public administration, both in terms of the recruitment and training of its personnel, and its formal organisational features. A second is the reform of what has recently come to be called the 'economic constitution', which includes so many issues (relations between public-sector managers and the political class; relationships between government, business, and labour; the scope and purpose of the public sector; the formation of public expenditure plans) that it can be identified as a *single* problem area only with some considerable imagination.

What is of interest about this latter group of issues, of course, is that the very fact that they are seen, at least by some, as 'constitutional' problems demonstrates the wide scope of constitutional laws and conventions in the political system. The need – if such a need there is – for a wide, even all-party, constitutional agreement to change aspects of governmental practice connected with, say, the public administration or the tools of economic management (areas which in some other systems are seen as fair game for straightforward policy [i.e. partisan] action by governments) shows how all-encompassing the debate has become.

However, as we shall see in the final section, by no means everyone shares this view. Some, at least, believe that the spirit of the constitution can be changed without changing its letter, through piecemeal reform, and by changes in political practice and political relationships. Clearly, in fact, this difference arises in part from contrasting reactions to the complexities of the political system. Those who despair of decisive government action, while there remains such a wide range of parties in Parliament exercising at least a partial veto, believe that the situation can only be rectified by broad inter-party agreement to change the rules of the game itself. Others are less pessimistic about the prospects for decisive action, if only the appropriate political will to make proper use of the existing rules can be injected into a politically more homogenous majority.

The Bozzi Commission
To date, the most notable fruit of the great debate on constitutional reform has been the parliamentary commission of inquiry known, after its chairman, as the *Commissione Bozzi*. The idea of an all-party,

bicameral, investigative commission was first mooted in September 1982, but its progress was interrupted by the general election of the following year. It was taken up again by the incoming Craxi Government, and finally started work in November 1983. The Commission was charged with identifying the common ground between the parliamentary parties on the question of institutional reform, broadly defined, and with setting out proposals for action. As an attempt to establish all-party agreement, or something reasonably close to it, the Commission proved a failure, and perhaps this was inevitable, given the bitter relations prevailing between the government coalition and the Communist opposition while the Commission was in session. Eventually, in fact, only 16 out of 41 members voted in favour of the final report.[8] The Communists withdrew in protest, and the left independents, the small far-left Proletarian Democracy Party, and the MSI voted against; two Social Democrats and one Christian Democrat abstained.

The 'common ground' presented to the two chambers of parliament in February 1985 thus consisted of little more than a series of seven minority reports, the main one of which, claiming the status of *the* Bozzi report and agreed among the governing majority (or most of its constituent parts), was in itself rather bland. Not surprisingly, therefore, the follow-up has been extremely slow, and in relation to the constitutional text itself, that the Commission has been a failure. At the level below this, however, and particularly in relation to the powers of the executive, there are some signs of progress, particularly in the past year, as relations between government and opposition have started to thaw. Moreover, the Bozzi Commission has at least had the virtue of charting the positions of the various Italian parties in the constitutional debate, and for this reason it is worth considering its work in a little more detail.

The Commission held seven major sessions dealing, in order, with: parliament, government, '*fonti normativi*' (roughly, the nature and sources of legislation), the electoral system, parties, the head of state, and a final miscellaneous category including civil rights, justice, public administration, industrial relations, and local government. The fundamental disagreement between parties of the majority and the Communist opposition was, however, clear even in the broad orientation of the opening session. The majority saw the essential problem as one of restoring 'governability' (even if they were singularly lacking in conceptual clarity about the nature of the expression)[9] as is shown in the introduction to the main report:[10]

... the Commission has set out a set of integrated proposals to revise the constitutional framework based on a new division of labour between the institutions, beginning with parliament and the government, and on a structuring of democratic power at various levels compatible with the primary need of overall governability within the system ... (author's trans.)

The Communist minority report, in contrast, takes issue with this fundamental objective:[11]

(the need) in any way possible, to guarantee speed to parliamentary proceedings and predictability (*sicurezza*) to parliamentary outcomes, is asserted as a basic aim (in the main report). From this, it was concluded that such an aim should dominate an inquiry focused on the delicate theme of the relationship between power and responsibility, between the governing function, and the sharing out of the powers of legislation, scrutiny, and participation. Apart from being a misconceived way of looking at government ... this orientation was accompanied by an assumption that power should be restored to the centre, against the trend which, since the early 1970s, has seen a dispersal of power and the legitimation in the decision-making process of actors other than the political parties themselves. (author's trans.)

Faced with such a contrast of outlooks, it is not surprising that, on the main themes of the governability debate, broad agreement proved elusive. However, agreement frequently proved elusive even within the government majority. In particular, on the key question of the reform of the electoral system a rationalisation limiting the effects of proportionality, or constraining parties to hold together more effectively in coalitions, could not be agreed. Four of the smaller parties (Republicans, Liberals, Social Democrats, and the MSI) were opposed to any major change at all beyond the generally agreed proposal to limit, if not abolish, the preference-vote mechanism. The Christian-Democrats, in contrast, favoured a system providing an incentive for the formation of stable majorities: in effect a premium of 10 per cent of the total seats in the Chamber, divided 60/40 between the largest and second-largest coalition lists. The purpose of this proposal was to bind troublesome minor parties to the dominant Christian Democrat leadership in government, thus reducing their contractual power. More generally, it was intended to provide some form of moral commitment to coalition cohesiveness by the parties before the electorate, and thereby to raise the electoral cost of disruptive behaviour. As a mechanism for strengthening the ruling majority through increasing its size, however, it was, as Agosta has pointed out, a more modest proposal than its authors had realised.[12]

In any case, the proposal obtained no support from the Communists, who favoured a modified version of the West German system. Even more significantly, since it had originally professed support for a more majoritarian system, the Socialist Party was against the

Christian Democrat proposal. Other than the Christian Democrats, in fact, the only support for a real change away from the existing degree of proportionality came from the 'independent-left' intellectuals. Notable here was the political scientist Gianfranco Pasquino, whose wider concern was to introduce alternation into the political system. He proposed a double-ballot system with 80 per cent of the seats distributed through a PR-based first ballot, followed, for the second, by the formation of party alliances and the designation of 'Prime Minister candidates', with the winning team taking three-quarters of the remaining seats.[13]

Given such a diversity of proposals, it was not surprising that the Bozzi Commission declared itself completely beaten by the problem of electoral reform. It admitted tamely that even minimum common ground had proved elusive, and restricted itself to a stark listing of alternative proposals 'as a contribution to the parliamentary debate'.

On the other key issues, there was at least some common ground – especially in relation to the debate on the powers of the executive. First, the main report concluded that there should be major changes in the position of the Prime Minister. Amendments were proposed to articles 92–95 of the Constitution, by which the Prime Minister would become the sole recipient of the parliamentary vote of confidence installing a government. To obtain this vote, the Prime Minister would present his programme, and the composition of his *inner* cabinet, to a joint session of the two chambers. Thereafter, he would be free to appoint *and dismiss* his ministers as he saw fit. The only constraint would be what was politically feasible. This might in practice be a major constraint, but as a first step towards increasing the Prime Minister's freedom, at least to reshuffle his Cabinet once formed, article 94 was to be amended to stipulate that in the case of the resignation of the government, there would have to be a formal explanation to a joint session of the two chambers of parliament by the Prime Minister. One main purpose of this would be to shed light on the precise causes of the crisis should it be precipitated not by Parliament itself, but by the Prime Minister's own detractors in the Cabinet. This would help to make clear who exactly was responsible for bringing about the collapse of the government. The procedure would obviously not be as strong as a constructive vote of no-confidence, on which there was much discussion in the Bozzi Commission but no agreement. But it might provide some assistance against speculative ministerial provocation if it could be institutionalised (most Cabinets, after all, tend to fall in this way, so it would be used frequently) and if public attention could be focused on it.

A second set of proposals aimed at strengthening the government touched on the blocking powers of parliament. In return for an effective surrender of the widespread use (and abuse) hitherto made by governments of the power, under article 77 of the Constitution, to rule by decree, the Commission proposed a revision of article 72, providing the government with preferential treatment for any legislation it declared urgent, providing that such treatment were approved by an absolute majority of the relevant chamber. The Commission also agreed in principle on the need to limit the scope of secret voting, especially on financial legislation, and proposed (without specifying the precise wording) that this be done by transferring the power to regulate secret voting from the regulations of each chamber to the Constitution itself. Not surprisingly, such a move was vigorously opposed by the Communist Party, which derives much of its parliamentary power from the provision for secret voting. Finally, the Commission proposed two modest measures to free parliament from a small part of its workload, and thus increase the prospects of legislative proposals getting through. The first was at least some division of labour between the two houses, making it unnecessary for all bills to pass through the Senate (although as a safeguard, the Senate could in principle request any particular bill). The second was an addendum to article 77 intended to increase the possibilities for generalised framework legislation, to be filled out by government decree, and for delegated legislation.

The full text of the main Bozzi report contains many other proposals, too numerous to analyse here. What have been described are the main proposals addressed to the overall problem of governability. It is clear, as the report acknowledges, that the intention was not to provide a framework for a 'Second Republic' with radical changes in the relationship between the public powers, and even in the form of government itself (direct election of the President of the Republic or the Prime Minister: abandonment of proportional representation etc.). The main outlines of the 1948 Constitution are accepted. Rather the aim was to introduce a series of limited adjustments improving the overall governability of the existing system.

As we have already seen, however, even in this limited aim the Bozzi Commission has met with little success. The narrow political basis (Christian Democracy, and the Socialist, Liberal, and Republican Parties) on which its report was constructed was seen as inadequate for the rigours of a process of constitutional revision. The Constitution requires that amendments be passed by absolute majorities of both houses in two successive sessions, at intervals of not less than three months. Unless approved by majorities of over two-thirds at second reading, they may then be subject to a referendum if one-fifth of the members of either house (or 500,000 voters or five regional councils) so request. In short, no government can seriously contemplate the risks of such a process without the consent of the Communists. Revising electoral law is, of course, a different matter, but that runs up against not only the Communists, but also most of the smaller parties of the centre.

The prospects: governability, but not from constitutional reform?

Ten years on from the firing of the first shots in the battle to reform the Constitution, the war continues – less fiercely than before, but with no sign of a conclusion. Some of the contestants appear over time to have changed sides; others to have lost sight of which side they are on. For the present the prospects for constitutional reform look poor. Relations between the Communists and the governing majority have improved from their low ebb in 1984/5, but are nowhere near the point where major constitutional revision seems likely. Even the Socialists, in the late 1970s the great protagonists of drastic constitutional surgery, lost interest in the issue after winning the premiership in 1983 (although, as their tenure came to an end they showed signs of reviving the debate). The Christian Democrats would welcome certain reforms, but are unwilling to create political tensions to obtain them.[14]

The stalemate is not quite complete, however, for two main reasons. First, not all reforms of the spirit of the Constitution require *constitutional* reform. In some areas ordinary law is enough, and the most important such area is that dealing with the executive. Earlier, we observed that the law dealing with the organisation of the Presidency of the Council of Ministers, stipulated by article 95 of the Constitution, has never been passed. In 1986, however, arising out of the work done by the Bozzi Commission, very substantial progress was made on that law. A draft was hammered out in the Constitutional Affairs Committee of the Chamber of Deputies, and passed through all its stages in the spring. By early 1987 it had reached the Senate (where, admittedly, its chances of further progress before a general election looked slim).

The Bill is wide ranging, and if eventually passed could have an impact on several of the issues discussed in this chapter. Article 5, Section 2 attempts to define the relationship between Prime Minister and Cabinet in terms intended to assist the co-ordinating role of the former. In particular, it aims to give him the authority to control public statements made by ministers, to suspend certain measures proposed by ministers, pending reference to full Cabinet, to interpret to individual ministers' (and give political directions to them on the basis of) general Cabinet decisions, and to co-ordinate (and resolve disputes between) the work of the entire Cabinet. According to the rapporteur of the Constitutional Affairs Committee of the Chamber of Deputies, this amounts to:

> a series of powers which should enable the Prime Minister to exercise the co-ordinating role attributed to him by the Constitution, but which has traditionally not been realised. In this way, long-standing and serious problems of disunity and lack of co-ordination may be overcome. It will be the first time, since the Zanardelli decree of 1901, that the powers of the Prime Minister have been anywhere defined. (author's trans.)[15]

The Bill also institutionalises a body which has been in existence since 1983, but without any legal basis: the so-called *Consiglio di Gabinetto* (Council of the Cabinet), a type of inner cabinet, consisting of seven senior ministers chosen not just for the importance of the ministries held, but for their role as coalition party leaders. Its purpose is to provide what the large and unwieldy Cabinet fails to provide: a genuinely collegial institution capable of discussing, within a restricted circle of authoritative party leaders, issues of central political importance to the overall strategy of the government, as opposed to the many technical and administrative issues which absorb the attention of the full Cabinet. Finally, the Bill provides authority for a complete overhaul of the structure of interministerial committees, makes the allocation of functions between ministries much more flexible, and, perhaps most important of all, for the first time installs a permanent Cabinet secretariat, with a substantial staff, to assist the Prime Minister in his work.[16]

There are, then, a number of measures in the Bill, which within the limits of what the law itself can do, assist the Prime Minister. There is, of course, a price to be paid to get the measure through, and that price is a commitment, enshrined in article 15, to impose limits on the government's use of decree-laws. It seems likely, in fact, that should the Bill eventually pass into law, it will do so within the framework of a wider agreement to change the regulations of the Chamber of Deputies to give preferential treatment to urgent government business, as a substitute for the present practice of issuing decrees. Such a change would represent a major improvement on the existing situation, not only because government decree powers are inherently undesirable, but also because Parliament would be less likely to be choked by a continuous stream of decrees requiring conversion into law. This improvement would be particularly likely if proposals for broader framework legislation also contained in the new Bill get through, and enable the government itself to present its legislation to Parliament in a more co-ordinated and orderly way.

Despite all these worthy proposals, however, it may legitimately be asked whether the detailed, essentially technical changes outlined either by the Bozzi Commission or by the Bill to reform the relationship between Prime Minister, Cabinet, and Parliament, can really do much to tackle problems which are essentially political in nature. In the short term, in fact, only the drastic constitutional surgery deliberately abjured by the Bozzi Commission (and possibly not even that) would hold out any prospect of a major change. Nevertheless, there may be some reason to suppose that, at the underlying political level, changes are taking place, albeit slowly. The most significant sign of this is of course the emergence of a trend, dating back to the late 1970s, towards at least some of the features of prime-ministerial government. Writing at the start of the decade, Sabino Cassese perspicaciously suggested that such a development could be discerned in the experience of the Andreotti Government of 1976–79.[17] The unhappy experiences of Cossiga, Forlani, and Fanfani in the following legislature made such a hypothesis seem premature, but the unprecedentedly long tenure of Bettino Craxi since the 1983 election, and in retrospect, the Spadolini premiership in 1981/2, both point in the direction indicated by Cassese.

The reasons why both these individuals can be seen as 'strong' Prime Ministers (at least in comparison to most of their predecessors) are complex, and I have outlined some in a recent article.[18] The essence of the argument is that changing relationships between parties and the electorate, and a greater personalisation of political leadership, are both serving to give the Prime Minister in Italy a much higher public profile, and hence a more direct relationship with public opinion, than has hitherto been the case. In Craxi's case, this has been combined with some unusual personal qualities and, perhaps crucially, an unusual configuration of relationships inside the coalition, in which the Prime Minister enjoys complete mastery of his own party, and his main ally (the Christian Democrat Party) is, or has been until recently, in an exceptionally weak position. Such circumstances have enabled Craxi to use his undoubted public popularity to put pressure on his Cabinet colleagues in a way not possible in the past. At the same time, and independently of any new legal powers granted to Palazzo Chigi to do so, there has been a gradual reorganisation and accretion of administrative powers in the Prime Minister's office, begun, as Cassese has argued, under Andreotti, but continued by his successors.

Speculatively, it may also be suggested that the Italian electorate – disillusioned by the instability brought by the rising strength of the Communists in the 1970s, and correspondingly grateful for the relative stability, and the remarkable economic recovery, of the middle years of the 1980s – is now ready to reward parties and leaders who provide that stability. Indeed, this may in turn act as an inhibition on those, whether in Cabinet or Parliament, who seek to disrupt the work of the executive. It is, to be sure, a rather slim and speculative hope, although there is at least some evidence from recent electoral behaviour that it is not an entirely unreasonable one. And if it is realised, then the greater political stability it may bring could either make the type of constitutional reform discussed in this chapter less necessary, or indeed create the very political conditions in which its introduction is possible.

It is, however, advisable to conclude on a note of caution about constitutional reform – even in the radical form which in the present political climate is beyond reach. At first sight it might seem intuitively obvious that had Italy adopted a different constitutional framework in the 1940s – a less libertarian document with an electoral system excluding the smaller parties, and perhaps (improbable though it was after two decades of tragi-comic Bonapartism) even a directly elected executive – then the system would have worked differently. Yet the strength and solid foundation of the Communist Party, established well before the 1948 Constitution was promulgated, and the anomic, alienated, politically volatile southern electorate, may well have precluded any stable, self-confident executive from establishing itself in power, even when bolstered by favourable constitutional conditions. The executive was stabilised in Germany (superficially an historical parallel) because the Nazi inheritance was far worse than its Fascist counterpart, because both the Western allies and the Russians took an active hand, in their different ways, in reconstructing German politics (while what was happening in Italy was largely ignored once the Communists accepted Italy's Western allegiance), because the country was partitioned, and because, socially and economically, it was far more advanced and homogenous. In Italy, in contrast, a strengthened executive could well have created such tensions that the end result would have been civil war and/or a classic Mediterranean military *coup*: an outcome far worse than the drawn-out, intricate, and continuous political balancing act dictated by the Republican Constitution itself. In this sense, the Constitution did *count*, but not necessarily with the costs supposed by those who wish that De Gasperi, the first post-war Christian Democrat Prime Minister, had been a de Gaulle!

Moreover, if at any subsequent date a Gaullist solution had been imposed, it is far from certain that Italy could have emulated the Fifth Republic. In recent years there has been much speculation about just how much 'necessity' there was in the eventual outcome of the 1958/62 constitutional revision in France. Had de Gaulle lost in 1962, or Poher won in 1969, the rules could have allowed for a rather different outcome, or so it has been widely argued.[19] Without an Algeria, and without a de Gaulle, it may well be suggested that the passage from the First to the Second Republic in Italy would be very different from that from the Fourth to the Fifth in France.

This does not *necessarily* invalidate some of the more radical constitutional solutions which have been advocated, in particular the Pasquino proposals for a second-ballot electoral system described above. In the late 1980s, Italy may indeed at last be able to cope with institutional engineering precisely because the underlying social and economic stability is greater, and the political dissensus less marked. Yet the risks of such changes having little impact, or worse a negative impact, are still not negligible, and it is for this reason, and because the existing system is tolerable, if only barely so, that few are willing to contemplate the leap in the dark that constitutional reform seems to entail.

Notes and references

1. The first section of this chapter outlines arguments found in greater detail in David Hine, 'Thirty Years of the Italian Republic: Governability and Constitutional Reform', *Parliamentary Affairs*, XXXIV, 1, Winter 1981, pp. 63–80.
2. See, *inter alia*, G. Pasquino, *Crisi di Governo e Governabilità*, (Bologna, Il Mulino, 1980).
3. For providing much useful material and assistance in the preparation of this section, I am indebted to Vincent Della Sala of Nuffield College, Oxford.
4. See M.L.M. Honorati, 'Le istituzioni in Italia: Il Parlamento: il modo del voto segreto', *Quaderni Costituzionali*, IV, 1, April 1984, pp. 143–47, and *La Costituzione della Repubblica e Il Regolamento della Camera dei Deputati* (Rome, Camera dei Deputati, 1984), art. 116, p. 137.
5. See *La Decretazione d'Urgenza* (Rome, Camera dei Deputati, 1985).
6. On the Italian executive see the special edition of *Quaderni Costituzionali*, 'Struttura del governo e ruolo della Presidenza del Consiglio', II, 1, 1982.
7. See S. Cassese, 'Esiste un governo in Italia?' in G. Pasquino (ed.), *Il Sistema Politico Italiano*, (Bari, Laterza, 1985), pp. 269–303.
8. The work of the Bozzi Commission is published as *Camera dei Deputati/Senato della Repubblica, Relazione della Commissione Parlamentare per le Riforme Istituzionali*, IX Legislatura, Doc. XVI–bis, nos. 1, 2, 3. A useful summary and commentary is found in *Riformi Istituzionali*, supplement to *Democrazia e Diritto*, 2, 1985, pp. 1–153.
9. See G. Pasquino, 'Teoria e prassi dell'ingovernabilità nella Commissione per la Riforme Istituzionali', *Stato e Mercato*, 15, December 1985, pp. 365–96.
10. *Relazione della Commissione*, op.cit., p. 13.
11. Ibid., pp. 606–7.
12. See A. Agosta, 'Sistema elettorale: obiettivi ed effetti delle proposte di riforma', in *Riforme Istituzionali*, op.cit., pp. 122–46.
13. Ibid., pp. 134–40. See also G. Pasquino, *Restituire lo scettro al principe* (Bari, Laterza, 1985).
14. For a summary of recent and current party attitudes to institutional reform, see P. Armaroli, *L'introvabile governabilità: le strategie dei partiti della constituente alla Commissione Bozzi* (Padova, CEDAM, 1986).
15. *Atti Parlamentari*, Camera dei Deputati, IX Legislatura, N. 1911–357–2184–349–1663–A, Relazione della I Commissione Permanente, p. XIII. This document

contains the bill as it emerged from committee, together with a commentary by the rapporteur, Alfredo Battaglia.

16. Ibid., pp. 1–35.
17. Cassese, op.cit., pp. 279–83.
18. See David Hine, 'The Craxi Premiership' in R. Leonardi and R. Nanetti (eds), *Italian Politics: A Review*, Vol. I (London, Frances Pinter, 1986).
19. See Olivier Duhamel, 'Les logiques cachées de la constitution de la Cinquième Republique', *Revue Française de Science Politique*, 34 (4/5), August–October 1984, pp. 615–27. In the same number see the articles by Parodi and Vedel.

11 The Federal Republic of Germany (1949): Restoring the *Rechtsstaat*
Kurt Sontheimer

The Constitution of the Federal Republic of Germany was passed on 23 May 1949. It will soon be forty years old. It is called the Basic Law (*Grundgesetz*) because the constituent assembly, the Parliamentary Council which deliberated upon it and passed it, wanted to reserve the title Constitution for a constitution for the whole of Germany. A constitutional document for only a part of the country was considered deficient. The Basic Law of the Federal Republic of Germany is, notwithstanding, a full-fledged constitution with no less than 146 articles. In fact, having existed for almost 40 years, it is now considered to be one of the best-functioning and most efficient working constitutions among the Western democracies.

The constituent assembly, called into existence in 1948 by the three military governors of the Western zones of occupation, had in mind the ill-fated experience of the first German democracy – the Weimar Republic – when it set out to deliberate on a new constitution for a new German democracy. It was keen to avoid the mistakes of the Weimar Constitution, so much so that the renowned constitutional theorist, Carl Schmitt, once called it an 'Anti-Constitution' to that of Weimar.[1]

In this attempt, the 'founding fathers' were hardly restricted by the guidelines of the Western military governments which ruled Germany until the Federal Republic came into existence in the autumn of 1949. They had asked for a 'democratic constitution', and more specifically for a 'governmental structure of the federal type which is best adapted to the re-establishment of German unity – and which will protect the rights of the participating states, provide adequate central authority and contain guarantees of individual rights and freedoms'.

What were the lessons that the vast majority of the 65 members of the Parliamentary Council, delegated from the *Länder* parliaments, had learned from Weimar?[2]

(i)   There should be a strong executive. This is why they made the Chancellor, elected by the Bundestag, the central figure in the political system. The Chancellor's authority was confined and enhanced by the unusual provisions in the Basic Law that the Bundestag could only vote him out of office by a 'constructive vote of no-confidence' in which it at the same time gave a majority to his successor; thus a purely negative majority *against* an incumbent chancellor would have no effect. This was to serve to prevent the Chancellor being overthrown by a coalition of incompatible parties as had occurred in the Weimar Republic. The President, potentially powerful in Weimar, as Hindenburg had shown, was to have no real power; his function was to be largely ceremonial.

(ii)   There should be a strong and authoritative constitution. Amendment of the Constitution, which requires a two-thirds majority in both houses, was ruled out altogether with respect to the fundamentals of the Basic Law, that is the democratic and federal character of the state and the guarantee of basic human rights. These principles were made the subject of entrenched clauses. Moreover, a constitutional court was to serve as the guardian of the constitution, even *vis-à-vis* the legislative bodies. Anti-constitutional parties and actions were to be forbidden.

(iii)   There should be representative party government. For the first time in German history parties were to be 'constitutionalised', that is, recognised in their democratic function by the Constitution (Art. 21). The people were deprived of any plebiscitarian instruments of the kind which had existed under Weimar which, it was held, had encouraged the growth of extremist demagogy, for example in the protest movement against the Young Plan in 1930, and had increased Hitler's popular appeal with the masses.

(iv)   As a further reaction against the experiences of the recent past (in this case the over-centralisation which had been latent in the Weimar Constitution and which had been carried to terrible completion under Hitler), the federal character of the new Republic was constitutionally guaranteed by the Basic Law. The links between democratic institutions at the federal and *Land* levels are embodied in part in the Bundesrat where representatives of the *Land* governments have a say in federal legislation.

It is widely accepted by most observers of German constitutional developments that these lessons of Weimar have been learnt well, although the successful working of the constitution has also, of course, been helped by ideological, social and political developments following the Second World War. These conditions, including the party system, a wide popular consensus on basic principles, and, it must not be forgotten, successful economic development, helped the constitution to work more smoothly.

What is the function of the Basic Law in the political life of the Federal Republic? As with every modern constitution, the Basic Law lays down the principles and provides the legal framework for the political process. It contains on the one hand the basic political orientations to which the country has committed itself; it also defines in detail the competences and the powers given to the different institutions of the political system, and lays down their possibilities and limits.

In reflecting on the forces that had brought about National Socialism and the ruin of the first German democracy, that of the Weimar Republic, the makers of the Basic Law were convinced that the constitution should be the ultimate point of reference in German political life and should provide norms for the political process. The constitution became the new sovereign of German politics.[3]

Understanding the Bonn Constitution

The Bonn constitution, as we have seen, is thus historically a response to the defeat of the first German democracy in 1933 and to Nazi dictatorship. That is why human rights have been given an eminent and important position in it; for the same reason the rule of law as a binding principle has been applied rigorously to all institutions of the new democratic state. By instituting the rule of law after the misrule of the *Unrechtsstaat* of the Third Reich, and by trying to amend the particular deficiencies of the Weimar Constitution, the founding fathers of the Federal Republic helped to create an instrument of government which was effective in producing as well as in maintaining liberal-democratic institutions in Germany. There have been some changes in the text of the constitution but they have not been so important as to give it a totally different direction. The constitutional amendments were adjustments to new situations rather than attempts fundamentally to alter the Constitution.

Although the Basic Law – being considered to be a provisional constitution – was not submitted to the German people for approval, but rather to the parliaments of the *Länder*, it quickly gained respect and authority amongst all political groups and amongst the population at large. This was remarkable progress compared with the Weimar Republic, where the constitution had never been fully accepted by many of the forces on the political scene nor by important segments of the general public.

The quality of the Basic Law

Why is it that the Basic Law is generally considered to be such a good and efficient constitution for the Federal Republic? The main reason is that the organisation and distribution of powers in the German state are regarded as acceptable and effective. The constitution, indeed, provides a legal framework for a free political system which gives all political forces subscribing to the principles of free and democratic government a fair chance to operate within the framework of the Basic Law. The constitution allows for a large amount of political freedom with respect to society and its groups, but on the other hand it provides for strong government when that is wanted or needed. Furthermore it renders possible a positive balance of power between the political forces at the different territorial levels of political life, namely, the communes, the States (*Länder*) and the federal organisation (*Bund*). A free democratic process, along with a high degree of governmental stability and social peace, are the main assets of German constitutional life.

According to a noted saying of one of the best known theoreticians of constitutional law, the late Professor Rudolf Smend, a constitution is at the same time 'a stimulus and a constraint' ('*Anregung und Schranke*');[4] it both liberates and binds. It is on the one hand an incentive to progress in public life but on the other a barrier to certain well-defined activities which are held to be unconstitutional. The Basic Law has not proved to be a very dogmatic, inflexible constitution which prevents political life from developing. It is, rather, a frame of reference of the kind which binds political forces together. The constitution is also sufficiently flexible to allow for adjustment to new situations without the need for constitutional amendment.

The Constitutional Court

The makers of the German constitution put the sovereignty of the Constitution higher than the will of the majority of the people's representatives. They instituted a Constitutional Court, at Karlsruhe, which serves as the guardian of the constitution. The *Grundgesetz* is, in a sense, what the Constitutional Court says it is.[5] If one wants to find out what a constitutional norm means, one has to refer to the jurisdiction of the sixteen constitutional judges, grouped in two Senates. Their decisions are binding for the other constitutional organs like the government and the parliament. The Court can nullify parliament acts if they are considered not to be congruent with constitutional norms, and it has often done so. It settles possible conflicts between the different political institutions, for example between the Federal State and the *Länder*.

The Constitutional Court is thus an important political institution within the framework of democratic government in Germany. It is the institution which is responsible for the understanding and interpretation of the constitution at any given moment. The Court, however, cannot act by itself. It has to be brought into action by one of the political institutions concerned. Nevertheless, on almost all important matters of constitutional law and political conflict, the Constitutional Court has made some pronouncement. There is by now a vast body of jurisdiction on all important aspects of the democratic state, from the interpretation of human and civil rights to the definition of the competences of the different organs of the federal state, and also in the judicial review of many policy issues. In 1983, for instance, the Court disrupted the government's plans to carry out a population census by ruling that some of the data to be collected represented an infringement of individual privacy. In 1975, it caused the SPD–FDP coalition government to modify its legislation on abortion, in the name of the 'right to life' guaranteed by Article 2 of the Basic Law. In 1984, it forced the government to repay several million Deutschmarks to well-off taxpayers who had been obliged to make a 'forced loan' to the government. And in 1983 it ruled that the stationing of Pershing II missiles in the Federal Republic was not unconstitutional, since it was the result of policies pursued by the Soviet Union.[6]

On the whole, one can say that in the Federal Republic of Germany the constitution serves the functions which are ascribed to it in constitutional theory. It allows for a relatively free democratic process, but relates this process to given rules and to the play of institutions whose powers are well defined and limited. It makes effective, though limited, government possible and its main provisions are accepted not only by the ruling political forces and by the central institutions of society but by the population at large. This gives the constitution great importance, although there has been no marked development in the direction of a particular constitutional mythology as in the United States.

But neither the existence of the powerful Constitutional Court nor the constitutional devices established in reaction to the apparent or alleged deficiencies of the former Weimar Constitution can completely explain the generally positive development and relatively efficient working of the Bonn constitution, although they have contributed to it. Unless the real forces in politics are in accordance with the potentialities and restrictions of the constitution, no constitution can become a 'living constitution' (*lebende Verfassung*). The *Grundgesetz* has become such a living constitution. The inherent antagonism between the constitution as a normative document and the reality of political life under such a constitution (the tension between *Verfassungsnorm* and *Verfassungswirklichkeit*) was never so strong as to produce serious conflicts which could threaten the stability of the political system.[7]

Changes in the Bonn Constitution

Although there have been some occasions when there was discussion of whether the Bonn Constitution was still good enough or whether it needed a thorough overhaul, it has on the whole been regarded as a good foundation for the democratic process in West Germany. A commission made up of parliamentarians and constitutional experts (*Enquête – Kommission*), which in the early 1970s investigated whether the *Grundgesetz* was in need of fundamental reform (with particular reference to the viability of the federal structure, but not its basic principles), did not suggest any major alterations, but confirmed the value and relevance of the constitution.[8] Nevertheless, the constitution has not remained unchanged.

In fact, the changes in the text of the constitutional document since 1949 have been quite numerous. There were 34 amendments up to 1986; 33 articles of the Basic Law have been newly formulated and others annulled. These bare statistics do not, however, say much about the substantive changes that have occurred. In substance there were *four* areas of state activity in which constitutional changes became necessary and were then put into practice.

The constitution can be altered only by a two-thirds majority in both the Bundestag and the Bundesrat. This (except in the unusual 'Grand Coalition' situation of 1966–69) means that the opposition parties must support any constitutional change; in any case, constitutional change requires general agreement. The areas of major constitutional change have been as follows:

(i)   the military constitution (*Wehrverfassung*);
(ii)   the emergency constitution (*Notstandsverfassung*);
(iii)   the federal relationship (*Verhältnis Bund-Länder*);
(iv)   the complex of internal security (*Innere Sicherheit*).

The Bonn Constitution of 1949 had been written under the assumption that Germany would not have armed forces at its disposal for some time. When rearmament became effective in the 1950s it also became necessary to include what is called the *Wehrverfassung*, namely all the constitutional rules regarding the military and its implications for the state and the individual citizen. The SPD opposition of the time finally agreed to the constitutional changes needed, because it wanted to preserve its influence on the spirit and organisation of the prospective army.

The emergency laws (*Notstandsgesetze*), passed in 1968, became necessary after Germany had gained full sovereignty as a state. They were elaborated in order to provide a legal framework for the political process in case of emergency, that is, in the case of an attack from outside or from within (civil war). For this particular eventuality, which had previously been under the control of the Allied Powers, the constitution sets up a number of norms and institutions which are designed so as to handle such a problem without completely putting aside the democratic and liberal character of the constitution. The emergency constitution was passed against the fierce hostility of the so-called extra-parliamentary opposition, which feared that the new law would be used against it. But at that time the CDU/CSU and the SPD had formed a Grand Coalition, commanding a two-thirds majority in both houses, which was resolved upon passing the emergency constitution. One concession to the opposition was the introduction of a resistance clause (Art. 20.4) which, however, has no real significance. The new article reads: 'All Germans shall have the right to resist any person or persons seeking to abolish that constitutional order (i.e. the Basic Law) should no other remedy be possible.' This article was devised as a concession to the opponents of the emergency constitution, by explicitly conferring upon them the right to resist. Under normal conditions, however, this right cannot be put into practice, since some kind of 'remedy' will always be available within the constitutional framework.

The heated discussion about this important extension of the constitution sometimes failed to see that the provisions of the emergency constitution were applicable only in the case of a real emergency. So far this has not come about. The emergency norms do not impinge upon everyday constitutional practice.

One of the most important fields of constitutional change is the relationship between *Bund* and *Länder*, i.e. the effectiveness and balance of the federal structure. This area was the subject of 25 of the 34 constitutional amendments mentioned above; in the case of every one of them (as in almost all other federal states) it was the federal level, the *Bund*, which gained more and more power in the process, because the demands of steering the economy and managing modern society made more uniform and centralised decisions essential. Some of the powers that had originally been left to the *Länder* were therefore now taken over by the *Bund*, partly through an extension of the concept of 'joint tasks' laid down in Art. 91a of the Basic Law. In other important cases *Bund* and *Länder*

formed a new kind of collaboration through a network of joint institutions – *co-operative federalism*, in Wheare's terminology, as opposed
to *co-ordinate federalism* or *administrative federalism*, in order to pave
the way for common measures acceptable to both of them. Thus,
even though there has been a shift of power from the *Länder* to
the centre, the federal element still remains strong.

Finally, some minor constitutional changes occurred in the field
of internal security, due mainly to acts of terrorism in the 1970s.
The implementation of a higher degree of *Verfassungsschutz* (protection of the constitution) has constantly been under discussion
since 1968.[9] There is a tendency on the part of the present conservative government (a CDU/CSU/FDP coalition) to value law and order
more highly than the protection of the individual rights of the citizen.
In particular, the right to assemble and to demonstrate is being
weakened by the increase in the power of the police. This was,
brought about by new laws, however, and not by constitutional
amendment.

Constitutional development, as reflected by these changes of the
Basic Law, can be taken as a more or less normal adjustment to
new situations and new challenges for the political system. Although
it has sometimes been said that the Bonn Constitution has been
transformed into an instrument of the executive, this cannot be confirmed by the facts. There have, however, been some situations
in which the traditional rights of liberalism were weighed against
necessities of state and the maintenance of law and order, with the
effect of succumbing to Raison d'État. Nevertheless, on the whole
the constitution of the Federal Republic of Germany has remained
what it was supposed to be, a liberal and democratic constitution
for a free society, combining a free democratic process with effective
government.

No present interest in new changes
At present there seems no need for further changes in the
constitution. Looking back on an almost forty-year-old constitutional
history, one finds that the Federal Republic has developed a rather
pragmatic outlook on the problem of constitutional change. The
majority of those in the established political parties want to avoid
constitutional change as much as possible. They are nevertheless
ready to consider change if the quality of political life and of the
political process is thereby improved.

Public debate on constitutional problems
One problem that has been under consideration for a long time
is the introduction of institutions of *plebiscitarian democracy* (such

as the referendum) into the almost totally representative nature of the federal constitution. Public discussion, especially within the FDP and even more within the Greens, has again and again made proposals for more direct democracy, but the majority has always been hesitant as a result of the bad experience of Weimar. It is therefore likely that, despite a stronger public interest in the participatory aspects of democracy, the Bonn Constitution will not make any changes in that direction.

The new party of the Greens would, if it had the power to do so, try to change the Constitution to introduce, for example, ecological obligations into it and even to demand the constitutional prohibition of nuclear energy for civil as well as for military purposes. There is not the slightest chance of such proposals gaining the necessary two-thirds majority, however. They are not, therefore, on the political agenda, nor is constitutional reform in general on the agenda of German politics.

There has also been, in connection with terrorism, a wide discussion about the problem of *Gewalt* (force, violence) and legitimacy in the modern state. The debate began in the students' movement, which had asked whether the power of the state was entirely legitimate and whether it should not be opposed by some kind of *Gegengewalt* (counter-power). The discussion was important for political and constitutional theory, because it contested the use of force by the state. It raised the question whether the use which the state made of its powers was always legitimate and justified. A similar discussion has been going in connection with nuclear power. It was questioned whether the state had, under the constitution, the right to build nuclear plants as long as it was not able to eliminate all the risks that nuclear power entails for human beings.

All these dicussions centred around problems of constitutional relevance, but since there is no majority for constitutional amendment, they were not likely to lead to constitutional reform. It is important to distinguish between the constitution as such and those special laws relating to the working of institutions such as, for example, the party law which regulates all matters connected with party life. Such laws are within the reach of a simple majority and can therefore easily be altered. But even in this field, apart from possible limitations on protest activity, no essential changes are in view.

The authority of the Constitution
Although there has been little pressure for fundamental constitutional change in the Federal Republic for some time, the opposing forces in the political arena tend to legitimise their political conceptions

by appealing to the constitution. It apparently gives more weight to a political argument if one can show that it is in accordance with the constitution. There are, however, two different ways in which the constitution can be brought into play: there are the conservative and the progressive approaches to the constitution. Conservative parties – the CDU and CSU – maintain that their policies and their political decisions are geared to the defence of the constitution. For them, the constitution is something to be preserved and defended against any attempt to alter it fundamentally. More progressive parties like the SPD or the Greens argue, by contrast, that new 'constitutional obligations', involving the obligation to carry out further reforms, must be met to ensure constitutional 'fulfilment'.[10]

The conservatives have a static conception of the constitution but progressive groups espouse a dynamic understanding of it; they see in it something which is still unfolding, and is at present not completely developed or fulfilled. The idea of the constitution as a mandate for the politicians, as a *telos* to be reached and completed, is generally inherent in progressive constitutional thought. When progressive groups speak about the development of the constitution they do not necessarily mean changes in the nature of the document but rather the realisation of some of the guiding principles laid down in the Constitution, for example, the principle of the *social state* which is indeed very important in German constitutional and social development. It is noteworthy that both the static and the dynamic conceptions use the constitution as a basic frame of reference. The constitution is common ground for both conservatives and progressives despite their different views, and this enhances its authority and the authority of that body to which constitutional guardianship is entrusted, the *Bundesverfassungsgericht*.

The political function of the Constitutional Court

The creators of the *Grundgesetz* had a deep mistrust of the wisdom and political maturity of the people and even of a majority of the people's representatives. They therefore restricted parliamentary sovereignty in order to keep legislation in accordance with constitutional principles. When a ruling majority passes a law it is always possible for it to be submitted to the Constitutional Court to investigate whether it is in accordance with the constitution. The Constitution takes precedence over the government's legislation: examples have been cited above.

This process of investigation, which is called *Normenkontrolle* (a form of judicial review), has gained great importance in German political life. German legislation can be investigated and struck down by the Constitutional Court. This means that the legislators normally try to ensure that the legislation will in the end be found constitutional, that is, they anxiously look to the jurisdiction of the Court when they make laws. It has also meant that political conflict between government and opposition has sometimes been carried over on to the benches of the Constitutional Court. Political conflict thus turns into a judicial problem. In a number of cases, the defeated parliamentary minority has successfully appealed to the Constitutional Court for a revision of the law passed by the majority. The existence and jurisdiction of the Constitutional Court therefore plays an important part in German politics; it is an undisputed power factor in the political process.

There have been observers of the Court's activities who believe that the political implications of its decisions are too important and too far-reaching in a democracy, and who therefore question its democratic legitimacy and powers. The members of the Court are elected by politicians, that is, by a commission either of the Bundestag or the Bundesrat, and by a two-thirds majority. This means that here, too, the two main parties have to reach agreement about whom to elect as a constitutional judge. Normally they go in for a package deal which takes the interests of the two main political parties into consideration. Despite the party political context of the nomination process, a distinct effort is made, however, by the elected members of the Constitutional Court to appear as independent judges, exclusively devoted to the task of pure jurisdiction with no political considerations.

The relationship between politics and constitutions
To sum up, there is an important relationship between politics and the Constitution in the Federal Republic of Germany. The Constitution is respected by the important political forces as the legal document by which the political process is to be channelled and organised. Although there are, of course, different conceptions of what the Constitution means and allows, all participants in the political process refer to it as their master, their guide and thus contribute to its widespread acceptance. There is no doubt, however, that this is partly due to the favourable external and internal conditions of German political life and especially to economic prosperity and the absence of strong social conflict.

Politics in the Federal Republic of Germany is closely tied to the Constitution, but the Constitution itself is not too much of a fetter for the politicians. It keeps government within certain limits, of course, but the boundaries of the Basic Law are wide enough to allow for a fairly free and open political process. One can perhaps put it this way – the German Constitution does not present serious problems for German politicians or for German democracy, and, conversely, the context of German politics does not create any serious problems for the German Constitution. The factors which have created this happy situation are so powerful that in the course of nearly forty years the Germans have come to take them for granted. In the light of the earlier instability of German constitutional forms, this is in itself remarkable.

Notes and references

1. Carl Schmitt, *Verfassungsrechtliche Aufsätze* (Berlin: Duncker und Humblot, 1958), p. 487.
2. For an investigation of the constituent assembly's reaction to the Weimar Constitution see K.F. Fromme, *Von der Weimarer Verfassung zum Bonner Grundgesetz* (Tübingen: J.C.B. Mohr, 1960).
3. For an interpretation of the constitution as it now stands see Theodor Maunz, *Deutsches Staatsrecht* (Munich, C.H. Beck, 1986).
4. Rudolf Smend, *Staatsrechtliche Abhandlungen*, 2nd edn (1968), pp. 119 ff.
5. Peter Häberle (ed.), *Verfassungsgerichtsbarkeit* (Darmstadt: Wissenschaftliche Buchgesellschaft, 1976) and M. Tohidipur, *Verfassung, Verfassungsgerichtsbarkeit, Politik* (Frankfurt: Suhrkamp, 1976).
6. See Gordon Smith, *Democracy in Western Germany*, 3rd edn (Aldershot, Gower, 1986), pp. 205–9. The Court's decisions appear under the title *Entscheidungen des Bundesverfassungsgerichts* (BVerfGE). As an important example of the political relevance of its decisions we may note the decision in the television dispute which made it impossible for the Federal Government (then under Konrad Adenauer) to establish a nation-wide second television network, because the competence in this matter was reserved to the *Länder* (the states making up the federation). See *BVerfGE*, Vol. 12, p. 205. All aspects of 'judicial politics' are treated well by the American scholar D. Kommers, in *Judicial Politics in West Germany* (London: Sage, 1976).
7. Contrasting constitutional norms with political reality is a recurrent pattern in German constitutional thought. On this particular problem see Wilhelm Hennis, 'Verfassung und Verfassungswirklichkeit' in M. Friedrich (ed.), *Verfassung, Beiträge zur Verfassungstheorie* (Darmstadt: Wissenschaftliche Buchgesellschaft, 1978).
8. Deutscher Bundestag: *Beratungen und Empfehlungen zur Verfassungs-Reform 1976/1977*.
9. The problem of 'Verfassungsschutz' in its full range is well treated by Konrad Hesse (a judge of the Constitutional Court and professor of constitutional law) in *Grundzüge des Verfassungsrechts der Bundesrepublik Deutschland* (Karlsruhe: C.F. Müller, 1985).
10. For a discussion of the programmatic character of the constitution see Robert Leicht, *Grundgesetz und politische Praxis* (Munich: Hanser Verlag, 1974).

12 France (1958): The Fifth Republic after thirty years
Guy Carcassonne

The Fifth Republic was born through a legal *coup d'état*. Its structure represents a reaction against the unsatisfactory working of previous parliamentary regimes. The circumstances of the Fifth Republic's birth heavily condition the working of the system, even today.

Engaged in a long-standing colonial war that it had neither the power to win nor the authority to finish, the Fourth Republic had little by little allowed the army to take the place of the government. The endemic weakness of successive governments had made them subject to military power at least in so far as Algeria was concerned. And when increasing hostility to the pursuit of the conflict in the metropolis made the government inclined to negotiate, the military leaders, more attached to French Algeria than to democracy and supported by local activists and by an important fringe of the parliamentary Right, reacted with violence, undermining civil authority and causing the crisis of 13 May 1958.

Entering into overt rebellion the majority of the insurgent officers did not, however, seek the permanent capture of power. They sought only to place power in hands which would not abandon Algeria. Encouraged by Gaullist militants, they naturally believed that they would find in Charles de Gaulle the ideal person. Put back into the saddle at 67 years of age the leader of Free France, who had waited twelve years for this moment, was ready to show his skill at manoeuvre.[1] Willingly embracing ambiguity he led everyone to believe that he supported them; he appeared to offer hope to the insurgent officers[2] at the same time as he offered hope to those who were against them.[3] He thus came to power in peculiar circumstances, some wanting him as a leader, others as a barrier to the army. But precisely because the circumstances allowed him to do what he wanted, he kept his true opinions to himself and took care to safeguard the forms of government quite scrupulously. He was legitimately invested as Head of Government on 1 June, profiting from the delegation of constituent power to the government of national union which he formed and which, again perfectly legitimately, elaborated a constitutional text, which was submitted to a referendum of the French people who massively ratified the new constitution so allowing his return to power.

Coup d'état this certainly was, but a legal *coup* since, despite the pressure of the insurgent officers, proper procedures were respected and the vote was free and unequivocal. There remained the Communist Party and some other isolated republicans who refused to accept this process and reproached General de Gaulle for conducting it in a factious way. They began a total and determined opposition not only to the Head of State but also to the institutions which he had created, although in other circumstances these institutions might well have suited them. Amongst these isolated opponents were the one with the most prestigious past, Pierre Mendès France, and the one with the most brilliant future, François Mitterrand.

To understand their attitude better, it is essential to bear in mind certain nuances. Critical of the Fourth Republic, they were willing to support revision of the Constitution. But they were frightened, absurd though it may seem today, that de Gaulle would be the hostage of the colonial Right. And by the time this anxiety had disappeared, they had already cast their lot with the Opposition on the basis of hostility to personal power – another Opposition motif.[4] Thus de Gaulle now came to be separated from the non-Communist Left, while the Socialists discovered a presidential reality behind the Constitution which they had supported in the belief that it was parliamentary. Thus the initial refusal of François Mitterrand and Pierre Mendès France became the common position of the Left as a whole, which forgot the legality of the procedures of 1958 and remembered only the *coup d'état*. So from the beginning of the 1960s, the Constitution of the Fifth Republic appeared to the Left to be directed against them and against the Republic. Nothing could diminish this hostility and even the exercise of power between 1981 and 1986 was not sufficient to make every Socialist politician admit that the institutions of the Fifth Republic were good ones. Whether they are good or not, however, there is no doubt that they appear reasonable to most people after thirty years. For, although born of a legal *coup d'état*, the Constitution has put right the faults of previous Republics.

Since the Revolution of 1789, French politics has reproduced in every generation the cleavages of the end of the eighteenth century. There were two conceptions of authority which found themselves in conflict for 170 years before the Fifth Republic put an end to it. The first, the revolutionary, was based on the theories of Rousseau blended with those of Montesquieu, without noticing the contradiction between them. From Rousseau, it took the idea of popular sovereignty, the idea that the law expressed the general will. Then this viewpoint fallaciously assimilated democracy with a '*régime d'assemblée*. Finally, and rather absurdly, republicans began to think that anything which limited or diminished the powers of parliament also limited or diminished democracy.

The second conception, which one may call 'directorial', put the principle of effective government first and this was to be secured by systematic reinforcement of the executive, whether democratically or not. And the constitutional history of France moved between these two conceptions, an alternation interrupted several times by periods of relative equilibrium but an alternation in which a momentary advantage for one conception provoked a contrary swing towards the other so that the dictatorship of the Assembly was succeeded by the dictatorship of the Executive. In 1958 it was, one might suggest, the turn of the 'directorial' conception to impose itself. The Third Republic (1875–1940), like the Fourth (1946–58), had been characterised by the dominance of parliament which, aggravated by the absence of a clear and disciplined majority, had led to chronic ministerial instability. But in fact, many conceptions jostled with each other during the elaboration of the Constitution of 1958, those of General de Gaulle himself above all. His conception of legitimacy comprised three elements:

- a military element: the leader. His whole apprenticeship, his whole past convinced him very strongly of the necessity of a leader, authoritarian, charismatic, inspired, in whom was incarnated the whole past of his country and also its future;
- a monarchical element: the Head of State. De Gaulle wanted to achieve a synthesis of Louis XIV and the Jacobins: he not only wanted the nation to have a leader, but that this leader should also be Head of State with important powers and an authority which could not be questioned;
- a democratic element – the Head of State must not only wield personal power. He also had to be accepted by the people. During the war it was essential for de Gaulle to lead only through the free choice of citizens. It does not matter whether this was a matter of calculation or conviction. All that matters is his belief that he was not legitimate in his own eyes unless he was accepted by the people.

With this willingness to break with the institutional mechanisms of previous Republics which gave only very feeble powers to the Head of State, were combined the ideas of Michel Debré, the chief architect of the 1958 Constitution and Prime Minister when it came into force.

Debré had been one of the most vigorous adversaries of the Fourth Republic. He had the ambition in 1958 of rebuilding a parliamentary and republican regime.[5] To this end he introduced mechanisms into the Constitution to allow the rationalisation of a parliamentary regime, and this constituted a clear break with French tradition.[6]

It is this double influence which gave the Fifth Republic its three basic characteristics: the power given to the President of the Republic, the role of Parliament, and the limitation of power through the Constitution. But it is a rather odd paradox, that these characteristics did not become established immediately, and when they did, it was for very different reasons from those envisaged by the authors of the constitution. Presidential pre-eminence owed less to the comparatively limited powers which the Constitution gave the President than to his election by universal suffrage following the constitutional revision of 1962. The subordination of Parliament owes much less to constitutional provisions than to the electoral system, which is not mentioned in the Constitution, but which is the main reason for the creation of a coherent majority. As for the limitation of government by the Constitution, this did not become apparent for some time, not until 1971 in fact, and the Constitutional Council was certainly not conceived with this purpose in mind.

Thus it is almost by chance that the founding fathers of 1958 attained their goal, and with weapons other than the ones which they had forged, for these weapons had been shown not to be very effective. It is worth illustrating how this came about.

As far as General de Gaulle was concerned, the spirit of the Constitution required that the pre-eminence of the Head of State be secured in two ways: by the method through which he was chosen and by the powers conferred upon him. Concerning the first, the new Constitution abandoned election of the President by the deputies and senators alone as in the Third and Fourth Republics, and replaced it with an electoral college comprising not only deputies and senators but also the numerous representatives of the departments and communes. Direct election by universal suffrage was not provided for in 1958 because it would have aroused violent opposition from those who already suspected de Gaulle of Bonapartist tendencies, and also because it risked making possible the election of a Communist President. But at least the considerable enlargement of the electoral body made it possible for the choice of Head of State to be removed from the exclusive arena of Parliament.

But it is also by the powers which the Constitution conferred on him that the President of the Fifth Republic is to be distinguished from his predecessors. In addition to Article 5 which defines his role, Article 19, breaking with tradition, gives him very important powers which can be exercised without countersignature, such as nomination of the Prime Minister, referendum, dissolution of the National Assembly, recourse to exceptional powers, etc. To these must also be added a number of powers which he cannot exercise on his own, but which cannot be exercised without him (he negotiates and ratifies treaties, appoints various civil and military functionaries, signs ordinances, presides over the Council of Ministers etc.)

The enumeration of these various powers is sufficient to show that the President is a figure of considerable importance. But it is worth noting that what these powers have in common (with the exception of the foreign policy powers) is that they do not, strictly speaking, permit him to do anything, but only to cause things to be done. Thus, he is not supposed to govern but to designate the person who governs, he is not supposed to settle differences between government and Parliament but to give the people the power to settle them through referendum or dissolution, he is not supposed himself to exercise control over constitutionality but only to appoint the members of the Constitutional Council.

Experience shows, however, that, except during a period of cohabitation, it is the President of the Republic who is the real ruler of France, that it is he and not the government, despite the text of Article 20, who 'determines and conducts the policy of the nation'. And if the division of functions between the Head of State and the Prime Minister varies, that is in virtue of the President's own wishes and inclinations rather than because the Prime Minister has any choice in the matter.

This was so from the very beginning of the Fifth Republic when the dominating personality of General de Gaulle made it inconceivable that any of his allies could resist him. But de Gaulle knew that this would not necessarily be possible for his successors who, by definition, could not benefit from his own personal legitimacy or prestige. That is why he argued that the President must be anointed by the people through election by direct universal suffrage. The constitutional revision of 1962 providing for this came into force for the first time in 1965.

De Gaulle's aim has certainly been attained. The 32 million French voters would clearly not like to elect someone who could only preside at official ceremonies and who had surrendered to government and Parliament the power to rule. Not only does the President exercise his powers to the full, but he can also impose his will upon the other organs of government.

France, however, is not the only country which elects its president by universal suffrage. How is it that the French President can exercise powers which are not exercised, for example, in Austria or Portugal?

This results from certain factors specific to France. The first is the method of election. The President is elected by the two-ballot system, with only two candidates participating in the second ballot, and every party has to choose which of the two candidates to support. Thus the presidential election structures the party system and so also divides Parliament into a majority and an opposition, the first defined primarily in terms of its agreement with the President; the majority is in fact his disciplined army. This also explains why the electoral system for the legislature – also a two-ballot system – has produced under the Fifth Republic a bipolarisation which it did not engender when it was used in the Third Republic. The legislative elections register and amplify a bipolarisation which has its source elsewhere: in 1958 and 1965 in support for or opposition to General de Gaulle, and after that in support or opposition to one of the two candidates in the second round of the presidential election.

The second element which has given French political life its particular flavour is the Bonapartist tradition incarnating the role of the leader, a deep-rooted tradition in French politics even when driven underground by everyday parliamentary practicality. Furthermore, the shadow of the first occupant of the presidency deeply affected its role; de Gaulle utilised his charisma to manufacture a strong presidency from which his successors continued to benefit.[7]

The third element, finally, is that the system feeds on itself; the stronger the President, the stronger the position and the greater its attraction. Because the presidency was strong at the beginning, it quickly became the point of reference – the ultimate power – and the President's power thus came to be increased even further; when France came to have atomic weapons, control of them was naturally given to him.[8] Because of this, because he is a constant point of reference, because he also controls France's nuclear weapons – and this is somewhat symbolic – he appears naturally as a republican monarch.

This seemingly omnipotent presidency, so characteristic of France with its liking for extremes, has also the advantage of giving the electorate great clarity of choice, although it has the corresponding disadvantage of producing a rigid bipolarity. This artificially accentuates the cleavage between right and left. Further, the President needs a political party which can steer his measures through; so political groupings have become much more powerful than ever before in France. Thus, by a strange reversal, the 'regime of parties' which de Gaulle tried to avoid by means of the election of the President by direct universal suffrage, has returned. In place of the kind of unanimous president that de Gaulle hoped for – an incarnation of the nation as a whole – the reality is that never have the parties been more indispensable, more powerful, and never have the French had to face so bipolar an electoral situation.

This has a further significance since it contributes to weakening even the role of Parliament. From the fact that, in effect, the parliamentary coalitions are formed principally on the second ballot of the presidential election, it is clear that the deputies who have supported the President are under an obligation to carry out the programme of the Head of State. The provisions of the Constitution allow the majority to impose discipline, and give even a minority government the opportunity of governing so long as there is no alternative majority.

Nevertheless, this is not the main reason for the reduction in the importance of parliamentarians. The main reason lies rather in the electoral system. The two-ballot system, which operated from 1958 to 1985, and again from 1986,[9] has had two important effects. The first has been to reinforce the second ballot of the presidential election and to give birth to two opposed coalitions, with the candidate of each party needing the benefit in the second ballot of the votes of its allied party.

The second consequence, perhaps even more crucial, has been to give the presidential power of dissolution real importance. Under proportional representation, the national leaders are in effect assured of re-election and so have no particular reason to fear a dissolution, while the two-ballot system, on the other hand, exposes everyone to the serious risk of defeat.

The combination of these two effects has also given France something which had always escaped it up to now – a clear parliamentary majority and, more important, a disciplined majority. Without any doubt, this was the indispensable precondition for the modernisation of the political system. What Michel Debré hoped to obtain by restricting the role of Parliament – governmental stability – was achieved more quickly and more efficaciously by the electoral system.

But there was a price to pay for this transformation. That price was a relative loss of influence on the part of Parliament – to the extent that the consequence of the new procedures together with the emergence of a majority, make the government, for practical purposes, the master of the legislative process. It controls the order of debate, it is the source of the vast majority of the laws, and it has the means to ensure that only those amendments which it supports are accepted. This leads to Parliament being removed from the centre of power.

This loss of influence should not be exaggerated, however. To give but one example, it is apparent that each legislative measure of the Fifth Republic has been amended by Parliament on average twice and the amendments were by no means always supported by the government.[10] This demonstrates that, contrary to what has long been believed and taught, Parliament continues to exercise its legislative function effectively. It remains the case nevertheless, however much one might regret it, that the executive is the dominant power, even if the instruments of this domination are not necessarily those which the founders of the Constitution had imagined them to be.

Nor did they contemplate a government limited by the Constitution, a limitation which, in 1958, was far from being the main preoccupation of the founding fathers.

Since 1789, France has known no less than seventeen regimes, and nearly as many constitutions. But none of them was able to provide the means to ensure that it was properly respected. Impregnated with the Rousseauist idea according to which the law is the expression of the sovereign general will, French constitutions had always rejected the idea of control of the constitutionality of laws, control which they saw as inherently illegitimate and opening the path to government by judges. De Gaulle subscribed perfectly to this tradition when he haughtily affirmed: 'In France, the people are the Supreme Court.' Nevertheless, it was under his authority that the Constitutional Council was created in the Constitution of 1958. The Council was, indeed, initially given the power to verify, before promulgation, the conformity of laws with the Constitution. But, in the spirit of those who had given birth to it, it concerned itself first with ensuring that Parliament could not trespass upon the acknowledged sphere of the government, and it did this in such a manner as to prevent the assemblies from escaping from their subordinate position.

In fact, the Constitutional Council acquitted itself well in this task for twelve years. It intervened only rarely, taking up no strong position, and so allowing François Mitterrand to comment of this period that the Council delivered, not judgments but services.

Two events, however, went far to change this pattern. The first was on 16 July 1971. On that day, the Constitutional Council, showing an unaccustomed audacity, annulled a law which the government had supported, because it was contrary to a principle embodied in the preamble to the Constitution. This decision was, of itself, extremely important in that, for the first time, not only was the preamble found to have a genuine juridical value, but the decision also revitalised the Declaration of the Rights of Man and of the Citizen of 1789. This decision suddenly showed that the Council could be a vigilant guardian of liberty. And thirdly, this spectacular awakening showed that henceforth neither government nor Parliament could do as they liked, and that they would have to respect the principles of the Constitution scrupulously.

This audacious action on the part of the Council might have had no sequel, had it not been for the second crucial event. The constitutional law of 29 October 1974, revising Article 61 of the Constitution, enlarged the role of the Council. Until that time, only the President of the Republic, the Prime Minister, or the Presidents of the National Assembly and Senate, could submit legislation to the Council. The significance of this is that, of these four, at least three are part of the political majority. From 1974, there was added to these four authorities, 'sixty deputies or sixty senators'; thus the power to submit legislation to the Constitutional Council was given to the parliamentary opposition.

Although voting against this reform, in favour of a more far-reaching measure, the Opposition immediately took advantage of its opportunity and obtained results which were not only satisfactory but even spectacular. Since that date, the Constitutional Council has become an important institution of the Fifth Republic, and has occupied a much greater role than it did in the 1960s. The French people have discovered the virtues of constitutional control, and of a state based upon law.

There are, indeed, those who fear that its more active role could put the institution under a cloud, especially because of the political character of its recruitment. Yet, paradoxically, its political composition (three members chosen by the President of the Republic, three by the President of the National Assembly and three by the President of the Senate), is part of the reason for its success. For the members of the Council have sufficient experience never to cross the line which would make it a third chamber imposing its will on the other two. Even more, the specific nature of its decisions and their responsible character means that, despite certain reactions of ill will, they are accepted by all. Moreover, both government and Parliament are careful to anticipate and to ensure that the legislation which leaves Parliament does not incur censure.

Because of this, for the first time in French constitutional history, the Constitution is effectively respected, it is effectively enforced upon all, and no person or institution can violate it with impunity.

Thus, an organ initially conceived of as a guard-dog of Parliament has today transformed itself into a real guarantor of the State based upon law. The creation of a majority was a necessity for political modernisation, but, in a country like France, an all-powerful majority could give rise to the danger of an 'elective dictatorship' which had not been present when there had been no majority. The role of the Constitutional Council is the healthy one of preventing such a majority from excessively exploiting its power.

The French people have fully understood this. They have suffered so much and so long from the total power of Parliament, which pretended that it was exercising its power in the name of the people even when the people had only limited confidence in it, that they have come to appreciate the prudent but decisive attitude of the Constitutional Council. Although quite new in the French political landscape, although a complete break with the doctrine of the sovereignty of the people as traditionally interpreted (the sovereignty of the representatives of the people), today the control of constitutionality assists considerably in maintaining that consensus which the Constitution has helped to create.[11]

Such are, briefly stated, the paradoxes which have given to the Fifth Republic its three basic principles: the power of the President, the subordination of Parliament, and the control on the constitutionality of laws.

After thirty years, the Fifth Republic has undergone many ordeals, but it has survived them all. It is perhaps surprising that it still continues to arouse controversy. But these controversies are limited, in general, at least since 1981, to politicians who are not leaders of the front rank. The Fifth Republic has survived its institutional ordeals as well as its political ones. Politically, it was able to achieve peacefully the decolonisation which the Fourth Republic had begun, and, above all, to face up to the problem of Algeria. Given the conditions under which the Fifth Republic was born, it was by no means clear that General de Gaulle would be able to find a reasonable solution. And in fact, even when one had been finally achieved, it had to be imposed in the face of violence. De Gaulle had to face not only the discontent of French Algerians, some of whom, with the aid of the OAS,[12] had resorted to terrorist violence, and to escape the attempts made on his life, but he also had to confront the generals' *putsch* of 21 April 1961. His own personal authority as Head of State, and the exceptional powers under Article 16 of the Constitution, allowed him to overcome these challenges, something which would not have been easy under the Constitution of the Fourth Republic.

May 1968, the departure of de Gaulle in 1969, the beginning of the economic recession in 1973, the alternation of power of 1981, are also events which could have led to the institutions being put in question. But the institutions have not only successfully resisted these challenges, they have allowed them to be met in the best way possible.

In particular, the change in the majority in 1981, bringing to power men who had always fought against the Constitution, rapidly dissipated their doubts, The Fifth Republic has been shown to be compatible with all political standpoints, whether of the right or of the left, even though some feared that it would place too many handicaps on the left, preventing them from achieving power. But these anxieties proved unnecessary. The left won in 1981, and governed as they had intended.

Gradually, as it came to be appreciated that electoral victory could be won by those who had been confined to opposition since 1958, the debate on whether the institutional mechanisms could accommodate themselves to this ordeal became more and more passionate. But, under the leadership of François Mitterrand, the left found no difficulty in working with the institutions which they had so often criticised. Not only was no constitutional revision proposed, but the left did not hesitate to use the powers which they had previously denounced. Indeed, they would have been foolish to deprive themselves of the means necessary for effective government.

There is, however, just one reservation. In 1985, the left reformed the electoral system and, although this was not a reform of the Constitution, it was at least as important. It provided for the adoption of proportional representation in the election of deputies. It proved, however, and its authors were under no illusion about its likely temporary nature, a new type of legislation which was christened 'law Kleenex', to be used only once. And in fact it allowed the left to minimise the effects of their electoral defeat in March 1986 before the right hastened to re-establish the two-ballot system.[13]

In the light of these experiences, it only remains for the Fifth Republic to overcome one further challenge, about which the law professors have speculated with so much concern over so many years – the challenge of 'cohabitation' characterised by the simultaneous presence of a President of the left face to face with a parliamentary majority and government of the right (or vice versa).

That is the position which has existed since March 1986 in France. It is indeed too early to tell for certain whether it will last until its natural expiry date with the presidential election of 1988, although there are good reasons for thinking that it will. But one thing is already clear: if by 'constitutional' one means a literal application of the text of 1958, the problems posed by cohabitation are not constitutional but political. For each of the protagonists is able to use the powers which the Constitution confers upon him, sometimes without ulterior motive, sometimes to try to put the other in difficulty. The Constitution does not allow either protagonist to exceed his powers nor to capture the powers of his partner-cum-adversary. The Fifth Republic has thus given the final proof which was lacking hitherto, that it could surmount this final challenge.

Professor Olivier Duhamel, in his indispensable work on *The Left and the Fifth Republic*,[14] argues that the position which the various parties take on the Constitution, although influenced by a number of factors – the party's tradition, its attitude on constitutional questions, its political programme, its immediate self-interest – is above all determined by their distance from power. In other words, political forces excluded from power make an appeal to constitutional tradition. Those nearer power set their political programme in the forefront; while those who actually exercise power are concerned only with the immediate translation into action of their programme.

It is this which doubtless explains the comings and goings of the right in the last ten years. The left, naturally, only found faults in the Republic when they had not been able to attain power within it. They sought to blame the institutions rather than admit that they had more than their own share of responsibility for the fact that the French people had not given them a majority.

But it is striking how this hostility weakened as the left approached victory. By the eve of the 1981 elections, their proposals for change had been reduced to a few vague promises, without any precise timetable, on strengthening the role of Parliament. Finally, as soon as they arrived in power, the socialists abandoned their critique of the Constitution, since they were preoccupied with exploiting its advantages. But it did not take them long – since they were defeated in the legislative elections of March 1986 – to rediscover the defects of a system which they had once before been so eager to denounce.

In justice to the Communist Party one must say that its hostility to the Constitution has never changed. This is perhaps explained by the fact that the Communists, in contrast to their Socialist allies, were never really in power. Having elected one of their own as President of the Republic, the Socialists endorsed the Constitution, and could not have been more gaullist when, invoking the name of the General, they reproached the right for seeking to weaken the role of the Head of State.

The right have been no less opportunistic. After 23 years spent extolling the virtues of the Constitution which de Gaulle had given France, its utilisation by their adversaries revealed to them its excesses. Discovering the delights of opposition, members of the opposition outbid each other in irresponsibility and impudence. Irresponsibility since, holding the view that the left was inherently illegitimate so that anything which embarrasssed it could be justified, they did not hesitate frenetically to practise parliamentary obstruction, in both chambers. This had two important consequences. First, the most important legislation, which was also the most controversial, was not properly discussed, and fear of obstruction obliged the government to resort to methods to expedite business as laid down in the Constitution. Secondly, anyone who, in opposition, has practised obstruction, is hardly in a position to reproach his successors for doing the same, and thus the precedents invoked lead to the devaluing of Parliament as an institution.

Irresponsibility then, but impudence also, to the extent that too many members of the right attacked what they had previously worshipped and denounced what they had themselves practised. The most symptomatic example perhaps relates to the Constitutional Council. For, while the right had sung of the beauties of a state under the law when the Council in 1982 annulled a nationalisation law of the left, certain representatives of the right did not hesitate to raise the spectre of a government of judges when the Council recently declared that various proposals of the new government did not conform with the Constitution.

It is worth noting that neither the President nor the Prime Minister, nor any of the likely candidates in the next presidential election, has questioned the Constitution or suggested that it be modified. It is rather those at lower levels of influence in political life and various constitutional specialists who have put forward views of this sort.

One large reform has been discussed recently – the introduction of a presidential system. Whether because of a fascination with the American example, or because of a belief that it is in the interest of the President, or alternatively simply to have something to say, a number of politicians of the centre-right and, more recently, the left, have pronounced themselves in favour of a rigid separation of powers in which they believe that they will find the solution to the problems of the Fifth Republic.

But they forget that, prestigious as the American model is, one is bound to conclude that it is difficult to export since it exists hardly anywhere else, save in a caricatured form under certain dictatorships. Two things are in any case certain in so far as they concern France. The first is that the deep gulf which separates right and left is quite different from that between Democrats and Republicans in the USA and conflict between legislature and executive in France would quickly lead without any doubt to a paralysis which has been avoided in the USA. Further, the USA is federal, and there is no equivalent in France in the recent measures of decentralisation; thus there exists in the United States a counterbalance to which there is no equivalent in France, which is why the Federal President has been given such great power.

The second factor is even more decisive. Even if all the experts reached the conclusion that the American model was the best for France, putting it into effect presupposes a massive constitutional revision which no individual, party or political movement could promote, even if they wished to, for the excellent reason that the French people, as is shown by the opinion polls,[15] and by their electoral participation, are very much attached to their institutions and see no necessity to change their method of working.

The only other serious reform sought by the French people, if one believes the opinion polls,[16] is to reduce the presidential term from seven years to five. People want this partly because the term is perceived as being too long, but also because in aligning the presidential term with that of the legislature, even without necessarily making them simultaneous, the risks and dangers of cohabitation are reduced. The presidential candidates are not hostile to this reform for they have well understood that they have a chance of winning two terms of five years each, while they have less chance of winning two seven-year terms.[17] With this reform, therefore, they could remain president for 10 rather than 7 years.

If this change has not yet been made, it is because of the almost taboo character which has come to be attached to the text of the Constitution. Whoever proposes to modify it is immediately suspected of seeking some political advantage, and that is sufficient to arouse the hostility of opponents who are perhaps, at bottom, in agreement on the issue.

But it is on the whole significant that, after thirty years full of conflict, the only serious modification likely to command the support of the French people in a referendum is the reduction by two years of the presidential term. That is a clear indication of the success of the institutions of the Fifth Republic, and the extent to which they have become rooted in public opinion.

Finally, outside the ebb and flow of political life, it seems that France has reached the point, thanks to the Constitution and even more to the manner in which it has operated, of crossing the last barrier which separated it from a truly civilised political system – the achievement of institutional consensus. There is in fact sufficient material for political conflict without there needing to be conflict over the means of ruling as well. Since 1789, the French have never been able to reach complete agreement on the basic rules of the game. The greatest merit of the current Constitution is to have helped secure this consensus. It rests with the politicians to recognise this, rather than to continue periodically to act as if the institutions themselves were still really in contention. The institutions guarantee the democratic evolution of power, stability and efficiency. That is all that one is entitled to ask of them. Beyond that, they allow the evolution of political forces in whatever direction the electorate wishes. So it is not, for example, absurd to think that they will lead, in the end, to the existence of two moderate coalitions, one on the left, the other on the right, comparable to those which exist in other Western European countries. This would certainly affect the working of the political system in a number of very important ways. But that is another story.

Notes and references

1. See the remarkable biography by Jean Lacouture, *De Gaulle* (Paris: Seuil, 1986), vol. 2.

2. 'Today in face of the ordeal which again threatens the country, let it be known that I am ready to resume the powers of the Republic', Declaration of 15 May 1958.

3. 'The Republic! There was a time when it was disowned, betrayed by the parties themselves. I myself restored its arms, its laws, its name. I fought to obtain victory for France, and ensured that it would also be the victory of the Republic', Press Conference of 19 May 1958.

4. See Olivier Duhamel, *La Gauche et la Ve Republique* (Paris: Presses Universitaire de France, 1980), pp. 45–83.

5. See the very important talk which he gave in presenting the draft Constitution to the Conseil d'État on 27 August 1958, published in D. Maus: *Textes et documents sur la pratique institutionnelle de la Ve République* (Paris: La documentation française et le CNRS, 1985).

6. (i) Restrictions on parliamentary sittings. (ii) The search for a domain of the Law. (iii) A radical reorganisation of legislative and budgetary procedure. (iv) The introduction of juridical mechanisms indispensable to the effective working of the political system.

7. 'The President is clearly the sole source of authority in the State... It must be clearly understood that the indivisible authority of the State is conferred entirely on the President by the people who elected him, that there exists no other source of authority, neither ministerial nor civil, nor military nor judicial, which is not conferred and maintained by him.' Charles de Gaulle, Press Conference 31 January 1964.

8. Decree of 14 January 1964.

9. It is not unimportant to note that the initial choice of electoral system had been imposed by the Socialists who hoped to constitute themselves as a pivotal group, and that it was also the Socialists (but not the same socialists!) who reintroduced, though for a very short time, proportional representation.

10. See Guy Carcassonne, 'La resistance de l'Assemblée nationale á l'abaissement de son rôle', in *La Constitution de Ve République* (Paris: Presses de la FNSP, 1985), p. 330.

11. If the opinion polls are to be believed, 70% of the French people in 1978 were 'favourable towards the Constitutional Council, which supervised the regularity of laws and elections'. On the same question, 80% were found to be in favour in 1983. Sofres, *Opinion publique 1984* (Paris: Gallimard, 1984), pp. 113–14.

12. Organisation de l'Armée Secrète, an organisation of the extreme right, clandestine and terrorist, it sought at the beginning of the 1960s to overthrow de Gaulle by armed struggle so as to prevent Algerian independence.

13. For the first time, the question of constituency boundaries was put to the Constitutional Council, which declared that it conformed to the Constitution, but recognised implicitly 'the relevance of certain criticisms' of the drawing-up of boundaries which the opposition had criticised (décision 86.218 DC 18 November 1986).

14. See note 4.

15. On the occasion of the 25th anniversary of the Constitution, 57% of French

people said that the Constitution worked well or very well, 25% expressed the opposite opinion (Sofres, *Opinion publique 1984*, p. 104).

16. 35% of French people pronounced themselves in favour of maintaining the seven-year term against 60% who favoured the five-year term (ibid. p. 109).

17. Whether through chance or fate, no President of the Fifth Republic, up to now, has been able to complete two seven-year terms. The record for longevity in this position is still held by General de Gaulle (January 1959–April 1969).

13 Emerging from dictatorship: The role of the Constitution in Spain (1978) and Portugal (1976)
Guy Hermet

An Iberian paradigm

The cases of Spain and of Portugal contrast sharply with those of other democratic countries. This goes without saying for the old European or North-American democracies. But it is also true *vis-à-vis* those countries which emerged hardly more recently from authoritarian or colonial rule, such as Germany, Italy, Japan or India.

Four salient features distinguish both Spanish and Portuguese constitutional processes. Comparing them with older democracies, first is the fact that they were born following a period of dictatorship. Elsewhere, constitutions merely expanded political freedom from the background of a representative practice already tested over a long period, as in Britain or even in colonial North America and India. Or, in the case of continental Europe, constitutions consolidated the final stage of an eventful yet democratically oriented institutional trend. By contrast, the 1978 and 1976 Spanish and Portuguese Constitutions aspired to inaugurate the start of a new political era. At the same time, they sought to symbolise the final break from the misfortunes of a dire political past, and a once-and-for-all settlement of stable representative government.

A second peculiarity arises from the distinction which needs to be made between two sequences of emergence from dictatorship: on the one hand, the post-Second World War German-Italian-Japanese sequence; on the other, the post-1974 Iberian sequence. Both are late in terms of the history of Western democracy. But the first one concerns defeated and lacerated nations. In their case, the constitutional process largely reflects an external constraint linked with a military occupation, so that the initial political risk was reduced. Nothing of that kind occurs in the Iberian sequence. This sequence was endogenous and relied purely upon Spain and Portugal themselves, without the backing of any external power.

The third difference concerns the ambition of the new Spanish and Portuguese Constitutions to ensure a permanent democratic regime. This was more than wishful thinking. In fact, the constitutional record of both countries is a very long one. Spain endured six liberal or democratic constitutions up to 1978 (in 1812, 1834, 1845, 1869, 1876 and 1931). Among these, only one – the 1876 Constitution – lasted for any length of time, but it ended amid acrimonious bickering and finally gave way to General Primo de Rivera's dictatorship in 1923. Ephemeral and counterproductive, the other constitutions generated nothing but turmoil and disaster, to the point of undermining democratic legitimacy instead of fostering it. Portugal similarly experimented with five constitutions from 1822 to 1933 (1822, 1826, 1838, 1911 and 1933). But as in Spain, none was able to consolidate a stable democratic practice. The Iberian constitution-makers were rather like sorcerer's apprentices. They contributed only to the pendulum-like oscillation of alternating authoritarian government and unstable democracy. The basic aim of the Spanish and Portugese constitutional processes must be understood by reference to this ominous cycle. For it was designed to overcome such disturbing precedents by taking advantage of new circumstances and by avoiding the political pitfalls of the past.

Finally, the fourth feature of the Iberian constitutional paradigm is a methodological one. The current constitutional experiments have had a relatively brief duration up to the present day: not more than nine years in Spain, and eleven in Portugal. In such a limited time they obviously cannot be analysed in the same way as in countries with pluridecennial or even centennial constitutions. In the Iberian peninsula, the problem is less the controversy about constitutional reform than the simple implementation of institutional structures written down on paper. The actual debate deals with the introduction of new political norms rather than with their obsolescence or refurbishing.

The various shared features should not, however, obliterate the specifics of the Spanish and Portuguese constitutional landscapes. Even though there exists a close connexion between them in matters of timing, geography and culture as well as a common authoritarian heritage, they differ from each other in almost every other respect. The Spanish path from dictatorship to democracy shaped itself into a gradual political transition. Its guides took care to avoid a clear-cut institutional rupture and counterproductive ideological resentment against the previously dominating élite. They applied themselves primarily to undoing the Francoist framework which was still in force at the start of the democratisation process, in order to mitigate the fears of those who feared a revengeful and convulsive return to representative government. By contrast, Portugal extracted itself from authoritarianism thanks to a military *coup*, and in a climax of revolutionary gesticulation. The Portuguese rupture was dramatic and characterised by a manichean political and social frenzy. The Portuguese leadership took the contrary course to that of the Spanish. Intoxicated with the idea of turning the tables on the past, they fêted their miraculous coming to power by founding their frail legitimacy on the denunciation of actual or imaginary 'enemies of the People', in accordance with the old French revolutionary recipe.

This contrast involves a further paradoxical difference. In Portuguese, a *putsch* conducted by 'democratic' army officers installed a confusedly radical but overtly military semi-dictatorship (at least until the 1982 constitutional reform). In Spain, the bulk of a still mainly Francoist army did not obstruct a more genuine process of civilian democratisation. Even though the military remained influential for a long time in Spain, they were never so arrogant in Madrid as in Lisbon. Franco had already subdued the military in Spain, something which Salazar and Caetano had not done in Portugal.

There are other distinctive contrasts. In Portugal, the revolutionary thrust which mobilised the energy of one section of the population, terrified the others. With no history of civil war, the Portuguese let themselves become enraptured by the lyrical illusion of a radical overthrow of society, without assessing the risks it involved for liberty. Painfully aware of the dangers of civil strife, the Spaniards preferred to relinquish political adventures and accepted the only type of democracy realised up to the present, i.e. our commonplace 'formal' democracy, which is real precisely because of its formality. In addition, there was the monarchical restoration in Spain. Nevertheless the process in Spain was not entirely smooth. For, in spite of its historic past, Spain remains a heterogeneous and unfinished nation. The very idea of a fully sovereign national state is no longer accepted by a large number of 'Spaniards'. Hence the special nature of the constitutional challenge in that country. In Spain, the institutions must not only establish a regime, the Constitution must also implement a new formula of coexistence acceptable to all regions, and rebuild a state fit for this purpose. Portugal does not suffer from this problem. It counts as one of the oldest nations in Europe. The power of the centralised Portuguese state is beyond serious argument, or reduces itself to a rather academic discussion on the government of the island provinces of Madeira and the Azores.

The analysis of current Spanish and Portuguese constitutional experience is conditioned by these two interwoven sets of common elements and divergent factors.

Spain

The Fundamental laws which served as the institutional framework of the Francoist dictatorship remained in force after the death of General Franco on 20 November 1975. These were: the March 1938 Charter of Labour, the Cortes Act of July 1942, the July 1945 'Bill of Rights', the Law of Principles of the National Movement of May 1958, and, especially, the July 1947 Succession law and the January 1967 Organic law of the State, regulating the nomination of the dictator's heir (Spanish Constitution 1971).

These laws made of Spain a corporatist kingdom without a king, ruled at pleasure and for life by the 'Caudillo by the grace of God'. It was in accordance with this legislation that Prince Juan Carlos was designated as Franco's presumptive successor in July 1969, after swearing loyalty to the regime's undemocratic principles. During the summer of 1974, while his cumbersome political godfather was suffering a first heart attack, he assumed the direction of the state under the same conditions. And he was kept once again to this constraint when he was installed on the throne on 22 November 1975, swearing once more his loyalty to the Francoist Cortes. All the new king could do in the speech he delivered on this occasion was to allude to the 'major improvements' the regime needed as well as to the necessary implementation of 'the exercise of all regional liberties and particularisms'. But Franco himself would probably not have disavowed so hazy a phraseology. More significant perhaps was the second enthronement ceremony held five days later, in the presence of democratic witnesses such as President Giscard d'Estaing and President Walter Scheel. This time, the king refrained from confirming his oath to the former authoritarian rule.

The truth is that Juan Carlos stood at that time practically alone in front of the authoritarian state structure. This was true also with regard to his relationship to public opinion both at home and abroad, which generally took him for some kind of crowned puppet. He consequently had to stoop to conquer: his first task was to avail himself of trustworthy men at the reins of government. That is why the king maintained Carlos Arias Navarro – head of Franco's last cabinet – in office for a few months more, though everybody knew he was no friend. Later on, it was by virtue of the same prudential reverence for the Francoist legal armour that he appointed Navarro's replacement after 1 July 1976. He had to comply with the regulation which obliged him to make his choice from a list of three, already picked out by a Council of the Kingdom still dominated by dignitaries of the authoritarian old guard. Two of them – Gregorio Lopez Bravo and Frederico Silva Munŏz – could be considered as compliant but not fully liberal ex-Francoist; they would be willing to admit the extreme-left opposition and the Communist Party into the democratisation process. The third man – Adolfo Suarez – seemed harder to define politically. On the one hand, Suarez's past characterised him as a young political climber pure and simple, with a very creditable performance in the Francoist apparat. He had won an important post of responsibility in the authoritarian single party (the Falange); and Franco had designated him as governor of the Segovia province a short time before he died. Yet, on the other hand, Suarez was the same age as the king, was on friendly terms with him, and appeared as one of the brightest political hopes of the new generation trained in the authoritarian seraglio. It was he whom the king called for on 3 July 1976.

During the first months of his term of office, Suarez's flawed political record did not receive a good press in the foreign newspapers. At that time, no one dared to imagine that he would become the strategist of a painless escape from Franco's institutional and ideological legacy. But it was precisely his lack of democratic political credentials which protected him from the suspicions of more dangerous potential opponents: the members of the corporatist Cortes, the authoritarian higher officials, the old generals still imbued with the spirit of the civil war. Suarez availed himself of their somewhat indulgent attitude to escape from the Francoist bunker. As early as 18 November 1976, he was able to get the Cortes to vote for his Law of political reform, with only 59 negative votes out of 438. This law implicitly put an end to the institutions of the dictatorship. Discouraged by this turn of fortune, the disheartened authoritarian élite, however, preferred to ignore it. Astutely indeed, the Law did not include any clause expressly derogating from the Francoist legislation it extinguished; and it avoided beginning with a solemn democratic declaration which could have outraged the authoritarians. But this discretion did not prevent the law from unshackling the democratisation process. Supported by 97.4 per cent of the voters in the national referendum of 15 December, it dissolved the moribund corporatist assemblies and replaced them by two representative chambers. These were to be elected through universal suffrage, within the framework of a pluralistic party system. Moreover, there was nothing to prevent these assemblies from arrogating to themselves a constituent role.

The very fact that the political reform law was supported by an overwhelming majority also disarmed the leftist and pro-republican opposition. Hostile to the monarchy which had arisen from the

Francoist political machinery, both Communists and Socialists had advocated abstention at the referendum. Disavowed by the voters, they could only save face by putting away the republican flags they had picked out of the dust a few months before. The Left, which coveted a democracy won by the People over the ashes of dictatorship, had to conform to a democratic regime granted by the heirs of Franco's authoritarianism.

Publicly announced on 9 March 1977 after much hesitation, the legalisation of the Communist Party looked like a handsome gesture made in answer to the radical opposition's forced political thaw. The Communist Party's secretary-general Santiago Carrillo had just explained to Suarez: 'If you don't legalise the Communist Party, you won't implement the reform because we shall wreck it.'¹ It seems that the Prime Minister understood the message: paradoxically enough, recognition of the Communists was to authenticate the transition to democracy. On that condition, punctilious democrats could no longer object to the legislative elections to be held six months after the promulgation of the Reform Law, on 15 June 1977. These elections could actually open the constituent process, in the perspective of the democratic legitimation of a monarchy initially established by General Franco. Moreover, the elections made the unofficial governmental party – the *Union del Centro Democratico* – the first political force in the Congress of Deputies and the Senate. Though lacking an absolute majority, Suarez was able comfortably to elaborate a new constitution.

It must be added that part of the constitution wrote itself even before the deputies considered it, at least in respect to the rebirth of provincial autonomous governments. Suarez wanted to ward off the danger of a unilateral and unlawful restoration of the Catalan Generalidad, whose 1931 statute was abrogated in 1939. The Catalan autonomists were getting nervous. In the spring of 1977 it was rumoured that they would carry out a surprise *coup* shortly after the election, so as to proclaim the restoration of the Generalidad. Adolfo Suarez prevented these manoeuvres by allowing the exiled former president of the republican Generalidad, J. Tarradellas, to return to Spain. Immediately, he negotiated a provisional but effective agreement with him. This would have seemed a mere dream only a few weeks before, because of the fear of a military reaction. But the Generalidad was revived nevertheless on 9 September. And the same procedure operated in the Basque provinces a short time later.

The working out of the constitutional project took place between July 1977 and summer 1978. Partly thanks to the flexible attitude of both the government and the UCD representatives, it was developed on a consensual basis by all parties. Both Right and Left shared a fundamental concern to escape from the mistakes which had led to the collapse of the Second Republic. Accordingly, great caution and a no less impressive moderation characterised the discussions in the parliamentary committees of the Congress and the Senate (eventually assembled in a joint committee in October 1978); hence the acceptance of the monarchical principle by leftist representatives, still republican in their hearts but none the less conscious of the value of monarchy as a factor of national cohesion. Hence also, symmetrically, the recognition of several nationalities inside the same state, on the part of rightist deputies whose unitary creed dissolved in face of the irreversible thrust of the autonomists.

In order to conciliate these conflicting attitudes, the king himself may have extracted some ideas from the Belgian model of institutionalised regionalism inside a centralised state; he has strong personal ties with Baudouin. And there is no doubt that the government's experts became supporters of the Italian constitutional model for organising regional autonomy. Italy is a country where the regions enjoy various degrees of governmental power within the framework of a unitary state, following a formula located between German federalism and traditional French centralism. The Spanish project goes further in that direction by extending the right of autonomy to all the provinces which wish to exercise it. In so doing, institutionalised regional particularism is supposed not to be inconsistent with the maintenance of the state, even though the state had to govern with several self-governing regions. And making the autonomy statute routine by allowing it to be extended in principle to all provinces was intended to make the older Catalan and Basque separatisms less dangerous. Moreover, autonomy was achieved through a two-stage referendum procedure which was an original constitutional innovation.

The codification of the power of a parliamentary monarchy was less controversial. This time, the model drew upon the inspiration of both the Swedish and the French Fifth Republic Constitutions. No longer the head of the executive, the king is entitled (Art. 56) to reign as a symbol of national unity and to ensure the correct functioning of the institutions. He is also the nominal commander of the armed forces, with all the difficulties of interpretation to which this can give rise (Art. 62). On its side, the government 'conducts domestic and foreign policy' (Art. 97) according to the usual practice of parliamentary regimes.

The text of the Constitution was approved almost unanimously by the Congress of Deputies on 21 July 1979, with 258 recorded positive votes, 14 abstentions and only 2 negative votes. It was also passed by the Senate on 5 October. And it was finally adopted

264 Constitutions in Democratic Politics

by national referendum on 6 December, with no less than 87.7 per cent of the voters in favour and only 7.8 per cent opposed to it, though 12.9 per cent abstained. This result owed much to the Prime Minister's tactical skills. It was also due to the great willingness to compromise shown by the Socialists and the Communists, the former following the advice of moderation given by the German Social Democrats who financed them, the latter still imbued at this time with the quasi-democratic doctrine of Eurocommunism.

In fact, the Socialists could not help displaying some of their ideological themes for honour's sake, and to claim credit for the constitutional recognition of some so-called social rights.[2] But this was really reciprocal back-scratching with the Union of the Democratic Centre. What they obtained in this sphere was more rhetorical than real. Thus the first paragraph of Article 1 of the Constitution stipulates that 'Spain constitutes herself as a social and democratic state'. Yet this assertion of the Spanish democracy's social ambition does not really pervade the detail of the Constitution. Spain remains faithful to the flexible rules of the free market, both in the political and economic spheres, despite Article 128, that 'all wealth in the country, whatever it is and whoever it belongs to, is subordinate to the public interest'.

Later on, the very ambiguity of these constitutional arrangements was to lead, as they were implemented, to strife. This was particularly the case with regional autonomy. It is no surprise that Suarez did not recover from his tactical success. Article 2 of the Constitution, which he inspired, assumes two contrary things at the same time. On the one hand, it proclaims 'the indissoluble unity of the Spanish nation as the common and indivisible motherland of all Spaniards'. But on the other, it contradicts this principle by acknowledging and guaranteeing 'the right of autonomy of nationalities and regions which are parts of the country'. Sticking to logic, that means that Spain is a nation only in so far as its citizens are willing not to avail themselves of another nationality. Consequently its citizens are not equal, since some of them use this facility while those who do not are reduced to the meaner estate of Spanish subjects pure and simple. And finally, even if these paradoxes were nothing but fussy hairsplitting, the fact remains that the unitary state's disunited faces inevitably generate endless conflicts about the respective competences of the central and regional powers. The constitutional machinery created by Suarez and his advisers can be interpreted as something which neither friends nor foes of regional autonomy can truly welcome. On the whole, the Prime Minister's fall which occurred on 25 January 1981 can be interpreted as the deferred price paid for his previous political artfulness.

Indeed, the main dispute over the Spanish Constitution since 1978 has been on this issue. But it must be added that the outrageous conduct of the Basque secessionists has distorted matters. The goodwill of the king and government were beyond doubt. Without waiting for the promulgation of the Constitution, provisional arrangements were made so as to foster the emerging regional authorities between the autumn of 1977 and the end of 1978. Later, the implementation of the Constitution led to the installation of nineteen regional governments up to 1983: in Catalonia and the Basque country first, in December 1979; Galicia in 1980; then in Andalusia, Aragon, Asturias, the Canary Islands, New Castile and Mancha, Old Castile and Leon, the Cantabrian region, Murcia, Navarre, the Rioja region, the Valencian provinces, Ceuta, Melilla and Madrid itself in 1982–83.

This revolutionary change in political and administrative structures necessarily involved serious practical difficulties and some passive resistance on the part of the formerly centralised Civil Service. Officials were allowed to choose between remaining with their department or being transferred to the corresponding regional agency. Most senior civil servants, and many of the best of them, opted for the centre and consequently left the provincial assignments to which they had been posted. In these uneasy circumstances, the regional agencies which inherited the local structures but not the right men had to improvise a hasty recruitment policy based on political patronage rather than on considerations of technical expertise. For this reason, inefficiency and useless duplication of responsibilities often characterised the disorderly proliferation of the new regional administrations. These defects led to a budgetary mess which complicated still further the tricky allocation of fiscal resources between the distrustful central state and the spendthrift regional governments (their accumulated deficit amounted to 130 billion pesetas up to 1983 alone).

These factors account for the growing gap which developed between the constitutional ideal and its translation into action, before and after Adolfo Suarez's term as Prime Minister. In 1980 the Minister of Home Affairs, Martin Villa, repeatedly declared that negotiations on the sharing of powers between Madrid and the regional capitals would start shortly. But the discussions actually initiated in April 1981, after Suarez's fall, involved only the two dominant national parties: the Union of the Democratic Centre (UCD) and the Socialist Party (PSOE). The reluctant autonomist groups and in particular the two main ones, the Basque Nationalist Party (PNV) and the Catalan *Convergencia: Unio*, were excluded from the working-out of the first draft of the law on regional autonomy (initially called LOOPA). Moreover, the crowning misfortune occurred when the rightist *Alianza Popular* and the Communist Party left the discussions almost immediately in June 1981. Rebaptised LOAPA, the new draft was submitted to the Congress on 16 October. The same day, the PNV convened a rally of 100,000 people in Bilbao. Later, the secret talks that Leopoldo Calvo Sotelo's UCD Government had been holding with moderate Catalan and Basque nationalists came to a dead-end after they were condemned by the Socialists. Examined by the Congress and the Senate during the summer of 1982, the project reached its end when the Constitutional Court declared 14 of its clauses unconstitutional in August 1983. Already in power for one year after their victory at the October 1982 legislative elections, the Socialists were not at all dissatisfied with this outcome. Though heirs of the UCD's difficulties, they preferred to let them vanish into infinity.

The worsening of the economic recession and the growth of Basque terrorism provided a kind of vindication of this sitting-on-the-fence policy. From then on, the major problem with the policy of regional autonomy was to become the issue of the police. More precisely, a debate ensued on whether complete responsibility for the police should or should not be granted to the Basque government. This meant that the core of the political question no longer dealt with the Constitution's implementation or interpretation: the constitutional dispute transformed itself into a different sort of issue, in the face of which the legal refinements amounted to little.

For the time being, the present Spanish constitutional experiment has had too short a life to allow a serious evaluation to be made. All that can be said tentatively is that the constitution-makers flung themselves into a restless irresponsible rush towards an undiscriminating recognition of regional autonomies. The spill-over of public funds generated by this somewhat demagogic policy was intended to drown the louder voices of the Basque and Catalan secessionists. But the use of this costly political device was not really justified for the majority of regions which were not pressing for autonomy. Granting a separate government to provinces which were not thinking of it beforehand did nothing but generate extra bureaucracy without any corresponding gain. It delighted the local party bosses without damping the spirits of the Basque separatists. On the contrary, the general concessions made to everybody exacerbated Basque bellicosity, both as regards terrorist activity and also Euskadi's attempt to outbid the central state.

Nevertheless, these flaws must not conceal one basic fact – the unquestionable relevance of the choice made in favour of the monarchy. The constitution-makers had no real choice, and therefore no great credit attaches to them. But they were at least aware of its benefits, and so did not obstruct a restoration which was at first sight anachronistic. Monarchists for the sake of convenience but not out of conviction, a great many members of the Spanish political class acted like non-ideological realists. They took the royal institutions as the only possible democratic antidote to be opposed to the regionalist implosion. Moreover, the monarchy gained in strength in virtue of the partial failure of the other basic element – the autonomist element – of the Spanish constitutional framework.

Portugal

If the Spanish political élite displayed some taste for apparently old-fashioned institutional arrangements, the Portuguese constitutional process is quite exceptional in modern Western societies. One reason for this lies in its origin, which derives from a political revolution and a would-be social revolution. The other reason lies in the constraints imposed on the Portuguese democracy until 1982 by the military after their 'revolution' of 25 April 1974. Under such a trusteeship, civilian opposition to the relatively mild Caetano's dictatorship could for a long time do nothing but try to play some part in the political space allotted to it by the revolutionary warlords. For eight years in fact, the Portuguese Government remained authoritarian to some extent, though more tolerant than before. The civilian opposition had to confine itself either to the powerless protest symbolised by the suspension of the newspaper *República* in 1975, or to some kind of opportunistic flirtation with one of the divided army's political coteries. On the whole, the fundamental logic of the 1976 Portuguese Constitution was that of a semi-authoritarian radical democracy controlled by the armed forces, in the same manner as the Salazar regime was a reactionary civilian semi-dictatorship. But there was this difference – that the core of the previous civilian authoritarianism showed itself much more coherent than its post-1974 military counterpart. Even though a substantial part of the officers' corps stubbornly ignored what democracy meant as a system of government, the majority adhered in theory to their democratic faith while turning their back upon it in practice. Hence their blundering permissiveness, which led finally to the emergence of a representative regime slipping its martial leash.

There were therefore many traps on the Portuguese path to democracy. The idealisation of the 1974 revolution on the part of various European intellectuals did nothing but display their own attitudes. The intellectuals did not seem very fond of democracy as a mere regulator of the political market. Following Rousseau, they were far more fascinated with the idea of democracy conceived as the paramount end of human destiny, as the ultimate instrument for the total overthrow of society. The Portuguese stage provided them with the lively entertainment of Utopia in motion, of a People's redemption led by military demiurges. The Portuguese 'iron surgeons' were to be exalted because they were clearing the road to happiness.

The assumption was correct in so far as it concerned intentions. Portuguese military officialdom mustered a large number of ingenious idealists. Portuguese officers did not display the same conceited *esprit de corps* as their Spanish colleagues had done. Indeed, they frequently shared a liberal and even socialist tradition quite uncommon in other armed forces. They genuinely did not want power just for its own sake but as a means to do good. This generous purpose was the source of their authoritarian behaviour (which contrasts, for example, with the discretion of the Brazilian armed forces in the current democratic transition in that country). But such an attitude also enabled them to revise their judgments, undo their excesses and tolerate the decent civilian democracy which was finally let loose to flourish in such seemingly unpromising ground. In this respect, the decisive step occurred when the General-President Ramalho Eanes handed supreme power over to the Socialist leader Mario Soares in 1985. This put an end to the purgatory which the Portuguese military had imposed on their fellow-citizens in the cause of freedom.

The beginning of the story must be remembered. In the days after the military *putsch* of 25 April 1974, a decree-law conferred a monopoly of power on the Armed Forces Movement (MFA). This self-enthronement created a Junta of National Salvation, which was complemented by a military President of the Republic, a provisional military government and a no less martial non-elective Council of State. But if the army had control over all these institutions, its dissensions and internal conflicts caused modifications in their power structure. General-President Spinola and his Prime Minister, Palma Carlos, were defeated in the first crisis of July 1974, after they tried unsuccessfully to reinforce the position of the executive power in the face of the Armed Forces Movement. The crisis recurred in September, when President Spinola resigned after his attempt to rest on the 'silent majority' in order to delay the decolonisation process. General Costa Gomes, who replaced him, did not hinder the MFA's radicalism. But his indulgent policy towards the military Left did not prevent a third crisis, in the shape of an abortive *coup* instigated this time by rightist officers with Christian Democrat civilian support.

This new incident intensified the political education of the pro-Communist military hardliners. The Junta and the Council of State were replaced by an Armed Forces Assembly and a Council of the Revolution which were to become the real organs of the government. At the same time, the military radicals confirmed their intention to remain in charge of the democratisation process for a period of three to five more years. And so as to be in a position to assess their popularity, they instructed their supporters to register blank votes at the Constituent Assembly election of 25 April 1975. For them, these blank votes were to be interpreted as a plebiscite in favour of the Armed Forces Movement, as well as an expression of distrust towards the political parties. The miscalculation is obvious. The 'rank and file' voters disclaimed the radical officers' ambition. Electoral participation amounted to 91.9 per cent of the registration census; the Socialist Party and the Moderates won the election with scores of 37.9 per cent and 33.9 per cent respectively; on the opposite side, the Communist Party and the pro-military MDP together gained only 16.6 per cent of the vote while the blank voters amounted to 6.9 per cent.[3]

The turning-point had come. The next step was taken between July and September 1975, when a fourth crisis led to the dismissal of the pro-Communist Prime Minister, Vasco Gonçalves, and to the nomination of a proxy-Socialist cabinet headed by Admiral Pinheiro de Azevedo. Assuredly, the reaction of the military radicals was not unexpected, as a further abortive *coup* had taken place on 25 April 1975. But the way was now sufficiently clear for the elected Constituent Assembly to slip its military leash and begin the work it was elected to do.

Like their Spanish colleagues, the Portuguese constitution-makers wanted to escape from the pitfalls of past constitutional experiments. They were partly inspired by the institutions of the French Fifth Republic in the organisation of the state. Accordingly, they designed a semi-presidential regime with a single chamber called the Assembly of the Republic. However, the President's powers are less extensive than in France. The President is not allowed to conduct Cabinet meetings and he is not entitled to appoint the Prime Minister without the previous agreement of the Assembly. The constitutional draft was cautiously innovating in a pre-emptive way, by granting autonomy to the provinces of the Azores and Madeira. But the Constitution's most salient features concern less these rather classical arrangements than the large role reserved to the armed forces and the orientation towards State socialism.

The Armed Forces Movement interfered directly and publicly in the constitutional process. On 26 February 1976, it obliged the parties to sign an agreement confirming the existence of the Council of the Revolution, and containing a new element concerning the election of the President of the Republic. Although the most influential military leaders were not the same as those in 1975, their less radical inclinations did not prevent them from exerting similar political pressure. First, they imposed the constitutional upgrading of the Council of the Revolution as provided for in Article 143. Comprising the President of the Republic, the Chief of the General Staff, the commanders of the three armed forces and fourteen officers elected by their colleagues, this Council was to advise the President in matters of war, peace and defence. Above all, it acted as a supreme constitutional court, and was entitled to approve the choice and dismissal of the Prime Minister. In so doing, it played a role which is not consistent with the normal practice of democracy.

In the same fashion, the MFA interfered, amazingly enough, in the system of election for the President of the Republic. The civilian constitutional draft provided for indirect election by a body nominated by the Assembly. With the agreement of February 1976, the military arranged to have him elected by universal suffrage, as in France. This idea seemed to convey a democratic intention. In fact, it was aimed at retrieving the chances of military candidates in the face of their civilian challengers; this change displayed the Bonapartist logic rather than the revolutionary appeal of the nascent MFA. Whatever the intention, it showed that the army had not dropped its 'right' to maintain ultimate sovereignty, and that it continued to contend against the political parties.

The constitution's ideological orientation was completely different from that of the other constitutions of Western Europe. The 1976 Portuguese Constitution contradicted the standards of free market societies. It dedicated itself to the revolutionary prospect of the transition of Portuguese society towards State socialism. The 311 clauses of the Constitution look like scrupulous disciplinary regulations, almost in the manner of the 1795 *Allgemeines preussisches Landrecht*. In content, they sought to articulate a situation of no return for the alignment of Portugal in a position located somewhere between Third World societies and Eastern European 'socialism'. Having been unable to dominate their own colonies, the Portuguese military used the constitution as a substitute, to colonise their fellow-citizens. As a constraining framework for the nation's future, the Constitution begins in this spirit with two parts dedicated respectively to specific rights 'in a classless society' (Art. 1), and to an economic organisation based on the socialisation of production, authoritarian planning and agrarian reform. Only the third part deals properly with the political structures, as if it were accessory or subordinate. Moreover, this Constitution promulgated on 2 April 1976 is totally barred and bolted for the mutual benefit of the military and their leftist civilian allies.

In fact, the legitimacy of a possible conservative shift is denied from the start as unconstitutional. The Portuguese are free, but they have no choice other than to maintain what was settled in their name once and for all between 1974 and 1976. The Constitution was not to be revised until 1982, while its fundamental principles were declared irreversible, especially with regard to agrarian reform and nationalisation, which went so far as to include the press which thus fell under the government's pleasure.

In December 1979, however, the moderate parties joined together in Democratic Action won the legislative elections. Francisco Sa'Carneiro was the leader of the new majority which comprised the Social-Democrat Party (PSD) reformists and the Democratic Social Centre (CDS) conservative Christian Democrats. It was known far and wide that their main purpose would be to reopen the constitutional debate despite the many obstacles raised in the way. After Sa'Carneiro's death in an unexplained air crash, the Pinto Balsemão Cabinet started the revision process on the symbolic anniversary date of 25 April 1981. Its reform project was quite radical.[4] It provided for the abandonment of the socialist model: it reduced the President's powers and suppressed the Council of the Revolution. But the eessential changes could not be achieved and there was no chance of a repeal of the constitution succeeding. President of the Republic since June 1976, Ramalho Eanes was diametrically opposed to it. Furthermore, Pinto Balsemão could not obtain the two-thirds majority which was required for such a reform.

A compromise between the Right in the Democratic Action and the Left-Centre in Mario Soares' Socialist Party was nevertheless agreed. It led to the adoption of the constitutional law of 24 September 1982. The first eleven articles of the law repealed most of the 1976 Constitution's fundamental principles. In particular they nullified all allusions to a revolutionary process of transition to socialism. And they suppressed the army's political ambitions by abolishing the Council of the Revolution. Henceforth, a civilian Supreme Court would have the power to control the constitutionality of legislation, while a new Council of State would have a more modest advisory role *vis-à-vis* the President. At the same time, the reform law expanded the powers of the Assembly to amend the Constitution. But the victory was not complete. The President's powers remained on the whole unchanged, while the economic provisions of the Constitution were untouched. Though no longer sustained by the same ideological assumptions, the State financial and industrial sectors remained entrenched inside their constitutional fortress. This was the price extorted by the army and the radical Left for Portugal's democratic consolidation.

Today Portuguese economic and political recovery is still handicapped by these unresolved constitutional conflicts. The product of an abortive ambition, the Portuguese regime is less semi-presidential than productive of strife between the President and the Prime Minister or the Assembly. Either the President acts like General Eanes by nominating technocratic cabinets which are largely antiparliamentary; or he is forced to act like Eanes' successor, Mario Soares, by accepting a difficult cohabitation with a more or less hostile government. The result is harmful whichever option is chosen, because it paralyses public policy and baffles public opinion. Presidential pre-eminence maintained with the assistance of obedient technical ministers ignores the parties' voice, while cohabitation tends to contradict the spirit of the Constitution when it becomes the norm instead of the exception. In short, the Portuguese constitutional construction generates instability and political uncertainty. It is no secret that the renascent democracies need to offer certainty to their citizens who have just been relieved of unpredictable and whimsical dictatorships. In considering the recent circumstances of Portuguese politics, Walter C. Opello Jr describes them as *Portugal's Political Development*[5] instead of using the common expression of a return to democracy. He is probably right, since Portugal has still not achieved reliable democratic stability.

Are constitutions enough?

Yet constitutions should not be made scapegoats for every political defect. In 1964, General de Gaulle was right to observe: 'Une constitution c'est un esprit, des institutions, une pratique.' In so doing, he noted, like Juan J. Linz[6] that some para-constitutional elements are at least as crucial as the constitution itself. Among these, in the case of Spain and Portugal, are the armed forces' attitude in the face of civilian authority, the quality of the democratic leadership, the cohesiveness and depth of the new party systems, the influence of the memory of prior dictatorship, and the maturity of the electorate or conversely its excessive sensitivity to political demagoguery.

In all these respects, both Iberian countries have been confronted with great difficulties. But these were especially pressing and difficult to surmount in Portugal. The Portuguese had not endured the sufferings of a civil war as had their Spanish neighbours. Perhaps this is the reason why they relished the dangerous delights of revolutionary Utopia and political hatreds. For this reason, their country has been torn between conflicting passions from the beginning. For its part, the Portuguese army obviously aspired to play more of a political role at the very moment when the Spanish military retired to its tents having convinced itself of the obsolescence of martial political surgery. Moreover, even though both party systems are still fairly brittle, the Portuguese have suffered more than the Spanish from the intolerance of leftist radicals who arrogated to themselves a monopoly of democratic sentiment.

But the historical wounds of the civil war were still painful in Spain. Perhaps that was why Spain accepted a transition to democracy which initially took place in secret, and which was not itself brought about by democratic processes. In fact, the central actor in the democratic transition in Spain was the UCD; and this party was nothing but an artificial creation imposed from above.

Finally, it seems almost reasonable to conclude that constitutions exert more influence on political life when they are ill-adapted than when they function well. Clumsily put together by squabbling parents, the Portuguese Constitution could not create a satisfactory political equilibrium. Put together by more skilled craftsmen, the Spanish Constitution established a satisfactory framework of compromise, at least as regards the level of central government. But the dangers of the policy of regional autonomy cannot be denied. Moreover, the builders of Spanish democracy were not heroes at all. The King, as well as his Prime Minister, Adolfo Suarez, were indeed more anxious about the enemies of democracy than about its friends – or rather, they considered that the friends could be kept waiting, while the enemies needed to be conciliated by a democratic process engineered from above. This appeared an effective principle of political strategy. But it had nothing in common with democratic philanthropy. Perhaps this should not surprise us, for it would be an illusion to suppose that constitutional questions can be divorced from political self-interest.

Notes and references

1. Lilly Marcou, *Le Communisme malgré tout* (Paris: Presses Universitaires de France, 1984), p. 84.
2. Miguel Martinez Cuadrado, *La constitución de 1978* (Madrid, 1982), pp. 8, 116.
3. Jorge Gasper and Nuno Vittorino, *As eleiçũes de 25 de Abril* (Lisbon: Livros Horizonte, 1976), p. 29.
4. See *Revisão constitutional* (Lisboa Assembleia da Republica, 1981).
5. Boulder, Col.: Westview Press, 1985.
6. *The Breakdown of Democratic Regimes* (Baltimore: Johns Hopkins University Press, 1978).

PART D
THE CONSTITUTIONS
OF THE SMALLER
DEMOCRACIES

14 Switzerland (1875): Constitutionalism and Democracy
Christopher Hughes

A Constitution came to Switzerland in 1798, together with a French invading army. But, as was the case in the British seaboard colonies in the United States, the way had been prepared by certain features of the Swiss *ancien régime*. The sovereign cities of Switzerland – Berne, Zurich etc – were governed by an indefinite number of charters, sworn letters enactments and providing for and thereby limiting the institutions of government. The texts of these were not widely known and were largely irrelevant (though a few winged phrases taken out of context were current) as with Magna Carta in England. In the English sense, these can be regarded as constitutions.

The countryside was rather different. The subject towns and many former lordships and communities had also received charters from ruling counts etc. before they were purchased or otherwise annexed by the sovereign republics or any one of them. The Swiss rulers obtained thereby only limited powers, and swore on acquisition to observe the limitations on the powers they had purchased. But time, and the *Policey-Staat* which Protestant and Catholic cantons alike introduced after the Reformation, had pushed these ancient rights to the fringe. However, there remained a memory of the good old law as a higher law infringed from time to time by modern proclamations imposed by force. That appeal to a pre-existing law is the essence of constitutionalism.

The Helvetic Constitution of 1798 was from the outset rejected by traditional Catholics, who called it 'the hellish booklet', and the disorder and oppression which followed its introduction caused a more widespread revulsion. Napoleon imposed a more conservative Instrument of Government, which included terse little constitutions for each canton; his authority stood behind it. The problem of authority is inherent in a government which a nation imposes upon itself. It is a problem which republican federal government side-steps; the Union enforces cantonal constitutions, and itself disposes of the army and can find friendly cantons or sections of the population to enforce its own edicts. (In a monarchy, on the other hand, the problem is to limit authority.)

The old ruling classes thrust Napoleon's federal constitution aside when the dictator was defeated by the Allies in 1813. But the Allies insisted on the newly-again sovereign cantons giving themselves constitutions guaranteed by the Union and in the last resort by the Allies themselves. These cantonal constitutions were little more than Instruments of Government. True constitutions, with a Catalogue of Rights and directive principles incorporated, appeared in 1830 when revolutionary enthusiasm moved around each canton in turn. The Union was left with its Federal Treaty of 1815 (which one could argue to be a constitution – in a confederacy the directive principles override the guarantees and the sphere allocated to majority rule) until 1847; at any one time only a bare majority of cantons had governments of Liberal-Radicals.

The Constitution of 1848 was again imposed by war, this time a civil war, which the cantons with liberal governments, i.e. most of the Protestant cantons, won. Puppet governments were installed in Lucerne, Fribourg and Valais, the three largest seceding cantons and, emboldened by this, a Senate (the Council of States) was installed as a House of the Legislature. In this house there was implicit a blocking majority whenever the religious minority (the Catholics) and the language minorities (French and Italian) made common cause.

By this concession, the imposed Constitution of 1848 became a true constitution acceptable both to conquerors and defeated. The liberals did indeed lose control over the internal politics of the secessionist cantons (Lucerne broke free in 1870, the last one: it never again had a liberal government). Nevertheless, the liberals maintained control of the Federal Executive until 1919; the introduction of proportional representation at the federal level then cut them down to their true strength of the party – around one quarter of the electorate, though it was and is the politically, economically and intellectually dominant quarter. 1870 was the year of German unity, and of the 'Fourteenth Amendment Constitution' of the United States, and of Supreme Court rule. Switzerland also started anew and submitted the result to a plebiscite: after a first defeat in a referendum, the revised document that became the Federal Constitution of 1874 came into effect. This, 'as amended' since, is the Constitution of today.

In the interval between 1848 and 1874, the cantons became politically mature. There is a law of political symmetry whereby government and opposition are nearly precisely equal over the years. A constitution can be made a device to enable the party which drafts it to juggle the electorate to its advantage and secure power for itself almost into perpetuity – a victorious party collects supporters through patronage. The patronage of the cantons was a matter of life and death to the fortunes of a family, in law, teaching, infantry officering, church and elsewhere. The rewards of a *coup d'état* were large and for a time (varying from one canton to another) power passed by violence. Then one by one cantons passed over to coalition and sharing the good things between the parties, and to a relatively neutral electoral system, always weighted in favour of the liberal-radicals because they held federal power. The Kulturkampf gave a short advantage to the Protestant-liberals, and this was used to get the new Constitution of 1874–75 past the plebiscite. But there was a new factor, the Referendum, which came fully into play on the federal level after 1891, and has profoundly transformed Swiss political life.

The Referendum had two effects relevant to our argument. In the first place, the liberals never managed to fudge the referendum as effectively as they controlled the elections to the Assembly. Although the Catholics and the socialists did not obtain positive control of the referendum, they had an effective negative destructive power that forced the liberals to make concessions, notably conceding a seat in the Executive to moderate Catholics. Secondly, the referendum has proved to be a tool not of the political parties so much as of the pressure groups: it called forth the great pressure groups (industry, retail trade, agriculture, trades unions, the Catholic Church) and they became its masters.

This is why the words 'as amended' are so important. In 1891, it was the popular initiative for *partial* amendment which was introduced. The full panoply of referendum rights already existed on the cantonal level, i.e. voting on Total Revision, Partial Revision, Laws, Finance, and initiative of constitutional revisions and laws. But there is still *no popular initiative of Federal Laws*. And the great pressure groups want laws passed in their favour. So they amend the Constitution. This was at first usually done under the form that the Constitution was amended to give the legislature power to pass a particular law hitherto inhibited by the Constitution. But then when at long last these projects of laws were drafted by the Assembly, as often as not they were defeated at referendum. It is much more profitable to encapsulate the proposed law in the form of a constitutional amendment, short-circuiting all complications and difficult to repeal or stultify (though stultification is a fine art in which considerable skill has been shown).

The Constitution is therefore getting longer, more chaotic, in places more ridiculous every year. This is democracy indeed but not constitutionalism. It is bulldozing sectional interests, in defiance of 'the Constitution', through normal legal hurdles.

There are other ways in which the document called the Federal Constitution falls short of the concept of a constitution, in addition to the two ways already considered (i.e. a misuse of power by a political faction or vested interest, and as the product of democracy but not of the idea of a permanent moral law).

First, the Constitution is imperfectly justiciable. So far as the cantons are concerned, the federal constitution is indeed a sovereign act, in that it also goes into effect as cantonal law. If the Federal Constitution proclaims that there is freedom of trade and commerce or freedom of conscience and belief, cantonal courts must apply this, because federal law prevails over cantonal law. The harshness of this rule is disguised because cantonal constitutions themselves proclaim high-sounding rights which duplicate the federal constitution. But the legislation passed by the Federal Parliament is not subject to annulment by the Courts. Courts being courts, and judges enjoying power, this immunity is somewhat precarious – after all the US Supreme Court arguably seized this power for itself in defiance of the Constitution – but it prevails. There has been some restiveness about this on the Federal Tribunal, which has requested a larger administrative staff, in order presumably to interfere more; but this request has not been fully met. The laws once passed may be challenged in a referendum, so no tears need be shed over the theoretical loss of cash value of the constitution.

However, very much is still left to the cantons, including the administrative stage of central government legislation. Federalism is weakening in Switzerland, but cantonalism is strong. Local particularism, and much raw power exercised personally and enjoyably by cantonal statesmen, remain. It is the constitutional position that has eroded. Because so much is left to the cantons, the imperfect justiciability of *federal* law is not so significant as it might seem.

Secondly, when judges apply themselves to widening their jurisdiction, they take some trivial flower of phraseology (such as 'due process of law') and make a whole judge-made constitution out of it. This has happened in Switzerland with the inoffensive-looking Article 4 of the Constitution – 'All Swiss are equal before the law'. At one time this boasted that the hereditary privileges of family and place (but not of the male sex) under the *ancien régime* had been abolished. But now it has become the rule of general fairness, palm-tree justice. This is itself formally a denial of constitutionalism, of marginal importance for the total balance of the Constitution indeed, because the Federal Tribunal is not at the centre of power. For there is only one set of Federal Judges residing in Lausanne:

the system is not like that in the USA where there is a whole parallel structure of courts deciding in matters of federal law, more respected and less corruptible than State judges.

Nevertheless, the Federal Tribunal is not negligible. A selection of its judgments is published officially, and in a country that does not revere legal precedent, they form precedents that create law, going well beyond the letter of the Constitution, even creating new categories such as 'the Guarantee of Property' long before this was added to the constitutional document.

As against this, Switzerland stands within the continental tradition which makes it unlikely that the judiciary would form the wish to hijack the constitution. Federal judges are 'elected by the Assembly', i.e. chosen by a committee of party leaders, for six years, and are re-eligible, and re-elected. Impartiality as a bench is secured by their party-political balance, not by guaranteed tenure, prestige or mumbo-jumbo. The legal profession itself is immensely powerful, but the judicial career within it is not glamorous. The marginal position of the Federal Tribunal and its anonymity are psychologically unfavourable for lawyers who nurture ambitions. The solicitude of the Federal Tribunal is to maintain legality, the rule of law, the *Rechtsstaat*, and perhaps to extend this, e.g. in the control of excessive legislative delegation of power to administrative bodies, a typical 'lawyer's' issue and a proper one.

An extreme issue in theoretical terms was the extension of equality to political equality between the sexes, to female suffrage. Faced with this demand, the Tribunal found itself unable to take the step, which the wording of the Constitution would seem to allow. It would even have been a breach of the constitution to introduce equal suffrage by simple legislation, and it required an express amendment, confined to the federal level, leaving the cantons to find their own way at their own time.

However the Federal Court and the cantonal legal profession have not since 1848 faced the ultimate test of national revolution or despotism. The same must be said of the army, and of the whole establishment wherein army, officialdom, the press, law, education, finance, and trade unionism collaborate. In 1918, and in 1940, the brink was approached, but as in Great Britain, the sum of things has always been saved.

Thirdly, there are also other ways in which the Constitution is not supreme. In wartime, that is, in times when neighbours are at war, the Constitution is, illegally, suspended, or at least it was suspended in 1939 and had been, to a much less extent, in the last years of the First World War. This was done by a simple decree of the two Chambers conferring Full Powers on the Federal

Executive. At the end of the war much of this Full Powers 'legislation' remained in force for up to a decade, some of it finding legality and permanent anchorage by constitutional amendment. Sovereignty, it has been said, is where the emergency power resides. In Switzerland the emergency power resides not in the Constitution, nor in the people (whose referendum rights were virtually suspended in 1939), but probably in the executive, or perhaps in the Assembly. But in normal times it is indeed the People in referendum which is the lawful sovereign, that is, in theory and in mythology. In Britain, the conjuring trick is to reconcile the sovereignty of Parliament with the Rule of Law, as the ideological shield behind which the dictatorship of the Prime Minister in Cabinet operates. In Switzerland, it is the optical illusion of the reconciliation of constitutionalism with democracy which shields the supremacy of the Federal Council from the eye.

Moreover, it is not only democracy which takes precedence over constitutionalism, nationalism also takes precedence. It takes three forms, xenophobia, neutrality, and national security.

A dislike of foreign influence as such (but not of individuals who are guests) is natural and healthy, the underside of affection for one's own kind, but it is not easy to manage under the rule of constitutionalism. Human rights belong to humans, not just to Swiss adults. Foreigners temporarily on Swiss soil cannot expect these rights. But when the whole proletarian working class of a country is foreign, and in practice debarred from acquiring citizen rights (in extreme cases for several generations) then the limits of constitutionalism are overpassed. Switzerland is not today quite in that position, but it is perhaps more nearly so than any other European country (though not by a great margin). The exclusion confines constitutionalism to the privileged many, who hold full citizenship. Most immigrants are Catholics, most would in Switzerland vote socialist, many speak Italian as their mother tongue. Trade unions would be more aggressive if immigrants had the guaranteed right of residence and association. The enviable balance of the country would be threatened by including these workers and their families within the pale of constitutionalism, even though one might doubt whether the balance would be destroyed. But the issue here is constitutionalism. Constitutional amendments are regularly proposed to expel as many as feasible of these aliens. The Swiss establishment is deeply humanitarian, but it came near to a defeat in a referendum contest on 7 July 1970 with the maximum turnout of voters (the Schwarzenbach initiative to limit the size of the immigrant workforce). The threat of the referendum (the initiative and the challenge to a vote of a newly enacted law) brings the coarse and unregenerated minds of normal people, nationalist and even racialist, into political calculations in Switzerland in a way that is unfamiliar in Britain, where the prejudices even of a majority can be conveniently ignored.

In federal countries, the internal status of international law is a constitutional issue, even if (until recently) a minor one. An international agreement (e.g. on Human Rights) can make hay of the classic division of powers into central and local; the central power can make a treaty infringing cantonal rights. There is a treaty referendum in Switzerland, relatively easy to side-step, which occasionally creates a slight embarrassment in relations with neighbours. But Switzerland is permanently neutral as a principle of foreign policy, though neutrality is not imposed by the written Constitution. It pleases Switzerland to regard many matters which are infringements of national self-interest as matters concerning neutrality: any derogation of national sovereignty is considered to be an infringement of neutrality. It is logical, but not quite constitutional, to submit proposals which are disputed, such as close co-operation with the European Community or membership of the United Nations (or in its day, of the League of Nations) to a preliminary referendum. But what is unconstitutional is the practice of making the referendum a 'constitutional' one, counting the votes of the cantons as well as the votes of the majority of voters as required for approval: the recent project to apply to join the UN was in fact rejected both by a large majority and by every single canton, so it hardly mattered. But this illustrates my theme that both nationalism and democracy take precedence over constitutionalism as a principle in Switzerland.

It also draws attention to another aspect of constitutions. Almost everywhere in the world certain pre-constitutional norms are considered more of a constitution than the constitutional document itself – the USA Declaration of Independence, the French Declaration of the Rights of Man, for example. In Switzerland, neutrality is a pre-constitutional but not a constitutional norm. Religion, on the other hand, is a central preoccupation of the constitution, though the militantly anti-Catholic provisions were early stultified and have rather recently been repealed. However, the linguistic balance *is* regarded as supra-constitutional – the Constitution *lists* the three 'official' and the four 'national' languages (Romanche, spoken in one canton only, has this status). The management of the French-German language frontier is left to the three cantons through which the frontier runs. The principle employed is the geographical one, a right to use French for all public purposes on one side, to use German on the other, no geographical shift in status normally being allowed. Italian is a special problem, and here the Ticino government has stepped in with a Law on Notices: these must be publicly exhibited *in Italian* (e.g. on shop windows). This law is unconstitutional, a breach of the freedom of trade, but has been permitted by the Federal Tribunal in an unpublished judgment because of the pre-eminence of the language principle. Canton Grisons, with German, Italian and Romanche, has the most complicated task of all, and has delegated to the communes the policing of Romanche language rights.

The words of the constitutional document declare that the cantons themselves are pre-constitutional, but this can no longer be considered the case when a new canton, Jura, French-speaking and Catholic, has been created out of the living body of Canton Berne and given standing thereby both in the Council of States and in the constitutional referendum, by simple amendment of the relevant federal constitutional articles. The basis in contract between cantons has disappeared; such rights as the cantons have now are under constitutional *law* and not under pre-constitutional *contract*: the principle of national interest has prevailed. A further innovation, the claim of the new canton that its citizenship extended to those whose families were Jurassian – the claim made on behalf of the South African Homelands – has been resisted by the Federal Chambers. Meanwhile, Protestant French-speaking Jura communes have opted to remain in Canton Berne, and so, by a slender majority, has the Catholic German-speaking Laufenthal. Moreover, there are other linguistic and religious minorities elsewhere in Switzerland, which might one day claim the same status as Jura.

Since 1875 all aspects of life in Switzerland have changed. The written constitution has also changed. As said, it has been much cluttered about with additions from the special pleading of interested groups, and by legislation masquerading as constitutional reform, particularly in recent years. In losing its elegance it has lost its popularity; it has become unreadable, though it remains very Swiss. There is also some clutter from pre-1848 days, when the country was a confederacy. Have the changes since 1875 been effected by reform of the document or have they happened because life and society in nearly every particular of which law takes cognisance has suffered a sea-change since then, even when the same words are still employed?

Three changes of substance have been made in the form of government, in 1891, in 1918 and in 1978 in the Jura amendment. Those of 1918 and 1978 were pushed through by the threat of extra-constitutional action, e.g., revolutionary strikes or terrorism. In a long constitution, some two dozen words effecting substantive change have been added, and of these the introduction of eight words in

1918 has changed life most, viz., 'these elections [for the National Council] shall follow the principles of proportionality', together with words making cantons the electoral constituencies. Behind the eight words lay seventy years of discontent. The cantonal constituency was included almost absent-mindedly, yet has had the effect of keeping the political parties (apart from the socialists) as cantonal parties primarily, and federal parties only secondarily. This remains today the most important residual aspect of a federalism which has become rather unified (apart from the French-German dichotomy which is the *raison d'être* of Switzerland).

Proportional representation in the Lower House of Parliament was a big step in the long dynamic of homogenisation which reached its peak about 1975, a system of total proportionality in every aspect of life, referred to now as *Konkordanzdemokratie*. In principle, all life is regulated on the 'magic formula' of 2:2:2:1, exemplified by the composition of the Federal Executive cabinet, composed of two liberal-radical ministers, two Christian-democrats, two socialists, and one conservative-agrarian. The formula is a constitution in itself, but the continued equal membership of the social democrats is once again under discussion.

The magic formula, by excluding the idea of opposition, is at once the culmination and the denial of the British idea of a constitution. It brings discussion round again to the topic of who is left out in the cold and what are the forces of anti-constitutionalism.

The exclusion of the large foreign workforce and their families from political activity (though not from basic juridical rights) has already been mentioned. Today there are also Swiss groups who feel excluded from the political consensus – the young, the Jurassians, the Greens, and, more seriously in spite of the magic formula, the socialists.

For the moment, the protests of the young Swiss have ceased to worry the public conscience, and seem likely even to disappear from the public scene. The Greens, notably the anti-nuclear movements, are much in the public eye, using unconstitutional methods, perhaps for preference, but also enjoying local political successes. The Jurassian outburst no longer threatens a Swiss Ulster, but still smoulders and occasionally flares up. As for the alleged growing exclusion of main-line democratic socialists from the political process, there are particular cases and anecdotal evidence. There is some erosion of voting strength, and the trades unions are more and more on the margin of being a serious factor, from causes well known to us in Britain as well as from local causes and the long disuse of the strike weapon. There has been talk of socialist withdrawal from the Federal Executive, so that there would once again be a socialist opposition party in parliament, but the erosion of voting power makes this dangerous. On the extreme left, the main-line 'Moscow' communist party is said to be losing ground to a wilder left wing. The commitment of the sober left to constitutionalism, and of constitutionalism to the left, are clearly important matters. There seems also to be some polarisation on the right wing of politics, and friction over refugee status claimed by Asians. But all these extreme groups, on occasion, claim constitutional protection and, in fact, give tolerance and the constitution a field of activity without which one would be unconscious of both. A more insidious enemy is abstentionism, both in the literal and the emotional senses – not bothering to vote, not understanding the issues, and not giving affection or respect to constitutionalism and the free-capitalist society which it maintains. Votations (elections and referendums) often nowadays bring voters to the polls only in the range of 25–40 per cent of those entitled. Membership of political parties, and readership of the party-political press, are difficult to maintain. Compulsory military service has come under discussion. Democracy has lost its vigour, and become a habit rather than a cause; this is not necessarily a criticism, and there is still enthusiasm for moral and political crusades abroad, sometimes altruistically, sometimes self-indulgently, sometimes specifically directed against the USSR.

Constitutionalism, indeed, reckons to be a method of dealing with anti-constitutionalism. In one aspect it is the dead hand of the past. But in another aspect, the constitution claims to be, as amended, a codification of the best practice of the present and, as amendable, a procedure for effecting change. In all these, it is making use of the full coercive power of the state, and legitimising itself by moderating that power, delaying change, postponing problems – political problems are not solved, but often change their form if solution is delayed – while providing a means of change.

The Swiss Constitution is a sober document, speaking little about subjective rights of the individual, and it places these into a specific political environment; the right of petition, the right to form associations subject to cantonal legislation to prevent misuse of the right, the right to live in other cantons on completion of the necessary documentation, *provided* . . . The normal phrase is the grant of a right to legislate upon a topic to the central power, or for the individual to 'exercise a freedom'. Collectively, these rights are called 'freedom rights', not rights of man – though in the new draft of constitutional total revision the term 'Basic Rights' has been borrowed from the Federal Republic of Germany. The situation resembles that of Britain: at first reading one would be tempted to deny that this constitution is very free or very democratic at all.

But then, who does read the Swiss Constitution? The expectation is that the Swiss enjoy a scarcely paralleled liberty, and the general opinion of mankind confirms this reputation – freedom is a Swiss thing. It is the same with Britain, freedom is a British thing. The surprise in both cases is that so many reservations exist. This chapter has been full of reservations, because the expectations of informed opinion are, rightly, so high. It is a happy country which has to defend itself against the charge that it rates democracy higher than constitutionalism.

Postscript: Is Switzerland *sui generis?*
It is often suggested that Switzerland is *sui generis*, i.e. so 'one-off' that no lessons could be learned by other nations, or by Great Britain, from Swiss political experience. The same claim is sometimes made in Switzerland itself; applied to Neutrality it is the official doctrine and received opinion. The task here is to deny its application to the Swiss Constitution.

In a sense, each country is unique; there are not many USAs, or Israels, at any one moment of time. This is not entirely a trivial statement; a nation, like an individual person, incorporates an imperishable moral value. But we can talk about men and nations nevertheless, seek to understand them, while allowing something mysterious at the heart of things, a factor x. Put in another way, one cannot learn everything from any country, but there is no country from which nothing can be learned. Within this spectrum we must place Switzerland: it is a question whether Switzerland is exceptionally interesting, with clear, extreme, results of unique experiments, or whether these taken together form a polity which is incomparable.

In several respects Swiss society is indeed an extreme example. First, it is a paradigm of cross-cutting cleavages, where three languages and two religions co-exist in deadlock, but do not coincide. Secondly, it has exhibited historically an extreme time-lag in some respects (e.g. votes for women) but been in advance of the time in others (e.g. republicanism, manhood suffrage, the referendum). Thirdly, the corporative solution has been applied to labour/ management/ownership relations, with extreme success.

Switzerland is also an extreme example of federalism, and of the referendum. With the referendum, a distinction must be made between 'plebiscites', and the 'procedural referendum'. The Common Market and devolution referendums in Britain were 'plebiscites', and some Swiss referendums must be classified under the same head, e.g., the Jura referendums, and the cases treated illegally as being people-and-cantons matters when by law they are simple-majority questions, such as the EEC and UN referendums. The big turning-points of the past – bringing in the Catholics in 1891, and the working class in 1918, and rejecting Nazism in the 1930s – are to be counted along with matters 'unconstitutionally' submitted to referendum in Britain and France, and are comparable in number. But in Switzerland there is also the regular procedural referendum, which is a local quirk, just as Questions in Parliament at Westminster are quirkish in one aspect, but profoundly revealing and necessary in another aspect.

When it comes to the structure of the Executive Cabinet, Switzerland is also indeed on an extreme flank, along with the 26 cantons (plus Liechtenstein), but comparable to English local government, and, at one time, to Uruguay and Ceylon. The institution is all the more interesting in that only half of it is in the constitutional document, the remainder being a rule of practice. One may observe that the magic-formula period has coincided with, but outlasted, a consensus period at Westminster (i.e. two parties with scarcely distinguishable records) and the Great Coalition in Austria.

Having said this, it must be conceded that when a whole series of data – refrigerators, strikes, car owners, savings accounts, urban crime, divorces, military service, atom bombs, terrorism, church attendance, Picasso paintings, Nobel prizes – are fed into a computer, Switzerland 'always' stands out from correlations. When I have seen this done, the *time-lag* factor has not been fed in, a lag on occasion of fifty years. The *sui-generis* charge must be kept open, but in the meanwhile Switzerland can continue to be compared with South Africa, India, Belgium, Ireland, Canada, and with purgatory and paradise.

Appendix

In 1987 a move to Total Revision of the constitutional document enjoys much official support. The idea surfaced in the early 1960s, became a stimulating topic in university seminars, particularly in Basle, and escaped from there to a wider public. Consultations have been completed, but the project has not yet fructified in a submission to the electorate by way of a referendum backed by the government and the Federal Assembly. Indeed, consultation has been so wide and so painstaking that the most favourable moment for acceptance has passed, and the project itself is lichened up with compromise, reading once again like a committee decision rather than a work of art such as the Canton Jura constitution. However, the results of these consultations are an excellent source for the attitudes of the Swiss vocal classes on the 'constitution and what it means today'. There is some ambiguity as to whether it is a more beautiful version of the existing Constitution, as too much amended, or whether indeed it is a sort of Vatican II. It started life in an atmosphere of the recasting of the living ideas of the traditional constitution and has finished up as a sober refurbishing, making minimum alteration to the play of political forces. Many cantonal constitutions have been completely revised as a by-product of this movement, and federalism itself has been rethought. Details may be found in: *Revising the Federal Constitution of Switzerland*, by Charles F. Schuetz, Department of Political Science paper, distributed by the University Bookstall, Carleton University, Ottawa, 1983. This has the text, a commentary, a summary of the Opinions of Experts, together with the political background.

The Israeli political public, living in a state without a constitution, nevertheless highly values constitutionalism and constitutions, perhaps precisely because of the absence of the latter. Israelis enjoy a constitutional[1] government in the popular sense of the term, which entails, as a minimum, limited government, the sharing of power and the influence of public opinion. But as to a formal, or codified[2] constitution, those who favour the introduction of one, and even more so those who reject it, agree in their conviction that it would entail far-reaching changes, transforming Israel's political system. Fundamentally, the conflict is between two basically contradictory conceptions of the source of legitimacy of a constitution and of the political order which it enjoins: on the one side is the conception of a constitution based on popular sovereignty and given in the name of the people, and on the other side are those who will not accept anything other than a theocratic constitution, one which lays down God's commands as interpreted by them.

In more practical terms what is primarily at stake has to do with the role of religion in the state and in its legal system, or more specifically the (so-called) status quo in religious matters. The religious camps and their allies are staunch supporters of the existing status quo, even more so of the principle of status quo politics in these matters, and hence unwilling to enact a constitution which would have to abrogate, so they are convinced, the special and very central role of the religious institutions in Israel's public life. And it is, of course, for the self-same reason that the other side is so anxious to press for the adoption of one.

By the same token, however, one has to admit that the constitutional issue is not a live one at present, nor has it stirred up serious public debate since the early days when the enactment of a constitution was debated by the Knesset at great length.[3] At present, the existing constitutional situation is more or less taken for granted, and the supporters of a codified constitution raise the issue only very rarely. This is particularly so among those who seem to be motivated by a rather naive view that with a constitution much that they disapprove of would disappear overnight. These are the people who sigh, 'if only we had a constitution'.

I

At independence, in 1948, the speedy adoption of a constitution was thought of as almost certain. The Declaration of Independence of 14 May 1948 boldly asserted that a constituent assembly, to be elected by 1 October of that year,[4] was to enact a constitution. The then prevalent view was that a constitution was an integral component of a respectable newly independent state. Furthermore, the people then preparing the draft constitution were mindful of the UN resolution on Palestine of 29 November 1947, which had not only stipulated the convening of democratically elected constituent assemblies (in both the states to be established in Palestine), but had also enjoined the adoption of democratic constitutions, and had even specified some of their provisions, such as human, civil and religious rights and rights of minorities. However, the War of Independence then raging as a result of an invasion by Israel's neighbours, delayed the elections, which were ultimately held almost four months later, on 25 January 1949, when most of the fighting had ceased. By the time the Council of State, which at that time functioned as the legislature, debated the Constituent Assembly Bill (13 January 1949) a significant change of mind had taken place, however. When introduced for discussion, the bill provided for the adoption of a constitution by the assembly about to be elected, and allocated no more than two years for this purpose. However, in the law as finally enacted no reference to a constitution appears at all, and the newly elected Constituent Assembly in its first piece of legislation formally transformed itself into the First Knesset, i.e. the first regularly elected legislature, thus proclaiming by the change of its name that it would not necessarily pursue its constituent (i.e. constitution-making) function.

By that time the major parts of a draft constitution had been prepared by a committee of politicians and legal experts. The Knesset debated this draft intermittently for almost a year and a half, but most of this time was devoted to a discussion of the preliminary point of principle concerning the desirability and feasibility of adopting a constitution at all.

This controversy was finally resolved by the so-called Harari Resolution, adopted by the Knesset on 13 June 1950, which was presented as a compromise supposedly providing the best of both worlds. However, the more perspicacious antagonists on both sides must even then have sized up that decision for what it was, namely a victory for the opponents of a constitution. Nevertheless, not even the most perceptive observers could have foreseen that thirty-five years later no constitution would be adopted. The Harari resolution affirmed on the one hand that a constitution would ultimately be adopted and charged the appropriate Knesset committee to prepare the draft of one. But the constitution would be pieced together from individual chapters, each one to be initially a basic law by itself, which were to be prepared and enacted *seriatim*.[5] Although the First Knesset so instructed its committee, it must have been clear even at the time that this task could not be accomplished in one legislative period, however long. It is instructive to present the arguments on both sides of this constitutional controversy, because, by and large, they have not changed very much since those early years.[6]

One should, however, distinguish between publicly voiced arguments on the one hand and undivulged motivations on the other. To be sure, there was nothing very original, for quite obvious reasons, to be found on the side of the advocates of the immediate adoption of a formal, normative,[7] constitution. Other than the legal argument, that the above-mentioned documents made this almost mandatory, and the trite one that constitutions are 'baptismal certificates for newly-independent nations',[8] five main contentions were produced in support of this demand. These five were as follows: the first, the universalist argument, simply claimed that good reasons must have persuaded almost all states, especially all democratic states, to have a constitution, and Israel which prides itself on being almost a model democracy, cannot remain without one for long. The second argument was the educative one, regarding the constitution as the best and most authoritative guide-post for the purposes of civil and political education, as well as a sort of state identity card for others to see. Then there was the obvious argument from the restrictive function of the constitution, namely that it was an instrument guaranteeing constitutional, i.e. limited, government, the preservation of the civil and political rights of individuals and groups, and the proper operation of the different branches and levels of government.

Others stressed the stabilising effect of a constitution, which is particularly necessary in a dynamic and volatile population. This leads finally to the last argument, which contained elements of originality, namely that in a newly independent state, as yet inhabited by only a fraction of the nation, and soon to be filled by people coming from all over the globe and with very diverse cultural and political backgrounds, the constitution had to perform an important integrative role, contributing crucially to the nation-building process which was then getting under way.

With a few significant exceptions, support for the constitution came from the opposition parties; by the same token, a few prominent members of the main government party, the Israel Labour Party (Mapai), vigorously defended the need for one in the Knesset debates. The leaders of the opposition, both from the left and the right wings, made use of the self-same points, partly for different reasons, of course, but, less openly, they also voiced other arguments.

Thus the prevailing underlying assumption at that time, after the first national elections in which the major party, Mapai, gained only a plurality of votes and seats but all others were left far behind, was that for a long time to come Mapai could hardly be dislodged from power and so no real change of government could be envisaged. In addition, and in spite of all evidence to the contrary, the opposition, and perhaps others, had at least some forebodings concerning the Prime Minister's genuine commitment to democratic procedures. A constitution, apparently almost any constitution, was considered capable of overcoming such supposed anti-democratic predilections. What is more, a notion was afoot that the constitution could not be anything other than an expression of middle-of-the-road, moderate and perhaps centrist tendencies, which, although seemingly uncongenial to both the main wings of the opposition, yet seemed to offer the right wing the prospect of preventing socialism, while the left could consider it as some sort of bulwark against eventual right-wing, populist inclinations. Also, left-wing and other secular groups were convinced that the constitution would bar any possibility of strengthening clerical or theocratic tendencies, and would perhaps even proscribe the then emerging status quo in religious matters.[9]

Paradoxically, however, what certainly should have been the most cogent argument of all favouring the immediate adoption of a constitution, namely that this would best indicate the revolutionary character of Israeli independence (which as some scholars would have it was the moment of the return of the Jewish people back into history)[10] was only very weakly expressed. Thus the constitution could and should have been presented as the manifestation of renewed Jewish sovereignty, which would have implied a renunciation of, or at least a full severence from, past Jewish history. Indeed it could have symbolised the total transformation of Jewish collective existence.

The non-adoption of a constitution not only implied a reluctance, actually an unreadiness, to break the pattern of previous Jewish experience as a subjugated minority, but more specifically it signified the continuation, with little substantial change, of the milieu and the regime which had prevailed in the small Jewish community in Palestine before independence. In other words, the opportunity to avail oneself of a constitution in order to institute statehood legally and symbolically was passed over. There are some who, although they do not deny that the rule of law is more or less maintained in Israel, attribute to this omission whatever manifestations of illegality have appeared in the Israeli polity.[11]

The main opponents of the constitution were the major parties which composed the governmental coalition. These can be divided into two camps according to the firmness of their opposition. There were first those who rejected the very idea of a modern secular constitution out of hand, but there were also those who went on record as objecting only to the adoption of a constitution at that time, most of whom would be reconciled to its ultimate adoption (but *sine die!*). By and large, the first of these two camps can be identified with the religious sector, especially the ultra-orthodox, who claimed that Israel had no need of a 'new' constitution since it already had an old and venerated one, the Torah, i.e. the body of traditional Jewish learning, and more specifically the halacha, i.e. the body of Jewish (religious) law. Nothing but the halacha will do as the law and the constitution of a Jewish state, and especially a man-made and Godless one was unthinkable in Judaism.

Pushed to its logical conclusion, this argument really entailed the establishment of a full-fledged theocratic polity. The more moderate orthodox politicians of the national religious (i.e. Mizrahi) persuasion, although they hesitated to adopt this extreme line, rejected a constitution because they considered the likelihood of the adoption of one which they could live with, as very low. They were ready in theory to accept a man-made constitution, i.e. one given in the name of the people and enacted by a secular law-giver, as long as the state did not come into conflict with the halacha and would fully accept the jurisdiction of all relevant religious institutions and uphold the exclusiveness of orthodoxy as the sole recognised Jewish persuasion. But such a constitution, they thought, was not likely to be forthcoming. With hindsight, it seems to me that this was a misreading of the situation on their part, because in fact these demands were all met, most of them at the time and some a little later. It would seem that over this issue, as on so many others, the moderate orthodox wing of religious Zionism deferred to the militancy of the ultra-orthodox and accepted their theological guidance.

Uri Zvi Greenberg, a non-religious member of the Knesset who was considered by many, certainly by the more nationalistically inclined circles, to be the national poet of his generation, expressed himself with his customery grandiloquence in comparing contemporary constitution-making with the Torah-giving act at Sinai. He doubted whether the mastery and originality needed for the task

were available and whether it could be accomplished without resorting to foreign models. Other spokesmen doubted whether the necessary God-inspired spirit was indeed motivating the constitution-
makers.

The secularists pursued a number of different lines of argumen-
tation, which may be grouped into the following categories: the legal-
historical, the sociological, the conflictual and the efficient or
operational.

The legal-historical anti-constitutional arguments claimed, first,
that constitutions had had their day, as part of the transformation
from autocratic and authoritarian to liberal-democratic regimes, in
which clear limitations of governmental power and the safeguarding
of human rights were of the essence. Nowadays, however, with the
widespread consensus concerning limited government, constitutional
affirmation of these principles was considered superfluous.

The Prime Minister, Ben Gurion, argued contrariwise that what
he called democratic republicanism had been deeply entrenched in
Judaism for ages, and that therefore no constitution was necessary.
And, then, strange as this may sound to British ears, the favourable
British precedent was produced as convincing proof not only that
a constitution was unnecessary but that not having one was actually
much to be preferred. This widespread admiration for English constitutionalism, at least among the Israeli political and legal élites,
was only part of a much wider positive attitude towards what were
seen as the art and craftsmanship of British domestic governance.
This is all the more remarkable coming as it did at the time of
the debate within a year or two after the final denouement between
the United Kingdom and the Palestinian Jewish community. The
counter-argument which was also produced, to the effect that inasmuch as Israelis lacked the necessary propensity for self-restraint
and the long historical tradition which created it, the British case
was totally irrelevant, did nothing to disparage this supposedly
exemplary British feature.

Others argued that from a legally material point of view Israel
already had at least a constitution-surrogate, both by its Declaration
of Independence, which although not strictly a legal document had
been accorded by the courts the status of a guiding and binding
declaration of principles of free and democratic rule, and by the
Law of Transition of 1948, also called 'the small constitution', and
other organic laws which had provided for the main offices of state,
thus making a constitution quite superfluous.

Still others stressed the dangers of a rigid constitution, and the
likely calamities ensuing from a reactionary supreme court with
powers of judicial review, particularly in a dynamic society, and

also the likelihood of parliamentary minorities obstructing the enactment of emergency measures so essential for a state under siege.
It goes without saying that the majoritarian argument that a minority
would use the entrenched constitution to obstruct the wishes of
the majority, was common to almost all opponents of a constitution.

The sociological argument of the nation-building of an immigrant
society is a mirror-image of that presented by the supporters of
a constitution. Here the claim was made that the then existing nucleus
of early pioneers had no right to pre-empt major decisions concerning
the regime for the masses of the Jewish people yet to come. The
state had been established for these and not for its present inhabitants. But this argument had very little credibility, even at the time.

The two remaining groups of arguments, however, came much
closer to the real core of the opposition to speedy constitution-
making. The first of these, which may be called the conflictual argument, runs as follows: constitution-making demands a far-reaching
consensus, at least among most of the sectors of the population,
because without it the legitimacy of the regime would be at stake.
In newly-established Israel a consensus prevailed as to the very
existence of the state, but at the same time there were deep cleavages
concerning the cultural foundations, and more particularly about
the role of religion in state and society and the religious conception
of the polity. This state of affairs did not bar, as had already been
shown, a political *modus vivendi*, based on the status quo in religious
matters, to allow for collaboration on the governmental level, but
at the same time it made an agreement on the legitimising principles
of rule and authority most unlikely.

Such a conflict over the ideological and moral fundamentals of
the constitution would not only have introduced vehemence and
passion which would have considerably deepened the already existing
political and social cleavages, but it would have severely affected,
or more likely actually put an end to, the existence of the governmental coalition. The two main coalition partners, namely the Labour
Party (Mapai) and the religious bloc, would have been the major
protagonists over the constitutional issue. The presentiments of such
a conflict were frequently depicted as the Israeli Kulturkampf, a
haunting simile at that time.[12]

Undoubtedly this was to be the most telling anti-constitutional
argument. The religious camp supported it to defend its *raison d'être*
and the Labour Party for *raison d'état*. As to this last point, strange
and contradictory as it must appear to those unfamiliar both with
Ben-Gurion's statemanship and with the details of the state-religion
interrelationships, Ben-Gurion seems to have believed that it was
precisely by way of the prevailing legal and political set-up that

he, i.e. the secular or even laicist governmental authority, would be able to control and perhaps subdue the religious establishments, whereas a new constitutional arrangement would have entrenched their privileged prerogatives. With hindsight it is hard to deny that on this point he was off the mark.

There was, however, another rationale on the opponents' side, here termed operational, which had little of a theoretical stance but was of great practical import, and yet could claim some sort of constitutional or ideological justification. What was at stake here was actually the preservation of the unobstructed freedom of action of the government, over and above the obvious constraints of the rule of law, including the tests of judicial control. A constitution was considered as imposing what were seen, from the governmental point of view, as unnecessary institutional limitations, which would severely impede the smooth operation of the government's business. Implied in this contention was what one might term a parliamentary majoritarianism,[13] in the simple sense that a government enjoying a parliamentary majority should not be subject to any institutional restrictions whatsoever. Given the then prevailing parliamentary partisan composition, this meant that Mapai, as the dominant party with no overall majority but with a plurality of less than 40 per cent of the vote, actually commanded a working majority in parliament and in the cabinet with the help of its small coalition partners.

Without this being articulated at the time, the ruling élite, and especially Ben-Gurion, perceived the growing diversification of Israeli society, its deepening cleavages and sectoral and sectarian tendencies, which would dangerously have enervated the exercise of governmental authority and affected its efficiency, if there was no vigorous counterbalance.

These social and political impediments were therefore considered serious enough, without any further encumbrances of unnecessary constitutional limitations. A constitution, or in this case a non-constitution, was looked upon, at least by the opponents, as a corrective to the political power structure or as a curb on its perceived, baneful results, but not as an instrument capable of actually changing that structure. This train of thought was at the time quite widespread even though politically there was an obvious unwillingness to express it openly in so many words. What was, on the other hand, frequently brought forth as a telling argument was that Israel's precarious security situation, being at war with all its neighbours, made it imperative that the government should have a totally free hand to cope with it and that a too libertarian constitution would not only be detrimental but could even endanger its very existence.

The conclusion regarding the 1950 constitutional debate and the 1950 Knesset decision is, then, that in the final analysis pragmatic and opportunistic considerations overruled the principles of what Sartori has called *garantiste* (or strict, or substantive) constitutionalism.[14]

II

Since the 1950 resolution there have been a number of developments relevant to our subject. For our purposes these may be subsumed under two headings, as follows: (i) the progress in constitution-making in accordance with the 1950 resolution; (ii) the operation of constitutional government without a formal constitution.

The years since independence may be viewed as the post-revolutionary period in Israel's history. Some observers, using the Weberian vocabulary, see them as the years of 'the routinisation and demystification of the original revolutionary vision'.[15] What could have become, constitutionally speaking, the capstone of the Zionist/Israeli revolution, namely the adoption of a constitution, was never achieved, and thus the opportunity was forgone to create a truly 'revolutionary' political order. Instead, the existing power relationships, the political culture and the principles of the institutional structure of the pre-independence Jewish community in Palestine were preserved, after some slight adjustments, as the framework for the newly-established state, i.e. they were routinised.[16] This was achieved by formal status-quo accords in matters of religion, and by indeterminate and tacit status-quo understanding in other political matters, including constitutional and legal concerns. Within the framework of our interest here what has been happening is the impact of the 'living' constitution on the constitution-making process.

Since the 1950 resolution eight basic laws have been passed by the Knesset, namely those entitled: the Knesset (1958), Israel Lands (1960), State President (1964), the Government (1968), the State Economy (1975), the Army (1976), Jerusalem, Capital of Israel (1980), and the Judiciary (1984). As their titles indicate all these basic laws are organic in character, and it is to be expected that ultimately they will all be included in the constitution. Although progress is very slow indeed, the constitution-making process is continuing. None of these basic laws amounted at the time of their respective enactments to a real constitutional *volte-face*, although speculatively one can say that had a constitution been adopted soon after independence some of the paragraphs in these basic laws, and at least one basic law in its entirety, would not have been part of it at all, or only in a substantially different form. The modifications implied by this may partly be attributed to a gradual legal learning process leading towards improvements in the legal draftsmanship, and partly to changing specific needs.

The main institutional basic laws, i.e. those dealing with the Knesset, the Cabinet and the State President, were codifications and elaborations of previous legislation, and hardly any innovation which they contained can be looked upon as of constitutional significance. The same is true of the other basic laws, each of which affirmed the respective legislative and *de facto* situation. The exceptions to this, namely, the entrenched clauses contained in some of the basic laws, are discussed below, but let it be said here that these represented a real change in the legal conception of the lawmakers. Of the other basic laws, that dealing with the army actually did no more than spell out civilian control and responsibility of the army and the procedure of the appointment of the Chief of Staff. In this case legislation was the result of the report of a commission which had inquired into the unpreparedness and non-alertness of the army on the eve of the Yom Kippur War, and had found ill-defined allocations of responsibility between the highest political-civilian and military levels. On the other hand, the basic law on the judiciary refrained even more stringently than had been originally intended from any constitutionally significant change. And the Jerusalem basic law had no more than a declaratory effect, without any normative consequences.

As already mentioned, the one real innovation was in the entrenchment clauses of some of the basic laws. Most of them provide against the abrogation of these laws or some of their paragraphs by way of emergency laws, thus safeguarding the continued existence of the major democratic bodies even in times of emergency. This may of course be of immense importance some time in the future, but of much greater interest is the one substantive paragraph entrenched by the need for an absolute majority. This refers to paragraph 4 of the Knesset basic law, specifying the principles of the electoral system; more specifically this paragraph was entrenched in order to preserve the principle of the nationwide, one-constituency proportional representation system. This entrenchment has been of immense constitutional and practical importance for two reasons. First, it has up to now achieved its original purpose of preventing any change from the extreme PR system used in Israeli elections, in spite of intermittent efforts, some of them quite sustained, to have it altered. It is very likely that the structure of the party map and their interests as conceived by most parties would in any event have prevented any change in the system, but the availability of this legal provision has put everybody on notice that only in very special circumstances could such a change be feasible. But in 1984, when as a result of the elections of that year and the creation of the National Unity Government (about which more below) there seemed to be some opportunity for reform the enthusiasts for electoral reform were quickly disabused of their hopes. What had seemed a feasible compromise, acceptable to both major parties, between the present extreme nationwide PR version and a constituency system with reduced proportionality – namely a system of multi-member (3–5) constituencies with nationwide additional seats to ensure maximum PR – proved in the end unattainable, because each of the two major parties feared for the representation of its satellite parties. Even the much less extreme corrective of the system, by way of an increase of the minimal threshold from the current 1 per cent to, say, 2 or $2\frac{1}{2}$ per cent, was turned down for the same reasons. So far, in any event, a change of the electoral system, which in the eyes of many observers in Israel and elsewhere is the single most crucial constitutional change essential in itself and as a catalyst for other systemic changes, seems quite improbable. The one change of consequence relating to proportionality, namely the switch from the highest remainder formula for allotting seats to the highest average formula (the so-called Bader-Ofer formula) in 1971, which resulted, as anticipated, in a slight strengthening of the parliamentary representation of the two major parties, cannot really be considered as being of any particular constitutional significance.

The single most important word in all the basic laws from the point of view of constitutional change seems, contrary to original expection, to be the word 'equal' in the same entrenched paragraph 4, dealing with the principles of the election law. Ten years after the passage of this law the constitutionality of another ordinary law providing for state financing of parliamentary and local elections was challenged in the High Court of Justice, with the claim that this law discriminated against, i.e. treated unequally, new parties which were not represented in the outgoing Knesset and were not therefore to receive any financial help from the Treasury. The court, in accepting this challenge, created very stringent norms of equality, ruling that the equality guaranteed by the basic law had to be interpreted as applying not only to the equal weight of each vote cast[17] but also to the equal chance of getting elected, which because of the Israeli list system referred to the equality of all candidates' lists participating in the election. The crucial constitutional element in this judgment was that the court assumed here the power of judicial review, but, unlike the US Supreme Court in *Marbury v. Madison*, without actually ruling on its competence, which however remained unchallenged and has been accepted as established by this precedent ever since.[18] Neither the Knesset nor the government demurred. Undoubtedly this case has been a turning-point in Israel's constitutional history. From the relevant draft basic laws which have been tabled subsequent to this ruling, it is pretty clear that there is far-reaching agreement to provide judicial review of a restricted nature in any future constitution, i.e. to empower the Supreme Court, in whatever capacity, to disallow ordinary legislation on procedural grounds, that is, if not passed with the requisite majority.[19]

Over the years a considerable number of ordinary laws have been enacted, which in content should be considered as basic laws without, however, carrying that title. Indeed, back in 1964 the then chairman (i.e. speaker) of the Knesset spoke of 22 such ordinary laws 'of a constitutional nature', one of the very early ones being the Law of Return (1950). This law stipulates that every Jew has the right to immigrate (*la'alot* in Hebrew, literally: to ascend) into Israel, and is thus commonly considered to be the enactment of the fundamental rationale of the Jewish state. This law has for years been the focus of two of the most fundamental constitutional conflicts concerning the very nature of the Israeli polity. On the one hand it has been criticised, mainly from outside the country, that, inasmuch as it grants this right to immigrate automatically to every Jew, but not to anyone else, it is discriminatory against non-Jews, i.e. against Arabs. However, this privilege does not affect the population residing in the state, where equal civil rights prevail for all national and religious sectors, and it thus does not constitute a legal discrimination. Yet it illustrates the difficulties inherent in the collision between two organisational principles of statehood, the one being that of equal citizenship irrespective of communal affiliation, and the other that of the primacy of the national element. This inevitably affects the constitutional safeguards guaranteeing the co-existence of a majority and a minority sector, differing nationally, culturally, in religion and political aspirations, within the framework of a democratic polity based on common citizenship.

The other constitutional issue raised by the Law of Return is internal to the Jewish community. The law is being challenged by the ultra-orthodox groups on the ground that as enacted and interpreted by the courts the right to immigrate into Israel is accorded to anyone claiming to be Jewish, whereas they demand that it be restricted only to those who are recognised as Jews by the orthodox establishment according to its interpretation of the halacha (the Jewish law). As it happens the domestic legal situation, primarily in matrimonial matters but in others as well, already follows this interpretation, and the status quo in religious affairs does not allow any change in this whatsoever. The endeavour by the orthodox sector to include even immigration within this ruling as to 'Who is a Jew?' is presented by it as an attempt at legal streamlining, but really strikes at the root of the constitutional conception of the source of legislative authority and thus of sovereignty.

It is at present the accepted opinion that two more basic laws are necessary and sufficient for the completion of the component parts of the constitution, in addition to the inclusion in the constitution of some of the ordinary laws, such as the Law of Return just mentioned and the State Comptroller's law, and perhaps some others.

One of these yet to be enacted basic laws is that dealing with the legislative process (the Basic Law: the Knesset deals only with institutional matters). This will have to determine the procedures for amending basic laws and ultimately the constitution, thereby providing for whatever legal supremacy and rigidity it will be accorded.

The other yet to be enacted basic law is the one dealing with human and civil rights. Needless to say, that is the most controversial of all the parts of the future constitution, and it is the one which at this stage does not seem likely to pass soon into law. Considerable preparatory work has been done on such a law since the mid-1950s, both by the Ministry of Justice, the appropriate committees and sub-committees of the Knesset and by a number of private members as initiators and draftsmen.

Some of these drafts have passed the early reading stages, but so far have not got anywhere. Even the exclusion of all existing legislation from the application of the repugnance clause, so that only new legislation incompatible with the provisions of the basic law would not stand – something which would actually entrench constitutionally all the existing religious legislation, i.e. the status quo – has not sufficed to convince the orthodox sector to recant its staunch opposition. The orthodox are not in fact satisfied with the status quo (compare the opposition to the existing Law of Return) and are bent on abrogating all legislation unacceptable to them. Moreover, they are convinced that, in spite of their parliamentary weakness, they will ultimately succeed in securing majority support.

But there are other kinds of hesitation with regard to a fully-fledged civil rights law, which account for the restriction of the repugnance clause to new legislation only. This, again, is because of Israel's precarious security situation, and therefore this basic law had to be drafted to allay the apprehension that its strict enforcement would render existing legal provisions, such as defence and emergency regulations, illegal. And, incidentally, this security argument has been urned on its head by those who claim that the present times are inopportune for a truly liberal constitution, precisely because the security needs of the country would inevitably dampen sensitivity on individual rights.

Finally, a few words should be said here about at least two major constitutional changes which do not have much support. The first refers to the switch from Israel's parliamentary system to a presidential one, whether American or French style. The background is the supposed need for strong leadership and stable government, dissatisfaction with the multi-party system and the small likelihood, as we have seen, of a change in the electoral system. Nevertheless, other than a very few intellectuals and even fewer politicians, there seems very little enthusiasm for such a change of regime.

The other change, for which no demand at all has been voiced, is the introduction of some provision for direct democracy. In the early years of independence it was a generally accepted part of the political wisdom that plebiscites and referendums were dangerous, anti-democratic tools of popular manipulation by populist leaders, to be avoided at all costs. Early on there was also the notion that, in a small society made up of intimate communities, political leaders and their local affiliates really knew what people thought and wanted. Strange as this may sound, these notions still seem to prevail.

III

Finally we have to discuss how Israel fares without a formal constitution. As will be seen, it is extremely difficult to be certain whether a constitution would alter much; and it is really impossible to say whether it would be an improvement. The view expressed above, that a constitution would have been advantageous as a stabilising, legitimising and educational factor, is really no more, at best, than an educated guess.

As we have seen, government and governmental institutions have been functioning reasonably well, even without a constitution, nor can any malfunctioning reasonably be attributed to the absence of one. Thus, for example, parliamentary responsibility of ministers and of the government including the application of political sanctions, and collective responsibility were never strongly developed and have actually deteriorated over the years, but not for the lack of a specific paragraph in the law. Indeed, these principles of parliamentary government have been adapted to the specific reality of coalition government, without sacrificing the individual responsibility of ministers. The quite tenuous equilibrium arrived at in governmental practice on these matters may not be to the liking of some observers, or even comprehensible to purists of the Westminster style (whoever these may be), but the point made here is simply that a constitution might actually have been a hindrance, at times, to the smooth running of the system.

On the other hand, it cannot be denied that the absence of a serious legal, i.e. constitutional, barrier has created abuses. Thus, for example, the original law provided for the cabinet to consist of a Prime Minister and any number of ministers. Later, and for internal party reasons, the need was felt to appoint one Deputy Prime Minister, and so the law was amended to allow for this contingency. That, however, was not the end of the story; later still, coalition-making was deemed to make it necessary to appoint two Deputy Prime Ministers, and so the law was amended once more. It might or might not have been more difficult, and perhaps also more awkward, to go through the motions of a constitutional amendment; but it is likely that, given the prevailing political culture, this proliferation of deputies might just have been avoided. Actually, this story is all the more striking in view of the creation, in addition, of a vice-premiership, and that without any legal provision at all for this innovation. This last new appointment was part of the agreement which brought forth the National Unity Government of 1984, a real innovation in parliamentary government. Its main provision – the rotation of the premiership between the two heads of the two main coalescing partners in the middle of the 4-year legislative term – was not dependent on any special legal procedure but utilised the existing procedure of resignation of the outgoing and appointment of the incoming Prime Minister. This points to the likelihood that with a constitution, probably no different on this score from the present basic law, not much, if anything, would have been handled differently. And the fact that with such a wide coalition the opposition has been severely cut down in size, which might be considered inimical to the proper functioning of a parliamentary government, is constitutionally irrelevant. Similarly, it is an open question whether the innovation of a 'Cabinet' of ten members (called by this word in Hebrew for the first time) as a sort of inner cabinet (or overlords) of an unwieldly government of 25 members would have been established differently, if at all, with a constitution.

The main burden of the question as to the working of a democracy without a constitution should, however, be directed not towards the functioning of government but to the preservation and enhancement of human rights. A combination of four rather disparate factors is at work here. The first comprises generalised notions of human dignity and decency, civic morality and interpersonal civility which are parts of Jewish cultural traditions deriving from a miscellany of sources; needless to say, there are also other traits in Judaism, some contradictory to these.

The second factor is the not inconsiderable original Israeli legislation in the fields of human, communal, civil, social and political rights, which has substantially improved the position in this area since Israel's independence.[20]

Next, Israel inherited on independence, by way of the British mandatory regime over Palestine, major elements of English law, including the common law and the doctrine of equity, court procedure and practice and other legislation. Since independence, original Israeli legislation has abrogated a few of these legal precedents and provisions, but in 1980, by the Foundation of Law Act, the recourse to these elements of English law has been abrogated for the future, although the continued viability of those principles of English rules that had been incorporated into Israeli law prior to the adoption of this law was specifically asserted.[21]

Last, but possibly foremost in our concern, comes the role of the courts, and more specifically, the Supreme Court sitting as High Court of Justice, as the supreme guardian of the constitution, such as it is. In the field of individual and collective rights, as well as in other areas, the court has been much more than a guardian, preserver and expounder; it has been an initiator and creator and has thus been actively engaged, at some times more than at others, in law-making and constitution-making. The court has been courageous in overruling and criticising the government, and as we have seen, the Knesset as well, and in seizing the power of judicial review even without a real legal basis for this acquisition.

Parallel to its central concern with the relations between the authorities and the citizen, the work of the court has been of special significance in the area of minorities' rights and relations between the majority and minorities. It has been eager, within the quite narrow confines of the law and the wide powers which the legislature has as a whole given to the executive, to come to the help of the underprivileged, the abused and those discriminated against. At the same time, it has almost always had a solid understanding of the needs and demands of good government. It is usually seen as sympathetic to the problems of the Arab minority, and after 1967 it extended its jurisdiction to the occupied territories, which have ever since remained some sort of an extra-sovereign territory due to the legal void which emerged as a result of the occupation. The court deemed this extension necessary for the administration of justice. The court likewise has all along played a crucial role in the conflict over religion, and has usually protected the civil, i.e. non-religious, law and civil institutions, the freedom both of the religious and irreligious as well as a full implementation of religious rights within the framework of the law. All in all, it can safely be asserted that the single most important factor guaranteeing democracy without a constitution is the Supreme Court.

Does Israel need a constitution today? From the discussion above it should be evident that no firm answer is possible to this question, one way or the other. The present legal set-up permits the introduction of piecemeal legislation rather more easily than a codified constitution would. Thus, although most unlikely in existing circumstances, a far-reaching revision of the cabinet system, providing, for example, for a legally established prime-ministerial government, could be introduced without needing to overcome the hurdles of special majorities, and so on. But the fact that such changes have rarely taken place seems to prove that given a certain balance between countervailing political forces and a corresponding political culture, the so-called dangers of unrestricted majoritarianism unfettered by a constitution are rather limited. In other words, the fact that no formal constitution exists allowed the Israeli political system more freely to develop its own very special blend of elements of the Westminster model with those of a quasi-, or perhaps semi-consociational, system,[22] and to continue to experiment with this combination during the years of the Government of National Unity. The Westminster model has provided some of the formal features of Israel's political system, and to that extent it must be considered to be beneficial to the development of its parliamentary democracy.[23] The consociational portions reflect Israel's domestic power structure and its ideological and cultural outlook, as well as its (Jewish) solidarity in face of external threats. All told, the existing system has served Israel well, in spite of the general tendency to bewail the deterioriation of political culture and morality, and of governmental performance.

These considerations by themselves are, however, not decisive as far as the constitution is concerned. Two further factors should be given their proper weight in this respect. The first is a growing threat, in recent years, to the principles of the rule of law, as generally understood in the West, which seems to be emerging in spite of the vigorous surveillance of the courts and most of the legal profession. There are, of course, many reasons for this. But on balance it would seem that a more rigid constitutional framework could serve as one more safeguard of the rule of law.

But there is a second point at issue, of more serious implication for Israel's body politic, at least in the long run. This concerns the apparent approaching breakdown of the status quo over religious matters; not so much over single religious-legal issues, however important, but over the spirit of acceptance of the national covenant on religion. What is at stake here is the major segment of the national consensus, and thus of the consociational set-up. A new consociational pact will have to be reached ultimately, and it is of secondary importance what exact legal form(s) this will take. But, again, on balance it might be advantageous to write this pact into a constitution. Whether this will be politically feasible is, however, another matter. Thus we have come back full circle to the realisation that the crucial question is not whether Israel should get itself a constitution but whether it can survive as a liberal and consensual democracy.

Notes and references
1. Carl J. Friedrich calls this the 'ideology of constitutionalism', irrespective of whether there is a constitution or not. See his *Limited Government, A Comparison* (Engelwood Cliffs, N.J.: Prentice-Hall, 1974), p. 37.
2. Leslie Wolf-Phillips, *Comparative Constitutions* (London: Macmillan, 1972), pp. 32–33. This study contains an exhaustive survey of classifications of constitutions.
3. Samuel Sager, *The Parliamentary System of Israel* (Syracuse: Syracuse University Press, 1985), pp. 36–39.
4. The relevant clause of the declaration is phrased rather ambiguously, so that some read it as stipulating that the constitution should have been adopted no later than this date. See e.g. Meir Shamgar, 'On the Written Constitution', *Israel Law Review*, Vol. 9, No. 4, 1974, p. 470. It is, however, very unlikely that the drafters of the declaration, even taking into account the enthusiasm of that moment, could have expected, with a war on their hands, to elect a constituent assembly to debate and adopt such a constitution all within four and a half months. Clearly this moot legal point is today of no more than passing historical interest.
5. This terminology was undoubtedly influenced by the then recently enacted West German (Bonn) Constitution. But whereas there the one basic law proved a substitute for an ultimate constitution, to be adopted at some uncertain time in the (distant) future, in Israel each one of an unspecified number of basic laws would become a chapter of the final constitution.
6. For brief resumés of the major speakers in the parliamentary debates see Emanuel Rackman, *Israel's Emerging Constitution* (New York: Columbia University Press, 1955), *passim*.
7. In the sense first suggested by Karl Loewenstein in *Political Power and the Governmental Process* (Chicago: University of Chicago Press, 1957), pp. 147 ff.
8. William G. Andrews (ed.), *Constitutions and Constitutionalism* (New York: Van Nostrand, 1961), p. 24.
9. The major protagonist for a constitution on the left was the Mapam party, the left-wing socialists. Daniel Elazar's assertion that they were opposed because they realised that the constitution would not embrace their Marxist vision, is contrary to the facts. See D.J. Elazar, 'Constitution-making: The Pre-eminently Political Act' in K.G. Banting and Richard Simeon (eds), *Redesigning the State: The Politics of Constitutional Change in Industrial Nations* (Toronto: University of Toronto Press, 1985), p. 238. Nor can I accept his contention there that Israel's constitution may be viewed as a modern adaptation of an ancient traditional constitution. This may be wishful thinking on his part. In my view the emerging constitution, so far in any event, contains anti-traditional and non-religious elements, and as such it may be said even to contradict, at least in part, the existing legal system.
10. S.N. Eisenstadt, *The Transformation of Israeli Society* (London: Weidenfeld

and Nicolson, 1985), p. 560. See also B. Halpern, *The Idea of the Jewish State*
2nd edn (Cambridge, Mass.: Harvard University Press, 1969).

11. Ehud Shprinzak, *Every Man Whosoever is Right in His Own Eyes* (Sifriat Poalim,
1986), chapter 5 (Hebrew).

12. In the constitutional debate this term was usually used in the original German,
and must have stirred up vivid emotions. Strictly this historical analogy is not
quite accurate for two reasons. First, the original Kulturkampf was a dispute
between state authorities and a minority church, whereas in Israel the controversy
was basically one between the Jewish secular majority and the observing,
orthodox minority. Second, and perhaps more important, in the Prussian case
what was primarily at issue were the role, legal status and authority of the
(minority) Roman Catholic church, while in Israel all these matters were indeed
affected with regard to the Jewish orthodox religious institutions but in addition,
the wider problem of state-church separation was involved, as well as the entire
range of human (i.e. individual) rights and civil liberties in their confrontation
with the halacha (the religious legal codex).

13. As explained later, this (normative) majoritarianism fully accords with what
has been termed the 'anti-majoritarian philosophy' of the quasi-consociational
coalition system. See Daniel Shimshoni, *Israeli Democracy* (Free Press, 1982),
p. 57.

14. Giovanni Sartori, 'Constitutionalism: A Preliminary Discussion', *American Political Science Review*, LVI, 1962, pp. 853–64.

15. Eisenstadt, *op. cit.* p. 564.

16. D. Horowitz and M. Lissak, *Origins of the Israeli Polity* (Chicago: Chicago
University Press, 1978). Also Yonathan Shapiro, *Democracy in Israel* (Massada,
1977) (Hebrew).

17. One may speculate that the court would almost certainly strike down any law
creating parliamentary constituencies, unless of course enacted with the necessary
special majority, because these would inevitably be of unequal size, and would
thus create inequality in the value of the ballots.

18. Sager, *op. cit.* pp. 43–44.

19. Bergmann vs. Minister of Finance, HCJ 98/69 231 P.D. 963 (1969).

20. For full surveys of this issue, into which we cannot delve here, see Gideon
Hausner, 'Individuals' Rights in the Courts of Israel', *International Lawyers
Convention in Israel*, Jerusalem, 1959, pp. 201–8, and other articles in this volume;
Amos Shapira, 'The Status of Fundamental Human Rights in the Absence
of a Written Constitution', *Israel Law Review*, 9, 1974, pp. 497–511.

21. 'Foundation of Law', *Laws of the State of Israel*, 34 (5740–1979/1980), p. 181.

22. Arend Lijphart, *Democracies, Patterns of Majoritarian and Consensus Government
in Twenty-One Countries* (New Haven: Yale University Press, 1984).

23. Leslie Wolf-Phillips, 'The "Westminster Model" in Israel?', *Parliamentary
Affairs*, 26, 1973, pp. 415–39.

Note: In August 1987, a team of law professors at Tel-Aviv University produced
a draft constitution for public discussion. Discussion there might be – especially
of the controversial bill of rights chapter which would considerably liberalise the
religious status quo, and the proposal for a directly elected prime minister – but
the likelihood of adoption of all or parts of it seems remote.

16 Sweden: The new constitution (1974) and the tradition of consensual politics
Olof Ruin

At the beginning of the 1970s, a new constitution was adopted in
Sweden: the 1974 Instrument of Government. It replaced the 1809
Instrument of Government which had for a long time been the
second oldest written constitution in force in the world. This fundamental law had contained many features inherited from a domestic
constitutional development of almost 400 years.[1]

The decision to replace a written constitution more than 150 years
old was not taken precipitately. On the contrary, it had been preceded
by almost two decades of deliberation. The process was begun in
1954 when the government decided to appoint a parliamentary commission with the task of conducting a comprehensive review of the
functioning of democratic institutions in Sweden; at that time there
was a discussion under way in the country concerning greater use
of the referendum and a different electoral system. During the course
of its work, the commission came to the conclusion that in attempting
to adapt the constitution to contemporary demands, it was no longer
possible to patch and mend the old 1809 Instrument of Government.
Thus, a proposal for a completely new constitution was presented
in 1963. The proposal aroused criticism on a number of points;
negotiations were immediately begun between representatives of the
different political parties, and in the spring of 1966, a new parliamentary commission was appointed. The tempo of the reform work
was intensified. In the spring of 1967, the commission presented
a proposal for a partial constitutional reform which affected the
most central aspects of the political system. The proposal was
approved by the Riksdag in 1968 and 1969. In March 1972, the
commission presented its proposal for a complete reform of the constitution, of which the more limited reforms which had already been
decided upon comprised a part. In 1973 and 1974, after further
revision in the Government Office, the Riksdag decided to adopt
this proposal for a completely new constitution, the 1974 Instrument
of Government.[2]

When the commission's work on the constitution was initiated at the beginning of the 1950s, there were not many in Sweden who thought that it would result as it did: in a completely new fundamental law. The new constitution differed from the one it replaced both in structure and in the wording of specific paragraphs. However, five changes are of particular significance; almost all of them were decided upon in connection with the partial reform at the end of the 1960s. It was also these which were the main focus of attention during the extended period when the work of the commission was carried out.

(i)   A unicameral Riksdag has replaced the previous bicameral Riksdag. The two chambers – the First Chamber and the Second Chamber – had in principle had the same sphere of responsibility and equal importance. The First Chamber was elected indirectly, by so-called county councils and a number of similar bodies. The Lower Chamber was directly elected. The present unicameral Riksdag is composed of 349 seats and is directly elected.

(ii)   Concurrent elections to the three levels into which the Swedish political system is divided – the municipal, the county, and the national levels – have replaced the elections to the municipal and county councils and the elections to the Lower Chamber which were previously held at different times. The present concurrence of elections has been called 'the municipal link'.

(iii)   The mandate periods have been shortened. For the municipal councils, county councils, and Lower Chamber they were previously four years. Members of the First Chamber served terms of office of eight years. Now everyone on the different levels serves terms of office of only three years. When the elections to the Second Chamber and the local assemblies took place at different times, there was a pattern of elections being held every other year on the third Sunday in September. Now elections are held rather more seldom – once every three years – but are held on all three levels at the same time. (It is possible to dissolve the Riksdag and call for a new election, but the next ordinary election must, notwithstanding this, take place at the prescribed time in September three years after the previous ordinary one.)

(iv)   The proportional nature of the electoral system has been further accentuated. The previous system was also characterised by proportionality. However, it led – primarily due to the manner in which the First Chamber was elected – to a certain overrepresentation for the largest party. Furthermore, small parties were underrepresented. Now, by means of a

national pool of seats, all parties are guaranteed complete proportionality in the distribution of mandates, but under one
very important condition: they must receive at least 4 per cent
of the votes cast. Parties which fall below this magic number
receive no representation at all in the Riksdag.[3]

(v)   The monarch as Head of State has been disengaged from the
formation of the government, i.e. the Cabinet in a parliamentary
system, and the principle of parliamentarianism has been introduced into the fundamental law. It is now incumbent upon
the Speaker of the Riksdag to nominate a new Prime Minister,
after conferring with the representatives of the parties represented in the Riksdag and with the Vice-Speakers. The Riksdag
has explicitly to approve the nomination; the person nominated
becomes Prime Minister if a majority of the members of the
Riksdag do not vote against the nomination. (The members
of the Riksdag are of course also entitled to abstain from voting.)
The Prime Minister then appoints the other members of the
Cabinet.[4]

A characteristic feature of the new Swedish Constitution, in comparison with the old, is that on point after point it encourages versa-
tility and drama. There is only one chamber; the elections to this
one chamber are held at a single time; the election periods are
relatively short; parties which are small lose all representation in
the Riksdag if they do not obtain a certain minimum percentage
of the vote, while other parties are guaranteed strict proportionality;
the Riksdag has to pass a vote of confidence before a new government
assumes office. It can be argued that the new Swedish Constitution
has contributed to making a conspicuously stable political system
more unstable.

The constitutional view of the Social Democratic Party
The much-discussed stability which has long characterised Swedish
politics flowed from the fact that one of the five political parties
in the country – the Social Democratic Party – dominated Swedish
political life. The party was in government from the autumn of
1932 to the autumn of 1976, with the sole exception being 100 days
during the summer of 1936. For the most part, the party governed
alone. During two periods it governed together with the Agrarian
Party, later named the Centre Party; during the Second World War
it governed together with the Conservative Party, the Liberal Party,
and the Agrarian Party in a so-called national coalition Government.
The fifth and smalllest party – the Communist Party – was always

in opposition. The Social Democratic Party generally received between 45 and 50 per cent of the vote in general elections; on a few occasions it either fell below 45 per cent or exceeded 50 per cent.

Quite naturally, the Social Democrats, who dominated Swedish politics within the framework of the constitution which was then in force, did not feel any need to change it. The party was fully occupied with extending and further developing the Swedish welfare state, and this reform work was not rendered more difficult by the existing constitutional framework. On the contrary, it gave the Social Democratic Party a favourable position in some respects.

In this situation it was not unusual for active Social Democrats to consider an interest in constitutional matters both superfluous and unnecessary. Nevertheless, the very process that gradually led to the formation of a completely new constitution was originally set in motion by a group of Social Democratic members of the Riksdag who in the early 1950s petitioned for a comprehensive review of the functioning of democratic institutions which the government decided to undertake. Furthermore, the leader of the party from the autumn of 1946 to the Autumn of 1969, Tage Erlander, harboured a genuine interest in constitutional matters.

This interest had been aroused during his years as a student in Lund in the 1920s; he had studied political science and had been seized by a sense of frustration under the influence of the political instability, characterised by a series of successive minority governments, which prevailed in Sweden at that time. This interest persisted even during the following decades at a time when Erlander himself wound up in the absolute centre of Swedish politics and when what had been instability changed into considerable stability. His thinking on constitutional matters both reflected the atmosphere within the party he led and also committed the party. It was focused on two areas: (i) the possibility of securing 'strong governments', i.e. strong parliamentary Cabinets, and (ii) the possibility of establishing a connection between national and local politics.[5]

Tage Erlander's involvement in the problem of strong governments was greatest during the 1940s and 1950s. His point of departure was that the citizens were dependent on an effectively functioning state apparatus for their welfare and security. The Cabinet was the only organ which could get the state apparatus, always difficult to manage, to function effectively. It had the power to intervene in most areas; it had the entire system of parliamentary commissions at its disposal; it had, as representative of the state, to hold discussions and negotiate with interest organisations. The Riksdag, on the other hand, was too large to provide effective leadership of the state apparatus. There was also too great a diversity of opinions within it.

However, the opportunities for a government to exercise its capacity for leadership for the good of the majority – as Erlander expressed it time and again – could only be realised under two conditions. First that the government be supported by a clear majority in the Riksdag. Such a government could adopt a long-term perspective in its work in a completely different way from a minority government; it did not run the risk of being forced to resign in the middle of its term; it could force unpopular measures through the Riksdag and stand firm against well-organised special interests.

The second condition was that the government be united by common values and preferably be formed on the basis of a single party. In any case, it had to be based on a clearly expressed programme. A government composed of many different parties, with different values on essential matters, and which was not united by a clearly formulated programme ran the risk of becoming ineffectual due to an excessive diversity of opinions.

Tage Erlander's central idea that governments should be based on a majority of the Riksdag and be united by common values would naturally be easier to put into practice if the traditional five-party system in Sweden were replaced by a two-party system of the classic English model. Tage Erlander was well aware of this relationship. Thus, he frequently referred to the fact that the existence of a large number of parties could make the formation of effective governments more difficult. Small parties, strategically placed, could gain an unreasonable degree of influence over government policy; they could block the political system, with dangerous consequences for the continued existence of the democratic system, as witnessed in Weimar Germany and during the Fourth Republic in France.

But, although Tage Erlander was aware that a two-party system could facilitate the formation of strongly cohesive majority governments, he was not prepared to work actively for the creation of a party system of that type in Sweden. In particular, he opposed majority elections in single-member constituencies, which some of his fellow party members supported, because under such a system the three non-socialist parties might feel forced to form a common non-socialist party. Social Democratic advocates of single-member constituencies thought that a two-party system would not only facilitate the formation of a government, but would generally lead to clearer political alternatives in Swedish society.

For Tage Erlander, a two-party system, even if it might facilitate the formation of alternative majority governments, was seen as something to be avoided in Sweden since it could limit the parties' room for manoeuvre. It would no longer be possible for the Social Democratic Party to attempt to co-operate with one or more of the non-socialist parties; it would thus be more difficult to create working parliamentary majorities. Conflict in society would increase. A unified non-socialist alternative to the Social Democratic Party could also be expected to attract new voters to the non-socialist side. A continued division of the non-socialist side into three parties was, in Tage Erlander's view, of value both for the Social Democrats as a party and for Sweden as a whole.

It should be added that there were reasons for Tage Erlander's opposition to majority elections in single-member constituencies other than their potential consequences for the party structure. One reason was that, given the electoral geography of Sweden at that time, such a system would have led to entire regions being represented in the Riksdag almost exclusively either by the Social Democratic Party or by the non-socialist parties. Another reason was that a small party like the Communist Party would lose its representation in the Riksdag completely. In such a situation, its supporters might be tempted to resort to the Social Democratic Party, with increased tensions within the labour movement as a result. Tage Erlander was constantly concerned about keeping his own party united and avoiding tensions and conflicts of the kind that have bedevilled the Labour Party in Britain. The Communist Party and Communist supporters were to be kept away from Swedish Social Democracy.

Tage Erlander's practical conclusion when he discussed his first main constitutional thesis – the need for 'strong governments' – was quite simple. His own party had the greatest opportunity, within the framework of the proportional election system which existed, for generating the type of government which was presented as the ideal: a government united by common values and based on a majority in the Riksdag. Under the existing electoral system, the non-socialist parties were not tempted to unite; very small parties remained underrepresented and a barrier was thereby established against an extensive fragmentation of the party system in the Riksdag. Most importantly, the Social Democratic Party, as the largest party, was slightly overrepresented as a result of the indirect method by which the First Chamber was elected. This overrepresentation was seen as defensible by Erlander since that party, because of its size, had a special responsibility in connection with the formation of a government. Constitutional ideology and the interests of the party coincided in Erlander's defence of the status quo.

It should be added that Tage Erlander, as well as the Social Democratic Party, also objected to the idea of establishing a governmental system on the Swiss model, i.e. a system of all-party governments. This idea was put forward in public discussions in the post-war period, mainly by Herbert Tingsten, a former professor of political science and editor-in-chief of *Dagens Nyheter*, the country's largest morning newspaper. Such a reform was looked upon as being in line with tendencies already inherent in Swedish political life: a consensual style and a high degree of proportional party representation at all stages of the policy-making process, with the exception of the Cabinet level. In arguing against these ideas, Tage Erlander again referred to his concern for 'strong governments'. A Cabinet composed of representatives of all the parties in the Riksdag was, in his view, bound to be weak, unable to govern effectively because of internal disagreements.[6]

Tage Erlander's concern for his second main constitutional thesis – preserving the connections between national and local politics – was developed primarily during the 1960s, the issue of 'strong governments' receiving somewhat less prominence at this time. This interest in preserving ties between national and local politics was based on an understanding of the functions of the state and of local government as being closely intertwined. The role of local authorities in Swedish politics had increased during the 1960s. They had for a long time been empowered with the right of taxation. More recently they had been given successively increased tasks in the administration of the Swedish welfare society and had also been drastically reduced in number in order thereby to make them more viable and efficient in the execution of their duties.

In arguing during the 1960s for the preservation of the ties between national and local politics, Erlander coined the concept – considered by many to be vague and difficult to interpret – of 'the municipal link'. The connection had to be maintained and, according to Erlander's interpretation, this meant that elections to the Riksdag had to be linked in some manner to elections to the local authorities. National issues always influence local election results just as local issues influence national election results; an election wind that is blowing should be able to make itself felt in the composition both of the local assemblies and of the Riksdag at the same time; local elections independent of elections to the Riksdag would lead to low voter participation. Erlander was afraid that this might damage the Social Democratic Party.

The practical conclusion which he drew from his argument on connections between national and local politics was, strictly speaking, the same as that from his argument on the necessity of 'strong governments': the current constitution met the demands made on it. A bicameral Riksdag, in which the members of one chamber are elected by local assemblies, guarantees that the local elections are connected to national politics at the same time as they have their distinct local orientation. Even in this respect the status quo appeared to correspond both to constitutional ideology and to the interests of the party. None the less, a comprehensive constitutional reform was implemented which the Social Democratic Party, still at this time the party in government, and Tage Erlander, supported and to a large extent designed. Why?

The constitutional view of the non-socialist parties
The three non-socialist parties – the Conservative Party, the Liberal party, and the Agrarian Party – had different traditions within this policy area. At the beginning of the century, constitutional issues had been one of the central dividing lines between Conservatives and Liberals. The Conservatives had some sympathy for the continuation of independent royal power and doubts about abolishing various restrictions on universal suffrage too quickly. The Liberals, in accord with the growing Social Democratic Party, had worked for a genuinely parliamentary system and for universal and equal suffrage.

At the beginning of the prolonged constitutional debates during the post-1945 period, there were still slight differences between the three non-socialist parties on how a modern constitution ought to be designed. However, the differences no longer involved parliamentarianism or universal suffrage; on these matters the parties were in agreement. Instead, they concerned the bicameral system and the electoral system. Among Conservatives and Agrarians, there was lingering support for some form of bicameral system, while the Liberals took the position that a Riksdag should be composed of only one chamber elected at a single time. Among the Conservatives, as opposed to the Liberals and Agrarians, there was some support for majority elections in single-member constituencies. Such an electoral system could promote a non-socialist coalition, for which many Conservatives felt particular sympathy. However, among Liberals and Agrarians, there was clear support for a proportional electoral system.

What united the three non-socialist parties from the beginning was the fact that, unlike the Social Democratic Party, their perspective on constitutional matters was in many respects that of parties in opposition. All three had been in the government during the war years; one, the Agrarian Party, had even formed a coalition government with the Social Democrats for six years during the 1950s. However, the view of all three was characterised by that of parties in opposition. They were thus sceptical of or uninterested in Tage Erlander's viewpoint on the need to create conditions for 'strong government'. Attention was focused more on the Riksdag. Furthermore, within all three parties there was support for a greater use of the referendum as an instrument for checking and balancing the power of the government, which was seen as fairly strong; advisory referendums decided upon by the Riksdag were already a feature of the constitution.

The discontent of the three non-socialist parties with the current constitutional system and with their position as opposition parties increased at the beginning of the 1960s. The Social Democratic Party had won clear victories both in the elections to the Second Chamber in 1960 and in the elections to the municipalities and counties (and thereby indirectly to the First Chamber) in 1962; in this latter election the party received more than 50 per cent of the vote. The non-socialist side's chances of ever assuming power within the framework of the existing constitutional system seemed increasingly remote. The Social Democratic Party, powerful in its own right, seemed to be favoured by a bicameral system which both rewarded the largest party and created a safety net for the incumbent government through the slow and gradual way in which the First Chamber was elected. In this state of mutual frustration, the previous differences of view between the non-socialist parties concerning the bicameral system and the electoral system steadily diminished. They jointly demanded that the First Chamber be abolished and also jointly supported the demand for a more proportional electoral system.

In this non-socialist atmosphere, Tage Erlander's argument for a 'municipal link', developed at the beginning of the 1960s, was also experienced as primarily a covert appeal for continued Social Democratic advantages. It was suggested that he seemed to want to preserve some form of First Chamber. The argument was also seen as vague and difficult to grasp. Local elections independent of elections to the Riksdag were seen by non-socialists in contrast to Erlander, as valuable in their own right. In purely local elections of this kind, there was no risk of strictly local issues giving way to issues of a more national nature, which, it was felt, could easily happen if the two elections were co-ordinated in some way.

The foremost spokesman for constitutional reform on the non-socialist side was Bertil Ohlin, leader of the Liberal Party for as many years as Tage Erlander for the Social Democratic Party. Through great persistence over the years, he established as his demand and that of his party that elections to the Riksdag should take place at a single time. The will of the people as expressed in elections should have immediate results. The distribution of mandates in the Riksdag should in principle be in proportion to the percentage of votes cast for the different parties. The Social Democratic Party, and most particularly its leader Erlander, was accused of protracting the issue and of being reluctant to bring about any change in the constitution. In the middle of the 1960s, after the parliamentary commission had presented its report, these accusations intensifed. The constitutional issue was thereby elevated to one of the major domestic issues of the decade.

The agreement

A political consensus was reached on a new constitutional system. This is not particularly suprising. During the post-war decades, Swedish politics was generally characterised by a great degree of consensus; decisions on many, though not all, of the great social and educational policy reforms had been taken with large majorities. Constitutional policy was one of the areas in which there was particular pressure to reach agreement. For it was argued that the parties should be in agreement over the framework of their activity; temporary majorities should not force new constitutional arrangements upon minorities.

However, a very important precondition for the achievement of a consensual agreement was the willingness of the Social Democratic Party to pave the way for a new system. This willingness became quite evident towards the end of the 1960s.

One reason for this was that the unresolved constitutional issue began to be perceived as a political liability. The accusations of the non-socialist opposition that the Social Democrats were intentionally protracting the matter were felt to be gaining credibility. The party, which had won spectacular electoral victories at the beginning of the 1960s, suffered a surprising and very considerable defeat in the 1966 local elections. Its share of the vote declined to 42.2 per cent, the lowest since the beginning of the 1930s. The defeat cannot be explained in terms of the constitutional issue; other issues had been of greater importance in the election campaign. However, after this election, the Social Democratic leadership felt strongly that they should not conduct another election campaign with the constitutional issue still unresolved and the non-socialist opposition accusing the government of protraction. Furthermore, there was a clear risk after the poor local election results in 1966 that the non-socialist parties would finally be able to gain power after the next election – that to the Second Chamber in 1968 – and thereby also gain a significantly stronger position in future negotiations on the constitutional issue. It was, therefore, perceived as important that the matter of the constitution be settled.

Another important reason for the Social Democrats' genuine willingness to negotiate toward the end of the 1960s was, however, the fact that even within the party certain features of the existing constitutional system were beginning to be regarded as unsatisfactory.

One of these was the position of the King. The Social Democratic Party was, as a matter of principle, a republican party, even if the party leadership never actively worked for the abolition of the monarchy. However, during the 1960s, dissatisfaction within the party increased over the strong position formally held by the King in accordance with the existing constitution. This dissatisfaction was based in particular on the fact that the popular King Gustaf Adolf VI was at that time slightly over 80 years old and was to be succeeded by a very young man, his grandson. There was a feeling of uncertainty as to how well the successor would be able to manage in his role as head of state. Therefore, the Social Democrats directed their efforts towards further limiting the active participation of the monarch in the governance of the nation, while maintaining the monarchical form of government.

Another feature of the current system which, surprisingly enough, began to be perceived as unsatisfactory from the point of view of the Social Democrats was the electoral system. Support had previously been expressed for an electoral system which, although proportional, to some extent favoured the largest party and disfavoured smaller ones. The commission on the constitution appointed in 1954 had also outlined in its report an electoral system for a unicameral Riksdag which included precisely these features. The growing doubts within the Social Democratic Party concerning an electoral system which tended to overrepresent larger parties and underrepresent smaller ones was based on a feeling, intensified after the 1966 local elections, that electoral systems with such effects could also create problems for the Social Democratic Party in the long run. This type of electoral system, just like majority elections in single-member constituencies, could lead to consolidation on the non-socialist side; the Social Democrats continued to worry about collaboration among the non-socialist parties. This type of system could also lead to an underrepresentation of the Communists in the Riksdag. The Social Democrats tried to avoid co-operation with the Communists and considered them to be divisive elements in the labour movement, but at the same time they realised that an underrepresentation of the Communist Party in the Riksdag favoured the non-socialist parties inasmuch as the total socialist representation would be correspondingly reduced.

The consensual agreement over the constitutional issue which was reached between the Social Democratic Party and the non-socialist parties – the decisive decisions were taken in the spring of 1967

- involved concessions from both sides. The Social Democrats secured a 'municipal link' inasmuch as the elections to the three levels of the political system were in future to take place concurrently. This would, it was imagined, mean that local and national politics would continue to be discussed in the same election campaign, that voter participation in local elections would in principle be as high as in elections to the Riksdag, and that the same electoral trend could be expected to make itself felt in the composition of the decision-making organs on the three levels with, as a result, advantageous consequences for co-operation between them. The non-socialist parties secured the abolition of the First Chamber with its built-in overrepresentation for the largest party and staggered change. The preference of the voters as expressed in elections was to have an immediate and direct effect on the composition of the Riksdag.

The Social Democrats gained a hearing for their second main constitutional principle – favourable conditions for 'strong government' – only inasmuch as a 4 per cent barrier was introduced into an otherwise strictly proportional electoral system. The non-socialist parties procured what many, though not everyone, on their side had for a long time struggled for: a proportional electoral system which no longer gave the large Social Democratic Party any special advantages in the distribution of mandates.

Finally, the Social Democrats also secured – this consensual agreement was reached somewhat later – further limitations on the active participation of the King in the governance of the nation. The non-socialist parties, amongst whom support for monarchy as a form of government has always been greater than within the Social Democratic Party, did not need to agree to a system which directly threatened the continued existence of the monarchy in Sweden.

In the bargaining which characterised the agreement on a new constitution, it can be argued that the Social Democrats made the most concessions, given their previous opinions. The First Chamber was surrendered: more important, so was the 'municipal link' through indirect elections to the Riksdag. The idea of an electoral system favouring large parties and facilitating the formation of a strong government was also surrendered. The non-socialist parties, on the other hand, won what appeared to be of greatest importance, given their long period in opposition: better chances for a change of power in Swedish politics.

The long debate over constitutional policy which took place in Sweden during the post-war period was not conducted under conditions of great conflict or of difficult social problems. An idyllic situation had prevailed. Nor does the agreement which was gradually

hammered out rest on any vision of the right constitutional framework for an advanced welfare society of the Swedish type. Rather,
the agreement was characterised by calculations from different
quarters of what maximally favoured and disfavoured their own political party. The Swedish version of constitutional politics appeared
as the interest politics of political parties *par excellence*.

An evaluation

For more than a decade and a half, Sweden has lived with the
central features of its new constitution. For, as already indicated,
the new Constitution was promulgated in 1974, but most of its politically important features – a unicameral Riksdag, concurrent elections,
a strictly proportional electoral system, and three-year mandate periods – had come into force by 1970. The parliamentary life of the
country during this period has been characterised by a greater degree
of instability than during previous decades.

First, a number of governments have followed each other: a Social
Democratic Government was in power up until the general elections
in the autumn of 1976; a non-socialist three-party Government was
in power for two years from 1976 to 1978; a non-socialist one-party
(Liberal Party) Government was in power for one year up until
the elections in the autumn of 1979; a new non-socialist three-party
Government was in power for one and a half years from 1979 to
1981; a non-socialist two-party (Liberal Party and Centre Party)
Government was in power until the elections in the autumn of 1982;
and a new Social Democratic Government has been in power since
1982.

Another closely related feature of instability has been the different
bases of support in the Riksdag which the various governments
have had. The only governments which have been formed on the
basis of independent majorities in the unicameral Riksdag have been
the two non-socialist three-party Governments (1976–78 and 1979–
81), while all the others have been minority governments. The Social
Democratic Government in power during the 1982–85 period was
based on the largest of these minorities, while the non-socialist one-
party Government between 1978 and 1979, formed by the Liberal
Party, was based on the smallest of these minorities, on only 39
out of a total of 349 mandates in the Riksdag. The 1985–88 Social
Democratic Government is based on 159 mandates, the party having
received 44.7 per cent of the vote in the 1985 general election.

The new parliamentary instability naturally cannot be explained
by the new constitutional system alone. Many other things have
occurred which have contributed both to a more versatile and to
a somewhat more exciting political climate. The country has suffered

from economic problems as the traditional branches of industry have lost their competitiveness in the world market, oil prices have risen, and the rate of growth has been low or nil; the comprehensive welfare system which had been built up during previous decades has become the object of criticism and even suspicion, the conspicuously peaceful conditions which previously prevailed in the labour market no longer exist; issues which cannot be located along a traditional left-right dimension in politics – in particular the issue of nuclear energy – have created new conflicts and new solutions. But even if it cannot be said that the new Swedish constitutional system is the sole reason for greater instability, it has none the less contributed to it.[7]

A consequence of the new system is that it seems rather improbable that Sweden will henceforth be able to obtain one-party governments based on independent majorities in the Riksdag, something considered by many to be the ideal in a parliamentary system. In the light of the strictly proportional electoral system, there is no reason for the three non-socialist parties to consider consolidation and thereby pave the way for a non-socialist majority party. The Social Democratic Party, which has historically been closest to having an independent majority in the Riksdag, can henceforth attain such a position only if it receives more votes than the three non-socialist parties and the Communist Party together or – if Communist Party support falls below 4 per cent and it loses all representation in the Riksdag – more votes than the three non-socialist parties. At present, following the 1985 election, the Social Democratic Party with its 44.7 per cent of the vote is smaller than the three non-socialist parties together but is able to form a government due to the fact that the Communist Party prefers a Social Democratic to a non-socialist government.

A majority government formed on the basis of a coalition between the Social Democratic Party and one or more of the non-socialist parties does not seem particularly likely at present. The division of Swedish politics into two blocs – a non-socialist bloc comprised of the three non-socialist parties and a socialist bloc comprised of the Social Democratic Party and the Communist Party – has, contrary to what many, including Tage Erlander, expected, become more pronounced under the new system. This is not only because of an increased level of conflict in the country but also because of a constitution which at least once every three years brings the issue of government formation to the fore. Demands are placed on the parties at frequent intervals to declare what kind of government they can consider being a part of after the next election; the non-socialist parties, for fear of losing votes if they suggest a willingness to co-operate in government with the Social Democrats, are thereby prompted more often and more strongly than before to emphasise a common bloc affiliation.

Another feature of the new constitutional system which to some extent fosters instability is the 4 per cent barrier. Its consequence is that a single vote can, in the extreme case, determine whether a party will lose its representation in the Riksdag completely or receive full representation. Furthermore, voters and closely related parties are faced with strategic problems. The Social Democratic Party has had this problem in its relationship to the Communist Party: on the one hand, a competing party which has historically been considered a divider of the labour movement, on the other hand, a party whose continued presence in the Riksdag is considered an important prerequisite for a Social Democratic Government. The non-socialist parties, though to a lesser extent, had this problem in relation to a sixth party not previously mentioned – the Christian Democratic Union. This party, established in the middle of the 1960s, has received between 1 and 2 per cent of the vote in general elections and succeeded in getting a representative elected to the Riksdag for the first time in the 1985 election through an electoral collaboration with the Centre Party, a collaboration which was highly criticised in various quarters.

However, the feature of the Swedish constitutional system which is particularly responsible for fostering instability is the short mandate period. A government which has assumed office after an election must count on the possibility of being forced to leave office after three years, if not sooner. This shortsighted perspective leads to discontinuity and hastiness on the part of the government.

An example of such discontinuity is the budget. A government assuming office after a regular election in September has only two months at its disposal in which to work out its first budget; the budget it presented in January and after consideration in the Riksdag takes effect from 1 July the same year. During these two months in the autumn a new government must attempt to execute much of what has been promised during the election campaign, even though it may be composed of many inexperienced ministers and, in addition, of different parties with different positions on various key issues related to the budget. The second budget for which a government has to take responsibility within a three-year period can usually be worked out in a more composed atmosphere. But the third has to be worked out once more under dramatic circumstances, for it will soon be time for a general election again. Thus it is also uncertain whether the government which has worked out this budget will remain in power during the financial year concerned.[8]

Another example of the discontinuity which has accompanied the

three-year mandate periods are the changes in the methods of operation of the Swedish parliamentary commissions. These were
historically renowned for their thoroughness and often yielded
comprehensive reports complemented by independent research.[9]
They have now had to become accustomed to working under severe
time limits. It can take some time before a new government is able
to appoint all the parliamentary commissions which it intends to
initiate. Once appointed, the commissions not only have to produce
their proposals before the next election but they must also give
the incumbent government a chance to act on the basis of the proposals. The tempo is hectic; the work is of necessity often cursory.
The Swedish commission system, which in its previous thoroughness
was sometimes said to grind perhaps too slowly and carefully, is
now beginning to be accused of being slipshod.

By way of summary, it can be said that a tension has arisen in
Sweden during the 1970s and 1980s between constitutional rules
and actual political developments. Rules and developments are almost
out of step with each other. On the one hand, the country has
received a constitution which, with its strictly proportional electoral
system and its short mandate periods, has clearly made it more
difficult for the winning side to obtain a majority in the Riksdag
and a reasonably long term of office. On the other hand, there is
a development in the direction of a two-party system in which two
so-called blocs oppose each other and compete over the government.

Possible new reform
The new constitutional system which has been in force for over
a decade has not only been criticised, it has also been followed
by explicit demands for change. These have concerned not only
the less essential features but also the central features, i.e. the electoral
system, the unicameral parliament, the concurrence of elections, and
the length of the mandate periods. In addition, a new parliamentary
commission was appointed in 1984 with the task of presenting proposals aimed at 'improving the conditions for democratic government
in Sweden'. The commission, which was led by a Social Democrat,
included representatives from all the three non-socialist parties and
from the Communist Party. The work was finished in late 1986
but disagreement remained on many issues.[10]

The electoral system will probably not be changed in any essential
respect. There have been individual commentators, in particular from
Social Democratic quarters, who have wondered if it would not
be reasonable, now that Sweden, despite the proportional electoral
system, has drifted into something which is similar to a two-party
system, to establish an electoral system which promotes decisive

results. Majority elections in single-member constituencies or proportional elections in small constituencies have been discussed. However, developments which have gone in the direction of strict proportionality – with the exception of the 4 per cent barrier – are not easily reversed. Agreement can only be reached over slight changes in the electoral system, e.g. an increasing degree of voting for individual candidates.

Nor is there any political likelihood of changing the system of a Riksdag comprising only a single chamber. However, there have been commentators who have called attention to the fact that in the old First Chamber there were politicians of another kind than in the unicameral Riksdag of today; on the one hand, national politicians with great expertise in special areas, on the other hand, politicians with a very strong local base. Discussion is under way concerning quality in the present unicameral Riksdag and also concerning its comparatively large number of members. Reforms are being considered which would increase the efficiency of the work of the Riksdag and the attractiveness of being a member. But the idea of once again creating some form of bicameral system would seem to be completely academic.

However, as opposed to the issues of the electoral system and the unicameral system, the issue of concurrent or separate elections continues actively to engage the political parties. The issue was also central for the parliamentary commission appointed in 1984. The non-socialist parties have continued to express reservations on this concurrence. Reference is made to the fact that specifically local issues tend to be completely neglected in current election campaigns; furthermore, it is noted that the propensity to vote for different parties on different levels seems to be increasing, quite contrary to what was expected by those who spoke of the value of the same electoral trend making itself felt on all three levels. On the other hand, the Social Democratic Party is still strongly committed to concurrent elections. It is feared that purely local elections would lead to decidedly lower voter participation in elections to local assemblies than to the Riksdag. At present, voter participation in elections to local assemblies is 1 to 2 per cent lower. (That voter participation is somewhat lower in local elections despite the elections being concurrent can be explained primarily by the fact that foreigners who have resided in the country for a certain period have the right to vote in elections to local assemblies but not in elections to the Riksdag and that they exercise their right to vote to a lesser extent than Swedish citizens.) Voter participation is on the whole relatively high in Sweden, around 90 per cent.

Finally, the issue of the length of the mandate periods also engages the political parties. There is rather broad agreement, regardless of party affiliation, that three years is too short a time. (Individual commentators have, however, claimed that frequent elections have a positive effect on the political system. With frequent elections, the parties are deterred from making irresponsible promises and taking opportunistic measures.) But agreement on lengthening the mandate periods is complicated by disagreement over concurrence on the three levels. The Social Democratic Party would consider an extension of the mandate periods to four years on condition that the three elections were held concurrently every four years. The non-socialist parties, on the other hand, oppose such long periods without elections of any kind being held. They seem to be saying, by all means four-year periods but on the condition that local elections and Riksdag elections are separated and that the country thereby has elections with more frequent intervals than once every four years. The situation would seem to be deadlocked.

Swedish constitutional policy is not characterised by frequent shifts. It took almost two decades to reach a decision to replace the 1809 Instrument of Government with a new one. During the period of more than a decade in which the new Instrument of Government has been in force, complaints over various features of it have been presented time and again. A new parliamentary commission on the constitution was appointed. However, no comprehensive change in the constitutional system which was created during the 1970s seems to be imminent. Constitutional policy in Sweden, even if the present constitution has contributed to a different and more versatile political system in the country, still appears as something slightly academic and peripheral. Conflicts and tensions of the kind which would force drastic changes in the constitutional system have not arisen; individual citizens and citizens' groups remain uninterested; the parties are still the major actors and act largely out of personal interest, at the same time aware of the fact that they must be in agreement if new changes in the current system are to be made. Sweden remains, after all, very stable.

Notes and references

1. The degree to which the 1809 Instrument of Government was the result of a domestic constitutional development was at one time a hotly debated issue in Swedish political science. Some scholars, foremost among them Fredrik Laggerroth in Lund, maintained that this constitution was almost totally formed by specific Swedish experiences during the preceding centuries; other scholars, among them particularly Axel Brusewitz in Uppsala, emphasised on the other hand the influence of constitutional ideas held generally in Europe during the eighteenth century. For a summary of this debate, see *Statsvetenskaplig tidskrift*, 1959, pp. 2–3.

2. For a treatment of the two decades of deliberations preceding the 1973 and

1974 decisions, see Björn von Sydow's forthcoming book, *Partierna inför författningen. En studie i demokratisk författningspolitik i Sverige 1944–1967*. Cp. *Statsvetenskaplig tidskrift*, 1976, p. 1.

3. On the development of the electoral system in Sweden, see Bo Särlvik, 'Scandinavia' in Vernon Bogdanor and David Butler (eds), *Democracy and Elections* (Cambridge University Press, 1983), and Björn von Sydow, 'Tage Erlanders första valsystem', *Scandia*, 1986, p. 1.

4. On the principle of parliamentarianism in the new Swedish constitution, see Fredrik Sterzel, *Parlamentarismen i författningen* (Norstedts, 1983).

5. A study of Tage Erlander as Prime Minister and party leader has recently been published. See Olof Ruin, *I välfärdsstatens tjänst. Tage Erlander 1946–1969* (Tiden, 1986).

6. See Olof Ruin, *Mellan samlingsregering och tvåpartisystem. Den svenska regeringsdiskussionen 1945–1960* (Bonniers, 1968). Cp. Olof Ruin, 'Patterns of Government Composition in Multi-Party Systems: the Case of Sweden', *Scandinavian Political Studies*, Vol. 4, 1969.

7. For a discussion of the factors behind the greater instability, see Olof Ruin, 'Sweden in the 1970s: Policy-Making Becomes More Difficult' in Jeremy Richardson (ed.), *Policy Styles in Western Europe* (London: George Allen & Unwin, 1982).

8. For a discussion of different problems of the present constitution, see *Makten från folket. 12 uppsatser om folkstyrelsen*, 1985.

9. For a presentation in English of the Swedish parliamentary commissions, see Rune Premfors, 'Governmental Commissions in Sweden', *American Behavioral Scientist*, Vol. 26, No. 5, 1983.

10. See the report of the commission, *Folkstyrelsens villkor* (Sou, 1987:6).

17 The State reform in Belgium (1970–): Positive and negative aspects
Robert Senelle

Belgium: an old nation

Abroad the question often arises whether Belgium is not an artificial state which owes its existence to the striving for political and military equilibrium on the part of France, Great Britain, Prussia and the Danubian Monarchy (the Austrian, later Austro-Hungarian Empire). Nothing could be further from the truth. Belgium is no more artificial than Switzerland, that other multi-lingual nation in Europe. The North and South Low Countries (i.e. the present-day Kingdom of the Netherlands and the present-day Kingdom of Belgium) formed a political entity, created during the fifteenth and sixteenth centuries, which consisted of various principalities and had, through the genius of the Dukes of Burgundy, been made into a particularly prosperous economic and political unit. We are not dealing here with the accidential joining together of miscellaneous principalities. The constituent parts of the Burgundian state spoke French and Dutch, but shared the same socio-economic culture and sovereign, who held all the constituent parts together within one personal union. The foolish wars of religion were to divide the North and South Low Countries for good. The reunion from 1815 to 1830 was to fail ingloriously.

Until the steamroller of the French armies was to force Jacobin centralism on them in 1792, the Belgian principalities had an almost federal structure within the Burgundian state. From Napoleon's time onwards, up to 1970, Belgium's structure as a state remained strictly centralist. Belgium however contains five and a half million Flemings who belong to the Dutch cultural area, three and a quarter million Walloons who form a part of French culture and about 70,000 German-speaking Belgians. The inhabitants of Brussels – nearly one million – speak one of the country's two most important languages, French or Flemish. This cultural diversity, owing to the rise of regional tendencies, made the reform of the structure of the Belgium state along federal lines inevitable in the twentieth century.

The course of the State reform

The State reform which has dominated political events in Belgium for the past quarter of a century may be understood as the gradual, but unavoidable transformation of a strictly unitarian state entity into a regional or federal state system. It is obvious that the language conflict has played, in its successive phases, an essential part in the historic development of Belgian society. The language legislation has developed as follows:

(i)   1831: constitutional freedom in respect of the use of language; laws and decrees are promulgated in French; there exist 'Flemish' translations, but only the French text has legal validity;

(ii)   1873: a law imposes the use of Dutch on the courts (in criminal cases) in the Flemish part of the country, unless requested otherwise by the accused;

(iii)   1878: a law imposes the use of Dutch on the government authorities in the Flemish part of the country, unless requested otherwise by the interested party;

(iv)   1883: in the Flemish part of the country part of the teaching in secondary education is henceforth in Dutch;

(v)   1890: magistrates must prove that they have command of Dutch in order to be eligible for appointment in the Flemish part of the country; at Ghent National University lecturing in some of the subjects (including criminal law and criminal procedure for future Flemish magistrates) is henceforth in Dutch;

(vi)   1898: laws and decrees are sanctioned, ratified and promulgated in Dutch as well as in French; both texts have legal validity;

(vii)   1912: at the Catholic University of Louvain, too, lecturing in some of the subjects is henceforth in Dutch;

(viii) 1913: military officers must henceforth also have command of Dutch;

(ix)   1921: law concerning the use of languages in administrative matters:
        – the central national administrations become bilingual, as do their officials;
        – local administrations become monolingual (the language of the region becomes the vehicular language);
        – the Brussels communal administrations have the choice between the country's two languages;
        – protection of the French-speaking minorities in the Flemish part of the country;
        – language censuses every ten years whereby a commune can change its language statute;

(x)   1928: training of soldiers is in their mother tongue, while military officers must be bilingual;

(xi)   1930: official use of the Dutch language in the Ghent National University. The free universities (Brussels and Louvain) are gradually being transformed into two separate linguistic entities;

(xii)   1932: abolition of individual bilingualism of officials of the central national administrations; matters must be dealt with in the language of the dossiers without resorting to translators. Officials are distributed over two language rolls (Dutch and French), with a fair balance in respect of appointments; in primary and secondary education in the Flemish part of the country bilingualism is abolished; Dutch becomes the vehicular language. In Brussels, the theoretical principle 'mother tongue, vehicular language' is applicable;

(xiii) 1935: law concerning the use of the country's languages in judicial matters: 'language of the region – language of proceedings' principle is applicable, but the accused may apply for the proceedings to be conducted in the other language; in Brussels: the language of the accused is the language of the proceedings.

The actual run-up to the State reform began with the so-called Harmel Centre, set up by the Law of 3 May 1948, under the name 'Research Centre for the national solution of the social and legal problems in the Flemish and Walloon Regions'. The final report, which was published on 24 April, 1958, in the form of a parliamentary paper, contained important conclusions on the regionalisation of the institutions: equal representation of Flemings and Walloons in the administration; definitive demarcation of the language boundary, and the setting-up of a Walloon Cultural Council and a Flemish Cultural Council for the purpose of conducting a cultural policy of their own; division of the Province of Brabant.

One of the first important consequences of the Harmel Centre were the new laws of 1962 and 1963 concerning the use of languages in administrative matters and introducing for the first time since 1831 the absolute monolingualism of the language areas. Furthermore, these laws contained amongst other things: abolition of the language census whereby communes could change their language statute; definitive demarcation of the language boundary; the congruence of the boundaries of the provinces with the language boundaries; the requirement that communal administrations of Greater Brussels become bilingual and an equal number of Dutch-speaking and French-speaking officials in the national administrations.

Under the Lefèvre Government (1961–65) the harmonisation of political relations between the two communities was to be definitively launched. After a working party had handed over on 24 October 1963 a report to the then Government headed by Lefèvre, a declaration concerning the revision of the Constitution with a view to reforming the institutions was made, for the first time, in the House of Representatives on 3 March 1965. However, the fall of the Lefèvre Government did not allow this revision to be brought to a successful conclusion. Subsequently various commissions had to advise the government on the reform of the institutions.

The Eyskens Government (1968–71) included for the first time a Minister of Dutch Culture and a Minister of French Culture, two Ministers of National Education and two Ministers with the status of Secretaries of State for Regional Economy. For Dutch culture, French culture and common cultural affairs separate budgetary laws were passed. The language laws, which were nearly always passed with a majority approaching or exceeding two-thirds and which were based on the territoriality principle, are in fact of a federal nature. Since 1960 the radio and television service has been provided by two autonomous public corporations.

The 1970 constitutional revision
So far, the reform of the Belgian state has occurred in two stages. The 1970 Constituent Assembly duly endorsed in its broad outlines, the programme submitted by the Eyskens Government, even though it was left to the legislature to lay down the competence and composition of the regional bodies. In doing so, the 1970 Constituent Assembly sought to preserve the unity of general state policy and at the same time to reconcile this unity of policy with the recognition of cultural communities, language areas and regions.

To establish cultural autonomy, Article 32b was incorporated into the Constitution. In the cases specified by the Constitution, the elected members of each House were divided, in the manner laid down by the law, into Dutch and a French language group. This article is still valid. The elected members were assigned, albeit in a limited field, as members of the cultural councils and in specific cases were given an extensive area of legislative authority from which the national legislature was excluded, and which in principle only applied to the members of the community for whom they acted.

Article 3c provided that the Dutch, the French and the German cultural communities should be able to exercise powers which are conferred by the Constitution or by laws passed by virtue of the Constitution. The cultural councils were the bodies of the Dutch and the French cultural community. The cultural council for the

Dutch cultural community (consisting of the members of the Dutch language group of both houses) and the cultural council for the French cultural community (consisting of the members of the French language group of both houses) received the necessary authority to lay down legally valid provisions in the matter of cultural affairs, cultural co-operation, educational matters (to the exclusion, however, of the subjects summed up by the Constitution) and the regulation of the use of languages in the field defined by the Constitution.

According to Article 3b – which is still applicable – Belgium comprises four language areas: the Dutch, the French, the bilingual Brussels-capital and the German language area. Every commune of the realm forms a part of one of these language areas. No modification or correction may be made to the boundaries of the four areas other than by a law passed by special majority. The Constitution laid down as a rule that the decrees of the cultural council for the Dutch cultural community in the Dutch language area and the decrees of the cultural council for the French cultural community in the French language area had the force of law and specified in which cases it was possible to deviate from this rule.

According to what is stated in Article 107d Belgium comprises three regions: the Flemish region, the Walloon region and the Brussels region. This article is still in force. The law confers upon the regional bodies which it sets up and which are made up of elected members authority to deal with the matters to which it (the law) refers, to the exclusion of those mentioned in Articles 23 (use of languages) and 59b (cultural affairs), and this within the definition and in the manner laid down by it. The law must be passed by a qualified majority. From this it is apparent that the Constitutional Assembly has given a clearly defined content to the autonomy of the cultural communities, while relying on (ordinary) legislation as far as the regions are concerned.

In the House of Representatives and in the Senate the majority rule was retained, but its application was tempered by the so-called 'alarm-bell procedure' (Art. 38b) for the purpose of avoiding conflict between Flemings and Walloons, and by introducing equal representation of Flemish and Dutch speakers in the Cabinet (Art. 86b). The 1970 constitutional legislation clearly sought to achieve a balance between the newly created state institutions and the existing structure of the state.

Although Article 32 (whereby the members of both Houses represent the nation) had remained unchanged, it no longer applied without reservation, as in the cases specified by the Constitution the elected members of each House were divided into a Dutch and a French language group (Art. 32b) and only the members of these language groups, acting as the organ of a cultural community, made the legally effective decisions mentioned by the Constitution, which in principle were only applicable in the Dutch and the French language areas respectively. In the exercise of this authority, the members of the cultural councils were holders of rights of sovereignty, as they enacted the law in the field of the subject-matter reserved for them.

A qualfied majority was required when voting on draft laws and bills submitted in pursuance of Article 1, paragraph 4 (withdrawal of an area with its own statute from the division into provinces), 3b (modification of the boundaries of the language areas), 59b, sections 1 and 2 (laying down of the manner in which the cultural councils exercise their authority, the cultural matters which fall within the scope of the cultural councils, as well as the forms of co-operation) and article 107d (laying down of the manner of composition and of the authority of the regional bodies).

It is obvious that after 1970 Belgium was no longer a classic unitary state: (i) the national legislature retained full authority. The authority of the cultural councils and that which could be assigned to the regional bodies was an assigned authority; (ii) according to the explicit provisions of Article 32b the division into language groups is effected (solely) 'in the cases specified by the Constitution'; (iii) according to the second paragraph of Article 3c each cultural community possessed (only) those powers which were conferred upon it by the Constitution or by laws passed by virtue of the Constitution; (iv) subject to application of the unaltered Article 32.

Yet Belgium had not become a classic federal or regional state. The federal form of government implies the existence of two legal systems, a federal and a regional legal system, which clearly differ from one another. Apart from the cultural councils, the cultural communities of 1970 did not have the necessary structures and competences; they lacked judicial and executive bodies of their own. The rules passed by the cultural councils were confirmed, proclaimed and implemented by the King.

The 1980 Constitutional Revision

Only a few years after the Constitution had been changed in 1970, however, it was called into question again. Between 1970 and 1980 there had indeed been a remarkable gathering of momentum on the political plane. An overall and definitive settlement of the regional problems was demanded by all political parties. The State Reform issue had reached a stage where its pace was quickening.

During the negotiations for the formation of the Tindemans II

334 Constitutions in Democratic Politics

Government (June 1977–October 1978) a new political agreement, the so-called Community Pact, on a fundamental reform of the Belgian state system was confirmed by most of the parties. This pact was subsequently further supplemented by the so-called Stuyvenberg agreement and gave rise to the tabling, on 11 June 1978, of a draft law containing various institutional reforms. But, due to the dissolution of Parliament, this draft law lapsed.

Under the political agreement which, after the parliamentary elections of 17 December 1978, led to the formation of the Martens I Government (April 1979–May 1980) it was agreed that the state reform should be carried out in three phases: a first phase, during which special executives for the communities and regions were to be established; a second so-called provisional and irreversible phase, whereby a number of legislative competences in various fields were to be assigned to the communities and the regions; and lastly a third phase, during which a definitive state reform was to be worked out by the Parliament and the government. The first phase, which remained limited to policy at the executive level, was carried into effect by a number of royal decrees on the basis of the law setting up provisional community and regional institutions. To implement the second phase, two draft laws were submitted on 1 October 1979. Parliamentary resistance to these draft laws resulted in the resignation of the government on 3 April 1986.

During the negotiations which led to the formation of the Martens III Government in May 1980, agreement was reached on the principles and main lines of a definitive State reform, except for the Brussels problem. With a view to the implementation of the agreement, the government immediately tabled proposals for the revision of a number of constitutional provisions, together with two draft laws for the reform of the institutions: a first draft grouping together the provisions which had to be sanctioned by a special majority and a second draft containing those provisions which could be sanctioned on the basis of an ordinary majority. Articles 3c, 26b, 28, 59b, 107c, 108, 110, 111, 113, and 135 of the Constitution were amended or inserted and the special law and the ordinary law on institutional reforms were proclaimed on 8 and 9 August 1980, respectively.

The special law of 8 August 1980 on institutional reforms settles, as a transitional measure, the boundaries of the Flemish and the Walloon regions, lays down the competence and composition of the Executives, fixes the competences mentioned in Articles 59b and 107d of the Constitution and regulates the composition of the councils.

The ordinary law of 9 August 1980 on institutional reforms deals mainly with the problem of the financial resources to which the communities and regions are entitled.

The 1980 Constituent Assembly has limited the revision of the Constitution to those articles which were strictly necessary for the approval of the draft of the special law and the draft of the ordinary law on institutional reforms. The purpose of the constitutional changes was mainly: (i) to extend the communities' competence to 'personalised' matters, amongst others, medical care, social services and education'; (ii) to enable the community organs to exercise the powers of the regional bodies; (iii) to create the possibility of statutorily regulating the legal force of the rules issued in regional matters.

The extension of the communities' competence to 'personalised' matters led, for the sake of the parallelism with Article 59b, to an adaptation of Article 3c. The word 'cultural communities' was replaced by the word 'communities', and the three communities were henceforth called Flemish, French and German-speaking communities.

Article 26b, which was inserted into the Constitution, deals with the manner in which the legal force of the regional rules is determined. The text affords the possibility of conferring (legal) force on the regional rules on the basis of a law which must be passed by a special majority. The special law of 8 August 1980, on institutional reforms provides that for the Flemish and the Walloon regions rules called decrees can be issued with the force of law.

Article 28 was supplemented by the authority of genuine interpretation, which, in the matter of laws, devolves on the national legislator, also to be conferred on the decree legislator in respect of the decrees which are issued, whether by virtue of Article 59b or by virtue of the new Article 26b.

The amendment of Article 59b is the cornerstone of the new state structure. The cultural communities become communities, the communities' competences are extended to 'personalised' matters and the right of initiative is conferred on the Executive and the members of the Community Council. Article 59b makes it henceforth possible for the regional powers mentioned in Article 107d to be exercised by the Community Councils. The special law of 8 August 1980 on institutional reforms regulates this immediately for Flanders, while the possibility is created of this being done for Wallonia.

Article 107c relates to the prevention and settlement of conflicts of competence between the law, the decree and the regional rules referred to in Article 26b, as also between the decree and the regional rules. For this purpose a Court of Arbitration is to be set up, and the legislator is instructed to determine the composition, competence and operation of this court. On 28 June 1983, the law concerning the institution, competence and operation of the Court of Arbitration was enacted. Article 108 was supplemented by a decision which makes it possible to delegate the organisation and exercise of administrative supervision of provincial and communal institutions to the communities or to the regions.

The aim of the revision of Articles 110, 111 and 113 is to provide the communities and the regions with a fiscal system of their own. In pursuance of this, the ordinary law of 9 August 1980 provides for the following financial resources for the Flemish Community, the French Community and the Walloon Region:

(i)   non-fiscal resources of their own;
(ii) credits chargeable to the National Budget (= endowment);
(iii) rebates on the yield of certain taxes and levies imposed by the law;
(iv) a fiscal system of their own;
(v)   loans.

Owing to its limited size, no decree-making authority was conferred, in the 1970 Constitutional Revision, on the German cultural community. In the 1980 Constitutional Revision the designation was admittedly changed to 'German-speaking community' (Art. 3c of the Constitution), but its position still remained unchanged. Only in 1983 was Article 59c of the Constitution inserted to grant it autonomy wholly equivalent to that of the other two communities, including decree-making authority. The new constitutional provision requires, for its implementation, an ordinary law, which was proclaimed on 31 December 1983, as the law on institutional reforms for the German-speaking community.

As already mentioned earlier, only the Brussels Region remained outside the implementation of Art. 107d of the Constitution because of the lack of the majorities required for this purpose. The Brussels Region, then, is not as yet a legal person separate from the state and continues to be governed by the co-ordinated law of 20 July 1979 setting up provisional community and regional institutions and the decrees implementing them.

Where are we now?

The 1980 State reform is wrongly regarded by some as the definitive structure of the Belgian state. This state reform is, however, simply the extension of the cultural and regional autonomy begun in 1970. It is no more than an important transitional phase, a second step towards the ultimate goal, that is, the Belgian federal monarchy.

That this development is progressing fairly slowly need not surprise us. In states with a federal tradition, the revision of the structure of the state is not a speedy process either. The overall revision

The State reform in Belgium (1970–) : Positive and negative aspects

of the Federal Constitution of Switzerland took more than ten years. The system for the financing of the *Länder* in the Federal Republic of Germany materialised after five years of parliamentary activity and even so represented but a fraction of the problems raised by the need for reform. Belgium, however, does not have a federal tradition. Where most federal states have come into existence from a joining together of previously independent and autonomous territories, just the opposite is happening in Belgium. Here, starting from a Napoleonically centralised state, self-government is now being conferred on parts of that state.

It goes without saying that the reform of the unitary Belgian state into a federal form of government might have been effected simply through the remodelling of the present nine provinces into Swiss-style cantons. The great advantage of this constitutional structure would have been that in this way a federalism consisting of two or three component parts might have been avoided. Oddly enough, a solution of this kind never had any real chance. The political division of the country along the language boundary, which separates the Dutch-speaking from the French-speaking population, was to appear unavoidable to the majority of politicians. As a result, the State reform was to be effected on a cultural and not on a provincial basis. For almost ten years now the provinces in Belgium have once more been under discussion in the political forum. The 1970–71 State reform had passed the provinces by although the final settlement of the institutional question in a new federal Belgium entailed the abolition of the provinces as political entities. Ten years later a revaluation of the provinces as intermediary administrative bodies seems once more conceivable. It should nevertheless be noted that the Communities and Regions have so far not yet spoken out on the definitive position of the provinces in the new form of government. Only time will tell whether a cantonal solution for the institutional problem of the Belgian state is still a possibility.

Criticism may, however, be levelled at the composition of the Community and Regional Councils. The members, elected by direct suffrage, of the central Belgian Parliament make up the Flemish, Walloon and French 'Parliaments', respectively, albeit according to the language group to which they belong and their place of residence. These members of Parliament thus have (on the Flemish side) a twofold and (on the Walloon-French-speaking side) even a threefold capacity as sovereign legislators and political organs of supervision of the executive power. This brings about a delicate situation.

The citizen casts his vote, at elections, on the basis of his preference for a specific political choice at the Belgian level, and decides on possible coalitions for the central government. Indirectly, and in most cases unconciously, he thereby also determines the political relationships and possibilities in his Region and Community. Once the government coalitions have been formed for the central government, the members of Parliament are landed in a hybrid situation in which they must decide on coalitions and political choices at regional or community level. Their attitude at that level inevitably has repercussions in the central Parliament, on the stability of the central government and vice versa. Bearing in mind the obvious tensions on points of competence and interests between the central government and the newly created state institutions, communities and regions, any unequivocal assumption of political responsibility at any level becomes hard to realise. Thus it may happen that, for example, members of the Flemish Parliament approve a specific point of view on the Council and that the same members take up a different position in the central Parliament because they do not want to embarrass the central government there. Moreover, this state of affairs acts as a brake on the inner dynamism of the Community and Regional Parliaments, respectively. One can well imagine that a directly elected Flemish legislative body would experience different political conditions from the present-day Flemish Council and would take up a more independent position *vis-à-vis* the national authority.

Not only at the level of the institutions can the existing structure of the state be criticised. The 1980 legislation did not entirely succeed in establishing a clear demarcation of competence between the central government and the communities and regions. At first sight the distribution of competences is simple: the communities and regions possess exclusive powers granted to them, while the central government retains the residual competence. In practice, however, this distribution of competences may provoke conflicts. When devising a distribution of competences within a federally organised state, it is a fundamental condition that one should have clear insight into the criteria (key) according to which one wants to redistribute the tasks devolving upon the authorities and that these powers should be defined in straightforward, unequivocal terms. It is difficult to claim that the existing Belgian law fully comes up to this. The distribution of competences carried out in 1980 is the result of many a compromise. A lot of competences – especially at regional level – were distributed in an arbitrary manner between the central government and the regions.

The financial arrangement, too, is open to criticism. The fact is that the financial resources consist for the most part of an endowment and only in a very incidental way of so-called shared taxation revenue, while a fiscal system of their own was denied to the communities and regions until the end of 1984 and can only have an impact in the future.

The result is that the financial resources of communities and regions are very inflexible and that a direct connection between the policy conducted by communities and regions and their financial circumstances is lacking. Budgetary and fiscal mechanisms should be improved so that the communities and regions can become genuine policy instruments.

In addition to the small volume of financial resources, another, more fundamental disadvantage of the existing financing system comes to the fore – the manner in which the financial resources are made available to the various areas making up the whole. The financing system of most federal states is based on the principle that each of the areas is itself responsible *vis-à-vis* its population for the financing of its expenditure policy, on the basis of its own fiscal system. The central subsidising system, founded on the idea of mutual solidarity, is incidental and designed solely to correct any excessive imbalances between the regions.

In Belgium this arrangement has been reversed. The provision of financial resources under the Belgian state reform is not in keeping with the principle of financial responsibility. At the moment a discrepancy between the expenditure and the proper financial means is manifest. This is an absolute negation of the basic rules of sound financial policy.

It is, then, also obvious that the provision of financial resources to the regions as organised at present is not capable of supporting and guaranteeing the autonomy of the regional authorities. Proper regionalisation requires that the national government should, parallel with the competence to spend, delegate to the regions equivalent authority to raise revenue.

Whither Belgium?

It is generally accepted that the basic principles of federalism can be summed up as follows: the co-existence of two legal systems with their own legislative and executive power; respect for the principle 'Bundesrecht bricht Landesrecht' (Federal law sets aside state law); the existence of a supreme constitutional court; participation of the individual states in the federal legislative process; federal solidarity, amongst other things in the financial field.

The three communities in Belgium are already recognised as genuine people's communities. They must have their own legislative assembly which they themselves have elected, so that the relationship between the individual state and the federation can be fully operative and internal tutelage of regional political initiatives inside the unitary party-political structures should diminish in importance.

There can be no well-being for the Flemish and Walloons outside a genuinely federal Belgium with a strong central authority. It is necessary to fall back on the classic criteria which are applicable to any federally organised state. These criteria have up to now made possible peaceful co-existence of the different constituent parts in foreign federal states. Swiss and German federalism serve as models in this connection. Belgium must become a genuine federal monarchy.

The financial and economic relations between the communities must be based on the full responsibility of each of them, supplemented by interregional and national solidarity to be calculated in an objective, but indispensable manner.

Every federal state has a Constitutional Court which sees to it that the laws, regional decrees and acts of political bodies are in line with the Constitution. The Court of Arbitration is quite correctly solely authorised to deal with conflicts of competence between, on the one hand, the national and the regional authorities and, on the other hand, the regional authorities themselves.

Particularly important is the change in the technique of distribution of competence, traditionally applied in Belgium, via the technique of exclusive powers. Indeed, experience abroad and the development there towards what is conventionally called co-operative federalism teaches us that a technique of competing powers, coupled with the existence of a genuine Chamber representing the individual states (e.g. Bundesrat) should make for a more flexible system of co-existence than the existing rigid Belgian competence distribution system. It is also a striking fact that even if the rule of the preponderance of national law over regional law has not been expressly written into all federal constitutions, all federal countries nevertheless apply this rule, if only to promote indispensable legal security over the whole territory of the federation.

No radical transformation of the state structure has ever been carried out in any country at a stroke. The 1980 State reform, however, needs to be brought to a successful conclusion. This naturally involves laying down the definitive statute of Brussels-capital and the reform of the Senate.

The State reform must continue in a federal direction because there is no turning back. We must ensure that the South Low Countries do not disintegrate into a number of mini-states without international prestige.

More than ever is the role of the monarchy fundamental for the harmonious transformation of the Belgian state entity. The King must continue to exist as a moderating figure above the political struggle. It is not a good thing that in a country without a federal tradition the electorate should have to be periodically consulted on the choice of the Head of State. The result of that choice would, even if the latter were trilingual, always be open to challenge in the eyes of those individual states making up the whole from which the elected Head of State does not come. Without the monarchy Belgium is not viable today.

A federal monarchy? Why not? The popular King Baudouin, who has been caused many worries by the Belgians, but who, with dogged perseverance and an unflagging sense of duty, embodies the cohesion between the communities amid the constitutional storms, is the last bond between the component parts of the Belgian state. Owing to an unexpected repetition of history, this sovereign must do the work of his Burgundian predecessors over again albeit in the opposite sense, i.e. by ensuring the transition from a unitary state structure, which has proved intolerable, via a regional, towards a federal model. A genuine federal structure, with the preservation of the country's political unity, is the only possible lasting solution for the further co-existence of Flemings, Walloons and German-speaking Belgians in one and the same state.

Despite the occasional high tide of verbal violence, the Belgians live peacefully side by side and take a philosophical view of the slowly, but steadily, progressing State reform. The large majority of Belgians wish to continue to live together in one and the same federal state. They are too wise not to realise that cultural diversity may also constitute intellectual enrichment.

18 The Netherlands (1983): The failure of constitutional reform
Jan Vis

The development of Dutch constitutional history has followed a relatively even course. There have not been any revolutions in the traditional sense of that word since the day the monarchy was founded; constitutional reforms generally took a long period of preparation before they were realised, and once introduced, they never became the subject of fundamental debate. The constitutional climate is characterised by an inclination towards pragmatism and little need is felt for theory, so that the more fundamental issues receive little attention. With a few exceptions, the reforms of the Dutch Constitution have been essentially codifications of a broad political consensus.

Given this evolutionary character, the most important characteristics of the Dutch Constitution can only be understood in the light of its historical development. In a period of 170 years or more, this development shows a gradual shift of power from the hereditary sovereign to the three main political movements in the Netherlands: the Liberals, the Christian Democrats and the Socialists. The most significant moments in this development are the years 1815, when the principles of constitutional monarchy were laid down; 1848, when the liberal-dominated Parliament discarded the personal power of the king; 1887, when the position of the political parties became stronger; and 1917/22, when universal suffrage was introduced. In the last few years there have been a few minor constitutional changes, and a major constitutional revision in 1983. This last alteration had a dual character: (i) the introduction of a social and economic Bill of Rights; (ii) the express confirmation of the representative (party-) democracy.

The significance of the historical moments
The Constitution of 1815 – the basis of the constitutional monarchy and one of the oldest operative constitutions in Europe (Norway whose constitution dates from 1814 is the oldest) – was the result of a number of relatively unrelated circumstances.

The first is the existence of the Orange-Nassau family, which already during the Republic of the Seven Provinces exerted some hereditary power, but never managed to achieve a sovereign position on account of the resistance of the Dutch mercantile aristocracy. The return of the 'Hereditary Prince' from England to the liberated Netherlands was part of the national reveille, which made the monarchy of the Oranges inevitable. The discussion between the prospective sovereign and the aristocracy resulted in a Constitution, which was described by contemporaries as an 'agreement between Sovereign and People'. In other words, in the Netherlands it was not a question of a Charter, presented by the sovereign to his people (as in the case of the French Restoration Monarchy).[1] The fact that the Constitution had the character of a treaty is possibly one of the reasons why it did not (and does not) indicate in which organ sovereignty is vested. Dutch constitutional theory is extraordinarily reticent about this matter, which is understandable, considering that at least one-third of the present parliament rejects the monarchy for reasons of principle. The fact that nevertheless nearly everyone supports the monarchy on practical grounds is a completely different matter; this practical support is entirely the result of the circumstance that the Dutch royalty is still in the hands of the Orange-Nassau family. Should the line of the family run out (which is highly unlikely in view of the present size of the royal family), a powerful republican movement would immediately manifest itself.

The second influence was the French occupation during 1795–1813, in which period the Netherlands became acquainted with the benefits of a unitary state. Thus, in accordance with the Constitution of 1815, the Netherlands became a unitary state with all the consequent advantages in administration, law, finance and economics.

The third influence was the union of the North and South Netherlands, as imposed by the Congress of Vienna; that is, the union of the former Republic of the Seven Provinces and the former Austrian Netherlands. For various reasons, the constitutional and political culture of the South (later Belgium) was more sophisticated than that of the North. The South had been much more influenced by French ideas: interest in a parliamentary system as well as in liberal fundamental rights was much greater in that part of the country. Whatever thoughts and opinions were rejected by the North on account of their foreign (French) origin were accepted without much resistance by the predominantly French-speaking southerners. On the other hand, Belgian influence also resulted in a reinforcement of the aristocratic and feudal element. The South, which had belonged to the Spanish or the Austrian Crown for centuries, had an extensive nobility; in the originally republican North, there was hardly any nobility. It was essentially under the influence of the

Belgian nobility that the new Constitution introduced the bicameral system; in addition to the indirectly elected Second Chamber (comparable to the British House of Commons), the First Chamber (comparable to the House of Lords) was chosen, consisting of members who were appointed for life by the King, and was intended as a bulwark in defence of the Crown.

The strong Belgian influence on the Dutch constitution (which was issued in both a Dutch and a French version and ordered Parliament to meet in The Hague and Brussels alternately) can be demonstrated from a comparison of the Constitution of 1815 and that of 1814, which was designed solely by Northerners but was no longer operative from the moment at which the union of the North and the South was decided on in Vienna. In contrast with the Constitution of 1815, this northern Dutch Constitution did not contain any provisions concerning, for instance, the bicameral system, the separation of Church and State, the right of free assembly and public meeting, or the publicity of parliamentary meetings. However, the Belgian influence could not prevent the Constitution of 1815 from giving shape to the personal rule of the King. Also, with the help of the States-General, legislation remained of little importance; by right of his executive power, the King dealt with many affairs of a legislative nature, supported by docile ministers, who only held meetings presided over by the King, and who fulfilled an official rather than a political function. Whereas the establishment of ministerial responsibility was already well on its way in France, and often proposed by the Belgian parliamentarians,[2] it was put off for more than thirty years in the Netherlands.

1848

After the separation of Belgium, which, in 1831, established a Constitution to be envied by the progressive-liberals of the (North-) Netherlands, attempts at innovation proved in vain. The great breakthrough took place in 1848, following the February Revolution, which, in his own words, turned King William II 'from a conservative into a liberal overnight'. The liberal reformers gained ample opportunity to make up rapidly for Dutch constitutional arrears. The revision of the Constitution yielded a radical shift of power towards the liberal bourgeoisie through the introduction of ministerial responsibilty, direct election of the Second Chamber, and the rights of amendment and inquiry. The First Chamber continued to exist but was from now on to be chosen by the members of the provincial representative organs. The elections of the two chambers took place partially (for the Second Chamber: one half of the membership every two years). Naturally, a wider suffrage

was introduced as well as a constituency voting system, according
to which candidates were eligible by winning an absolute majority.
The maintenance of the First Chamber was clearly a compensation
to the conservative powers, who, however, continued to interpret
it themselves as 'a bulwark of the Crown' and 'a protection against
the folly of the day'. The introduction of the royal right of dissolution,
presented as an important extension of the King's power, can also
be regarded as a compensatory gesture towards the conservative
powers. The constitutional history contains some ironic moments:
the right of dissolution was introduced in the Netherlands on practically the same day as that on which the French Constitution discarded this right on the ground that dissolution of a sovereign
people's representatives was to be considered as an act of high treason.

The changes in 1848 were on the whole a distinct break with
the past and put an end to the personal rule of the King through
the introduction of the cabinet system and ministerial responsibility.
Yet, it would still be another twenty years before a virtually parliamentary system, in the sense of a relationship of confidence between
government and parliament, took shape. Due to internal disagreement amongst the liberal majority in parliament, there continued
to be royal cabinets from time to time, and as early as 1868, after
a sensational dissolution of Parliament and an election result which
put the King and his ministers in the wrong, it became clear that
in the case of a conflict between government and Parliament, the
latter would have the better of it.

The events of 1868, are generally seen as the final establishment
of the 'rule of confidence', although this was never inserted in the
written Constitution. The lasting, more or less 'conventional'
character of the rule can be seen as an illustrative expression of
the undecided question of ultimate sovereignty.

1887

The primacy of Parliament thus established offered room for an
intra-parliamentary discussion instead of a discussion between representatives and King. In the 1880s there came new distinct alignments within parliament, which, however, were severely hindered
by the limited suffrage which meant that parliament never reflected
the actual electoral proportions in the country. The constitutional
reform of 1887 finally included the introduction of integral elections
to the Second Chamber (once every four years), which strongly
encouraged the alignment of political parties. The elections became
a national and political touchstone on which the continuation or
discontinuation of cabinets became dependent. Other essential
elements of this constitutional reform included a serious restriction

of the King's legislative power, a wide extension of the suffrage, and the introduction of a constitutional article concerning education, which would present quite a few difficulties of interpretation in the years to come, but would finally allow for the co-existence of public and private education. In the course of the following decades, the conflict about the interpretation and application of this article, which lasted for years on end, would turn out to be one of the most important elements in the determination of the structure of the Dutch political families. In particular, the formation of the Christian-Democratic alignment took place predominantly in connection with the 'matter of education', the Dutch variant of the German 'Kulturkampf'. The change in political relations in 1887 became particularly clear from the falling into disuse of the parliamentary right of inquiry. In the period when Parliament regarded the government as its chief opponent, this right had often been utilised; however, by the time that Parliament (more precisely, the parliamentary majority) had gained a certain preponderance over the government, this right fell abruptly into desuetude. If a parliament has the daily opportunity of controlling the government, the exertion of special powers is no longer necessary; attempts on the part of the opposition (the minority) to re-introduce this weapon from time to time have been (categorically) rejected by the majority.[3]

In the parliamentary history of the Netherlands, the period after 1887 has often been described as 'la belle époque' of the parliamentary system. The two-ballot electoral system forced related parties to co-operate (in the interval between the first and the second round of the elections) and created two political coalitions in Parliament: the Christian coalition and the co-operative union of the Liberal and early-Socialist groupings. In the terminology of that time, the Christian block was referred to as 'right-wing' and the other as 'left-wing'. For a quarter of a century, the political pendulum swung quite regularly from left to right alternately, but the movement ceased when, after a number of extensions of the suffrage, the left wing managed to attain a majority in parliament, but failed to co-operate in harmony. In 1913, a conflict between the Liberals and Socialists was revealed and it has never been healed. This conflict led to a dominant position for the Christian Democrats, who have continuously governed the country either alone or in coalition since 1918, and have given the Netherlands a social, economic and cultural infrastructure which differs considerably from that of the surrounding countries. The Netherlands is one of the very few countries in Western Europe in which the Socialists have never formed a single-party government of their own. Since the introduction of universal suffrage (in 1918), the Netherlands has had three Socialist

Prime Ministers (who ruled for a total of fifteen years), thirteen Christian Democratic Prime Ministers (with a total of fifty-three years of government), and not a single Liberal Prime Minister.[4] Nor has there ever been a coalition cabinet in which the Socialists formed the majority.

1917

The constitutional revision of 1917 (the first after that of 1887) can be compared to that of 1848. Just as in 1848 shape was given to the parliamentary system, in 1917 a political democracy was formed according to principles which have not lost their validity. The most important principle is probably not so much the introduction of universal suffrage for men and women (because, for years, both left- and right-wing politicians had considered this as an inevitable and natural final stage of the many extensions of the property-based suffrage), but rather the introduction of proportional representation with its strong emphasis on party lists. The decision to turn to proportional representation was not solely the result of a desire for arithmetical justice.[5] For at least two political parties there were essential advantages connected with it. Since the support of the various confessional parties is rather unevenly distributed over the Netherlands (most Roman Catholics in the South, most Protestants in the North), the Protestant and Catholic parties experienced serious disadvantages in the system of absolute majorities. The numerical superiority of the Catholic electorate in the south of the country (Limburg and North Brabant) was so strong that the other parties refrained from nominating opposing candidates. The political managers of the Confessional parties were right in relying on the expectation that the introduction of proportional representation would put a sudden end to the distorted picture caused by the constituency voting system. What was expected became reality. At the first elections held under the system of proportional representation, the Confessional parties gained a collective majority which they managed to keep until the election of 1967. The Liberals knew that their position was seriously threatened by the abolition of the property-based suffrage, for the frequent reductions of the qualification had continually weakened their parliamentary position. The introduction of universal suffrage combined with the system of absolute majorities would lead to their elimination from Parliament. A combination of universal suffrage and proportional representation would indeed weaken their position, but not destroy it. This expectation became reality too: at the first elections held under the system of proportional representation, the total of Liberals returned fell from 39 to 19 (out of the 100 seats in the Second

Chamber). For the Socialists too, the introduction of proportional representation would yield some advantages, though their main interest lay of course in universal suffrage.

Apart from these strategic considerations, there were definitely some institutional interests for the parties concerned as well. It is true that the system of proportional representation encourages the rise of small parties and hardly allows for the existence of majority parties, but it also stimulates party centralisation.[6] This is the result in particular of the method of nomination and the binding force of the election programme. Since the order of the list of candidates is generally determined by the party (the party conference, the party committee, or a special board), the foundation of the prospective representative's power lies inside the party, and not outside it; this is also the case if regional party organisations take part in the nomination. Deviant behaviour on the part of a candidate is rapidly punished by putting him in an ineligible position on the list. Loyal behaviour is rewarded. The most important touchstone for the judgment of behaviour is the election programme, which, consequently, soon becomes an essential element both for the representative in parliament and for the party as a whole. Deviant behaviour on the part of junior representatives is also prevented in the Netherlands by the fact that the electoral law discourages preference votes, and because some parties are familiar with the internal prescription of the party that elected candidates are not allowed to accept their mandates themselves, but are obliged to have this done by the party committee. The candidate who has already been elected but happens to fall into disgrace with the party committee may therefore run the risk of not becoming a member of the Second Chamber after all.

Proportional representation offers an opportunity to political parties of accentuating their character, so increasing the differences between them. Since there have to be negotiations after the elections in order to create a more or less artificial parliamentary majority and because these negotiations are naturally conducted by the party leadership, the latter gets a firmer hold of the party. Moreover, since the majority is an artificial one, created merely to produce a coalition cabinet for a limited period, negotiations are necessary after every election. The possibility that the coalition partners might maintain their majority makes no difference. Even if the coalition succeeds in maintaining its majority, the internal relations within that majority will have altered.

Such negotiations as have been conducted in the Netherlands since 1917 have had a consequence which tends to be ignored. If the negotiations are successful, they lead to the acceptance of a 'package deal', which consists in part of compromises, meaning that the participating parties get only part of what they had bargained for – a situation comparable to that of a sales market, where the parties agree on a final sales price which lies somewhere between the supply and the demand price. The package deal also contains a series of agreements in which a demand of one of the two parties is expressly met in its entirety; the price to paid by this party is to agree on and comply with a demand of the opposing party. Obviously, in this process of negotiation not all wishes of the parties involved are satisfied, but those that are, are always met entirely, that is, not partially.

The consequence of all this is that for a number of options of policy, which would be unlikely to get the support of an electoral majority, parliamentary majorities are created artificially, thus enabling even parties which are in a permanent minority to play a major part. It is obvious that the Christian Democrats, who were prepared and in a position to negotiate with the Liberals and the Socialists, would have the greatest success in realising these desires; the fact that the Dutch social infrastructure has a strongly Christian Democratic character is a major result. This process by which minority parties mutually support each other has caused the typically Dutch denominational segregation or 'pillarisation'. In addition, it has led practically all the political parties in the Netherlands to be opposed to every form of direct democracy, such as, for instance, the referendum and the election by popular vote of executive government functionaries. Dutch democracy is an outstanding example of an exclusively representative democracy; it is one of the few democracies in the world in which there has never been a plebiscite on a national level; it is the only democracy in which burgomasters and provincial governors are not appointed by the electorate, but by the central government. A telling example is the appointment of the burgomasters of the four largest cities of the Netherlands (Amsterdam, Rotterdam, The Hague and Utrecht). Though the Labour Party is by far the largest in all these four cities, and with the support of radical left-wing groupings and the Communists would definitely have a majority, it is an unwritten law that the Labour Party is allowed to occupy only two of the four burgomaster's offices (Amsterdam and Rotterdam), that the Christian Democrats provide the burgomaster of The Hague, and the Liberals that of Utrecht. This distribution is fixed and remains unaltered even if the coalition government changes.

To return to the main aspect of the constitutional revision of 1917, the introduction of political democracy led to a proportional distribution of power among heavily centralised party organisations and the exclusion of every form of direct democracy. This of course had consequences for the functioning of the government as well as Parliament. If the number of political parties is great and, in addition, differences of opinion are numerous, Parliament will have little influence and the power of the government will depend primarily on the personal prestige of ministers.

In proportion as the number of parties is smaller and mutual differences decrease, Parliament gains more influence. However, if the chief members of the Second Chamber give up their seats in order to become ministers (as is usual in the Netherlands because the offices of people's representative and minister are incompatible), Parliament becomes more and more populated by backbenchers, who view their membership essentially as a stage in their career structure.

In the past half century the Netherlands has gone through both situations. Until the Second World War the first situation prevailed (a large number of parties and little agreement); after that, the second situation gradually became prevalent (a smaller number of parties, less discord, some loss of parliament's quality). The more recent discussions about the revision of the Constitution have ensued from a dissatisfaction with both the first and the second situation.

Post-war attempts at innovation

During the Second World War, the experiences of the 1920s and 1930s stimulated many thoughts about innovation, which were generally intended to decrease political discord and to consolidate the government's position. Feelings of solidarity inspired the formation of new and larger parties and an extension of the political role of the royal Head of State. However, the reality of post-war politics did not offer any opportunity for the realisation of these two ideas. Attempts to break the pre-war political relationships failed when the parties which existed before the war rose again very quickly and comparatively prosperously. The only result was a few name-changes. In addition, the reborn pre-war parties resisted a strengthening of the government's position, or rather that of the Head of State. During her stay in London Queen Wilhelmina had indeed become the 'Mother of the Fatherland' (just as William the Silent had been nicknamed 'Father of the Fatherland' three centuries before, also in a period of national distress), but once back on her native soil, she found that what had been preserved for her was hardly more than a symbolic function.

Yet, the Constitution had to be revised – though not with a view to political renewal. The conferment of independence on Indonesia and, somewhat later, the constitutional emancipation of the former colonies in the West Indies, brought a number of constitutional changes requiring much political energy, and even forced the Socialists and the Liberals at a certain moment to a (malfunctioning) coalition government, but did not yield any substantial reforms. The advice of a revision committee set up in 1950 was reverently received but quickly filed away in the drawers of government desks. Only two of the proposals were realised: first, the proposal to increase the membership of both chambers of the States-General (in the case of the Second Chamber from 100 to 150, and in the case of the First Chamber from 50 to 75): second, the proposal to reinforce the function of international treaties in the Dutch legislature. The second proposal in particular was and still is of some importance; it has had the result that provisions of international treaties, in so far as they are of direct influence on the position of individual citizens, no longer have to be translated (transformed) into the Dutch national legislature, but are immediately valid.[7] Furthermore, these provisions are given priority over Dutch justice, including the Constitution. As far as is known, there is no other country which has allowed such an intrusion of international law into its national legislature.

In the 1950s the pre-war complaint about political dissension and the relatively weak position of the government appeared no longer relevant. Though the formation of governments was still a laborious and mysterious process, the coalitions nevertheless proved capable of effective government. The need to rebuild the country, to repair the ruins of the war as well as the disastrous floods of 1953, required co-operation, which relegated discord to the background. The attempts at renewal did not become current again until the 1960s with, on the one hand, rapidly rising prosperity, and on the other, a growing desire for emancipation and democratisation. Constitutional changes and revisions suddenly became major issues in the late 1960s and brought about the formation of several new progressive parties,[8] causing the government to set up a broadly based revision committee (which became known under the name 'Cals-Donner Royal Commission', after the two chairmen). The several interim reports of this committee as well as their final report (published in 1971)[9] have largely determined recent constitutional discussion in the Netherlands. The committee discussed and proposed a number of drastic reforms but the final result (the constitutional revision of 1983) was a poor one and regarded by many as a failure. The revision, unlike those of 1848 and 1917, did not essentially alter the constitutional[10] and political infrastructure, but merely adapted parts of it.

The revision of 1983
The main changes in the constitutional revision of 1983 were as follows:

(i)   Terminological adaptations and a different arrangement. From
        an editorial point of view, there is hardly any correspondence
        between the old and the new text. In many articles the new
        text reads 'Government' where the old text employed the nine-
        teenth-century concept 'King'. Also by means of the new
        arrangement, more justice is done to the constitutional reality.
        There is, for instance, a separate chapter on 'Fundamental
        Rights' (which was lacking in the old version) as well as a
        separate chapter on 'Government', in which the existence of
        the Prime Minister is recognised for the first time. Further-
        more, the new text is markedly shorter than the old one (142
        articles versus 215), since many outdated regulations have been
        cancelled.

(ii)   Introduction of a great number of social fundamental rights
        and extension of the political fundamental rights already extant
        in the old text. The new text begins with an article prohibiting
        discrimination on grounds of religion, philosophy of life, po-
        litical convictions, race, sex, or 'on any other ground'. The
        social fundamental rights relate to such matters as the advance-
        ment of employment, social security and the spread of welfare,
        protection of the environment, public health, housing accom-
        modation, and social and cultural development.

(iii)   The introduction of a new article, reading: 'Capital punish-
        ment cannot be imposed'.

(iv)   Constitutional confirmation of the previously introduced office
        of Parliamentary Commissioner (Ombudsman).

(v)   Conferment of suffrage for municipal elections on inhabitants
        of foreign nationality.

(vi)   A different voting system for the First Chamber. The partial
        election (the election of half the membership every three years)
        is replaced by integral election (once every four years). The
        method of indirect election (by members of the provincial
        representative organs) is maintained.

(vii)   Extension of the compatibility of the offices of minister and
        member of the Second Chamber. The old text prohibited
        combination of the two offices for a period of longer than
        three months, the period generally needed for the formation
        of a government. Should the formation take more than three
        months, those ministers who had also been elected members
        of the Second Chamber were faced with a hard choice, which
        was usually made in favour of the office of minister. The
        problem of this choice no longer exists, for the combination
        of the two offices is now allowed for the whole period required
        to form a government. This change is a concession towards

the practice of long-term formation of governments, and offers more political elbow-room to the leading politicians.

Though these changes are certainly not insignificant – I shall go into their meaning later – the reforms proposed by the commission as well as by others, but which never materialised, were of far greater importance. The most important were:

(i)   Modification of the system of proportional representation by means of the introduction of a constituency proportional representation voting system.
(ii) Direct election of the Prime Minister, or premier-designate.
(iii) Direct election of the burgomaster.
(iv) Introduction of a system of judicial review.
(v)   Introduction of the referendum to give the electorate the opportunity to veto bills which have been already passed by the two chambers.
(vi) Provision for setting up a parliamentary inquiry if the request for it is supported by a minority in each of the two chambers. (According to the present Constitution, an inquiry is only possible if a majority agrees to it.)

It is not difficult to point out the differences between what was and was not achieved as well as the significance of those differences. First of all, the editorial innovation and the cataloguing of the social and political fundamental rights. Actually, both these changes are merely of cosmetic importance; what is now for the first time put into words in the Constitution already existed for a long time in actual practice and/or in the legislature. The constitutional shape of the office of Parliamentary Commissioner is nothing more than a codification of a previously established (though not very successful) office.

More important is the conferment of suffrage on foreigners. Foreign voters (particularly Turks, Moroccans, Surinamese and South Moluccans) made use of this right for the first time in 1986. The poll exceeded 60 per cent, which is little less than that of the Dutch electorate. The foreigners showed no inclination to set up their own ethnic parties, but tended mainly to vote for the Labour party or the Christian Democrats, parties which had put foreign candidates in eligible positions. (It may cause some surprise that a Christian Democratic party also accepts Muslim candidates – an illustration perhaps of the relatively high degree of Dutch tolerance.)

The different electoral system for the First Chamber – which consists of part-time politicians – presumably makes this institution somewhat more important than it used to be. As a result of the abolition of partial elections, this chamber also becomes a reflection of prevailing electoral opinion. Immediately after its election the First Chamber is even more 'topical' than the Second Chamber, which increases its self-confidence. Friction between the two chambers thus becomes more likely.

Virtually all the rejected proposals have something in common (certainly i to v): their realisation would increase the influence of that part of the electorate which is not committed to a political party, and would weaken the established political parties. With a constituency voting system and direct election of the Prime Minister or premier-designate (both proposals have always been presented in combination), this would certainly be the case. A constituency system of proportional representation would diminish the power of the central party organs: a directly elected Prime Minister/premier-designate would have his own electoral legitimacy, which would make him more independent of his party than the Prime Minister is at present. He will be chosen on his own platform, which, in order to obtain more electoral support will occasionally deviate substantially from the programme of the party he belongs to. This proposal failed mainly on the question of whether Parliament should maintain the right to dismiss an elected Prime Minister or premier-designate and whether in case of the exercise of that right, Parliament itself should be dissolved and re-elected. The advocates of the proposal generally answered these questions in the affirmative. The Royal Commission proposed a modified form of the original proposal (the Prime-Minister/premier-designate would only be elected if he obtained an absolute majority in one round), but even this was unacceptable to the majority of the Second Chamber.   The same can be said about the election of the burgomaster: direct election would have weakened the hold of the political parties. The rejection of the two proposals is presumably connected with this aspect – though it must be said that direct election of a burgomaster would also imply a drastic revision of the division of authority between central and local authorities. A burgomaster appointed by the government has a number of powers (among which is the maintenance of public order) which a locally elected burgomaster would probably not be able to exercise.[11]

Roughly the same can be said about the issue of judicial review. The possibility of the judiciary pronouncing legislation invalid because it is in conflict with the Constitution necessarily implies loss of power on the part of the legislator – and thus of the political establishment. One of the arguments used for the rejection of the proposal was that its acceptance would lead to the politicisation of the judiciary. But this is somewhat hypocritical since even at present the political colour of candidates occasionally plays a part in the assignment of important judicial functions. The electoral veto of bills through the referendum also implies a loss of power for the legislator. The parties' traditional aversion to direct public influence, as well as the arguments for the primacy of the representative system, meant that this proposal did not stand a chance.

The only exception in this series of proposals is in fact the right of inquiry for minorities. By means of this right (which exists in Germany and is used occasionally), the position of the parliamentary minority was intended to be consolidated. What was remarkable was that practically the entire Second Chamber was in favour of the proposal, but that the First Chamber voted against it.

Current constitutional issues

The preliminary conclusion of this survey is that the prevailing political order has warded off the attempts at change rather successfully. Does this mean that the entire constitutional discussion is now a matter of the past? Are there political forces which will continue to keep constitutional issues under discussions?

(a) Of a number of proposed reforms it can be said that even though they have been rejected, the problems they were intended to solve have not disappeared; they may even become more significant. This is especially the case with respect to the position of the Prime Minister, the formation of government, and the relationship between government and Parliament.

As a result of a number of developments in the past ten to fifteen years, the function of the Prime Minister has become increasingly more important. Though constitutionally he is merely the chairman of the Council of Ministers and as such does not have more influence than his colleagues, his function has become extended to that of head of the government, comparable to the German 'Bundeskanzler' and the British Prime Minister. In the European Community's European Council he acts as their equal, which has provided him with a tactical and psychological preponderance over the Minister for Foreign Affairs and, in a sense, over the Ministers of Finance, Economic Affairs and Social Affairs. In the opinion of the Dutch public he is without question the head of the government. After every weekly meeting of the Council of Ministers (on Fridays), he appears on television as the sole spokesman of the government and as defender of the government's policy. Furthermore, it has become increasingly customary for Parliament to call to account first the Prime Minister, even when dealing with issues which fall primarily under the responsibility of a particular departmental minister.

The enhanced role of the Prime Minister has caused him to be in effect leader of his party, although the Dutch constitution prescribes that he is not allowed to be a member of parliament at the same time. It is therefore inevitable that the parliamentary representation of his party is led by someone with considerably less prestige, which means that parliament as a whole suffers a certain loss. A comparable phenomenon incidentally presents itself in the other party (-ies) of the coalition. The most prominent figure of such a party becomes vice-premier. Therefore, the parliamentary section of the other coalition party is also led by a second-rate politician.[12] Thus the leading politicians disappear from parliament after the elections in order to become ministers; in parliament they are replaced by politicians of second-rate quality who were not able or allowed to become ministers. As a further result, the Dutch Parliament has become a mere staging-post. Being a member of parliament is the initial stage of one's career, not the final stage. A former minister hardly ever returns to parliament; he becomes the burgomaster of one of the big cities, or a provincial governor, or a member of the State Council or he accepts a position in a business firm.

Research has shown that the rate at which members of the Second Chamber leave parliament after a relatively short period is higher in the Netherlands than in any other Western democracy, and comparable to the rate of departure of members of parliament in countries of the Third World.[13] The dominant position of the Prime Minister (and to a lesser extent that of the government as a whole) is hardly compatible with the presuppositions of proportional representation. The main presupposition of proportional representation in the Netherlands, is that the voters vote for party lists and decide on their votes by means of party programmes. In proportion as the electorate begins to vote more and more for persons instead of parties and political principles, there comes to be a lack of balance. The parliamentary elections turn in fact into elections of a head of government; the political composition of parliament becomes more and more a matter of secondary importance.

However, the so-called 'governmental' elections do not provide a clear answer; this is a result of the second presupposition of proportional representation, namely that a proportionally composed parliament ought to lead to a likewise proportionally composed government. This is a purely theoretical presupposition, however, and unacceptable to the political culture of the modern Netherlands. In general, the so-called 'governmental elections' are without results. The consequence of this is that the prospective Prime Minister has to acquire his position by way of complicated long-term negotiations, so as to secure a parliamentary majority. The elections do not give the future Prime Minister a great deal of legitimacy; he reinforces his legitimacy at the expense of parliament (of which he, in his newly acquired position of Prime Minister, is no longer a member). The argument that in the Westminster model the Prime Minister is also in control of the parliamentary majority is not very convincing. In the first place, the British Prime Minister is a member of parliament. But, more important, the Westminster model offers the possibility of an alternative government, a possibility virtually lacking in the Netherlands. In the Netherlands there is an ever growing awareness that the strong emphasis put on the role of the Prime Minister seriously impairs the power of parliament. In parliamentary elections an attempt is made to choose a Prime Minister, but because this attempt is never entirely successful, the second part of the process takes place at the expense of parliament.

The awareness that something is wrong here led in 1982 – during the parliamentary discussion of revision of the Constitution – to the establishment of a Royal Commission to advise on this problem. The Commission proposed[14] that every newly elected parliament should choose a premier-designate by a majority of votes and release the Queen from appointing this functionary. In this way the Commission hoped to strip the negotiations on the formation of a new government of their mysterious aspects and to increase their public and parliamentary character. Although the Commission, composed of representatives of all the leading political parties, had reached this advice almost unanimously, the proposal was largely ignored, to the intense annoyance of the Commission and, particularly, its chairman, former Prime Minister Biesheuvel.

The Commission's proposal did not offer a total solution of the tension between the principle of parliamentary elections on the one hand, and the appointment of a Prime Minister on the other. It was pre-eminently focused on political feasibility and was merely intended to remove some of the objectionable aspects. The fact that it was nevertheless almost completely ignored without much specific explanation caused some discord, but this soon died away. However, the problem itself is unlikely to disappear

The issue of judicial review has not lost its topicality either. The reason for this is the NATO decision to modernise nuclear weapons in Western Europe which has, as far as the Netherlands is concerned, been elaborated into an agreement between the Netherlands and the United States. On the basis of this agreement – which has the validity of a treaty for the Dutch contractual partner – the American President is authorised to launch cruise missiles from Dutch territory. During the parliamentary discussion of the treaty, the inevitable question arose to what extent the American President's authority could be combined with the sovereignty of the Netherlands, as formulated in the Constitution. According to the Constitution, the answer to this question must be given by the legislature, which has to approve the Dutch-American treaty. The majority of both chambers considered the content of the treaty to be in line with the Constitution. But during the extensive parliamentary discussion of the issue, many realised that there was a somewhat unfortunate blend of interpretation of the Constitution with political judgment. A negative answer to the question of compatibility would not only have brought about the rejection of the treaty, but also a cabinet crisis and new elections. Consequently, the political pressure was extraordinarily high; in interpreting the Constitution, parliament also had to take into account the interests of the coalition. The issue of judicial review, which had not received much public attention so far, became quite suddenly very topical. From that moment on, the issue has come to be discussed more and more within the political parties.

Interest in the idea of the referendum shows a similar development. In its final report (published in 1985), the above-mentioned Royal Commission under the leadership of Biesheuvel firmly and unanimously pleaded for the legislative veto referendum (the possibility of rejection by popular vote of bills already accepted by parliament as in Italy). The Commission's primary intention was to increase the legitimacy of legislation. Because of the nature of coalition negotiations, it is not unusual in the Netherlands for laws to materialise which have indeed been accepted by a parliamentary majority, but which may not always be, and sometimes are quite unlikely to be, acceptable to the majority of the population. Shortly before the Commission reported, the leader of the smallest government party had declared that this party had voted for a significant and highly controversial Bill, merely because this had been agreed upon at the government formation stage. In a free vote, his party would have rejected the Bill.[15] Just like the proposal concerning the formation of governments, the (extensively elaborated and motivated) suggestion on the issue of referendums by the Biesheuvel Commission was largely neglected by government and parliament alike. The obvious counterargument was that the introduction of the referendum would impair the representative system. Meanwhile, many analysts have pointed out that the referendum as such does not impair the system of representation, but that it compels the representatives to pay more attention to extra-parliamentary opinion, thus limiting the elbow-room of the representatives *within* parliament. But this should not be confused with the room for manoeuvre of parliament itself.

The discussion about the possibility of referendums is still current. The Labour Party and two of the smaller parties (D'66 and PPR) have included the issue in their party programme; within other parties, advocates raise their voices from time to time.[16] The possibility of local referendums (also proposed by the Commission) receives increasing attention. The remarkable thing about the discussion of the referendum is that it is not confined to the traditional political and constitutional environment. Many other socially committed groups also appear interested in it; the view that the referendum is mainly a tool employed by dictatorial regimes, or that it is a means of allowing 'backward' Swiss farmers to prevent female suffrage, is disappearing. The introduction of the referendum in the Netherlands seems to be essentially a question of time.

(b) The new Constitution has also given rise to two new constitutional problems: (i) the relationship between the Second and the First Chamber; (ii) suffrage for foreigners.

As regards (i): In the relationship between the two chambers of the States General, the Second Chamber, that is, the directly elected chamber, has traditionally enjoyed a dominant position. Apart from the right of parliamentary inquiry, which it has never used, the First Chamber is entitled to the right of veto on legislation. Primarily because the partial elections provided the First Chamber with only a weak legitimacy, it hardly ever used this right. The integral elections (which were introduced in the constitutional reform of 1983) provide the First Chamber with a composition which is by no means inferior to that of the Second Chamber with respect to its topicality. Since Dutch coalition governments tend to be supported by majorities which becomes increasingly smaller in size, it is by no means unthinkable that the elections to the First Chamber will yield a majority of votes for those parties that occupy a minority of seats in the Second Chamber. In view of current developments, the reticent role of the First Chamber will soon come to an end; important bills, accepted by the Second Chamber, will be thrown out by the First Chamber. Whether the First Chamber will ever dismiss a cabinet remains to be seen, but even if that does not happen, an extremely difficult situation could arise. Dissolution of the First Chamber will be of no avail, for the voters of the First Chamber (the members of the provincial representative organs) will undoubtedly choose a new chamber with exactly the same political composition as that of the previous one. In bicameral systems the problem is not a new or unfamiliar one, but it will become rather acute in the Netherlands, because the composition of the chamber cannot be altered rapidly and because the legislative right of veto applies to all those matters to be settled by the law (it is thus different from the German Bundesrat, for the authorities of the latter organ are slightly more limited in this respect). It is not clear when the problem of the different compositions of the two houses will arise: that it will arise sooner or later is beyond all doubt.

It may be wondered why this problem was not prevented in the revision of 1983. It was in fact largely neglected as well as underestimated. The most obvious solution (direct election of the First Chamber) was unacceptable to the Second Chamber, because it would reduce the latter's status. It goes without saying that the problem is mostly raised by the opposition; the attitude of the government and of the parties represented in the government is one of 'wait and see'.

As regards (ii): The conferment of the municipal vote on residents of foreign nationality (in the constitutional revision of 1983) implies a partial abandoning of the nationality principle as well as a partial introduction of the territorial principle. The argument for giving up the one principle in favour of the other at municipal elections especially, was that the position of foreigners is especially influenced by municipal policy. But, on second thoughts, this argument does not appear very convincing; the foreign vote is indeed heavily concentrated in a limited number of large municipalities, but, nevertheless, its position is mainly dependent on government policy. The quality of accommodation, employment, education (to mention a few examples) depends on the policy of the central government, not on that of the municipal council.

Immediately after the first elections in which foreigners participated (March 1986), this argument was put forward, particularly by left-wing parties (which happen to attract most of the foreign votes). Since the argument is in fact irrefutable, there is a fair chance of the extension of the suffrage of foreigners. However, there are some problems, such as, for instance, the question of compulsory military service. Does a total acceptance of the territorial principle also imply the introduction of compulsory military service for foreigners in the Netherlands? Is it acceptable to impose compulsory military service on foreigners with the risk that they lose their nationality and acquire the status of 'displaced' persons? Should the government exempt foreigners from military service and thus create different kinds of voters? An additional complication is that conferment of complete suffrage is only possible by means of a constitutional reform, which has to be accepted by a two-thirds majority of each chamber. It will be a long time before the parliamentary support has reached the required size.

Conclusion
The conclusion of the foregoing may well be that post-war attempts at renewal have predominantly failed, but that many old problems

retain their relevance while a number of new problems have arisen. The Dutch constitutional order still largely reflects the 'Pacificatie' of 1917, when the three main political movements gave shape to the Constitution and, consequently, created the typically Dutch system of political and social denominational segregation – pillarisation or *Verzuiling*: pacification by means of a proportional distribution of power. The increasing polarisation of the political parties and a growing tendency to vote for persons rather than parties reveal the flaws in the system, but it has not yet broken down. Should the system really break down (for instance, owing to an unexpected conflict between the two chambers), the failure may prove to be a catalyst for more fundamental changes, because, at that moment, it is the credibility of the system that will be put under discussion. Although the Constitution is still by and large respected, and liberal constitutionalism is still a strongly held value, it has become part of a rapidly changing political culture. Until the 1960s the pluralistic political system had time and again allowed the rise of formal oppositions without violent reversals of the constitutional order. Almost never did any political group have a strong and convincing reason to advocate a major change of the constitutional order. *Homines novi* made their way at the local level and in the various parts of the 'pillarised' society, until they became part of the collective leadership of national political society.

But in the 1960s, with the first post-war generation coming to adulthood, the pillars lost a great deal of their support. The floating vote became a structural element in Dutch politics; a number of 'pillarised' organisations lost membership and money; they claimed government subsidies and became more or less part of the governmental bureaucracy. Government spending as a percentage of gross national income, in 1950 still one of the lowest in Western Europe, rose to 70 per cent in the 1980s (higher than in any other Western European country). A substantial part of this amount was spent via 'pillarised' organisations, related to the governmental bureaucracy. The dangers of this situation are becoming visible: budget reductions tend to hit subsidised organisations more than governmental departments. Moreover, budget cuts tend to go hand in hand with more (instead of less) regulations.[17]

Pillarisation, for more than seventy years one of the most integrative elements of Dutch political, economic, social and cultural society, is thus losing its *raison d'être* and its basis. This kind of pillarisation can be counterproductive, just as pillars without foundations can be harmful.

All the post-war attempts to modernise the constitution came perhaps too early in a society still convinced that the values of pillarisation would last forever. This conviction is melting away gradually, creating a more dynamic situation. Anyone who asserts that the Dutch constitutional reform has failed is probably stating a very temporary fact.

Notes and references

1. P.J. Oud, *Het constitutionele recht van het Koninkrijk der Nederlanden I* (Tjeenk Willink, Zwolle, 1947), p. 7.
2. R. Kranenburg, *Het Nederlandsch Staatsrecht I*, 3rd edn (Tjeenk Willink, Haarlem, 1928), p. 61.
3. Recently the Dutch Parliament showed more interest in the parliamentary inquiry. In 1984–85 an inquiry was held into the spending of huge government subsidies by the Rotterdam Shipbuilding Company RSV. The outcome was rather negative for the Minister of Economic Affairs but had no political consequences. In 1986 Parliament started preparations for an investigation into investment by the Government Pension Fund. Both inquiries were mainly the result of outside pressures on Parliament, in 1984 exerted by former RSV-workers and in 1986 in relation to the prosecution of Pension Fund management.
4. Catholic Prime Ministers:
   Ruys de Beerenbrouck 1918–25 and 1929–33
   Beel 1946–48 and 1958–59
   De Quay 1959–63
   Marijnen 1963–65
   Cals 1965–66
   De Jong 1967–71
   Van Agt 1977–82
   Lubbers (CDA) 1982–

   Protestant Prime Minisers:
   Colijn (ARP) 1925–26 and 1933–39
   De Geer (CHU) 1926–29 and 1939–40
   Gerbrandy (ARP) 1940–45 (exile gvt. in London)
   Zijlstra (ARP) 1966–67
   Biesheuvel (ARP) 1971–73

   Socialist Prime Ministers:
   Schermerhorn 1945–46
   Drees 1948–58
   Den Uyl 1973–77
5. See A.M. Donner, 'Iets over kiesstelsels', *Mededelingen Kon. Ned. Akademie van Wetenschappen*, Vol. 30, No. 5, 1969.
6. Arend Lijphart's *The Politics of Accommodation* (Berkeley, 1975) gives a profound analysis of the Dutch political culture since 1917.
7. Art. 93 and 94, Constitution 1983.
8. For various reasons the year 1966 may be considered as a watershed in the development of the Dutch political and constitutional culture.
   (a) In October 1966 the centre-left Cals Government was toppled by a motion of no-confidence introduced by the Catholic Party (KVP). All later cabinet crises (1972, 1977, 1982) were the result not of a parliamentary vote but of internal disharmony within the various coalition governments. The strong relationship between the parliamentary parties and the cabinet members of those parties on the one hand and the general acceptance of the convention 'No cabinet formation without dissolution of parliament and new elections' on the other has so far prevented the use of this final parliamentary weapon.
   (b) The 1966 cabinet crisis stimulated the already existing interest in consti-

tutional and political reform. The 1967 Parliament comprised a new party, Democrats '66 (D'66), with a party programme mainly concentrated on constitutional reform. In 1968 left-wingers of the Catholic Party and the two major Protestant Parties (Anti-Revolutionary Party and Christian Historical Union) founded their own party, PPR (Politieke Partij Radicalen). In 1969 the New Left in the Labour Party (Partij van de Arbeid) gained a substantial number of posts in the party leadership, which in 1970 resulted in the creation of a more right-wing Social-Democratic party DS'70.

PvdA, D'66 and PPR held a majority of portfolios in the Den Uyl Government (1973–77) which proposed a number of constitutional reforms based on the final report of the 1967 Royal Commission; most of these reforms were rejected by a parliamentary majority of Liberals and members of the confessional parties. Attempts to create a Progressive People's Party (a merger of Labour, D'66 and PPR) failed in the course of the 1970s. In 1980 KVP, ARP and CHU merged into the Christian Democratic Appeal, now under the leadership of Prime Minister Ruud Lubbers. During the centre-right governments of Van Agt and Lubbers (1977–) the movement for constitutional reform lost its impetus. D'66 and, to a lesser extent, PvdA, are the strongest supporters of constitutional reform.

The election returns of the main political parties in the last two elections (September 1982 and May 1986) were as follows:

	1982		1986	
	%	Seats	%	Seats
CDA	29	45	35	54
PvdA	30	47	33	52
VVD (Lib.)	23	36	17	27
D'66	4	6	6	9
Others	14	16	9	8
Total	100	150	100	150

9. Final Report of Royal Commission 1967, The Hague, 1971.
10. A.M. Donner, one of the two chairmen of the Royal Commission, wrote an interesting article on the 1983 constitutional reform. See A.M. Donner, 'Tussen het echte en het gemaakte', Zwolle, 1986, pp. 90–103.
11. Interim report of the Royal Commission 1982, *Relatie kiezers-beleidsvorming* (The Hague, 1984), pp. 195–207.
12. J.J. Vis, *Regeerakkoord 1986* (The Hague, 1986), p. 90.
13. P.L. de Vos of Rotterdam University is preparing a study on this subject. Interviewed by one of the leading Dutch weeklies (*Elseviers Magazine*, 8 March 1986), he mentioned a flow rate of 18.5% in the period 1974–83, compared with 13 for Belgium, 8.3 for FRG, 7.4 for UK, 9.9 for USA, 7.1 for Canada.
14. *Final Report of the Royal Commission 1982* (The Hague, 1985).
15. J.J. Vis, 'Regeerakkoord dupeert kiezers', *Namens,* August 1986, p. 251.
16. The referendum, as proposed by the Royal Commission, was recently rejected by the Liberal Party Congress. The Christian Democrats, although not having taken an official stand, are probably not in favour.
17. According to Van Schendelen, The Hague is the number two law-making factory of Europe, only exceeded by Italy. M.P.C.M. van Schendelen, *Over de kwaliteit van de Tweede Kamer* (Rotterdam, 1983), p. 20.

PART E
THE EUROPEAN
COMMUNITY

19 The European Community: The constitution of a 'would-be polity' (1957)
Roger Morgan

In the political life of an established state, constitutional issues have usually played a fairly predictable part. In theory at least, the constitution lays down the framework of rules for the conduct of politics, and political pressures only occasionally threaten the nature of that framework. In times of revolution, to be sure, moulds are broken, but most of the time they adapt flexibly to new circumstances: constitutional issues are rarely at the centre of political life. One of the premises of this book, indeed, is that the present time is unusual in seeing the political life of many countries heavily influenced by constitutional issues. In the politics of the European Community, by contrast, such issues have quite often dominated the agenda. For some of the actors in the politics of the Community, it is true, the matter is simple: the Community is an international organisation of sovereign states which delegate specific powers to central institutions on a pragmatic and strictly circumscribed basis. For others, however the Community is the embryo from which a European polity (often designated by the ambiguous term 'European Union) should, and will, develop; for them, this teleological dimension provides the yardstick for judging its day-to-day political activities. In any case, the perspective differs from that of the political concerns of a state with an established constitution.

The question whether the Community can strictly be said to have a constitution, and even the question whether it ought to have one, is highly contentious. The Community, as a political institution, has been the subject of aspirations and expectations, hopes and fears, of the most diverse kind. Even though many other organisations in the course of history have generated voluminous controversy – the Holy Roman Empire, for instance, the Holy Alliance, the League of Nations, or the institutions of individual states – the Community must hold the record for the greatest *annual* output of speculation, advocacy, denunciation, proposals and counter-proposals for its future direction. Ever since the 1950s, the period between the

Schuman Plan of 1950 and the Rome Treaty of 1957, the debate about the institutional development of the Community has been influenced by arguments – often passionate – about whether it should be more supranational or less, the instrument of a European planned economy or an agent of free competition and deregulation, a military power or something else. Each of these fundamental issues has implications for the Community's institutional structure.[1]

It is in any case clear that the member states of the Community have joined together in something more than a conventional international treaty. The questions of how much more, or what the declared goal of 'European Union' means, or might mean, are matters of continuing debate. The constitutional compromise embodied in the Single European Act of 1986, the latest development in the Community's institutional development, can only be assessed in the light of the long earlier history of constitutional debates which has accompanied the Community's institutions since their origins.

Even those who are sceptical, or hostile, towards the idea that the Community should develop into a political unit, agree that it has developed a new legal order, distinct from those of the member states and in some ways superior to them: by virtue of the Treaty obligations which the member states have undertaken, and the accepted authority of the European Court of Justice in enforcing them, the principles of the supremacy of the Community law over national law, and of the direct effect of Community law on those subject to it, have been generally accepted. This means that, in terms of constitutional law, the 'constitution' of the Community has become part of the constitution of each of the member states. But how far does this give the Community a constitutional standing in its own right? The Treaty of Rome, in contrast, say, to the Constitution of the United States, is quite distinctly an agreement between states, which agreed to pool their sovereignty in strictly limited spheres of public policy (we should never forget that the budget of the European Community, a rough measure of its area of authority, amounts only to 1 per cent of the member states' GDP, or about 2 per cent of their *national* budgets): this is in stark contrast to the US Constitution, which represented a 'compact' between individual *citizens*, and thus allowed for a dynamic growth in the authority of the central institutions, which has no parallel in the European Community.

If we ask how far the Community has been able to develop the constitutional attributes of a 'polity' (which, in the circumstances, could only take the form of a federation), the answer might be as follows: the Community institutions do possess some of these attributes, including certain policy instruments (e.g. authority over agricultural policy, the legal power to try to enforce non-discrimination in general, and the common commercial policy for external trade), but these fall far short of the powers of a 'normal' national government. There is also the Community's command over its 'own resources' in the financial sphere (though these are strictly limited and precisely circumscribed by the power of the member states); there is the independent civil service working for the Commission (though it is clear that in practice the Commission's staff has by now been to a considerable degree dominated, or infiltrated, by the national bureaucracies of the member states); there is the 'federating' role of the European Parliament (though again its powers have been drastically limited by the consensus of member governments); and there is the European Court of Justice, to which many observers have attributed a role similar to that of the US Supreme Court in advancing the cause of integration along federal lines (but which has, in practice, been limited in its scope for action by the need to base its judgments on the interpretations of the existing Community treaties).

Indeed, it is clear that progress towards constitutional integration, which must take place according to the treaties establishing the Community and the inescapable process of inter-governmental bargaining between the member states, has so far left the Community far short of anything that could be called a political entity with a constitution in the accepted sense. This explains why the nature of the Community's institutions, and their future development, have been constant matters of controversy and debate, so that the whole history of the Community has become a continuous seminar in constitutional law.

The fundamental constitutional issues, which have played a part throughout, may be summarised as follows:

- What should be the role of the European Commission, as a notionally supranational representative of the general interest of the Community?
- What powers should belong to the European Parliament (elected indirectly up to 1979, and since then directly)?
- What reforms should be introduced in the status and functioning of the inter-governmental parts of the Community machinery (the Council of Ministers, the Committee of Permanent Representatives or COREPER, and since 1974 the European Council)?
- How should the pursuit of the policy aims already assigned to the Community be related to broader common objectives, such as diplomatic co-operation ('European Political Co-operation'), joint action against terrorism, etc.?

These four issues, and a proliferation of others stemming from them (often interpreted by the European Court of Justice, which has itself become something of a political force), can be traced through the debates of the last third of a century: the proposed European Political Community of the early 1950s, the 'Fouchet Plan' of the early 1960s, the 'Luxembourg Compromise' of 1966, the conflicts over the 'first enlargement' when the UK, Ireland and Denmark joined in 1973, the Tindemans Report on European Union in 1975, the report of the Three Wise Men in 1979, and so forth.

The living constitution of the Community, as it has emerged from all these debates (and more significantly from the clash of political wills of 1965–66, which produced the so-called 'Luxembourg Compromise'), is one in which the power of the 'supranational' Commission has been severely circumscribed, and that of the member-states powerfully enhanced, if the situation is compared with the institutional scheme designed by the Community's founding fathers. To be sure, the legislative process prescribed by the Treaty of Rome is still followed, outwardly: legislative proposals proceed from the Commission, via the 'opinion' of the Parliament (and of the Economic and Social Committee, where appropriate) towards a decision by the effective legislature of the Community, the Council of Ministers. It is also true that, in budgetary matters, the European Parliament, especially since the first direct popular election of its members in 1979, has striven to make the most of its constitutional role as a partner in the Community's budgetary authority (together with the Council), in the sense both of exercising its existing rights and of extending them. Yet despite these outward signs both of continuity in the legislative process and of parliamentary assertiveness in budgetary matters, the underlying reality has been the steady growth in the authority of that Community institution which represents the member-states, namely the Council of Ministers (supported by a normally very powerful COREPER and now regularly reinforced by the summit-level European Council). In the actual functioning of the legislative process, and in the annual bargaining on the budget, it has become increasingly clear that the Council of Ministers (or rather the array of the national capitals that lie behind it) is the main locus of real power. The Commission nowadays rarely makes a new proposal without having first checked its acceptability most carefully with the national government or their Brussels representatives; and the Parliament, even in its most daring bursts of self-assertiveness, has been obliged to pay attention not only to the Court of Justice, but also and more importantly to the Council of Ministers, COREPER, and the principle of inter-governmental bargaining for which they stand.[2]

In summarising the actual constitution of the Community then, we could say that its institutions fall far short, in their functioning, of those of a true federation. The method of integration being pur-

sued is not federal, in that there is no precise definition of states'
rights (so that national objections to the Community majority have
to be expressed in the negative form of the veto). There is an overwhelming 'democratic deficit' in the sense that the Parliament, even
though now directly elected, is excluded from a decisive say in legislation, taxation, or the appointment and control of the executive.
And the fact that the three central organs – Council, Commission
and Parliament – are appointed to their offices by very different
means, is a built-in source of conflict and deadlock.[3]

The Single European Act

The constitutonal pattern of the Community thus appeared to be
firmly set – in an essentially inter-governmental mould – when new
life was brought into the debate by the European Parliament's Draft
Treaty of European Union, instigated originally by the veteran
Italian federalist and MEP Altiero Spinelli in the early 1980s. In
the latest phase of the debate, the key documents are the Draft
Treaty of European Union ('Spinelli Treaty') approved by the European Parliament in February 1984; the Report of the European Council's *ad hoc* Committee for Institutional Affairs ('Dooge Committee')
of March 1985; and the Single European Act signed by the twelve
governments in February 1986 which entered into force (once ratified
by the national parliaments) in July 1987.[4]

All of these documents are explicitly concerned with constitutional
reform. The full title of the 'Spinelli Treaty' speaks for itself; the
members of the Dooge Committee (including Malcolm Rifkind as
Mrs Thatcher's representative) declared their aim of turning the
Community into 'a genuine political entity'; and the ministers who
signed the Single European Act committed their governments 'to
transform relations . . . among their States into a European Union'.
Lord Denning, as the House of Lords voted to ratify the Single
European Act, commented that it 'ushers in a new constitution for
Europe'.

But what kind of constitution (in contrast to the 'old' constitution
of the Treaty of Rome and the ensuing customary law and practice)
is it? What bargains and compromises went into its construction?
And what balance between 'constitutional' and 'substantive' issues
does it represent?

The text of the Act, which occupies over a dozen pages of small
print, commits the signatory governments to progress on a wide range
of policy issues, ranging from the completion (by 1992) of a free
market for the exchange of goods and services throughout the European Community to an intensified co-operation in matters of foreign
policy, including 'the political and economic aspects of security'.

At first sight, the Single European Act looks like a triumph for legalism: many of its clauses refer to detailed amendments to the text of the European Community's founding document, the Treaty of Rome, in which details of voting and other procedural matters are set out. In reality, the agreement reached in February 1986 goes beyond legalism: it represents a delicate and highly significant compromise between two of the fundamental strands of thinking about how Europe could be more closely united – the pragmatic and the constitutional – which is likely to determine the development of the European Community for a long time to come.

In the discussions of the first half of the 1980s, there appeared to be a gap that was impossible to bridge between the pragmatic concerns of someone like the British Prime Minister, Mrs Thatcher, with her insistence on practical results and on financial equity, and, on the other hand, the current of thought which favoured a new and legally binding commitment to the goal of closer institutional union for the Community. The latter view appeared to be shared not only by 'extremists' such as Altiero Spinelli, the veteran pioneer of federalism in the European Parliament, but also, in varying degrees, by the governments of the Federal Republic, Italy, the Benelux countries, and France. There were times, during the early 1980s, when there appeared to be a fundamental gulf between the original six countries of the European Community, who were determined to reaffirm their commitment to the closer political union of their peoples, and on the other hand the three new member states who had joined in 1973: Ireland, concerned to preserve its neutrality in international political matters, Denmark, worried about the risk of seeing its national identity submerged in a supranational European union, and Britain. Britain appeared not only disdainful of what Mr Callaghan had called 'institution-mongering', but also preoccupied with the fact that its payments into the Community budget were not fully offset by receipts from the Community's agricultural, regional and other spending programmes.

These two strands of thinking – the institutional and the pragmatic, for short – appeared incapable of reconciliation. Yet the inter-governmental discussions of 1985–86, which led to the signature of the Single European Act in February, amounted to a striking example of the diplomatic skill of Europe's professional negotiators in bringing together apparently irreconcilable points of view in a synthesis where each side saw that it could only get its way by an agreement with the other. The protagonists of institutional reform saw that this in itself, without agreement on substantive policy issues, would be meaningless, while the pragmatic supporters of reform in policy saw that this could only be achieved by agreement to important changes of procedures and institutions. What was the influence of these rival schools of thought, in the critical year 1985–86, and how was it possible to reconcile them?

Both the start of the negotiating process which produced the Single European Act and the manner in which it was finally adopted gave clear indications of differences between the member states of the Community. At the meeting of the European Council in Milan in June 1985, when it was decided to call a formal inter-governmental conference (which would work for several months on the plan), the decision was taken against the wishes of the United Kingdom, Denmark and Greece, who had misgivings of various kinds about where the process might lead. Eight months later, when the European Act was submitted for ratification, Denmark and Greece feared that the proposals went too far in the direction of supranationality, while in Italy the national parliament criticised the plan for not going far enough. It was only after further discussion, and a national referendum in Denmark which approved the proposal (and enabled Denmark remarkably to be the first country to notify ratification), that these countries gave it their formal agreement. In the intervening eight months of debate, which had ranged over every aspect of the policy of the Community (past, present and future), over the whole range of international political and military issues confronting the countries of Western Europe, and over many proposals for the institutional reform of the Community, the degree of consensus, and its limits, had become clearer.

What were the main points on which the countries of the Community finally agreed in the Single European Act? The two main areas concern, first, the development of the European Community as an economic unit, particularly the commitment to achieve a completely free internal market by 1992, and secondly, the area of political co-operation between the Community's member states, with special reference to diplomatic and international security issues. In relation to both these policy areas, as will be seen, important innovations in the decision-making process of the Community have been agreed.

The agreement to turn the EC into 'an area without internal frontiers', by removing all remaining obstacles to the free movement of goods, persons, services and capital, was underlined by the commitment to achieve this by the end of the year 1992. It should be noted that this precise timetable is not in fact one of the legally binding elements in the Single European Act: it is, however, meant to set a target to be used in planning by the business firms of Europe, as well as to put pressure on the specialist government departments in national capitals, who will have a large say in carrying the programme out. The most important innovation in this connection is that, for certain specified matters, the Council of Ministers will take decisions by a majority vote (in place of the unanimity required by the original provisions of the Treaty of Rome), thus removing the possibility of a national veto. It must be stressed that this change will apply only to certain carefully specified policy areas. For instance, unanimity will still be required for sensitive issues such as tax harmonisation (VAT and other indirect taxes), and also for many aspects of labour market policy: for instance, issues of vocational training and recognition of professional qualifications.

Despite these reservations, the realisation that progress towards freeing the internal market can only be achieved by majority voting has been clearly recognised in many areas of policy. For instance, in the harmonisation of commercial law in the different countries, and in the reduction of bureaucratic barriers to trade across European frontiers, great progress should be possible. Even though national governments keep the right to regulate trade by insisting on national standards of quality, the Commission may now require such procedures to be justified before the European Court of Justice.

The remaining provisions of the Single European Act, in the field of economic integration, include the commitment to develop the European Monetary System (for the first time there is a formal Treaty commitment to an 'Economic and Monetary Union'), and to improve the use of the Community's structural funds (the Fund for Agricultural Guidance, the Social Fund and the Regional Fund) in doing something to reduce the differences in the economic level between one region of the Community and another. There is also emphasis on developing a collective European effort in the field of research and technology, related to the non-Community EUREKA plan for high technology.

As far as the area of diplomatic co-operation is concerned, the Single European Act breaks new ground in linking the existing system of European Political Co-operation formally with the institutions of the Community. Surprising as it may seem, the system of consultation between the foreign ministries of the Community countries has hitherto been conducted under completely separate rules from those of the Community itself. Henceforth, the institutional basis for this co-operation will be strengthened by the setting-up of a small permanent secretariat (another example of the interdependence between institutional development and the growth of substantive policies), and it is clearly stated that security issues, including arms control and disarmament, should be considered by Foreign Ministers and their officials alongside the economic issues for which the Community is responsible.

The general institutional changes associated with the commitment to new policies are of varying kinds. The most important is certainly the breakthrough which has been achieved by the agreement to carry out certain aspects of economic and legal integration by majority vote in the Council. At the same time, the European Parliament has received a small concession – certainly not significant enough in the eyes of many of its members – by being formally associated with the process of completing the liberalisation of the internal market. According to the Single European Act, this process is to be carried out 'in co-operation with the European Parliament' (incidentally, this is also the first occasion on which all the member states of the Community, including the British Government, have agreed to refer to 'the European Parliament' rather than use the more disparaging title of 'European Assembly'). At the same time, the Parliament has been given new possibilities of exercising influence in the development of policies designed to develop the economic and social cohesion of the Community, to improve working conditions and to carry out the new commitments which have been reached on research and technological co-operation. For these areas of policy, a new decision-making procedure is being introduced, providing for the Parliament to express its opinion in a 'second reading' before the Council of Ministers takes the final decision. Both the European Parliament and the Commission will be given greater possibiliites of influencing the decision-making process, although the last word remains, as before, with the Council of Ministers. It should again be stressed, however, that a Council of Ministers in which important decisions are taken by majority vote will not be the same as the old Council of Ministers, in which decisions could be held up or prevented by the exercise of national vetoes not only at ministerial level but also – often with very serious effects – by junior officials representing their governments in Council working-parties.

The Single European Act has been attacked in some quarters as the precursor of an all-powerful European superstate which will destroy the sovereignty of European nations: as we have seen, this was the original reaction of Danish public opinion (although the Danish people approved the European Act in a subsequent referendum), and it has also been expressed by opponents of supranational integration in the United Kingdom. In reality, we have only to compare the actual provisions of the Single European Act with the vastly more ambitious designs for European Union which were supported by the European Parliament in 1984 to realise how limited the new reforms actually are. The process by which the Single European Act came into existence was a classic example of the bargaining, compromising and reconciliation of national interests, which have marked the process of European integration from the beginning.

It is significant that member governments of the Community quickly agreed to carry through the new reform package on the basis of Article 236 of the Treaty of Rome, the Article which allows member states to take on additional commitments if they all wish to do so. In other words, the long-declared readiness of certain member states (particularly Italy, the Federal Republic, and the Benelux countries) to take decisive steps towards a more supranational Europe, even if this meant leaving Britain and other laggard partners in a peripheral second-class status, has been put to the test. If the countries concerned had been seriously inclined to go in this direction, they would have ignored Article 236, called an inter-governmental conference outside the EC framework and opted for a new European Union among themselves, rather than for the new commitments which all twelve member states have been able to accept.

The Single European Act thus represents a collective decision to move towards closer integration in a pragmatic rather than a dramatic way. There is clearly general agreement that the decision-making procedures of the Community have to be simplified and speeded up, particularly in view of the increased risk of national vetoes blocking agreement now that the membership has increased to twelve through the accession of Spain and Portugal. The Single European Act, while it clearly provides for majority voting on the kinds of issues specified above, leaves the unanimity rule intact for other purposes. On balance, the acceptance of majority voting may have broader implications than appear at first sight: if the member states take seriously their commitment to move towards an integrated market by 1992, the fact that some decisions will be taken by majority vote will probably create a new climate for the conduct of Community business generally, in which member states will feel under greater pressure to reach agreement even on issues where they might have blocked it. Much depends here on the way in which the Commission will use its enhanced influence, and how the European Parliament exercises its enhanced influence on policy-making.

The Single European Act contains a new commitment by all concerned to the goal of 'European Union', but no precise definition of what this means. In contrast to earlier commitments of this kind – for instance, the pledge given by Heath, Brandt, Pompidou and the others at the Paris summit of 1972 that a 'European Union' would be created by the year 1980 – the treaty-makers of 1986 have wisely left the term 'European Union' somewhat vague. This further underlines the point that the European Community has now reached a stage where neither the proponents of institutional grand designs nor those of pragmatic *ad hoc* progress on policy matters can have things all their own way. The development of 'European Union', it is now clear, must be seen as a pragmatic process of growth and development, rather than as a dramatic step brought about by some new Treaty of Rome. On the other hand, however irritating this may be for the out-and-out pragmatists, it is clear that serious progress on the substance of policies – economic, social or diplomatic – is not possible without a simultaneous development of the institutional framework.

The constitutional settlement embodied in the Single European Act thus reflects the consensus now obtaining among the Community's member states about the direction and speed of its substantive policy undertakings as well. The Act is a constitution for a Community in which the member states are still concerned to place strict limits on the competence of the Community institutions, but one which also provides for a certain increase of their authority in some directions. In terms of the fundamental issues listed earlier, the Act provides for a slight enhancement of the authority of the Commission; a rather more significant increase in the powers of the Parliament; some diminution of the power of member states in the Council (through the weakening of the unanimity rule); and tightening of the links between 'Community' affairs on the one hand and the remaining agenda of a European Union (political co-operation etc.) on the other. Finally (though this is not in the Act itself), the increased authority given to the European Court of Justice implies a consolidation and closer integration of the Community.

The debate of 1985–86 has greatly clarified the central issues, and has indicated the degree of commitment with which various actors in the process – national governments and parliaments, Community institutions, and political parties – will support this or that proposal. This phase of the story has also provided a basis from which the future attempts at constitutional change will have to start.

The main force for further change will continue to be the European Parliament, which will combine the adaptation to its enhanced role in current policy-making with continued bids for the role of Constituent Assembly. Future bids are unlikely to be as dramatic as the Draft Treaty of 1984, but they will be pressed in the same direction by the many MEPs disappointed with the watering-down of this treaty in the Single Act. The argument has already been advanced, by an influential German member of the Parliament's Political Committee, that the volume of Community legislation now being approved by the Council of Ministers, without democratic control either by the European Parliament or by the Bundestag, infringes the principles of the Federal Republic's Basic Law of 1949.[5]

Arguments for reform couched, like this one, in terms of the unconstitutionality of existing arrangements, represent a cautious and pragmatic approach to the problem. There have also been a number of proposals for much more radical change. One of these is the stimulating argument that the way to remedy the manifest failure of direct parliamentary elections to create a transnational party system would be for the voters of Europe to have the chance to elect the *Commission* directly: under this proposal, rival candidates for the Commission's presidency would present themselves to the electors, accompanied by ministerial 'teams' representing their respective political standpoints. The view that this proposal is utopian is countered by its supporters with the argument that without the campaigns of such 'utopians' as Spinelli the Community would not even have made the limited advance embodied in the Single European Act.[6] More drastic reforms, such as this one, may be acceptable in time, but one of the clear lessons of the debates of 1985–86 is that even modest institutional innovations only stand a chance of success if they are seen to be necessary to achieve specific policy objectives (e.g. the completion of the internal market).

In the shorter run, constitutional change in the Community is more likely to come about through the pragmatic development of existing institutions, as advocated by Christopher Tugendhat: the exercise of more authority by the European Council; better co-ordination between the different specialised Councils; more imaginative trade-offs between national interests; the creation of a truly unified internal market; greater co-operation in industrial policy, monetary affairs, and defence; and an acceptance that the idea of European Union has to take the form, in the short run at least, of a union of states.[7]

Mrs Thatcher may be wrong in the prediction she made to a French audience in 1984: 'I do not believe that we shall ever have a United States of Europe in the same way that there is a United States of America.'[8] Recent history should teach those who expect dramatic progress towards such a goal that, as another realist said of 'visions of a world federation or blue-prints of a more perfect League of Nations': 'Those elegant superstructures must wait until some progress has been made in digging the foundations.'[9]

If the foregoing analysis of the linkage between Europe's 'substantive' and 'constitutional' issues is correct, the inconspicuous progress represented by the Single European Act may prove to have been a significant contribution to the foundations of a 'genuine political entity.'

Notes and references

1. For an early but penetrating account of the issues, see Leon Lindberg and Stuart Scheingold, *Europe's Would-be Polity*, Englewood Cliffs (NJ: Prentice-Hall, 1970).
2. A clear account of the Community's institutions is given by T.C. Hartley, *The Foundations of European Community Law* (Oxford: Clarendon Press, 1981), especially Chapter I. Richard Mayne, *The Institutions of the European Community*

(London: Chatham House/PEP, 1968) analyses the situation created by the 'Luxembourg compromise', which still prevails today.

3. See Vernon Bogdanor, 'Why Europe is Deadlocked', *Encounter*, March 1986, and *Britain and European Union. Report of a Study Group*, Chairman: Lord Ezra, Rapporteur: Vernon Bogdanor, London, European Centre for Political Studies, PSI, and Federal Trust for Education and Research, June 1985.

4. The story is well summarised, and the key documents up to 1985 are printed, in House of Lords Select Committee on the European Communities, Session 1984–85, 14th Report, *European Union* (London: HMSO, July 1985). The text of the Single European Act is in *Bulletin of the European Communities*, Supplement 2/1986. See also Richard Corbett, *The 1985 Intergovernmental Conference* (European Community Research Unit, Hull University, 1986).

5. This view is advanced by Klaus Hänsch, MEP, 'Europäische Integration und Parlamentarische Demokratie', *Europa-Archiv*, Vol. 41, No. 7, April 1986, pp. 191–200.

6. See the statement of this case by Vernon Bogdanor, 'The Future of the European Community', *Government and Opposition*, Vol. 21, No. 2, Spring 1985, pp. 161–76.

7. Christopher Tugendhat, *Making Sense of Europe* (London: Viking, 1986), especially pp. 128–230.

8. Franco-British Council, *Report on the Avignon Conference, 30 November–2 December 1984* (London: n.d.), p. 9.

9. E.H. Carr, *The Twenty Years Crisis: An Introduction to the Study of International Relations* (London: Macmillan, 1939), p. 307.

20 Conclusion
Vernon Bogdanor

I

There have been, since the adoption of the American Constitution in 1787, six major periods of constitutional upheaval. All of them have occurred amidst times of political turmoil, such as mark the beginning of a new historical era. The 1780s and 1790s were the years of the adoption and ratification of the American Constitution, the French Revolution and the various attempts in France to fashion a workable constitution, all of them abortive. The period at the end of the Napoleonic wars saw a further rash of constitution-building, as states sought to give themselves a birth certificate to mark their independence or the restoration of their sovereignty. Of these constitutions, only that of Norway (1814) survives today. The 1848 revolutions spawned a series of liberal constitutions, most of which were swept away in the period of reaction which followed that year of revolutions. As a result, Germany and Italy did not succeed in achieving unity until 1870 in the midst of the fourth period of constitutional upheaval, while genuine republican government in France also had to await the defeat of that false republican, Napoleon III, in the same year. The *Ausgleich* established a Dual Monarchy in Austria-Hungary in 1867, while 1874 saw the revision of the Constitution of Switzerland. Moreover, the years 1865–70 had seen the adoption of three amendments to the American Constitution – the 13th, 14th and 15th – sometimes called the '14th Amendment Constitution', extending, in theory at least, equality and equal protection to all American citizens, following the victory of the north in the American Civil War. It was the 14th Amendment in particular which was radically to alter the American Constitution by providing for the application, through judicial interpretation, of the first ten Amendments – the Bill of Rights – to the states, firmly subordinating the states to the federal government and ensuring the triumph of the federal concept.

The fifth and sixth periods of constitutional reconstruction followed each of the two world wars, but, whereas the constitutions adopted after the First World War tended to the over-optimistic and most of them proved but ephemeral creations, the 'negative' constitutions of the post-Second World War years have proved highly resilient and successful.

The developments of more recent years discussed in this book do not, by any means, establish that the current period is a seventh period of major constitutional upheaval. It is not. For the 1970s and 1980s have not been years in which constitutions have been radically restructured, or drawn up *de novo*; constitutional change and proposals for constitutional change have been incremental, building on existing values and institutions rather than seeking totally to replace the heritage of the past. By contrast with the years immediately following the two world wars, proposals for constitutional change have not been a response to breakdown, but rather an attempt to refashion and reshape constitutions in countries within which (with the exception of Greece, Portugal and Spain), constitutional values are felt to be secure. Constitutional change is being pursued within a framework of continuity, not discontinuity. Why, then, is it occurring?

II

It is easier to ask than to answer. The diverse patterns of constitutional change illustrated in this book resist summary in any easy formula. There is no *one* answer – unless it be in such highly general terms as to be of little use – to the question of why the constitution has become a matter of political controversy in so many democracies in recent years. What is, however, clear is that there comes to be pressure for constitutional change when the constitution of a country ceases to be congruent with changing social values and political tendencies; and that, in these circumstances, political parties will be able, with some degree of success, to adopt the reform of the constitution as an item in their programmes. However, the changes in values and attitudes which precipitate constitutional change will be very different in different countries; and it is not easy to discover any common factors.

There is, at the outset, something of a paradox in that those countries in which power tends to be concentrated – the executive-majoritarian countries in Lijphart's terminology – have undergone pressure to reform the constitution by dispersing power; while the countries in which power is diffused – those which Lijphart labels consensual democracies – find themselves under pressure to reform their constitutions so as to provide responsible party government along lines not so different from that of the classical model of British government.[1]

Thus, amongst the countries studied in this book, two opposing patterns of constitutional change can be discerned. In one group of countries – Britain, Belgium and Israel – constitutional problems have arisen because a basically majoritarian political system has concentrated power in the executive to such an extent that it is not possible to accommodate the major political forces in the country without some degree of dispersal of power, whether territorially or functionally. In Britain, constitutional reformers have sought to challenge the supremacy of Parliament which in their view serves as a mask for the omnicompetence of government, a condition which Lord Hailsham has described as one akin to elective dictatorship. The challenge to the supremacy of Parliament is both territorial in that it seeks devolution and decentralisation, and also functional in that it seeks, by means of such reforms as proportional representation, a Bill of Rights, and reform of the House of Lords, to limit the power of an elected government even within its own sphere of influence.

In Belgium, the community problem has compelled a wholesale reconsideration of the structure of a political system in which the basis of conflict became – for a time at least in the 1970s – linguistic rather than socio-economic. As a result of the State reform, the party battle in Belgium has become of less importance than the constitutional procedures, carefully crafted but still fragile, necessary to accommodate the two communities within one state. Belgium, together with Spain, has turned itself into a quasi-federal state, not in order to weaken central authority, but rather to strengthen it by seeking to show that allegiance to the state need not conflict with, but can, on the contrary, accommodate subordinate loyalties to sub-national communities – whether these communities are defined in terms of language or of territory.

Israel, a state whose institutions, as Emanuel Gutmann shows, owe a good deal to the British model, has also found itself with a system of government whose majoritarian elements are unsuited to the purpose of governing a society marked by ethnic, religious and national differences – differences between Ashkenazi and Sephardic Jews, between the orthodox and the secular, and between Jews and Arabs. The 1984 Government of National Unity was an unforeseen and improvised response to the tensions created by these conflicts, a consociational device of a novel kind unlikely to be replicated in the future. What Israel badly needs is a consociational pact, recognising the legitimacy of the diverse elements within Israeli society (including the Arabs), and their right to a political personality; but the entrenched interests of the parties make it difficult to be optimistic that this will in fact be the outcome of a period of constitutional questioning. For this reason a weakening of the stranglehold which the parties exert over Israeli political life – perhaps through electoral reform – is a precondition of constitutional change. But it is not easy to see how this can be achieved either.

In a second group of countries – the United States, Italy, France, and the Netherlands – the problem is, or in the case of France was, the opposite: how to achieve a greater concentration of power, in order to allow the formation of ideologically coherent governments whose policies can be sharply differentiated from those of the opposition. Such a model was given the label of responsible party government in the United States in the 1950s; and it bears some resemblance indeed to the idealised model of British government in the 1950s and 1960s celebrated in Samuel Beer's classic work, *Modern British Politics*.[2]

Sweden also perhaps falls into this category of countries since, as Olof Ruin shows, the new Constitution of 1974 has conspicuously failed to achieve the aims hoped for by the ruling Social Democrats of providing strong, single-party majority government. Indeed, little more than a decade after the adoption of the new Instrument of Government, there is discussion as to the desirability and feasibility of further constitutional change.

In countries in this group, constitutional reformers have complained that the system of government is one in which power is too widely diffused, making governments unaccountable, and depriving the electorate of that clear choice between alternatives which is the hallmark of democracy. In the United States, Italy, Fourth Republic France and the Netherlands, reformers raised the question of governability, of whether the political arrangements of these countries were such as could provide for effective leadership. Yet, in the United States, the Netherlands and Italy alike, constitutional reform is highly unlikely since it would be so contrary to the interests of the major parties and political leaders; while in France, it took the trauma of the Algerian war and the threat of a military *putsch* to bring General de Gaulle to power through a legal *coup d'état*. Without these events, the parties of the Fourth Republic would never have agreed to adopt Gaullist solutions to their problems, just as the parties in Italy have not. Yet, by a strange paradox which would not have appealed to de Gaulle, the very success of the Fifth Republic is based on its having created a 'régime des partis' of precisely the kind which de Gaulle despised, and which, moreover, now has its own vested interests to defend on constitutional questions.

There is a third group of countries discussed in this book – but not distinguished as a separate category by Lijphart – whose constitutions may be labelled hybrid. Australia, Canada and India have each sought to combine responsible parliamentary government, based broadly on principles derived from the Westminster model of government, with federalism, a form of political organisation whose whole *raison d'être* is the sharing and diffusion of power, a principle which can easily conflict with the strong executive leadership associated with the Westminster model. In each of these countries, constitutional problems have arisen in recent years as a result of the tension between these principles; and it is not yet clear that they have been satisfactorily resolved in any of them. Australia has established both a Constitutional Convention and a Constitutional Commission to seek answers to these intractable problems; in Canada, the process of patriating the constitution turned out to be a traumatic one and, since the final outcome has been significantly to weaken the influence of Quebec in the political process, it is by no means clear that the 1982 Constitution Act offers a final solution of Canada's constitutional difficulties. India has not seen any serious political attempt to change the constitution, but the seemingly gradual disintegration of Congress and the growth of regional pressures for autonomy are bound to put the political system under increasing strain. Moreover, both in Canada and in India, there has been a further source of tension resulting from the conflict between a Bill of Rights and what governments claim to be the needs of strong executive leadership. In Canada, the new Charter of Rights and Freedoms, like the 1960 Bill of Rights, offers a graphic illustration of how a Bill of Rights can be effective even with legislative override; but, nevertheless, it raises in an acute form the question of whether a common approach to language rights can be found between Quebec and the other provinces; while India, the first Commonwealth country to adopt a Bill of Rights, has been faced with the problem of whether the maintenance of some rights – and in particular property rights – are compatible with the policies which governments believe are necessary to promote economic development.

Of the other countries discussed in this book, the Constitutions of Portugal and Spain are too recent for serious judgments about their viability to be made, while in Japan, West Germany and Switzerland, there seems to be a considerable degree of satisfaction with constitutional arrangements – despite the attempt, probably a forlorn one, to seek a Total Revision of the Swiss Constitution. In Japan and West Germany, satisfaction with the constitution is clearly a product of the fact that their constitutions have made possible stable government, economic progress and the restoration of national self-respect; while in Switzerland, it is difficult to object very strenuously to the constitution because it is so very easy to change. Indeed, Switzerland is quite remarkable – and to this extent *sui generis* – in that its constitution is subordinate to democracy, and also indeed to nationalism.

III

In every democracy, constitutional change depends upon a perception by political parties and leaders that change would be in their interest. That in itself is hardly surprising. Constitutional rules are rarely neutral in their political effects, but so order political life as to favour some kinds of activity and hinder others. Men and women would not involve themselves in the rough and tumble of political life unless they genuinely believed that it is for the good of their country that the cause which they support, triumphs. Therefore, those in power will tend to take a favourable view of the rules which allowed them to achieve their position, and they are likely to be somewhat sceptical of proposals for change. Thus, in countries such as Britain and the Netherlands, where the entrenched parties find themselves challenged by new movements placing constitutional reform at the centre of their programmes – the Liberal/SDP Alliance and D'66 respectively – they will either, as in Britain, resist such proposals for as long as they can; or, as in the Netherlands, ensure that if change is forced upon them, it is channelled into safe directions so that it does not weaken the party system nor increase the power of that portion of the electorate not strongly committed to political parties. Similar reactions can be observed in Italy and Israel, two *Parteienstaaten* whose political leaders have skilfully resisted proposals for constitutional change which would challenge their prerogatives.

Constitutional change therefore is intimately linked with the rise and fall of political parties. In France, under the Fifth Republic, the political parties have become more entrenched, and they have strengthened their hold upon the French electorate under what has become a 'régime des partis'. But France is very much an exception. In most other democracies, the trend has been the other way. The hold of political parties upon society has been loosening, because the social structural factors – primarily class and religion – which enabled them to penetrate deeply into society have themselves been in decline as motivators of electoral behaviour. The processes of advanced industrial society have been such as to break down the simplicities of models of society based upon class or religious conflict. As the traditional loyalties upon which parties have relied come increasingly to be questioned, so a political space is opened up within which new issues come to the fore, and there is room again for constitutional questions to return to the agenda of politics, a place which they occupied in most democracies at the beginning of the century and indeed until universal suffrage was achieved.

It was the growth of tightly organised mass parties which, in many democracies, fossilised the movement for constitutional change. For these parties claimed to represent particular social or religious groups, and demanded the loyalty of their supporters as a precondition for effectiveness in the political struggle. Democracy, it was held, had already been achieved, and the agenda of politics would henceforth consist primarily of socio-economic issues; the constitution was merely a distraction. So it was that the sociological development of political parties and the ideological preconceptions of the parties themselves, came to reinforce each other.

It may not be too speculative to suggest that, in a number of democracies, changes in the character of political conflict and competition are leading to the development of new political patterns, in some respects more characteristic of the nineteenth century and the early part of the twentieth before the growth of tight party organisation. Commitment to political parties and to the social structures upon which they rested, has been steadily weakening. There has been a renewal of interest in new forms of political organisation, and a revival of individualism. Democracy has come to be seen, not as a form of organisation which has already been achieved, or indeed as something which *can* be definitively achieved, but as a conception of government capable of continual improvement. For, at bottom, the search for constitutional change is a search for more effective ways of securing popular control and accountability of government. It is precisely because liberal democracy is a peculiarly open and non-definitive method of government that constitutional change is likely to be a permanent feature of the politics of democratic states well into the twenty-first century. For, is there ever a time when one can say that the process of building a democratic state has been completed, that the task is at an end?

Notes and references

1. Arend Lijphart, *Democracies: Patterns of Majoritarian and Consensus Government in Twenty-One Countries* (New Haven: Yale University Press, 1984).
2. New York: Norton, 1982. First published in 1965.

Index